Nobody Men

Nobody Men

Nobody Men

Neutrality, Loyalties, and Family in the American Revolution

Travis Glasson

Yale

UNIVERSITY PRESS

NEW HAVEN AND LONDON

Published with assistance from the Annie Burr Lewis Fund
and from the Louis Stern Memorial Fund.

Copyright © 2025 by Travis Glasson.
All rights reserved.
This book may not be reproduced, in whole or in part, including illustrations, in
any form (beyond that copying permitted by Sections 107 and 108 of the U.S.
Copyright Law and except by reviewers for the public press), without written
permission from the publishers.

Yale University Press books may be purchased in quantity for educational,
business, or promotional use. For information, please email sales.press@yale.edu
(U.S. office) or sales@yaleup.co.uk (U.K. office).

Set in Fournier type by Integrated Publishing Solutions.
Printed in the United States of America.

Library of Congress Control Number: 2024950357
ISBN 978-0-300-25889-9 (hardcover : alk. paper)

A catalogue record for this book is available from the British Library.

Authorized Representative in the EU: Easy Access System Europe,
Mustamäe tee 50, 10621 Tallinn, Estonia, gpsr.requests@easproject.com

10 9 8 7 6 5 4 3 2 1

For Lucy, Hilary, and Ned

Contents

Introduction	1

PART ONE. "CRUGER AND LIBERTY!": 1760–1775

1. The Crugers' World	21
2. Stamps and People	44
3. Transatlantic Patriots	68
4. The Center Fails	91

PART TWO. "SOME MIDDLE WAY SHOULD BE FOUND OUT": 1775–1783

5. Whigs Killing for the King	117
6. The Price of Neutrality	142
7. The Search for Peace	166
8. Friend of Washington?	192

PART THREE. "MY HEART STILL CLEAVES TO NEW YORK": 1783–1800

9. Subjects and Citizens	219
10. Oblivion and Conciliation	242

Conclusion	267
Notes	275
Acknowledgments	343
Index	347

Introduction

In May 1779, as the war of the American Revolution dragged into its fifth year, a Pennsylvania newspaper printed a letter from a patriot writing under the pseudonym of "Bramin." The letter was revealingly addressed to "Messieurs the Tory-men, Moderate-men, Any-bodies-men, Every-bodies-men, No-bodies men, the Trimmers, Temporizers, &c. &c. &c. wheresoever dispersed throughout the Thirteen United States of America." In what might read as advice or a threat, the writer urged all these people that their only safety lay in embracing the revolution. It was a long and relentlessly pejorative list of names, one which simultaneously identifies the difficulty of capturing and categorizing the people that this book is about—those in the middle in the American Revolution—and indicates the long-term problems their presence posed for ultras on both sides.[1]

The patriot writer had good reason to be concerned because the "no-bodies men" were not a small group. One reasonable estimate suggests that "neutrals" accounted for perhaps 40 to 60 percent of the total colonial population during the revolutionary conflict.[2] Nevertheless, when writing about the American Revolution, historians have largely ignored those in the middle and concentrated on small minorities of the most violent and polarized populations in the future United States: militant patriots and loyalists. What follows aims to go beyond caricatures like Bramin's or the silences in much writing on the Revolution and analyze the experiences of people who were labeled variously as "neutral," "moderate," or "disaffected" during the conflict.

This book calls these people "nobody men," "nobody women," or "nobodyists" and contributes to their history by telling the ocean-spanning story of a single extended family. The Crugers were a New York–based merchant clan with strong ties to other places including England and the multinational Caribbean. In the decades before the Revolution, family members shipped, bought, and sold almost anything on which they thought they could turn a profit and also immersed themselves in local and transatlantic politics. The chapters that follow trace these people's paths into, through, and beyond the Revolutionary War. In doing so, they explore themes including how and why people came to be "in the middle" during the Revolution, the role of the family and other connections in people's decision-making, concepts of citizenship and subjecthood in an era of transformation, the impact of the conflict on people outside of what became the United States, and the centrality of violence and coercion to many people's wartime experiences. Through the history of the Crugers, this book offers wider ways to think about a large group of people whose experiences of the revolutionary era have often been ignored.

Together, the Crugers had a remarkable and revealing Revolution. John Cruger was a prosperous merchant, the popular mayor of New York City during the Seven Years' War, an effective opponent of the Stamp Act, and the last Speaker of New York's colonial assembly. Unable to contain a political firestorm over questions of sovereignty that he had helped create, in 1775 John joined the many colonial Americans of his generation who managed to ride out the war years by retiring quietly from public life. John had no children, but his brother and business partner, Henry Cruger, and Henry's wife, Elizabeth, did. These Crugers, members of the family's "revolutionary generation," ranging in age from their late twenties to late thirties when the war began, had their lives transformed by the conflict. Henry Cruger Jr. was American born but served as a pro-peace member of the British Parliament during the war years. Arguing for reconciliation from the floor of a Parliament that was waging war, he confronted repeated questions about his true loyalties. In a surprising twist, after more than thirty years of residence in England, he returned to the United States in 1790.

Other Crugers' experiences were more tragic. The younger Henry's sisters, Mary and Elizabeth, and several of Elizabeth's children, were among the thousands of civilians who died of wartime contagious diseases. Their deaths took place far from famous battlefields but still scarred those left behind. The book also considers the experiences of Elizabeth's husband, Peter Van Schaack, who was banished by New York's revolutionary state government as what later might have been called a conscientious objector. Struggling to reconcile his own moral code with the claims that competing governments made upon him, Van Schaack wrote eloquently of the challenges people faced in trying to navigate their ways through a war he regarded as a catastrophe. Returning to New York after the war, Van Schaack was one of the many people in the middle who reconciled themselves to the new regime.

The eldest member of the family's revolutionary generation was John Harris Cruger. He and his wife, Anne De Lancey Cruger, born into wealthy and influential families, shared their relatives' whiggish prewar politics, but John Harris Cruger became a loyalist army officer who might have been remembered as a hero had the British won the war. He was joined on campaign by Anne, who witnessed much violence firsthand. They ended up living in exile in a small Yorkshire town. Unlike most of their Cruger kin, the couple became loyalists, not nobodyists. But the story of how they came to fight for the king while sharing many of the same political commitments as their neutralist relatives illuminates the dynamics of personal and family decision-making during the war.

John Harris Cruger's younger brother Nicholas gave the family some of its closest ties to the patriots. A St. Croix–based merchant before the Revolution, Nicholas is most often remembered today for employing a young Alexander Hamilton. Nicholas's ties to Hamilton endured, but his own wartime politics were richly ambiguous. After profitably spending much of the war on a neutral island in the Caribbean, Nicholas moved to New York with the peace. There he burnished his bona fides as a patriot and took the lead in restoring the Cruger family's financial and political fortunes in the new United States (fig. 1).

On April 23, 1776, as the Second Continental Congress moved toward the adoption of the Declaration of Independence, John Adams wrote his wife, Abigail, to tell her about political divisions in Philadelphia. It was St. George's Day, and English-born men in the city had formed a club to honor their "national" saint and themselves. It was their day to celebrate, and they marked the day with a "a great Feast." However, "the Times and Politicks" imbued such public displays with new meanings, and there was a "schism" in the St. George's society: "one Part of them are to meet and dine at the City Tavern, and the other att the Bunch of Grapes, Israel Jacob's, and a third Party go out of Town." The reason for the division was that "one sett are staunch Americans, another staunch Britons I suppose, and a Third," he noted with sarcasm, were "half Way Men, Neutral Beings, moderate Men, prudent Folks." Everywhere in revolutionary America, this tripartite division was evident. The desire to keep the war at arms'

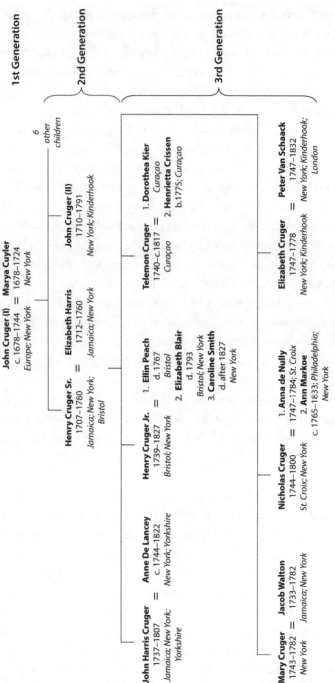

Figure 1. The Cruger Family in the Revolutionary Era.

length was common and crossed lines of race, class, gender, and geography. Adams professed that such divisions were to be expected, reflecting a historical rule of thirds. "Such is the Division among Men upon all Occasions and every Question" he observed.[3] Many years after the war, he would write that in 1774 "we were about one third Tories, one third timid and one third true Blue."[4] Adams saw the people in the middle, but like other hotter patriots and loyalists alike, he dismissed their motives.

Nobodyists have received little attention from historians and are almost never put at the center of books on the period. What even to call these people is not simple—there was no widely understood contemporary term for them that was not pejorative—and the continuing difficulty inherent in naming them reflects the conceptual hold that the binaries of "patriot" and "loyalist" have had on scholarly and popular histories of the Revolution. As Michael McDonnell has noted, "Historians still struggle to comprehend an extraordinarily wide array of peoples using such simple and ultimately opaque terms."[5] Nationalist paradigms continue to provide fundamental frameworks for the historiography of the American Revolution. In this book, nobodyists are defined as people affected by the American Revolution who were neither ardent patriots nor committed loyalists, but identifiable through their actions as differing from *both* the warring parties between 1775 and 1783.[6] This term is not intended to police the boundaries of revolutionary-era allegiance, but to encourage seeing the war as more than two-sided. It suggests a more flexible, less reductive way of considering people's attitudes, behavior, and experiences during the period. As a corollary to this, here the terms "patriot" and "loyalist" refer to people who actively supported one of the two warring parties in British North America. In the sense used here, there were no loyalists before the American crisis began its final descent into violence in 1774 and 1775. The meaning of the term "patriot" changed over time. In the period before the war "patriot" described a broad, oppositional political stance in the Anglo-Atlantic world. After 1775, while its prewar meaning continued to have salience in Britain and elsewhere in the British Empire, in rebellious North America "patriot" came to refer to Euro-Americans who supported congress, the war effort, and ultimately the independence of the United States.

Nobody men did not share a single, all-encompassing ideological position. Instead, like patriots and loyalists, nobodyists were motivated by a wide range of factors including understandings of the common good and self-interest; attachments to family and other groups; fear and other emotions; moral and religious attitudes and affiliations; political principles; and other forces.[7] This book uses some other terms—reconciliationist, conscientious objector, neutral, moderate, and others—to describe particular ways of being a nobodyist.[8]

The concept of nobodyism best describes a stance in relation to the militarized political violence of 1775 to 1783, rather than serving as a prewar, postwar, or lifelong identity. As examples from the Cruger family illustrate, wartime nobodyists often shared colonial and patriot political and economic grievances during the prewar period. Other wartime nobody women and men sympathized more with the British ministry before 1775. Still others might not have cared much. Moreover, because people after 1775 did not just make a decision about where they stood on the war once, but had to do so repeatedly over time and amid changing circumstances, it was possible to move in and out of affiliations like patriot, loyalist, and nobodyist. The long war wrought suffering, opportunity, and change. Its effects were neither chronologically nor geographically consistent; different people in different locations experienced the war in different ways at different times. Moreover, the conflict's overall nature and stakes were transformed at least twice, first by the Declaration of Independence in 1776 and then by France's entry in 1778. People's views of the past, present, and future changed between 1775 and 1783, and so too could their decisions about participating in the war.

Quakers have been essential to the understanding of neutrality in the Revolution and they are often the group that first comes to mind when considering the phenomenon.[9] However, the Quakers were numerically a relatively small group in British North America. One estimate is that there were around 50,000 Quakers in the thirteen colonies in 1775 out of a total non-Native population of about 2.5 million.[10] Most people in the middle were *not* Quakers or members of other, smaller pacifist denominations. Most nobodyists did not have access to the traditions of conscientious objection, carefully articulated rationales for their individual and communal choices, and institutional support that the Friends enjoyed. In this way, the story of the Crugers, who had ties to the Dutch Reformed Church but who had mostly joined the Church of England by the time of the Revolution, reveals wider dimensions of the nobody men's history.

Nobody men were described in various critical ways by polarized contemporaries. One term that was used especially by American patriots was "disaffected," and some historians interested in those in the middle have taken up the term.[11] I have preferred the terms "nobody men" or "nobodyists" because the term "disaffected" primarily describes people's relationship to the "patriot" cause and the new institutions that revolutionaries created. What American insurgent patriots cared about—and what "disaffected" reflects—was the failure of some people to actively support *their* military and political program. In using "nobodyists," I want to emphasize some people's acting to distinguish themselves from both warring parties—not just one—and avoid a term captive to either side's perspectives. The term "nobodyist" is also usefully more expansive than the term "disaffected." The patriots considered white Euro-American colonists who did not support their war effort and then independence to be disaffected because those were the people they most wanted to incorporate into their revolution. But there were nobodyists among a much wider group of people affected by the war, including Native Americans, African Americans, British colonists in North America outside the rebellious colonies, people in the multinational Caribbean, people elsewhere in the British Empire, and people in Britain itself. This book is not about all these varieties of nobodyists, but in proposing the term, I want to highlight commonalities among a large, widely dispersed, and diverse group of people.

Some patriots might have considered the people that I call nobodyists to have been loyalists; that is the warning given in the letter by Bramin that opened this introduction. Some historians have thought that some of the people I write about here should be considered loyalists too. Work on loyalists since the 1960s has revealed their experiences as more multivocal and less aberrant than they appeared in older US-centric literature focused on characterizing the Revolution as a unified and unifying national story.[12] Scholars have noted that loyalists were geographically, ethnically, socioeconomically, religiously, and otherwise diverse.[13] Related studies have detailed how Native American and Black people fought with and against the Crown, pursuing their own goals and freedom in the context of the imperial conflict.[14] There is an increasing awareness of how loyalist exiles and loyalism shaped the postwar British Empire.[15] Scholars have explored the histories of individual loyalists and groups of loyalists in specific localities.[16] Other work has explored the content of loyalist ideology and loyalist writing, seeing in them means for better understanding the Revolution and the postwar British Empire.[17] Some scholarship has looked to catalog various types of loyalism. Historians, for example, have differentiated between principled, doctrinaire, and accommodating loyalists;[18] "committed" or "vocal," "affective," and "passive" loyalists;[19] and "active," "reluctant," and "passive" loyalists.[20] Collectively, this literature has recovered loyalists as human beings rather than caricatures, documented the different ways that loyalists acted, and explored why loyalists made their choices.

Yet current broad—I might even say welcoming—definitions of loyalism accept and internalize the logic of the Revolution's combatants, particularly and ironically the patriots, in ways that seem limiting. For example, one recent expansive definition characterizes a "loyalist" as "an American who favored reconciliation with Great Britain during conflicts that began with the Stamp Act and concluded with the War of 1812."[21] Many people in this book might be considered loyalists under such a definition, but if "reconciliation"—rather than, say, allegiance to Britain, or activity undertaken to maintain imperial rule—is the operative concept, then it seems to me that "loyalist" is a misnomer, one encumbered by much historical and historiographical baggage. A generation previously, Robert Calhoon's influential, tellingly titled *The Loyalists in Revolutionary America, 1760–1781* took as its subject "all of those persons who may be described as *opponents* or *victims* of the Revolution," suggesting that loyalism was something that could either be chosen or imposed.[22] Militant patriots often insisted that there were only—could only be—two sides in the conflict because they wanted to compel the reluctant to join them. As insurgents, they required others' active participation to succeed, so they defined insufficient zeal as opposition. The British government and military were initially more willing to tolerate colonial inaction, but as the war deepened, they too increasingly insisted that any American who did not actively support the Crown's efforts to violently subdue the rebels was an enemy. A central aspect of the nobody men's wartime history was that both warring parties thought they should not exist.

By making the definition of loyalism so broad as to encompass anything short of active support for the Revolution, historians inadvertently incorporate this political rhetoric into their own categories of analysis. They also prioritize people's attitudes toward the political relationship between the rebellious colonies and the British Empire as the central feature of their wartime experiences and decision-making, rather than, for example, acknowledging that some people valued the return of peace more than they did any specific postwar constitutional arrangements. In doing so they assimilate people in the middle into the ranks of a cause they did not want to join.[23] So while this book owes a great deal to the scholarship on loyalists, it argues that we ought to consider the nobodyists as distinct from them, as worthy of consideration in their own right and on their own terms.

The Crugers were a merchant family, and commercial interests and links were important to their revolutionary-era politics and choices. That connects this book to other histories of eighteenth-century Anglo-American merchant families, most of which focus on exploring commercial affairs, but which have also sometimes touched on revolutionary-era politics.[24] In this book, unlike in some works on merchant families, my primary focus is not on reconstructing the Crugers' business practices for their own sake, but for how they affected their experiences of the Revolution. The Crugers' business operations were crucial to their history, but commercial considerations alone cannot explain why they became nobody men while some other similar merchants became patriots or loyalists. Self-interest was certainly part of the Crugers' revolutionary story—just as it was for many of their more militant contemporaries—but it was neither understood just in economic terms nor the only basis for their decisions.

Considerable scholarship has argued that the American Revolution should be understood as a civil war, and this provides a foundation for nobodyist histories.[25] John Shy laid out a basic reason for considering it as such. The "American Revolution was a civil war," he noted, because "in proportion to population almost as many Americans were engaged in fighting other Americans during the Revolution as did so during the Civil War."[26] Although these dimensions were long under-analyzed in nationalist narratives, the conflict was bitter, sometimes horrific, and violent.[27] The American Revolution also fits contemporary social scientific definitions of a civil war as "armed combat within the boundaries of a recognized sovereign entity between parties subject to a common authority at the outset of the hostilities."[28] Such definitions are agnostic about both the causes and the outcomes of civil wars, which have occurred for many different reasons and ended with widely varying settlements. In this respect it is useful to heed reminders like David Armitage's that "every great revolution is a civil war" and Alan Taylor's that "revolutions breed civil wars: triangular struggles in which two sides compete for civilian support."[29] Framing the American Revolution as a civil war puts the focus on the experience of the conflict itself rather than its causes or postwar consequences, but such framing is compatible with seeing what happened in North America between 1775 and 1783 as a radically transformative "revolution" or as a "war for independence" with quieter implications for subsequent Americans' and Britons' lives. Whether we think of the American Revolution as a civil war because "Americans" fought "Americans" or because it involved war between common subjects of the British Empire, it is clear that the struggle was something other than a national, interstate conflict between

Americans and Britons even if that idea continues to have a hold on the public imagination.

While they were clearly a very large group—the best estimates put them at between two-fifths and three-fifths of the total wartime population—the precise number of neutrals in the American Revolution remains elusive.[30] There were no referenda on beginning an armed insurrection or on the Declaration of Independence, no polls that offered "none of the above" as an option. Given this, one significant benefit of acknowledging the American Revolution as a civil war is that it puts its history into dialogue with scholarship that frames civil war as a painfully persistent global phenomenon.[31] A first point is simple but essential: civil wars across time and space feature large numbers of people in the middle. This was the case in conflicts with particular connections to the American Revolution: the British civil wars of the mid-seventeenth century, the French Revolution, and the American Civil War of the 1860s.[32] David Underdown, for example, memorably described the civil war in the English county of Somerset in the early 1640s as being "fought between two minorities, struggling in a sea of neutralism and apathy."[33] Such dynamics are common. As a leading study has put it, "an empirical regularity supported by considerable evidence is that only a small minority of people are actively involved in civil wars, either as fighters or active supporters." One well-regarded guideline is the "5 percent rule," which holds that only that much of the population in a civil war is made up of "active and militant supporters" of an armed group.[34] The number of active patriots in the American Revolution may well have been significantly higher than this norm, but this should not be assumed or read backward from people's acquiescence to the political order that emerged through the conflict. Most important, even if the rate of "active and militant" participation in the American Revolution greatly exceeded that typical in civil wars, the number of nobodyists in the conflict was certainly so large as to demand more thoughtful attention from historians.

Rather than characterizing the American population as divided between patriots and loyalists, we might instead think of it as split between militant partisans and "the rest," with engagement in or active support for making war— rather than an affinity for one warring side or the other's preferred political outcome—as the crucial marker of difference. Trying to keep a civil war at arm's length is also entirely normal behavior, and it has frequently been the case that collaboration, whether with insurgents or incumbents, is better understood as a *product* rather than a *cause* of military success (particularly the control of territory) in such conflicts.[35] Many people often described as loyalists remained in the United States after 1783; it seems likely that most colonial Americans would likewise have reconciled themselves to a return to imperial subjecthood had Britain prevailed in the war. As the final chapters of this book show, most of the Cruger family became American citizens after 1783. Scholarship on civil wars helps to suggest why they, like many others, made such choices.

A second related point, which comes out of work on civil wars, is that violence is central to their dynamics. Civil wars are not elections. Despite tendencies to regard choosing sides in the Revolution as akin to "voting" for a preferred political outcome, "election makes a poor analogy for civil war," in part because "war and peace are radically different contexts that induce and constrain violence in very different ways." Deciding if and how to participate in a civil war—to risk killing and being killed—is very different from pulling a lever on a referendum question behind a privacy curtain.[36] What drove the American Revolution, as Timothy Breen has put it, is that "insurgents" in America "accepted violence against the imperial state as a legitimate form of political resistance."[37] Others—the British government and military and their loyalist allies—deployed their own violence to preserve that state. In such circumstances, it is important to distinguish between people's "attitudinal support" or "preferences" and "behavioral support" or "actions."[38] While both sides in civil wars like the American Revolution welcome attitudinal support, what they need is behavioral support, and gaining this often depends on which side is able to establish territorial control. In such a situation, "people can be coerced, and violence is used to force people to alter their behavior and behave in ways that may not be consistent with their preferences."[39] Selective violence, or the threat of violence, plays a powerful role in such situations as combatants deploy a variety of tactics (i.e., loyalty oaths, local committees of inspection, imprisonment and banishment, partisan violence, militias and military call-ups, threats to property) to obtain people's compliance. These dynamics loom large in the history recounted here. Moreover, civil war is "a deeply 'endogenous' process" in which "behavior, beliefs, preferences, and even identities can be altered as a result of the conflict and its violence."[40] These strictures on the centrality of violence to civil war can aid in understanding nobodyists' choices.

Also useful is the idea that "microdynamics" are significant within civil wars.[41] Paradoxically, one of the benefits that historians of the American Revolution might gain by looking up at the literature on global civil war is a reminder to look down at the local level to recover who actually did what to whom during the conflict and why. As one scholar of civil war has observed, "the local is not the provincial or the parochial but rather the social, and most importantly, the empirical." This is in part because "civil war can be analyzed as a process that transforms the political actors' quest for victory and power, and the local or individual actors' quest for personal and local advantage into a joint process of violence."[42] This suggests that if historians of the American Revolution really want to understand how and why people made the decisions they did, then the answers likely lie in the particularities of time and place. This book gives considerable attention to specific communities in which the Crugers confronted the Revolution because local affinities and contexts were crucial to their wartime choices, and often as important as wider national or imperial ones.

Finally, comparative literature on civil war has implications for how historians of the American Revolution should read their sources. Historians are usually carefully attuned to the interests and forces that shape their sources, but the literature on global civil war flags particular issues. Most important, it suggests that while people who actively participate in civil wars largely do so for various nonideological reasons, they frequently *retroactively explain* their decisions in ideological terms.[43] This recurring feature of civil wars implies that historians of the American Revolution should be attuned to evidence of nonideological factors contributing to wartime decision-making, cautious about claims for ideological motivation that they find in their sources, and especially careful with post-1783 accounts that try to gloss wartime decision-making. These dynamics are powerful in the Crugers' story as, in the decade after the Revolution, different members of the family worked to reintegrate themselves into British and American societies transformed by the conflict. Staunch loyalists and patriots alike were rewarded with compensation, pensions, land grants, and influence by the political entities that emerged from the conflict, but there were no such incentives for having been a nobodyist. After the war, several of the Crugers looked to simplify their complicated pasts in ways that conformed to new expectations. The accounts that patriots, loyalists, and nobodyists told about themselves and others were shaped by the patterns of storytelling, remembering, and forgetting that are a feature of civil wars. After 1783, the nobodyists' history was inconvenient for others and themselves, which contributes to historians' difficulties with analyzing their experiences.

Unlike some of the most important older historiographical schools of thought associated with revolutionary scholarship, this book is not primarily about the conflict's causes. Rather it focuses on recovering and analyzing peo-

INTRODUCTION 13

ple's experiences of living through the era. Like much recent work, and influenced by studies of civil war, this book stresses that multiple factors shaped people's wartime decision-making. Considerations of political ideology alone do not provide compelling explanations for the choices made by the nobodyists in this book. To put it in a slightly different way, not all wartime political thinking was based on "political thought."[44] Indeed, at multiple points the Crugers' political principles seem indistinguishable from those of many of their patriot counterparts. In that respect this book departs from so-called neo-Whig interpretations of the Revolution. Yet, the nobody men considered here did not make their choices solely because of their socioeconomic position or their understanding of their financial interests, and that marks this book as distinct from various "progressive" interpretations of the Revolution that insist upon the explanatory power of class and class conflict.[45] Ideological and economic factors (as well as others) certainly contributed to what people did in the American Revolution, but—and this seems rather obvious—no single overarching explanation provides a golden key to understanding real people's behavior. Moreover, while this study focuses on a single family, the nobodyists, like patriots and loyalists, were a diverse group. I have drawn on studies from various interpretive traditions, sharing the view that "there is no single paradigm that can do justice to an event as multifaceted as the American Revolution."[46]

People typically made decisions not as atomized idealogues nor as miserly, Scrooge-like egotists, but from within dense webs of interconnection. Such groups—as opposed to almost mythically autonomous individuals—matter because as Kathleen DuVal noted "an individual or society that tried to act completely alone had no chance" in eighteenth-century North America and "*advantageous interdependence* was a more logical goal."[47] Because this book centers on an extended family, it emphasizes interdependence as a key feature of the lived experience and decision-making of the revolutionary era.[48] No trope of civil war is more familiar than the notion of "brother against brother," and such dynamics occurred during the American Revolution, but one theme that emerges from the Crugers' story is that family often endured rather than fractured in the face of such conflicts. Community ties could persist too, and this book traces the extended Cruger family interacting with a group of people—including many New Yorkers—across decades. Such relationships were marked by the war, but they were never solely defined by it.

If we put people in the middle at the center of the Revolution's history, we can understand its dynamics in less blinkered and ultimately more human ways. This book uses the Crugers' history to make five main arguments. First, it challenges how nobodyists' stories have been ignored or glossed over in many other histories. When it has been treated, nobodyism has usually been characterized as the product of some failing or deficiency: a lack of courage, an inability to think clearly, an absence of political commitment, or an insufficient regard for the greater good. People in the middle have usually been measured by competing national and historiographical traditions against either brave and visionary patriots or steadfast and self-sacrificing loyalists. In either case, they have usually been found wanting. Certainly, some nobodyists were afraid, irresolute, or conspicuously self-interested; so too were many active patriots and committed loyalists. More important, as examples from this book suggest, some nobodyists could—like some patriots and loyalists—be brave, coherent, profoundly political, and motivated by an interest in the common good. The book does not argue that the Crugers—much less all the nobodyists—were heroes. They were not. Nationalist mythologies of the Revolution also have given us far too many wooden caricatures already. Rather, tracing the Crugers' collective history demonstrates that efforts to steer a course between the two warring parties could be reasonable and comprehensible.

Second, the book argues that, as befitting such a large group of people, those in the middle did not all act in the same ways. Understanding how nobodyists experienced and shaped the period means exploring this variety, and the book does so through different Crugers' distinct but connected stories. Some nobodyists deployed strategies of silence, evasion, and retreat, trying to minimize their contact with British and nascent American officialdom alike. Uncovering these people's motivations and behaviors can be difficult because they avoided revealing their preferences. Other people in the middle were what some called "trimmers": occupants of the Revolution's middle ground who, like civilians in other civil wars, adhered to the warring side that exercised coercive power at a given moment and could switch allegiances as circumstances changed. Still other people made their desire for a position between the warring parties public, adopting an avowedly neutralist, independent, or pro-peace position, sometimes at great cost. The Crugers' story reveals that such behavioral variation was a crucial but understudied feature of the Revolution.

Third, the book argues that besides behaving differently, people in the middle had different reasons for being there. Most significantly, it uses the Crugers' experiences and builds on insights from civil war studies to show that ideological preferences were only one part of people's multidimensional wartime decision-making. Family, friendship, ties to local communities, understandings of the common good, economic self-interest, concerns about personal security, unwillingness to use violence to pursue political ends, and many other factors shaped nobodyists' choices. Moreover, some of the Crugers' most deeply held political commitments—such as their cross-generational dedication to New York City's development—map poorly onto the dichotomies of patriot and loyalist or national political narratives.[49] The Crugers' wartime judgments were not simply votes on their preferred constitutional outcomes; things were different once the shooting started and people had to make decisions about how to engage with the American Revolution not just once, but repeatedly, and amid diverse and changing contexts.

Fourth, the book builds on recent work in American, British, and Atlantic history by adopting a geographically expansive framework incorporating territories integral to the era's history but outside of what became the United States. The Crugers' wartime history shows how ties of interdependence crossed emerging international borders and how the Revolution affected spaces that remained outside the United States after 1783. The Crugers' postwar experiences also show that working out national identities in the post-revolutionary Atlantic was a gradual, contingent, and contested process that stretched into at least the 1790s.

Finally, this book introduces a new and more fully treated set of neutralist stories into revolutionary history. Individual lives and family histories have been crucial to how generations of readers have made sense of the Revolution. For many people, the canonical history of the Revolution *is* the story of "The Founders." There is power in narrative, and telling the Crugers' stories makes concrete some wider nobodyist experiences. While members of the family are known to historians, they have usually been treated briefly when their life stories intersect with some particular theme. The Crugers have never been fully considered as a collective, nor has any individual member of the family received book-length treatment since the nineteenth century. A major reason for this is that the Crugers left behind no single archive of family papers, a fact shaped by their tumultuous wartime experiences. However, in a testament to the extent of their personal, commercial, and political networks, traces of their revolution survive in many archives and libraries on both sides of the Atlantic.

The Crugers do not provide the last or only word on the revolutionary history of nobodyists. They are parts, not the whole. Their experiences, while revealing, are also the products of their specific places in the Atlantic world of the revolutionary era. The Crugers were merchants and urbanites. They closely identified with New York City and a few other port towns and were integrated into a wider maritime world. They held political offices and mixed with other elites in the places they called home. They were collectively very wealthy. They owned extensive property, including enslaved people, before, during, and after the Revolutionary War. Moreover, the Crugers whose lives are best documented, and therefore the most fully treated here, are the men in the family. This is partly a product of circumstance—the two sisters of the Crugers' revolutionary generation died during the war—and magnified by the absence of a family archive, which constrains the sort of material on the Crugers that survives. But, more widely the comparatively scant information on the perspectives and experiences of the Cruger women reflects gendered structures of power in the Anglo-American world of the period.

Were, therefore, the Crugers "representative" of the nobodyists? Given the large and diverse group of people that were in the middle during the American Revolution, no book focused on a single family can capture everything about the nobodyists' history. That said, the Crugers' Revolution reveals many themes, dilemmas, and dynamics experienced by others. Ultimately, this book is intended as a contribution to what I hope will become an expanding field of neutralist studies. Nobodyism, like patriotism and loyalism, cut across lines of geography, class, race, and gender after 1775. Other studies of the resulting conjunctions will make our collective understanding of the American Revolution richer and more compelling. The American Revolution begins to look different once we acknowledge that neither whigs nor tories had a monopoly on the truth, and that diverse groups of people sought other paths through the conflict.

What follows is organized into three sections on the prewar years, the war, and the postwar period. Part I treats the Cruger family's collective history and the political and economic world they inhabited between 1760 and 1775. In exploring the Crugers' significant parts in the prewar politics of patriot resistance, it makes clear that these future nobodyists were not isolated within colonial society. Part II examines the period between 1775 and 1783 as years of violence, turmoil, and dislocation. Its chapters branch out to consider particular family members' distinct wartime experiences, underlining the often highly contingent, local dynamics that framed people's choices when maneuvering through the Revolution. Through the Crugers' varied stories, it crystallizes what the war years were like for large numbers of people with allegiances that transcended the traditional patriot/loyalist divide. Part III, the final section of the book, brings the strands of the individual Crugers' lives back together and into the 1790s. It shows that while the Crugers welcomed the peace, it took them many years to build secure new lives in a world remade by the conflict. To do so, they left behind their wartime histories as nobody men and redefined themselves as British subjects or American citizens.

PART ONE

"Cruger and Liberty!"

1760–1775

1. The Crugers' World

In 1760, Cruger's Wharf was a bustling place: the center of a sprawling family commercial enterprise that put goods from around the world into the hands of New York's consumers and connected the province's producers to markets beyond the horizon. Superintending it all were two brothers—Henry and John Cruger—who ran their merchant firm from the Lower Manhattan dock and its warehouses. The Crugers' captains sailed their cargoes to far-flung destinations: Boston, Charleston, Jamaica, Curaçao, St. Croix, Bristol, London, and many other places big and small. On their returns, the Crugers' ships carried sugar and rum from the Caribbean, valuable woods from Central America, and cloth, pottery, and metal goods from Europe. As their trade flourished, the Crugers helped develop the wharf area, transforming it into a valuable block of the city. By 1760, Cruger's Wharf featured houses, shops, warehouses, a tavern, and a theater.[1] Patrons flowed in and out of these businesses, and the high and low of colonial society mingled in the shadows of the merchantmen's masts. New York was becoming a center of global commerce; the Crugers and their wharf were helping to make it so.

Understanding the Cruger family's revolution means understanding the world, encapsulated by Cruger's Wharf, they inhabited. Three interrelated factors were especially important. First, they were a family of merchants. This shaped how they made decisions individually and together. Trading made the family wealthy and, at times and in places, politically powerful. It also created a set of circum-Atlantic connections and promoted a particular set of attitudes toward the British Empire that contributed to their subsequent choices. Second, looking at the Crugers as a family reveals the centrality of collective action and mutual support to their lives.[2] In colonial America true "independence" was dangerously isolating while "interdependence" was a path to security and prosperity.[3] As a merchant clan, the Crugers long operated as a unit; none made their revolutionary-era choices in isolation. Rather, they did so as people tied to other people, and this was crucial to how they understood their responsibilities and determined their loyalties. The strongest of these bonds, which would be tested in the crisis of the 1770s, were forged in the years before 1765.

Third, by the time of the American Revolution, members of the Cruger family had been active within local, provincial, and imperial politics for more than fifty years. The Revolution brought new people into early American politics. The Crugers were among those who lost some—but not all—power as others gained it. Their choices after 1775 were influenced by older political commitments and strategies, some of which proved out of step with new realities but others of which proved more enduring. Because of their prewar prominence, the past often proved inescapable for the Crugers even as the world was being made anew.

John Cruger (c. 1678–1744) was the first male member of the family to settle in New York, where he arrived by 1696. His specific birthplace is uncertain. He may have been German, Dutch, Danish, or (less likely) English by birth; generations of genealogists and historians have been unable to determine exactly which. A man named Tileman Cruger, described as a "stranger, of Bremen," who died in London in 1694 was almost certainly John's close kinsman (perhaps his father or older brother) because the name Tileman—spelled variously—was passed down among the New York Crugers for generations.[4] Another relative, Valentine Cruger, was a London-based merchant who helped John get his start in New York. Although Valentine's country of origin is likewise uncertain, he too was not English by birth; his name appears in a 1688 list of foreign-born Protestants granted English residence. Operating out of Britain, Valentine had significant connections to New York prior to John Cruger's arrival there. In 1690 Valentine joined other "Merchants of London, trading to New York and New England" protesting fur trading privileges granted to the Hudson's Bay Company.[5] In 1692 Valentine was proposed, although not subsequently named, as a member of New York's Provincial Council in the wake of Leisler's Rebellion. Valentine died in England, recorded by a parish clerk as a "gentleman," in 1702.[6]

Wherever John Cruger was born, he certainly had strong Dutch connections. He may have spent his childhood in Holland and his early business correspondence mentions a man there, Hans Hansler, whom he called his "cosyn."[7] John Cruger knew at least the Dutch and English languages. He recorded his marriage and family births and deaths in Dutch in a 1688 Dutch-printed Bible and was a member of the Dutch Reformed Church in New York, where he married, his children were baptized, and he was buried.[8] Whether born in modern Germany, the Netherlands, or somewhere else, Cruger was part of a transnational mercantile family with roots in Protestant northern Europe.

The city of New York had been English for only a generation when John Cruger arrived. He joined a diverse trading community that included English newcomers, Dutch-descended holdovers, and Huguenot refugees. In 1696, Cruger appeared in New York tax records as a "factor" in business with a partner of Dutch birth and English connections, Ouziel Van Swieten. The pair likely acted as local agents for European merchants including Valentine Cruger. Also in 1696, both John Cruger and Van Swieten signed their names to the "Association Oath Rolls of the British Plantations" in New York, signaling their loyalty to the new monarchy brought in by the Glorious Revolution.[9]

Early English New York held opportunities for ambitious white immigrants like John, and he won himself a prominent place in it by taking and managing risks and by capitalizing on the exploitation integral to Britain's expanding empire. In 1698 he served as supercargo on a ship, the *Prophet Daniel*, on a slave-trading voyage to Madagascar. The ship, owned by a member of the De Lancey family, was seized by Madagascar-based pirates, but John found his way back to New York with his reputation intact. He was admitted as a New York freeman in March 1703, allowing him to legally retail goods, vote, and hold office.[10] A few days later, Cruger married Marya Cuyler (1678–1724), from an Albany Dutch family.[11] While he brought industry and transatlantic trading connections to the match, she had links to many other New Yorkers.

Marya's kinship networks—her father was an immigrant Dutch tailor, while her mother was likely born in America—were crucial to the Crugers' long-term future. Through Marya the Crugers were related to other New York families, including the powerful Livingstons. Both Marya and John called Philip Livingston (1686–1749), the second Lord of Livingston Manor, their "cosyn" when they wrote to him in Dutch.[12] The Crugers soon became people of consequence. In 1703 John Cruger was taxed as among the least wealthy third of New Yorkers; by 1708 he was one of the city's top forty merchants and on his way up.[13] He was selected as an assessor for New York's Dock Ward from 1707 to 1709.[14] In

1708, he also began serving as an auditor of accounts for Royal Navy ships in New York, suggesting a growing reputation for business acumen and increasing political influence.[15]

John and Marya had five daughters and three sons before her death in 1724. All were baptized in the Dutch Reformed Church. One daughter died in childhood. Three others, Anna (1704–44), Maria (1718–87), and Rachel (1721–75), evidently never married. These women probably spent their lives within relatives' households, but likely had money of their own. Maria and Rachel owned valuable waterfront property in Manhattan in partnership with their brothers on the eve of the Revolution.[16] A fifth sister, Sarah (1714–66), married Nicholas Gouverneur (1713–87), from another trading family, in New York's Dutch Church in 1755.[17] John and Marya's three sons, Tileman (1705–30), Henry (1707–80), and John (1710–91), would all become merchants.

The first John Cruger forged profitable connections across the cultural, linguistic, and political boundaries of the Atlantic world. New York customs and port records show him importing Barbados rum regularly in the first decade of the eighteenth century.[18] He also imported dutied European goods, either directly from London or Amsterdam or via Boston or Jamaica, in the early eighteenth century.[19] Besides retailing goods in the city, he was a middleman, connecting inland trappers, farmers, and traders with European merchants and markets. Between 1701 and 1709, for example, John regularly paid duties on bear skins and other peltries bound for London.[20] In the 1720s, John acted as a shipper for Marya's nephew Cornelius Cuyler, who operated out of Albany. Cuyler also did business with John's eldest son, Tileman, in the late 1720s, which included sending the Crugers flour sourced from Albany-area farmers for Caribbean export.[21] By the 1730s John Cruger's English correspondents included the London firm Storke and Gainsborough, whose extensive business included supplying goods for trade with Native Americans.[22] Cruger was wealthy enough by 1730 to have his house and land in the city's Dock Ward assessed as more valuable than some 95 percent of other properties there.[23] The Crugers came to live in increasingly prosperous fashion on "Broad street" in a house that became "notable for its elegance," and in 1740 he had his portrait painted by fellow New Yorker Gerardus Duyckinck (fig. 2).[24]

The Crugers of the family's first two American generations developed deepening ties with the Caribbean, including Dutch Curaçao. Located just off the northern coast of South America, which provided access to the silver and produce of the Spanish Empire, Curaçao became a key node for the Dutch West

Figure 2. Gerardus Duyckinck, *John Cruger Sr. (1677–1744)*, c. 1740. Oil on canvas. Gift of Edmund Astley Prentis, New-York Historical Society, 1957.64. Photography © New-York Historical Society.

India Company and the Dutch slave trade. The Dutch declared Curaçao's principal town, Willemstad, a free port in 1675. This enabled ships and traders of any nation, including New York and England's other Atlantic colonies, to visit and do business. Curaçao also provided a convenient, neutral site for conducting clandestine trade between the French, Spanish, and British empires.[25] These vectors of trade and Dutch toleration made Curaçao, even by Caribbean standards, a cosmopolitan place, home to merchants of diverse origins, including a prominent Jewish community.

Although some two thousand miles away, Curaçao was easily reachable by sail from New York. Many New York traders, especially those of Dutch extraction, did regular business with friends and relations on the island. Because it had poor soil and few natural advantages beyond its location, Curaçao relied on regular imports to meet its free and enslaved population's basic needs. As one island resident noted in 1747, if North American ships "did not bring us flour, butter, and other foodstuffs, half the inhabitants of the island would be on the brink of starvation."[26] The Crugers were collectively involved in the Curaçao trade by no later than 1730, the year in which young Tileman died from a disease contracted there.[27] It may be that the Crugers' trade with Curaçao and the rest of the Caribbean increased as New York's fur trade declined in importance. In 1739 John Cruger cooperated with several partners to send the brig *Union* to the island laden with flour and biscuit, butter, and planks.[28] By the late 1740s, Curaçao was second only to Jamaica in New York's commerce with the Caribbean.[29] During the Seven Years' War, one pamphleteer baldly claimed that "the merchants of New York have gotten their estates by the Curaçao Trade."[30] Trade with Curaçao became a multigenerational feature of the Crugers' business that stretched into the nineteenth century. More generally, the trading networks established by John and Marya Cruger, linking the port of New York to the North American interior, the Caribbean, and metropolitan English and European goods and markets, would be maintained and expanded by their descendants in the coming decades. Later Crugers inherited not only wealth and status in New York but also a set of commercial networks and practices that endured until the Revolution.

Although their eldest son died young, John and Marya's two surviving sons, Henry and John, lived to see the United States declare independence. Partners for decades in the firm Henry & John Cruger, they built on their parents' legacy and became two of New York's best-known merchants. They began their careers in common mercantile fashion, by voyaging to sea and living abroad. In 1724, seventeen-year-old Henry told a Livingston "cosin" that he was preparing to "sail for the Coast of Guinea in the sloop Ann." This voyage, likely taken with his father's guidance, gave Henry early exposure to the grim realities of transatlantic slave trading.[31] Henry then spent much of his twenties resident in Jamaica, where he arrived in 1731.[32] As they did with Curaçao, the Crugers forged enduring connections with Jamaica. The island, taken by England from Spain in 1655, was becoming a place dominated by planters and plantations. Under the British, Kingston became Jamaica's main port and urban center, and Henry resided there as it grew.[33]

THE CRUGERS' WORLD   27

Henry was quickly accepted into Kingston's burgeoning merchant community. In 1732 he was part of a partnership, Barry & Cruger, and doing some business with New York correspondents including Robert Livingston Jr.[34] By 1733 Henry was politicking to promote trade, joining other Jamaican merchants asking the Royal Navy to base more warships at Port Royal, closer to their Kingston business interests.[35] Slavery, climate, and disease meant life in eighteenth-century Jamaica was frequently short for Black and white people alike.[36] Henry married twice on the island in the space of less than two and a half years. In September 1734 he married Hannah (Sloughter) Montgomery, only twenty-one but already a widow with a young daughter. Within a year of joining the Cruger family, Hannah was dead.[37] Henry married for a second time in December 1736, this time to Elizabeth Harris, the daughter of a Jamaican doctor, Nicholas Harris, and his wife, Saye. Elizabeth and Henry's first child, John Harris Cruger, was born in Jamaica in 1737. That same year, Henry represented Kingston in the Jamaica Assembly.[38] Having already buried one spouse, however, Henry and his young family returned permanently to New York in 1738.[39]

In these years John Cruger II probably spent substantial time at sea and resided for a time in Curaçao, where he partnered with another New Yorker, Thomas Marston in the mid-1730s. The Crugers frequently traded alongside Thomas's brother Nathaniel in the ensuing decades.[40] In June 1738, John—then twenty-seven years old—was made a freeman of New York City and his occupation was described as "mariner."[41] In the late 1730s and 1740s, the elder John Cruger and his sons, now all based in New York, were engaged "in the import of occasional slaves, some fabric such as garline, and rather extensive importing of Madeira wine and Jamaica rum and molasses."[42] In 1741, the younger John petitioned New York's lieutenant governor for permission to send a ship laden with provisions to Curaçao.[43] By the 1740s, Henry was living in his own home near Manhattan's Hanover Square, and John came to live nearby too.[44] When the family patriarch, the elder John, died in 1744, his sons were well prepared to continue trading on their own.

While John of the second generation remained a childless bachelor, Henry had a large family with Elizabeth: four sons and two daughters.[45] John Harris Cruger (1737–1807) was born in Jamaica, but their five younger children were born in New York. The couple's two daughters, Mary Cruger Walton (1743–82) and Elizabeth Cruger Van Schaack (1747–78), known within the family as Bess or Betsey, remained in New York. Alongside John Harris, three other sons—Henry Cruger Jr. (1739–1827), Telemon Cruger (1740–c. 1817), and Nicholas

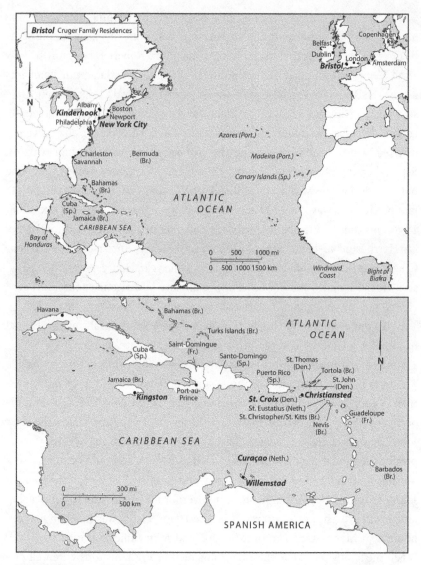

Figure 3. The Crugers' World, c. 1765. Bold text shows the locations where Cruger family members lived before the Revolution, and plain text shows other locations with which the Crugers traded or were connected.

Cruger (1744–1800)—all joined the family's sprawling circum-Atlantic commercial enterprise (fig. 3). As they reached adulthood, these Crugers were able to call on the support of their parents and their uncle John.

In the decades before the Revolution, the Cruger family took part in a wider anglicization and cultural refinement of colonial society.[46] Handwritten records in the family Bible switch from Dutch to English after 1728, and English was evidently the first language of the Crugers of the second and third generations. As their parents had been, John and his sisters of the second generation remained adherents of the Dutch Reformed Church.[47] Henry and his large family, however, entered the Church of England.[48] Given the care with which the Crugers would play the marriage market, their daughters probably were raised to be wives and mothers in wealthy merchant families of their own. Elizabeth Cruger Van Schaack was described by her husband Peter "as not having had much education" but, by building on her innate talents, she developed "a very considerable degree of accuracy in her writing." Despite having lost her own mother at relatively young age, Peter noted, Elizabeth was "judicious and economical" as a household manager and devoted to her Anglican faith.[49]

An object eloquently captures the family's increasingly refined world, which the Cruger women helped create. A particularly fine silver sugar bowl monogrammed with the initials of the Jamaica-born Elizabeth Harris Cruger, dating from around the time of her marriage to Henry Cruger, is preserved in the collections of Yale University (fig. 4). Inspired by Chinese porcelain but made by an American silversmith, the New Yorker Simeon Soumaine, the bowl captures the Cruger's mercantile cosmopolitanism and local pride. Celebrated by silver experts as attaining "the uttermost perfection of linear beauty and exquisite proportion" and as one of "the most distinguished objects in the whole range of American silver," Elizabeth's bowl is a testament to the wealth and refinement that the Crugers accrued through commerce by midcentury.[50] In its luxury and function, the sugar bowl is also a reminder that the family's prosperity was due in part to the Caribbean trade and the commodities that enslaved people produced. Henry and Elizabeth's children were given all of the advantages created by their grandparents' and parents' fortunes and circum-Atlantic connections.

Henry and Elizabeth's sons were destined to be merchants, but they also got the gentlemanly polishing that money could increasingly buy in colonial America. John Harris Cruger enrolled at the Philadelphia Academy, recently founded by Benjamin Franklin and others, from 1752 until 1755, when he left to enter trade.[51] As his father had done, he lived as a young man in Jamaica, where he was a resident merchant in 1761.[52] He may have split time between Jamaica and the mainland for a period, but in October 1765 he, alongside his brother Nicholas, was made a New York freeman and from 1766 advertised goods for sale under his own name in the city.[53] He lived there until the outbreak of the Revolution.

Figure 4. Simeon Soumaine, Elizabeth Harris Cruger's Silver Sugar Bowl, c. 1738–45. Mabel Brady Garvan Collection, Yale University Art Gallery, New Haven, CT, 1930.1056.

The founding of King's College, where Henry Cruger Jr. was part of the first class in 1754, was a milestone in New York's development. Established after considerable controversy, the college was simultaneously an assertion of civic pride, a symbol of royal authority and imperial belonging, and an Anglican counterweight to older dissenter-controlled American schools. Some non-Anglican New Yorkers and other colonists opposed the college's chartering, and for a time it was an emotive issue in provincial politics, but the Crugers put their considerable weight behind it. This was more likely because of a desire to see New York claim status and develop than a peculiarly sectarian motivation. Both the elder Henry and his brother John, despite the latter's membership in the Dutch Reformed Church, were among the college's original governors.[54] Young

Henry studied at King's College for three years, joined in 1755 by Telemon, who likewise stayed for three years.[55]

In 1757, aged sixteen, Henry left college and subsequently went to Bristol, England, to embark on a mercantile career.[56] Although he returned to New York on multiple occasions, he lived and traded out of Bristol for more than thirty years. Henry and Elizabeth's two younger sons settled in the Caribbean. Telemon lived in Curaçao by 1763 and resided there for the rest of his life, becoming the owner of a prominent house and wharves in Willemstad's Scharloo neighborhood. In his early twenties, Nicholas Cruger moved to the Danish island of St. Croix, where he was trading by 1766.[57]

Although the Cruger siblings dispersed, they remained connected for decades. In both the family's second and third generations, Cruger siblings seem to have regarded each other fundamentally as equals—a common colonial dynamic—and practiced "kin-keeping," the work of staying tied together as adults.[58] In 1772, Nicholas closed a letter to Telemon in Curaçao "with as sincere affection as one Brother can have for another, I am yours unalterable, & most affecteanately," and the effusive misspelling underlined his sentiments.[59] The Crugers did business together, worried for each other's health, and gossiped about friends and neighbors. They named their children after their siblings and cared for their nieces and nephews. When in 1774, the English-based Henry Cruger Jr. closed a letter to "my dear kinsman" Peter Van Schaack, by sending "my love to my dear Bess, and to Henry and Cornelius, and all friends, great and small, young and old," he was expressing an enduring, emotional family solidarity.[60]

As they established themselves as adults from the 1760s, the third generation of Crugers married and set up households of their own. Except for the poorest eighteenth-century colonists, "marriage was never just a private contract between a husband and a wife, it was an alliance of families and a linchpin in the social structure."[61] As merchants, the Crugers also knew that "commercial credit and familial credit were often one and the same."[62] The six siblings of the Cruger's revolutionary generation married between 1760 and 1772, and these unions had profound implications for how they experienced the conflict. These were one of two kinds of marriages, complementary in their effects on the Crugers' entwined status. First, some of the Crugers' marriages strengthened the family's position in New York. Mary Cruger's 1760 marriage to Jacob Walton (1733–82) cemented the Crugers' ties to another powerful family, as the Waltons were among the city's wealthiest merchants and political allies of the De Lanceys.[63]

The Crugers' links to the De Lanceys, who occupied the summit of New York society and became the chief rivals of the Livingston family in provincial politics in the two decades before the Revolution, were further strengthened by John Harris Cruger's 1762 marriage to Anne De Lancey. These New York marriages tied the Crugers to other colonial families in intricate, multigenerational ways. Anne's father, Oliver De Lancey, was among the wealthiest and most powerful men in New York, while her mother, Phila Franks De Lancey, was from a prominent Jewish transatlantic merchant family. The Crugers traded with Phila's London-based brother, Moses Franks, before the Revolution.[64] When Elizabeth "Bess" Cruger, aged eighteen, eloped with twenty-year-old law student Peter Van Schaack in 1765, the marriage caused a temporary rift—family lore has it that her exasperated father Henry threw his wig into the fire on learning the news—but Van Schaack was soon accepted, and his legal skills would be of repeated use to the Crugers in future years.[65]

In a second type of marriage, Cruger men found spouses who strengthened their mercantile and political connections in the communities to which they emigrated. Telemon married twice in Curaçao, first in 1767 to a widow, Dorothea Kier, and then, after the Revolution, to Henrietta Crissen. Nicholas Cruger married Anna de Nully in St. Croix in 1772. After her death, he married Ann Markoe, also from a St. Croix family with North American connections.[66] Henry Cruger Jr. married Ellin Peach in Bristol in 1765. Ellin's father, Samuel Peach, was a wealthy merchant-banker in Bristol. Although Ellin died in 1767 and Henry married twice more, Samuel Peach's local standing and fortune were crucial to Henry's career into the 1780s. There is distressingly little information preserved about Ellin, Henry's subsequent wives, Elizabeth Blair and Caroline Smith, or the other women of the extended Cruger family. Virtually nothing in their own words appears to survive in archives preserving material related to the Cruger men. It is revealing that sources have disagreed even about what Ellin's first name was, with some wrongly thinking she was named Hannah.[67] Yet, these Cruger women were central to the family's history and expanded the networks of interdependence central to revolutionary-era choices.

Following eighteenth-century norms, the Crugers living in different ports traded on their own accounts, often in partnership with other sons of New Yorkers. Outside of the enduring firm of Henry & John Cruger, the family members were not in formal partnership together. However, they frequently consigned each other cargoes; invested in voyages and other ventures together; provided each other credit, intelligence, and a host of services; steered each other business;

and generally showed "a high degree of family solidarity" in their dealings.[68] The Crugers were individuals, but they also benefited from being, and being known as, part of a mercantile dynasty.

The Crugers' collective business in the two decades before the Revolution centered on triangular trade between northern Europe, mainland North America, and the Caribbean.[69] It came to include an array of other profit-seeking activities that expanded and diversified as their wealth grew. One core component of the Crugers' business was importing British manufactured goods—textiles, pottery, ironware, and many other items—into the colonies, especially New York. The importance of this branch of the family's business likely underpinned young Henry's move to Bristol. The Crugers also probably participated in New York's "Dutch trade," the collective, somewhat imprecise name given to importation of goods including cloth, tea, and other products directly from northern European ports outside of Britain. Cargoes that originated in Amsterdam, Rotterdam, Copenhagen, and Hamburg all found willing buyers in New York's shops. While no merchant would openly avow violating Britain's Navigation Acts, there were many ways for continental imports to arrive in New York, and, according to the subject's leading historian, the Crugers, the Waltons, the De Lanceys, and many other commercial families were involved.[70] In the mid-1760s, for example, the firm of John and Henry Cruger did business with at least three merchants in Amsterdam, including the New York–born Daniel Crommelin, whose firm was a key Dutch trading partner for many New Yorkers.[71] Demand was strong, customs officials were easily bribed or circumvented, and such trade was ubiquitous and virtually impossible to stop.[72]

A second leg of the Crugers' trade was exporting North American products. These cargoes were principally from New York, but they sometimes loaded continental produce at other ports, including Boston, Newport, Philadelphia, and Charleston. Provisions, especially flour, destined for the Caribbean were central, and this export trade also included maritime stores, building materials, and much else destined for British and non-British islands. Between 1762 and 1768, for example, the firm of Henry & John Cruger sent fifty-six ships laden with flour, bread, and other foods to Curaçao, where Telemon and his partner acted as their local agents.[73] Nicholas Cruger's firm sold a wide variety of foodstuffs from North America to St. Croix customers including bread, flour, rice, pork, beef, fish, peas, corn, beer, and cider. He also imported working animals, building materials, and ships' supplies.[74]

The provision trade was directly connected to the third core component of the Crugers' business: the shipping of Caribbean plantation goods to New York, other American ports, and Europe, especially Bristol. Rum, molasses, and sugar could come from British colonies like Jamaica, or from other islands that participated in the gray economy of intra-imperial trade. Other goods supplemented sugar products. Curaçao, for example, was a source for cacao and silver specie.[75] Building on their Caribbean connections, from the 1750s the Crugers became heavily involved in shipping logwood, the source of a valuable textile and leather dye, and mahogany from the Central American mainland to North America, Britain, and the Netherlands.[76]

The Crugers also looked for opportunities outside of these main channels. In the 1760s, the Crugers sometimes shipped pig iron to Henry in Bristol or other correspondents. The Crugers imported wines from Madeira and the Azorean port of Fayal.[77] They developed a specialty in exporting flaxseed from New York to Bristol.[78] Henry and John Cruger passed on these practices and connections. In 1771, John Harris Cruger joined his uncle John in signing a petition from New York merchants trading to the Bay of Honduras asking for British assistance with the "disorderly and riotous" conditions there that were affecting trade.[79] Likewise shortly before the Revolution, John Harris introduced a merchant from Madeira to Boston associates as a "particular friend." Flexibility was the norm. In a 1770s experiment, Henry Cruger Jr. cooperated with Boston's John Hancock in a scheme to export New England whale oil to Britain.[80] If money might be made by putting something aboard a ship in one place and selling it at another, the Crugers were usually willing to give it a try.

New York port records for 1755 give a snapshot of Henry and John Cruger's business on the eve of the Seven Years' War. The Crugers were owners of thirteen different voyages made by five different ships recorded by New York customs official that year, six inbound and seven outbound. They solely owned just three of these, investing in nine with John Watts and one with John Riedelle. The Crugers received cargoes in 1755 from six different ports: "Mosquitos," (in modern Nicaragua), Bristol, Curaçao, Fayal, the Turks Islands and St. Thomas, and St. Christopher. They imported mahogany, logwood, and sarsaparilla from Central America; assorted "European goods," gunpowder, and earthenware from Bristol; and wine from the Azores. Tropical imports included lime juice and dyewood from Curaçao; salt, sugar, and the hardwood lignum vitae from the Turks Islands and St. Thomas; and sugar, cotton, rum, and molasses via St. Christopher's. The Crugers sent single outbound voyages in 1755 to Fayal and

Curaçao. Three of their seven outbound voyages listed St. Christopher as their destination, and two others were recorded as bound for "Mosquitos" or the Bay of Honduras. Their exports overwhelmingly centered on provisions, which were included in all seven outbound voyages. They also shipped wood products including staves, shingles, and planks to the Caribbean and reexported some goods such as Fayal wine, rum, and sugar to their mainland Central American correspondents. The Crugers were running a diverse business in 1755, much of which centered on trade with the Caribbean.[81] Records for 1762 present a similarly varied picture, but with Jamaica and Bristol, where John Harris Cruger and Henry Cruger Jr. were now based, becoming the most frequent destinations for Cruger voyages.[82] Across the 1760s, the firm of Henry and John Cruger looked to support Henry's sons in other ports as they built their own careers.[83]

As their Caribbean trading indicates, slavery was long integral to the Crugers' world. The New York–based Crugers were among the one-quarter to one-third of the city's merchants who owned shares in transatlantic slave trading voyages in the period between 1715 and 1764.[84] Henry and John Cruger's ship *Pitt* delivered seventy-two enslaved people from Africa to Kingston, Jamaica, in 1762 and nearly seventy other people to New York in a 1763 voyage.[85] Henry Cruger Jr. owned at least two ships that engaged in slave trading from Bristol. In 1768, the *Peggy* carried approximately 170 people away from the Bight of Biafra and delivered the survivors of the middle passage to Barbados. Henry's wealthy father-in-law, Samuel Peach, also invested in Bristol slave trading voyages. There are no signs that the Crugers were troubled by the slave trade's terrible human costs. In 1769, Henry Cruger Jr.'s Bristol-based *Nancy* brought some two hundred people from Africa to New York in chains; another forty or more people likely died during the voyage.[86] Nicholas Cruger was also heavily engaged in buying and selling people at points, especially in the early 1770s. He brought fifty-two African people into St. Croix for sale in 1770.[87] In January 1771, his firm Kortright and Cruger advertised that three hundred people who had been taken from Africa's Windward Coast would be sold at "Cruger's Yard" in Christiansted.[88] The following year, Nicholas handled the transport and sale of another two hundred and fifty people, this time from the Gold Coast.[89] In addition to the misery and death it wrought, large-scale human trafficking like this likely involved significant outlays of capital in pursuit of big profits.

The Crugers also bought and sold people singly or in small groups as part of their regular business operations and the intercolonial slave trade. Members of the family's first two generations were listed as owners or partial owners of seven voyages that brought enslaved people from Caribbean ports into greater New York between 1728 and 1751.[90] In 1772 Nicholas Cruger, John Harris Cruger, and Jacob Walton invested in a voyage that transported eight enslaved people for sale.[91] Like other wealthy New Yorkers, the Crugers also owned enslaved people who worked directly for them. These people labored as domestic servants within the Crugers' urban households or in other jobs on family properties. Accounts of the New York slave conspiracy of 1741, which occurred while John Cruger I was mayor, contain the names of several people, including the men Deptford, Hanover, and Neptune, owned by the family.[92] Isack, John, and Hammel and a woman, Catleen, were recorded as being owned by Henry Sr. on a 1755 Nassau County census.[93] A man named Piro, likely a personal servant, was manumitted in Henry Sr.'s 1780 will, on the condition that he not "quit or leave my service during my life time."[94] Some of these New Yorkers likely toiled for the Crugers for most of their lives.

The Crugers owned land and people in the Caribbean too. Henry Sr. held Jamaican property until his death. A 1753 tax list records that a Cruger—almost certainly Henry—possessed five separate parcels in Kingston, putting him in the top 10 percent of the town's property owners by value of rents.[95] He also obtained rural Jamaican land and held enslaved people to work it. In 1753, Henry owned 300 acres and 30 people in St. Andrew parish. This was not a sugar plantation, but rather a mountainous mixture of provision, grazing and wood lands, where some coffee and ginger was also grown.[96] Records for 1754 indicate that he owned a total of 778 acres in multiple parcels across Jamaica, including 250 acres in Port Royal, 513 acres in St. Andrew, and 15 acres in Dorothy.[97] When he died in 1780, Henry left his eldest son John Harris all his unspecified property "in the Island of Jamaica or elsewhere in the West Indies" and any debts due to him from the islands.[98] Nicholas Cruger owned sugar-producing land and people on St. Croix, periodically advertising for the return of those who sought their freedom. These people included "Joe, about 16 years old, well known in town and country," who ran away in May 1773, and the enslaved sailor named Tom, who escaped in 1775.[99] Philip St. Jago, whom Telemon owned in Curaçao, paid for the manumission of Anna Marianna, a mixed-race woman, in 1774.[100] Like other wealthy and prominent colonists of their era, including future patriots and loyalists, the Crugers profited from Atlantic slavery in multiple ways.

As the Crugers' wealth grew, their activities diversified. As an outgrowth of providing shipping services to other merchants, the Crugers occasionally invested in underwriting maritime insurance. From the 1750s, like other wealthy traders, Henry Sr. bought New York municipal bonds.[101] Most significantly, they became involved in urban property development, especially in New York. Soon after returning from Jamaica, Henry Sr. began developing Cruger's Wharf in lower Manhattan. In 1739, with financial support from a Cuyler relative and other partners, Henry contracted for the construction of a massive L-shaped wooden pier that jutted out into the East River, not far from their homes around Hanover Square.[102] As a commercial hub, it enabled the Crugers to move their own goods efficiently and to profit from the desire of other New York traders to do the same. The initial wharf was finished by 1740 (fig. 5). In a process that lasted until about 1765, the stretch of water now enclosed on three sides by the original Manhattan shoreline and the L of Cruger's Wharf was filled in and developed, creating a new city block. The Crugers and their partners further profited from selling lots or acting as landlords on this now prime part of Manhattan.[103] As New York City grew, the family's extensive property in it became increasingly valuable.

Several generations of Crugers also acquired land in today's upstate New York and Vermont. Trade rather than speculation in acreage was the Crugers' core business, but they joined other colonists in the process of systematically dispossessing Native Americans and expanding Euro-American settlement. In doing so they partnered with other well-connected New Yorkers in arrangements that spread financial risk and mobilized networks of political power to secure title to extensive blocks of "undeveloped" land. Henry Cruger Sr., John Cruger II, and John Harris Cruger, for example, were involved in land deals with the great upstate speculator and imperial power broker Sir William Johnson. Peter Van Schaack was his in-laws' lawyer in some of these transactions.[104] The Crugers were not themselves on New York's frontiers, but their money and influence became a presence there.

Together, these business interests shaped the Crugers' world. While intensely loyal to New York City, the Crugers had a much wider, cosmopolitan network of associates. Their trading made them wealthy, but its implications for their wartime decision-making were complex. While they prospered during the colonial period and had much to lose in the Revolution, they also built their fortune in part through forms of transnational trade that pushed against the boundaries and regulations of the British Empire. Moreover, considering their

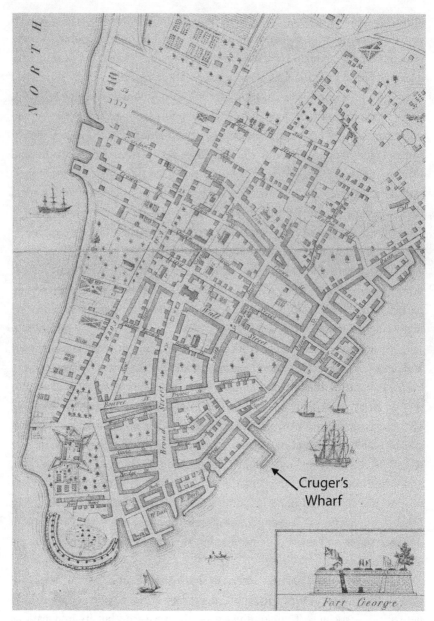

Figure 5. Cruger's Wharf and Lower Manhattan, c. 1743. Detail from "A Plan of the City and Environs of New York as they were in the years 1742, 1743 and 1744." New York Public Library.

future nobodyism, there was nothing in the Crugers' business activities to suggest that they were especially atypical in their trade, cautious, indecisive, or prone to the pangs of conscience.

Most North American merchants before 1750 were reluctant to enter politics directly, but John Cruger I began a family tradition of office holding.[105] Having been an assessor for the city's Dock Ward, he was elected its alderman in 1712. Cruger represented his home Dock Ward, the heart of the city's maritime trading, until 1734. In 1731, he also became New York's first deputy-mayor under the city's revised municipal charter. He capped his political career by serving five consecutive one-year terms as mayor, an office appointed by the governor with the advice of the Provincial Council, from 1739 until shortly before his death in 1744. Among other duties, this meant exercising significant local legal authority as both a justice of the peace and the presiding judge in the Mayor's Court, which had extensive jurisdiction over civil matters, including commercial litigation in the city.[106]

His sons built on this political legacy. Henry was first elected to represent New York City in the provincial assembly in 1745, holding the seat until 1758. These years saw Henry involved in the assembly's spiky disputes with Governor George Clinton over control of public spending.[107] The younger John was elected a Dock Ward alderman in 1754 and 1755. As elected urban politicians, the Crugers had to connect with New York's many non-elite voters. A 1752 advertisement encouraging voters to support Henry and allied candidates for the assembly noted that they "have at all Times, approved themselves in their Loyalty to his Majesty, and in a hearty and steady Attachment to the Rights and Liberties of the People."[108] In 1757 John was appointed as mayor of New York, an office in which he would serve for nearly a decade. In 1758, Henry stepped back for a period from provincial office holding, but John, while continuing as mayor, smoothly took over his place in the assembly as an elected representative for New York City in the 1759 session.[109] As a result, for many years John simultaneously occupied one office that relied on public support and another dependent on retaining the confidence of royally appointed officials. Collectively the Crugers were a force in municipal and provincial politics for several decades.

From 1756, the Seven Years' War presented dangers and opportunities, and several issues mingled the Crugers' particular concerns with much bigger questions. New York was a logistical center for the British Army, and the troops massed in North America needed to be paid and fed. Private merchants who obtained military supply contracts could earn significant commissions. As the Philadelphian Benjamin Franklin observed with a jealous twinge, "I can plainly see, that New York is growing immensely rich, by Money brought into it from all Quarters for the Pay and Subsistence of the Troops."[110] In 1756 John Cruger was named, alongside Oliver De Lancey and Beverly Robinson, as one of the "commissaries and paymasters of the provincial forces," a position of both responsibility and opportunity for profit.[111] In 1762, the Crugers joined John Watts and other New York merchants in trying to profit from provisioning the British troops that invaded and occupied Havana, but this venture proved a severe disappointment.[112]

Many colonial merchants outfitted vessels to attack French shipping. James De Lancey reported in 1758 that New York was experiencing a "kind of madness to go privateering."[113] Over the course of the war, New York–based privateers captured or destroyed over four hundred enemy ships, more than any other British American port. Henry Cruger had invested in a privateer during the earlier War of Austrian Succession, and now the Cruger brothers did so together alongside members of the Watts, Cuyler, and De Lancey families.[114] Privateering held out the promise of windfall gains for captains, sailors, and owners alike, and the Crugers joined fellow New Yorkers in trying to seize them. In doing so, their support for Britain's war effort and self-interest were hopelessly—or happily—intermingled.

Joining in provisioning and privateering did not mean that the Crugers saw the conflict in ways identical to those of British political and military leaders. New York's position as a hub for the British Army made military quartering a contentious issue. As mayor, John Cruger II clashed over quartering with British commander-in-chief John Campbell, fourth Earl of Loudon. Cruger helped facilitate a 1756/57 compromise about paying for the housing of British officers in New York City, spending that Loudon demanded but which the provincial assembly had not authorized.[115] Cruger and other town leaders, "countenanced by the conscious dread and impotency of the citizens," took up a voluntary subscription to cover the officers' expenses for the winter. An unauthorized "tax"—paying for demanded free quarters for officers—was thereby recast as a patriotic "gift" from the king's loyal New York subjects, preserving the colonial principle involved. Cruger seems to have been skilled at finding such clever and crisis-diffusing solutions. In these disputes, New York's people protested that Loudon's demands "were against the common law and the petition of right" and that "the colonists were entitled to all the rights of Englishmen."[116] In what became an increasingly regular feature of transatlantic politics, a practical dispute over expenses and inconveniences was framed in theoretical and "constitutional" terms. The truce that Cruger helped broker proved temporary, as tensions between the military and New Yorkers would return in subsequent years.

The Crugers' continuing involvement in trade contrary to the letter and spirit of Britain's Navigation Acts during the Seven Years' War also shows their markedly colonial and mercantile view of the British Empire. Many New Yorkers remained active in the so-called Dutch trade and in other forms of border-crossing business during the war.[117] Neutral ports like Curaçao and Monte Cristi ("the Mount") on Spanish Hispaniola facilitated ongoing trade with French and other islands in the Caribbean despite the fighting. According to these events' leading historian, mayor John Cruger was among those who did "business with the enemy during the war."[118] Jacob Walton, who married Mary Cruger in 1760, was a leader in New York's wartime commerce with the French. Walton used his wealth and influence to profit from such trade and to quash efforts by irate British political and military leaders to stop it.[119] In May 1762, Henry Sr. joined other prominent New York merchants in petitioning acting governor Cadwallader Colden to "abate the rigor of that resentment, which some of our fellow citizens at present labor under" for trading with the French.[120] John Harris Cruger may well have been involved too as he was partnered in legal business with Jacob Walton by July 1763, and they collaborated with the firm of Greg and Cunningham, which had also been conspicuous in trading with the enemy.[121] As merchants and politicians, the Crugers resisted British attempts to constrain trade and increase metropolitan control over the colonies. The Crugers wished and worked for a British victory in the "Great War for Empire," but they did not envision this as the prelude to a more hegemonic or closed Atlantic commercial system.

The Crugers' pre-revolutionary history raises questions about what they did and did not have in common with other colonial Americans of their era. The influential early twentieth-century historian Carl Becker, who emphasized the role of what he called the "aristocracy" in New York provincial politics before 1765, classed the Crugers among this elite. This New York aristocracy, Becker held, organized itself for political purposes primarily through "personal loyalty, rather than faith in a proposition," as expressed through relations between landlords and tenants and through marriage within the elite. For Becker, this aristocracy was central to the history of the coming of the Revolution because it was a dispute about both "home rule"—a constitutional transatlantic dispute—and "who should rule at home," the latter of which rested on "the latent opposition of motives and interests between the privileged and the unprivileged." Rhetorically, Becker's labeling of the Crugers as intrinsically antidemocratic pre-revolutionary "aristocrats" also served to make them—like other future nobody men and loyalists alike—seem less naturally "American" than those who later supported violent rebellion and independence. This way of understanding the operation of New York politics and, by extension, the Cruger family, proved powerful and enduring.[122]

Yet, from a less myopic, transatlantic perspective—one closer to how the Crugers probably saw themselves—characterizing them as part of an "aristocracy" is misleading. The Crugers were in mode of life far removed from the titled, landed elite who constituted the actual aristocracy that controlled the British Parliament and imperial politics. Like other colonial Americans, for example, the Crugers did not practice primogeniture, and they worked and expected their sons to take up middle-class professions rather than live off inheritances and estates.[123] When, in 1781, an anxious and exiled Peter Van Schaack wrote his fourteen-year-old son a long letter about the boy's future, he summarized the life he wanted for him. Whether his son became "a merchant, a lawyer, a physician, or a divine," Peter wished he would "aim at the more solid though less glaring character of a good rather than a great one; though I hope you will be *both* the one and the other."[124] In this way and others, the outlook of the Crugers and their associates was very different from that of British and other European aristocrats.

Moreover, rather than being inherently undemocratic, the Crugers were long active in the cross-class cause of promoting New York's commercial growth, joined other colonists in objecting to aspects of British imperial governance, and enthusiastically engaged in urban electoral politics. They believed in a communal political proposition that in the 1760s crystallized around the slogan "liberty and trade." Just as the ambition of provincial families like theirs was growing, they were recognizing their own distance from English centers of imperial power. While they might have been up-and-coming people, they were not regarded as peers by the landed oligarchs who held the British empire's reins. As we shall see, Henry Cruger Jr. instead fashioned a political career through critiquing aristocratic government from the later 1760s, and he shared his political principles with his New York relatives. From the perspectives of Bristol, Amsterdam, Kingston, and Christiansted—the wider world in which they moved—the Crugers looked more like successful members of a transatlantic middling sort.

Because of this, the Crugers are best understood as a family of creole traders, as people within rather than outside the mainstreams of colonial economic, social, cultural, and political development. Their natural habitat was the counting house, not a noble court, and the Crugers' peers were the other colonial merchants, planters, and professionals among whom they lived and worked, the very same groups that provided patriot leadership during the Revolution. Several subsequent "Founders," including John Hancock, John Jay, and Alexander Hamilton, were among the Crugers' associates during the prewar period. Like them, the Crugers' primary political loyalties were to the provinces they called home, and like them they saw the colonies as the field for their own futures. The Crugers had visions for how the British Empire should develop that were quite different from the real aristocrats who dominated Parliament and the ministry. In the decade after 1763, these views led the members of the family into influential roles in an emerging transatlantic resistance movement.

2. Stamps and People

In the years after the Seven Years' War, the Crugers were prominent in an interlinked and ocean-spanning series of controversies that roiled New York and the Anglo-American world. These disputes revealed cracks in the imperial constitution that bound Britain and its American colonies together and had major implications for the border-crossing commercial system in which the Crugers did business. Contrary to most people's expectations in 1763, these developments put thirteen colonies on a path that ended in the emergence of the United States as an independent republic two decades later. In the far-reaching crisis that developed in the mid-1760s, some Americans sided with the Crown and suffered for it. The Crugers did not. Rather, despite their subsequent wartime choices, their political sympathies during this period were entirely with the colonies, and their power grew because of it.

Scholars have long recognized how political movements in Britain and North America were connected and how the patriot cause that emerged in the colonies had roots in popular, oppositional English critiques of governmental corruption. Because of its transatlantic footprint, the Cruger family illustrates how the revolution that destroyed the first British Empire was largely a product of that empire's closer political and cultural integration after 1763. In these years, the Crugers pushed their way into the front ranks of a movement for reform and realignment around the Atlantic world. Most important, their multifaceted participation in the Stamp Act crisis shows how it laid the groundwork for their later revolutionary choices.[1]

Active in municipal and provincial politics since the 1750s, John Cruger II, aided by his brother Henry, exercised major political influence in New York in the 1760s. As the mayor of New York, a representative in the provincial legislature, and a delegate to 1765's Stamp Act Congress, John Cruger was as visible as any colonist in channeling mass anger at the Grenville ministry, which introduced the Stamp Act, into effective political action. Like other prominent New Yorkers, the Crugers also reckoned with emerging forms of popular politics. As Robert R. Livingston (1718–75, known as "the Judge") told his father in 1765, "Every man is wild with politics and you hear nothing but the Stamp Act talked of."[2] The Crugers were already wealthy and influential, but they were not directly opposed to this democratizing spirit. Rather they were immersed in the transformation, furthering it by their own embrace of popular activism when it suited their interests, and playing a changing game with skill that enhanced their own power.

Few who protested the Stamp Act thought they were threatening the constitutional underpinnings of the British Empire, but with hindsight they were. As a group, the Crugers were savvy people of experience. But in these years, even as they rose to increasing transatlantic commercial and political prominence, they were helping to weaken the imperial system under which they prospered. When the shooting started in 1775, the Crugers did not embrace the Revolution, but their actions in the mid-1760s helped make it conceivable for other colonists to do so.

After the costly Seven Years' War, people on both sides of the Atlantic looked to the future. When George Grenville, William Pitt's brother-in-law, became prime minister in April 1763, he faced the bill for years of global warfare and aimed to adjust British imperial trading regulations to help pay it. Colonial merchants constantly skirted the Navigation Acts, but few had historically disputed Parliament's right to superintend oceangoing trade. However, the bundle of new rules brought in by Grenville, known as the Sugar Act of 1764, was of immediate concern to merchants because it shone a light on murky but profitable commerce. The legislation affected the trade in many commodities and was best known for attempting to reset the trade in foreign molasses by lowering but actually collecting the duty levied on it. According to Grenville's estimate, the colonial customs regime annually earned the British treasury less than one-quarter of what it cost to enforce.[3] Improving revenue receipts was impossible if colonial merchants continued evading parliamentary duties, so Grenville planned a new super-vice-admiralty court based in Halifax.

The Crugers had prospered in the old system, so their interests were directly affected by many of the controversial efforts at imperial reform that arose in the mid-1760s. The New York General Assembly, where merchants including the Crugers were well represented and which had already been enflamed by wartime controversies over quartering, was prominent in articulating the wider principles involved in these disputes over commercial regulation.[4] In an address to acting governor Cadwallader Colden in September 1764, New York's representatives claimed that they intended to "secure that great Badge of English Liberty, of being taxed only with our own Consent, to which we conceive, all his Majesty's Subjects at home and abroad equally intitled" and asked for Colden's help in "pointing out to the Ministry, the many Mischiefs arising from the Act, commonly called, the Sugar Act, both to us and to Great Britain."[5] Colden refused to support this effort, but he could not quash it.

John Cruger II was instrumental in framing merchants' self-interested economic arguments as encompassing wider issues. The New York General Assembly had authorized a Committee of Correspondence to communicate with the province's London agent in 1761. In various colonies such committees, which initially drew legitimacy from the representative assemblies that created them, exercised increasing power. Their communications crystallized shared grievances and shaped the possibilities for collective action. By 1764 the representatives in the General Assembly elected from New York City constituted, ex officio, the members of this committee. John Cruger therefore served on this increasingly influential Committee of Correspondence as it exchanged letters with the assembly's agent in London over how to respond to the Sugar Act (fig. 6).[6]

The Crugers and other New York merchants and politicians tried to mobilize wider opposition to the Sugar Act by emphasizing how it affected people outside their own circles. In September 1764, John, acting on behalf of New York's Committee of Correspondence, presented the full assembly with a resolution calling for sending Parliament a petition on the Sugar Act and protesting the "many Inconveniences that must attend the infringing [of] the Liberty we have so long enjoyed of being taxed only with our own Consent."[7] The petitions sent to the king and Parliament a month later dropped detailed economic arguments against the Sugar Act to instead trumpet the principles involved.[8] The General Assembly's petition to the House of Commons said, for example, that while New Yorkers might expect continued exemption from parliamentary taxation as a "privilege" merited by their own fidelity, they did "nobly disdain" this option and instead insisted upon it as "the grand Principle of every free State"

Figure 6. Unknown artist, *Mayor John Cruger of New York City (1710–1791)*. Watercolor on ivory. Gift of Davida Tenenbaum Deutsch and Alvin Deutsch, LL.B. 1958, in honor of Kathleen Luhrs, Yale University Art Gallery, New Haven, CT, 2006.225.10.

and as a "principle even of natural justice." Freedom from taxation without their consent was something that New Yorkers could "glory in" as "their Right," which their "Ancestors enjoyed in Great-Britain and Ireland."[9] When the Board of Trade learned of these resolutions, they decided that the assembly's actions tended "to excite a combination in the several colonies" in opposition to parliamentary legislation.[10] In this way, debates over Grenville's efforts to address the empire's wartime debts were provocatively reframed as implicating fundamental principles, natural justice, and rights.

The Crugers and others were prone to raise the stakes when critiquing the Sugar Act partly because Grenville had suggested that a further revenue measure was to come: a colonial stamp act.[11] The Sugar Act could be framed as an extension of Parliament's largely accepted power to regulate imperial commerce, but a stamp act—an excise tax on documents and goods made of paper—was a revenue measure plain and simple. Rumors of varying truthfulness about ministerial plans gathered momentum in the colonies, and a few informants cautioned Grenville's government that a stamp tax would likely create a firestorm. They were, however, largely ignored. Adding to colonial fears, a postwar recession hurt traders, idled sailors, and damaged rich and poor alike. Many people were further angered by the April 1764 Currency Act, a measure that limited the ability of the colonies, where specie was scarce, to issue paper money.[12] Responding to these dynamics, in December 1764, New York merchants, including John Cruger, joined a wider politically inflected movement to improve local economies by establishing a provincial "Society for the Promotion of Arts, Agriculture, and Oeconomy," whose aims included stimulating linen manufacturing.[13]

The new restrictions on trade and paper money, a difficult business and employment climate, and the prospect of a stamp tax left many with the increasingly apocalyptic sense that Parliament was prepared to destroy colonial economies. Colonial legislatures urged their London agents to oppose a stamp act or other "internal" levies and some proposed raising alternative revenues, but these efforts failed. When Grenville moved the Stamp Act, a few eloquent speeches were made in protest, but no members denied Parliament's authority to enact it. The Stamp Act passed overwhelmingly, becoming law on March 22, 1765.[14] Grenville and other British politicians expected some colonial opposition, but few anticipated the scale and vehemence of the resulting protest movement.

In the ensuing crisis, the pace of transatlantic communications and governance created space for resistance. Because collecting revenue through the Stamp Act required appointing colonial agents and dispatching blank stamped paper to the colonies, the law was not scheduled to come into force until November 1765. When news of the Stamp Act's passage reached the colonies in the spring of 1765, there was time to mobilize opposition aimed at protesting the new law and blocking its implementation. Colonial legislatures, whose institutional roles were as threatened as individual rights, became key nodes of resistance. In early June 1765 the Massachusetts assembly sent a circular letter proposing that other colonial legislatures should send delegates to meet in New York in October and prepare a "general and united, dutiful, loyal, and humble" protest against the Stamp Act for submission to the king and Parliament.[15] The governors of Virginia, North Carolina, and Georgia, fearful of what such a meeting might yield, refused to convene their legislatures and thereby prevented them from electing delegates to it. The governors of Delaware and New Jersey tried the same tactic, but their assemblies gathered informally, ignoring proper procedure to dispatch delegates anyway.

In New York the assembly was out of session when Massachusetts' letter arrived, and the situation was likewise irregular. It had been in recess since October 1764 and Colden had no intention of recalling it amid the growing tumult. This left the assembly's Committee of Correspondence, which it had explicitly empowered to communicate with the province's London agent and other assemblies on the then rumored stamp act and other parliamentary measures, as the only legitimate embodiment of its authority. It was on this basis that the New York City representatives who constituted the Committee of Correspondence—William Bayard, Philip Livingston, Robert R. Livingston, Leonard Lispenard, and John Cruger—acted as New York's representatives to what became known as the Stamp Act Congress.[16]

John Cruger's part in the Stamp Act Congress is intriguingly uncertain, perhaps deliberately so. A man of business and political energy, Cruger's most notable personal traits were his lifelong bachelorhood, his decades-long partnership with his brother Henry, and his continuing connection to his extended family. With many years of experience as a merchant, an elected and appointed politician, and a judge through the Mayor's Court, John knew all of New York's major political and economic leaders. John was neither a celebrated orator nor someone who seems to have craved the political limelight, but his long career, including his subsequent post as Speaker of New York's assembly, suggests he was an effective dealmaker skilled at the cut and thrust of day-to-day politics. Lewis Cruger, a grandson of Nicholas, published a version of the Stamp Act Congress's proceedings in 1845. In that work, Lewis Cruger reported that his great-uncle, Henry Cruger Jr., who died only in 1827, had said the idea for calling a congress in 1765 originated with John Cruger and his fellow New York delegate, Robert R. Livingston. This pair, Lewis Cruger said, wrote to other colonies promoting the idea, which led the Massachusetts Assembly to issue its famous circular letter.[17] This may well have been a self-serving family myth; the foremost modern historian of the congress found no evidence for New York's supposed primacy.[18] However, there is little evidence available on much about the Stamp Act Congress, and it is notable that the Massachusetts circular letter proposed that a congress should be convened in New York on the first Tuesday of October 1765. This conspicuously specific proposal, in which the assembly of one colony called a meeting in another colony on an exact date, transformed the Stamp Act Congress from amorphous idea into concrete reality. Its terms strongly suggest that New Yorkers had already agreed to host the gathering and that the Massachusetts Assembly was coordinating with them, reflecting communication and cooperation within an emerging resistance movement.

Delegates began assembling in New York in late September 1765, and while this was widely reported, accounts of the Stamp Act Congress's deliberations were kept out of the colonial press. This was at least partly because many believed that the planned petitions to the king and Parliament would be undermined if they were publicly reported before being read by their intended recipients. Delegates may also have seen value in presenting a united front or feared the personal consequences of revealing individual positions. It appears that many of the delegates' important discussions and debates occurred at meals and otherwise informally. The surviving official journal of the congress is exceedingly brief because "the delegates obviously wanted their statements 'off the record.'"[19] Continuing uncertainties about what happened at the Stamp Act Congress reflect its participants' intentions.

Historians have usually assumed Cruger to have been among the more moderate, even "conservative" members of the congress, but the reality is that in the absence of much evidence, many characterizations of delegates' positions at the Stamp Act Congress have been read backward from their future actions in the Revolution. Later loyalists and nobodyists like John Cruger are assumed to have been moderates or conservatives in 1765. Besides the fact that many peoples' views changed as circumstances did in the tumultuous ensuing decade, what may well have been disagreements between largely like-minded people over effective tactics in 1765 are sometimes interpreted as revelations of profound and binary ideological commitments made manifest in 1776. This is a questionable exercise that says more about later desires for coherent nation-building narratives than it does about the events of the 1760s. The men who gathered in New York in October 1765 were neither rehearsing for the Continental Congress nor anticipating independence; they were trying to mobilize effective opposition within a political and economic framework premised on the colonies' continuing membership in the British Empire.[20]

Lewis Cruger claimed that John Cruger prepared the first draft of the Stamp Act Congress's "Declaration of Rights," the best-known document that came out of the meeting. There appears to be no other evidence for this claim, and this was probably family mythologizing.[21] John Dickinson likely wrote the Declaration of Rights, manuscript drafts of which have been found in his hand.[22] While separating the history of the mid-1760s from myths—family and national—is not easy, it seems likely that Cruger served as a de facto host of the congress because it is believed to have met at New York's city hall, which Cruger then occupied as mayor. The New York delegation also held meals for members and generally coordinated logistics, something in which its mercantile members, including Cruger, were well versed.[23]

Understanding the Crugers' part in the crisis of 1765 and how they were, in turn, affected by it, means juxtaposing the events inside city hall with what was happening on New York's streets and docks. The streams of formal, elite politics and popular protest mingled in North America after the Seven Years' War. In the summer of 1765, while legislators made public plans to formally protest the Stamp Act, other colonists took to the streets and began a campaign of intimidation aimed at preventing its implementation. In several port towns beginning with Boston, shadowy and only loosely related groups took "liberty" as their byword and channeled widespread anger into action. Collectively they came to be known as the Sons of Liberty, although in New York they were first called the Liberty Boys. Their behind-the-scenes leadership included merchants and lawyers with social standing, but these groups drew their energy and influence from the artisans, sailors, and other working-class urbanites who formed the crowds that their leaders could conjure but never fully control. Throughout the crisis, men with prestige, often including those who helped orchestrate crowd actions, then posed as peacemakers and preservers of public order. This proved an effective but inherently risky strategy for those with property and status. More privileged leaders could aim to control "the people," but that does not mean they always did.[24] Ensuing events in New York indicate that Mayor John Cruger knew this dangerous game well.

As reports arrived in late August 1765 of anti-stamp riots in Boston and Newport, the stamp agent appointed in New York, James McEvers, speedily reached the conclusion that he had far more to lose from selling stamped paper than he had to gain. He resigned his office before a crowd gathered before his own door.[25] Agents elsewhere also quit, complicating plans to implement the tax. Colden had made clear that, even as he understood colonial objections, he intended to enforce the Stamp Act as the law of the land. Having heard of what had happened in other colonies, he was also afraid of the potential power of the New York mob. Resolving "I shall not be intimidated," in September he started readying New York's Fort George for conflict: repairing its walls and coordinating an addition to its garrison. These military preparations, clearly aimed at the city's own people rather than a foreign enemy, added to the febrile atmosphere.[26]

The Crugers had known the McEvers family for decades, but they were also connected to the city's sailors and waterfront workers through their long-term presence as residents, merchants, and politicians in the Dock Ward. Relations between wealthy merchants like the Crugers and common sailors were neither simple nor always friendly, but they were conducted with much personal familiarity, and the lines between classes in New York were not as sharp as they would later be.[27] Sailors had a history of resisting agents of imperial authority through riots and other protests against impressment, and were often supported by merchants who resented the loss of their crews.[28] The Crugers also knew several of the men who emerged as leaders of the local Sons of Liberty. One key figure was Isaac Sears, a ship captain and a merchant, albeit one on a considerably smaller scale than the Crugers. Sears had worked as a seagoing officer for many local traders, including the Beekman family, with whom the Crugers did much business, and had been a successful privateer captain operating out of the city during the Seven Years' War.[29] His power lay in his ability to shape what happened on the streets and docks. "King Sears," as he was known, was believed to have as much influence as anyone with New York's common seaman and artisans. In the decade between 1765 and 1775, Sears became one of the most militant anti-British activists in the city, and he and the Crugers would have many future dealings, sometimes as allies and ultimately as opponents.

The Stamp Act Congress met amid this ferment from October 7 to October 25. Ultimately, its delegates approved the Declaration of Rights—an articulation of agreed-upon principles—and three different petitions to the king, Lords, and Commons. The Declaration of Rights asserted that the colonists owed allegiance to the Crown and "all due Subordination" to Parliament, but also insisted they had the same rights as other British subjects and could be taxed only by their own representatives, who were in provincial assemblies not Westminster. On this scaffolding, the declaration asserted that, in addition to being bad economic policy, the Stamp Act and other recent legislation had "a Manifest tendency to Subvert the Rights and liberties of the Colonists." The three petitions made the same substantive points, but were framed in loyal language. That to the House of Lords, for example, said colonists were "Animated with the warmest Sentimints of filial Affection for their Mother Country." On October 24, as the petitions and the congress's journal were transcribed, the delegates adopted the recommendation that the various colonies cooperate in appointing "special agents" to work on their behalf in England.

In a final episode of debatable meaning, the petitions were signed. John Cruger and the other New York delegates did not affix their names, reporting that since they had not been officially appointed by their provincial assembly to attend the congress, they did not believe themselves authorized to sign without its express approval. Given the New Yorkers' active participation in the congress—Robert R. Livingston and Philip Livingston even served on two of the petition-drafting committees—this was certainly a cautious argument. The thinness of the record again makes multiple interpretations possible. Perhaps it reflected a principled deference to the primacy of the assembly in provincial politics; upholding its prerogatives was consistent with the arguments embodied in the petitions themselves. Alternatively, perhaps the New York delegates disagreed about whether to sign or were alarmed by the content of the petitions or the discussions that produced them. While the decision not to sign the petitions seems strange, it was apparently accepted by the other colonies' delegations. Moreover, the New York delegation looked to obtain retroactive support for the Stamp Act Congress's work once their assembly reconvened. Connecticut and South Carolina's contingents followed New York's lead and similarly insisted that they had to present the petitions to their own legislatures. In the end, delegates from six colonies signed the petitions.[30]

Nothing the Stamp Act Congress might do in October could stop the new tax from coming into legal effect on November 1. Therefore, as the delegates worked, popular agitation and commitment to resisting the Stamp Act's implementation remained high. In several colonies a flashpoint in the fall of 1765 was the arrival of crates of stamped paper. New York's first consignment arrived on October 22, 1765 aboard the *Edward*, just as the congress was completing its proceedings. Thousands of people, alerted to the vessel's cargo, lined New York's waterfront to jeer its arrival. Merchantmen flew their flags at half-mast to mourn the death of liberty. Escorted by two warships, the *Edward* anchored off Manhattan's southern tip, and Colden had to decide what to do with the stamped paper. He sought to consult the Provincial Council, the small body that acted as a legislative upper house and advised the governor, but its members excused themselves from meeting on pretenses seemingly designed to protect themselves from public fury. Two nights later, the warships' boats ferried the stamped paper to New York's fort. A week of rising tensions ensued as the governor and the military prepared to enforce the Stamp Act and maintain control on the streets by force if necessary while New Yorkers grew increasingly determined to resist. Just as John Cruger and other delegates to the congress were finalizing their petitions in city hall, outside popular anger was reaching a boiling point.[31]

On October 31, the eve of the law's commencement, "a general meeting of the Merchants of the City of New York, trading to Great Britain" was held at Burns' Coffee House. More than two hundred assembled traders resolved not to bring in goods from England until the Stamp Act was repealed, the first use of nonimportation as a tactic in transatlantic disputes.[32] Given nonimportation's impact on merchants' livelihoods and the necessity of widespread agreement for it to work, it seems probable that leading merchants like the Crugers had previously discussed and agreed to it. Merchants elsewhere, including Philadelphia and Boston, followed suit and pledged to cease importing until the Stamp Act's repeal.[33]

There were strong elements of political theater in New York's response to the Stamp Act, and the Crugers acted multiple parts in the unfolding drama.[34] John Cruger was simultaneously a delegate to the Stamp Act Congress, a prominent merchant, a popular and well-known elected politician, and the city's appointed mayor, with official responsibilities for public order and the administration of justice. Each of these roles was important at certain moments; a major component of his power was his ability to shift between them. Because of the measured and respectful tone of the petitions that emerged from the Stamp Act Congress, the meeting's work has sometimes been contrasted with the more robust and effective actions undertaken by merchants and the riots that took place on New York's streets. There is some truth in this, but the Crugers' multisided involvement in the Stamp Act crisis also shows that the various efforts to oppose the widely detested law were interconnected.[35] Resistance was coordinated by many of the same people acting—and wanting to be seen as acting—in different capacities in different settings. There were, for example, merchants among the leadership of the Sons of Liberty and among those who met at Burns' Coffee House. Given that the interests of New York's traders appear to have been well represented in the formal and informal discussions of the Stamp Act Congress, it seems likely that the nonimportation campaign was conceived of as complementary to the congress's petitions and probably also to the unfolding street protests. John Cruger the Stamp Act Congress delegate, John Cruger the border-crossing trader, and John Cruger the mayor of New York were one person, but they could communicate his opposition to the Stamp Act in different registers.

This is well illustrated by his relationship to the developing street protests in New York. Popular desire for action was very high by the eve of implementation on October 31, when merchants agreed to nonimportation. Rumors were rife that a mob intended to storm Fort George to seize and destroy the stamped paper. Colden heard that some New Yorkers intended to bury alive Major Thomas James, a particularly detested artillery officer. Perhaps this was because, as James later admitted, he had "threatened to cram the stamps down their throats with the end of my sword."[36] Public notices were hung up menacing the property and persons of anyone who used the stamped paper. Colden, confined to the fort, wrote John Cruger, asking him as mayor and a magistrate to help prevent what Colden feared was an imminent riot.[37]

That night large crowds gathered in Manhattan's fall air. Several thousand people paraded by torchlight, breaking "some thousands of windows," and intimidating those seen as countenancing the new law. On the evening of the next day, November 1, with the Stamp Act officially in effect, even larger, angrier crowds assembled. People looted Major James's house, approached Fort George and taunted its defenders by urging them to fire, and hanged Colden in effigy before seizing and burning his carriage. The soldiers kept their cool, and a New York "massacre" was avoided, but Colden feared that the crowds would overwhelm the fort's garrison if violence broke out. Worried that outright rebellion was in the offing and in personal danger, Colden, encouraged by his council, promised publicly that he would do nothing to implement the Stamp Act before the province's appointed but not yet arrived new royal governor, Sir Henry Moore, took up his office.[38]

As long as the stamped paper was held at the fort, tensions between the townspeople on one side and Colden and the military on the other seemed likely to continue. On November 2, the garrison received notes threating Colden's life and the burning of the fort. Colden and his now very alarmed council asked Archibald Kennedy, captain of a Royal Navy warship anchored in the harbor, to take the boxes of stamped paper on board. Kennedy refused or at least demurred; different accounts later circulated. He may have been reluctant to become involved because he and his wife owned substantial property in the city, which he feared might be destroyed if he took possession of the boxes. Although Mayor Cruger also asked Kennedy to take the stamped paper aboard his ship, he still would not accept it.[39]

56   "CRUGER AND LIBERTY!"

Seeing the stamped paper—tyranny made manifest—ablaze on a bonfire would no doubt have been very satisfying for New Yorkers. But storming the fort would have been a dangerous escalation that carried the potential for mass casualties and major reprisals. Colden, for his part, could not consistent with his duty simply turn the stamped paper over to a mob, even if he was increasingly desperate to wash his hands of the matter. On November 4, he again pledged to do nothing to enforce the Stamp Act prior to Moore's arrival, and this promise was printed and witnessed by several prominent New Yorkers including Robert R. Livingston and John Cruger.[40] Popular anger, however, was not quelled. What was needed was a way out. In a deft maneuver that echoed his role in calming the previous dispute with Lord Loudon over the quartering of officers, Mayor Cruger and the Common Council, the city's municipal government, stepped forward on November 5 proposing a solution.

Claiming that the people would not be calm until the stamped paper was removed from the fort and that they wanted to avoid bloodshed, Cruger and the Common Council proposed that they would formally take possession of it and lodge it in city hall, where it would be kept under the watch of the city guard. The municipal corporation offered to be financially responsible for the revenue expected from the paper if it was destroyed or taken out of New York while under its protection. It was an ingenious solution, and all concerned quickly adopted it. Much of what ensued seems to have been done with an eye toward how the scheme would be received in London. Colden formally consulted the Provincial Council and General Thomas Gage on whether he could accept the proposal consistent with his duty, making sure to note in writing that he did so. Gage spoke that day personally with Mayor Cruger, and it seems that the general was promised that the municipal government would do everything it could to restore order on the streets once the paper was transferred to their control.[41] "The merchants" also acted their part by throwing their weight behind this proposal and easing Colden's surrender, waiting on him that day to appeal to him to adopt the plan.[42] The Provincial Council and Gage did their bits too, going on the record to provide the desired cover by stating that in their opinion turning the paper over to the municipal corporation was the best way to avoid bloodshed since, in Gage's words, if the soldiers were forced to fire, it would mark the "commencement of a Civil War." Colden wrote to the mayor and corporation of New York to tell them, in profoundly disingenuous officialese, that "in consequence of your earnest request" and because of their guarantees to be financially responsible for it, he would turn the paper over to them "to prevent the effusion of Blood and the Calamities of a Civil War, which might ensue by my withholding them from you." The city government took possession of the seven boxes of stamped paper, which were carried to city hall. Cruger sealed the deal in appropriately mercantile fashion by giving Colden a receipt, writing "I promise, in behalf of the Corporation of the City of New York, to take charge and care of [the boxes], and to be accountable in Case they shall be destroy'd or, carryed out of the Province."[43]

The bloodletting that all of the "responsible" figures—Colden, Gage, the merchants, the members of the provincial and municipal councils, and Mayor Cruger—involved in the crisis claimed to have feared was avoided, and the stamped paper remained in "official" custody rather than crackling atop a roaring fire. One interpretation of these events is that they were an "intervention" by the mayor and Common Council that "averted a riot that might have become an insurrection."[44] However, this underestimates the extent to which the different modes of politics, protest, and supposed compromise present in New York were symbiotic. The mob—a useful but shadowy power throughout the crisis—had been kept at bay, but what transpired was a humiliating defeat for the agents of imperial authority in New York. When Mayor Cruger and the city alderman arrived at the gate of Fort George to take possession of the stamped paper from Colden and the military, they were accompanied by "a Prodigious Concourse of People of all Ranks" who gave three cheers when the boxes were handed over and then processed along with them to city hall, where the Stamp Act Congress had just met to coordinate colonial resistance.[45]

Privately, and revealingly, Colden would subsequently air his view that the whole episode was a stitch-up, a solution engineered by the same people, including Mayor Cruger, that had been encouraging the street protests from behind the scenes. While professing to be responsible upholders of public order, they had stymied the acting governor at every turn and made a mockery of the law and its royal officers. Colden tended to see conspiracies everywhere, but here he was probably correct. Up and down the colonies, as the key study of the crisis of 1765 has observed, "the episodes of violence which defeated the Stamp Act in America were planned and prepared by men who were recognized at the time as belonging to the 'better and wiser part.'"[46] Even if this understates the power of the people, in New York there were clear signs of cooperation throughout the crisis between the so-called mob, the collective action of the city's merchants, and provincial politicians including Cruger. When, for example, sailors, mechanics, and other common people took to the streets on October 31, they paraded past the merchants meeting at Burns' Coffee House and, according to one source, rather than being concerned at what a mob might do "the Merchants were Exceedingly Pleas'd."[47] Likewise, the Provincial Council showed itself to be at least as sympathetic to the wishes of the people as it was to Colden and the military's dilemma. Its members refused to endorse a hardline stance and encouraged Colden to stand down.[48] Whether they were actively colluding with the protesters, intimidated, or motivated by genuine fears about bloodshed remains hazy, but their failure to support Colden is clear.

General Gage thought that New York's lawyers were the root of much of the trouble, and that the "whole Body of Merchants in general, Assembly Men, Magistrates, &c. have been united in this Plan of Riots." It was all, he thought, a coordinated effort, as "the Sailors who are the only People who may be properly Stiled Mob, are entirely at the Command of the Merchants who employ them."[49] New York's men of property and prominence, including John Cruger, may well have become genuinely alarmed at what other people might do if Colden did not give up the stamped paper, but they also benefited from publicly portraying themselves as figures of moderation even as they channeled street action on behalf of a common cause. There was, to be sure, some element of personal risk involved; there was always a chance that the tiger of people power might bite those who tried to ride it. According to one account, on the night of November 1 Cruger and several aldermen unsuccessfully attempted to block the parading of an effigy of Colden. They were warned by members of the crowd, who said that "they would not hurt them, provided they stood out of their way."[50] But Cruger was well known as an opponent of the Stamp Act, and New Yorkers at this point were largely united in their aim of preventing the law's implementation. For example, when Cruger wrote Captain Kennedy to urge him to take the stamped paper on board his ship—an act that might be interpreted as an attempt to preserve public order—he may have been acting in sympathy or even in concert with the Sons of Liberty. Colden later claimed that the Sons especially *wanted* Kennedy to have custody of the paper because Kennedy's New York property made him usefully susceptible to intimidation.[51]

The readiness of Cruger and the rest of the city government to assume financial responsibility for the stamped paper underscored his power and place in these events. Cruger did not run foolish financial risks, and he was likely confident the paper would be safe in his custody. Most tellingly, once the paper was transferred to the control of Cruger and the municipal government, the tumult in the city ceased. The New York crowds—supposedly so incensed they were on the verge of facing the soldiers, muskets, and cannon of the fort just to lay their hands on the stamped paper—now were content to let it sit in city hall. Calm ensued, and having been repeatedly outmaneuvered in the previous week, a flummoxed Colden recorded his thoughts on November 9. "It evidently appears now," he wrote "who were the Conductors of the Mob by its immediately ceasing in every appearance as soon as the Packages were delivered to the Mayor and Corporation."[52] New Yorkers' cooperative actions made a mockery of Grenville's plans for raising a new colonial revenue in their community.

The Cruger family's part in this resistance effort is underlined by what happened in the aftermath of these events. New York's new governor, Sir Henry Moore, finally landed in New York on November 13.[53] On his arrival, the Jamaican-born Moore had few personal connections in New York. According to Colden's son Alexander, Moore claimed he was a stranger to everyone but "Mr. Reade & Cruger whom he had seen in Jamaica," and Henry Cruger Sr. became increasingly conspicuous in provincial politics after Moore's arrival.[54] Moore wanted the Stamp Act repealed, but he endeavored to uphold royal authority and the rule of law by keeping the port and courts closed unless the required stamped paper was used in their proceedings. Moore's arrival, and probably the mutual desire of leading New Yorkers and the new governor to get their relationship off to a good start, affected how subsequent phases of the Stamp Act crisis unfolded in the province.

The provincial legislature, in recess since October 1764, finally reconvened at the outset of Moore's administration. On November 20, 1765, in one of its first pieces of business, the General Assembly approved the actions of the New York delegation to the recent Stamp Act Congress and resolved to submit petitions to the king, Commons, and Lords that were "as nearly similar to those drawn up by the Congress" as "the particular circumstances of this Colony will admit of."[55] The assembly's petitions addressed the Stamp Act and a wider set of grievances, including anger over the case of *Forsey v. Cunningham*, in which Colden intervened in ways that influential New Yorkers saw as an unacceptable derogation of the right to trial by jury.

Following Moore's arrival, the Crugers and other members of the province's and city's economic and political elite aimed to continue the campaign against the Stamp Act while ensuring that popular anger over it did not boil over. The operative question became how to get the law repealed. Not for the last time, the debate in New York about the way forward in a time of crisis became primarily about means rather than ends. On November 26, a very large public meeting of "about Twelve Hundred" of New York's "Freemen and Freeholders" was held. The meeting adopted a resolution addressed to the four men, including John Cruger, who represented the city in the General Assembly. It repeated grievances over the undermining of the right to trial by jury, the impact of recent duties on trade, and the imposition of "an internal tax upon the Colonies" through the Stamp Act. The freeholders told the city's representatives that they "most earnestly recommend it to you" to push the assembly to issue a "full Declaration" of the rights of the people to trial by jury and exemption from "Parliamentary internal taxation" as well as petitions to the king, Lords, and Commons. These "instructions," as they were termed in newspaper accounts, were signed on behalf of the people of New York by twelve well-known men. Henry Cruger Sr.'s name was at the top of the list, which also included prominent figures associated with both the Livingston and De Lancey factions in provincial politics and men who would be identified with directing the local Liberty Boys. The freeholders' instructions were then presented by these twelve men to New York City's representatives in the Assembly the following day.

Again, the elements of political theater were strong. Everyone involved knew that the lower house of the General Assembly had already begun drafting petitions in response to the Stamp Act. Nevertheless, the act of the "people" issuing "instructions" to their representatives was performed. This was partly an exercise in more elite figures steering popular energy into channels that they thought productive. According to one critical newspaper account, the original "Great Design" of this meeting was to obtain popular support for resuming business in the city and port of New York by simply ignoring the Stamp Act. Isaac Sears and some of his closest allies appear to have been behind this attempt to flout the law, but they were temporarily outmaneuvered.[56] Customs officials in several other colonial ports had been pressured to allow normal business to resume without requiring stamped paper, but evidently influential figures in New York thought such a step unwise. They may have thought so because reopening colonial ports was somewhat at cross-purposes with the nonimportation strategy already adopted by merchants, or because some New Yorkers hoped to avoid immediate conflict with the newly arrived Moore.

Despite the results of this public meeting, by early December the Customs Collector of the city's port was pressured to reopen it without using stamped paper anyway. Other ports, including Philadelphia, had all resumed operations without proper paper for ships' clearances and the Stamp Act was now effectively being ignored in much of North America. However, New York's trade did not return to normal because Captain Archibald Kennedy's Royal Navy vessel began seizing ships entering or leaving the harbor without properly stamped documents. More generally, for colonial merchants everywhere sailing without properly stamped paper increased the risks that their vessels might face troubles in the Caribbean or other ports or that they would not be able to collect insurance in the event of a ship's loss. These continuing impediments to trade were frustrating for wealthy New York merchants like the Crugers, but they had abundant resources to ride out lean times. For the shore-bound sailors deprived of the chance to earn their livings and other maritime workers in the city, it was a more serious hardship. High prices and short supplies of flour in New York in the winter of 1765 exacerbated their difficulties.[57]

Knowledgeable people on both sides of the Atlantic knew that the Rockingham administration, which came to power in July 1765, was far less invested in the Stamp Act than the Grenville administration had been. Therefore, even as the Stamp Act was coming into force, there were hopes that it would be repealed when Parliament reconvened in December 1765. The defiance shown by the colonists, however, complicated the situation for the "friends of America" in Britain because few politicians wanted to concede limitations on parliamentary authority over the colonies or be seen as bowing to lawlessness. Rockingham's ministry was also weakly supported in the House of Commons. On December 17, 1765, when the American situation was first discussed in the recently reconvened Parliament, William Pitt, who had resisted joining Rockingham's government, urged that the Stamp Act be repealed "absolutely, totally, and immediately." Even more powerfully, he asserted that "I rejoice that America has resisted." At the same time, Pitt argued, the "sovereign authority of this country" should be asserted over the colonies and extended to "every point of legislation whatsoever, except that of taking their money out of their pockets without their consent."[58] Pitt's denunciation of the Stamp Act and his vindication of American resistance was a major fillip to the colonists, but his seeming willingness to condone lawlessness shocked some of his parliamentary colleagues. Many colonials subsequently rejected Pitt's expansive conception of British authority over America, but in 1765 and 1766 his stance on the Stamp Act added to the luster of his colonial reputation. The Crugers and many others long admired him as the defender of their intertwined political and economic interests.

While the Rockingham administration agreed the Stamp Act was bad policy, repealing it was not simple. Pitt was a volatile and prickly ally at best, Grenville and his supporters were now in opposition and dangerous, the king was tepid on the idea of repeal, and most of the members of Parliament who had so overwhelmingly supported the Stamp Act's passage remained in their seats even though the ministry had changed. Likewise, neither the petitions of the Stamp Act Congress, which the Rockingham administration decided for tactical reasons not to use and which were not formally accepted by Parliament, nor communications from individual colonial legislatures appear to have carried much weight.[59]

As 1766 began, the Stamp Act was not being enforced effectively in New York, but it remained the law and continued to hamper trade and the administration of justice. People feared that the government might yet attempt to obtain compliance with it. In January 1766, Isaac Sears, acting apparently on behalf of a small group of like-minded men who had provided the most sustained but secret leadership of the city's Sons of Liberty since the November riots, entered into an agreement with James De Lancey and his allies, who were looking for popular support in their provincial political rivalry with the Livingston faction. On January 7, 1766, a "great number of gentlemen," most of whom were De Lancey supporters, formally affiliated themselves with the Sons of Liberty and pledged themselves to prevent any enforcement of the Stamp Act in New York. It is not documented that any of the Crugers participated in these events, but it is known that their friends and relatives including members of the De Lancey, Low, and Walton families did. Given this and the Crugers' subsequent dealings with Isaac Sears, it seems likely that they did too.[60] This was the origins of what proved a fraught and ultimately short-lived alliance between the De Lancey faction and Sears as an influential advocate for liberty on the streets.

Ultimately, what proved more influential in the actual repeal of the Stamp Act than colonial rights talk or petitioning was the intervention of British merchants, and by extension the economic pressure exerted upon the British political system by the actions of North American traders.[61] The colonists had insisted since early in their disputes with the Grenville administration that Britain reaped many benefits from the colonies' trade. As Parliament reconvened, the nonimportation movement, which began in New York, was beginning to worry British exporters. As in the American branch of this transatlantic movement, there were probably elements of preplanning at work. Henry Cruger Jr. told a Rhode Island trading partner in September 1765 that "it is very trying times with we poor North American Merchants, yet we'll die hard, and honourable."[62] In early December, a committee of London-based merchants met and sent a circular letter to trading communities in other British ports urging them to lobby for the Stamp Act's repeal. Bristol merchants may have spurred them into action. According to a London leader, Barlow Trecothick, "we were called on by the Bristol Merchants" and "this hastened our meeting for all the Merchants trading to North America."[63] Through the coordination of the London-based committee, petitions from trading towns across Britain duly arrived at Parliament. These petitions, which argued that the Stamp Act hurt the many people in England who relied on American trade, were more palatable to members of Parliament than the rights talk emanating from the colonies.

What emerged, therefore, in early 1766 was the Rockinghamites' plan to secure a parliamentary repeal of the Stamp Act justified primarily on domestic economic grounds coupled with the passage of the Declaratory Act, which asserted that Parliament "had hath, and of right ought to have" the power to legislate for the colonies "in all cases whatsoever," but which was deliberately ambiguous on whether this included the power to tax. As the administration strategized on how to move repeal through the Commons, it marshalled witnesses to testify to the act's pernicious consequences. Benjamin Franklin, then Pennsylvania's agent in London, was one, and he enhanced his growing reputation through his witty and effective explication of the colonial position. More of the witnesses, however, were representatives of British trading towns and the various branches of commerce that were being hurt by the nonimportation movement and declining imperial trade.

This was the context for the Crugers' exercise of their expanding political reach. In January 1766, Henry Cruger Jr. picked up his family's transatlantic campaign against the Stamp Act by serving in a delegation of Bristol merchants who traveled to London to register their objections to the law. The younger Cruger had only joined Bristol's Society of Merchant Venturers—the traditional collective voice for the city's traders—the previous month. He may have become involved because he and like-minded allies thought more established figures in local politics and trade were not as forceful or expansive as they should have been in protesting the Stamp Act.[64] He was, he subsequently reported, "no politician, but in this matter of America, and its Trade, I embarked body and soul."[65] The younger Cruger spent at least three weeks in London in January and February 1766, lobbying, attending the parliamentary debates over the repeal of the Stamp Act, and collecting information that was both commercially and politically valuable.

Because of these activities, the Crugers in New York were probably as well informed on the question of repeal as any colonial merchant family in this period, and they were receiving this information as they were helping calibrate colonial resistance. In a long letter that the younger Henry wrote to his father in New York in mid-February, he detailed what he had seen and heard during his three weeks in the capital and revealed how his family operated. He had been meeting "every Day with some one Member of Parliament, talking as it were for my own Life. It is surprising how ignorant some of them are of *Trade* and *America.*" He attended Parliament regularly and watched Trecothick testify for three and a half hours, noting his insistence on "Total Repeal" had "inflamed Grenville's Party." If Grenville's backers returned to power before a repeal was passed, Henry warned his father, "they'll certainly scourge you, altho, some English Merchants are ruined by it." Henry noted more positively that in the effort to show the economic consequences of the disruption of trade "we have proved the Debt from the Continent of America, to England is five Millions Sterling." In Henry's view, it was economic conditions that would lead to repeal, "especially if you stick to your engagements of having no English Goods untill it is effectuated."[66] Given the Crugers' interconnected business interests, Henry Jr.'s opposition to the Stamp Act was both "American" and "British," and another example of how various forms of resistance were symbiotic.

The Cruger family's prominence in the repeal effort was underlined by a February 1766 public letter tellingly addressed from the "Committee of Merchants in London, trading to North America" to "John Cruger, Esq. and the rest of the merchants in New York." The letter, one of several sent to colonial ports, was printed in New York and was said to have been signed by "Thirty principal merchants, residing in London." Written when repeal was certain but before it had been finally passed through Parliament, the letter urged calm in New York when the Stamp Act was rescinded and sought, through Cruger and his colleagues, to make colonists understand the impact of their actions on British politics.[67] Securing the impending repeal, the Londoners wrote Cruger, would have been easier if "various Ranks of people" in the colonies "had not by their Violence in Word and Action, awakened the Honour of Parliament, and thereby involved every Friend of the Repeal, in the Imputation of betraying the Dignity of Parliament." American disorder, the merchants wrote, had necessitated Parliament simultaneously putting forward the Declaratory Act in order to secure votes for repeal. Further disorders now would make things even harder for the friends of the colonies in England, including the Rockingham ministry. If, on the other hand, the colonists would take the occasion of the repeal to "express filial Duty and Gratitude to your Parent Country" rather than gloat or foment further disorder, then the hands of their British friends would be strengthened and the ministry might introduce other mutually beneficial measures.

The London committee closed by urging Cruger and his colleagues to "inculcate" proper conduct in New York. The letter cast moderated resistance as wisdom and, while it was in some ways a warning, it was almost certainly a welcome one. The Londoners simultaneously acknowledged and sought to strengthen Cruger's and other merchants' political influence. Given that their letter appeared in New York newspapers, it was probably an accurate reflection of the sentiments of the Crugers and others in their far-reaching circles at this moment of triumph.[68] If paternalistic in tone, it was also an astute reading of imperial political dynamics that accords with historical interpretations of the closing stages of the Stamp Act crisis.[69] An ocean-spanning coalition had won a remarkable victory; now all that was needed was the good sense to reap the rewards.

The repeal of the Stamp Act, legally enacted in March 1766, was celebrated across the trading towns of the British Atlantic world. Henry Cruger Jr. jubilantly wrote to Rhode Islander Aaron Lopez that "I hugg myself the Parliament will never trouble America again."[70] Enthusiastic crowds took to the streets to revel in their success and power, and those who had been prominent in the protests began rounds of choreographed mutual backslapping. Henry Cruger Jr. was conspicuous in Bristol's celebrations. In March 1766 he hosted a dinner in honor of Sir William Meredith, a leading parliamentary figure during the repeal effort. The other attendees were "a few of our principal merchants, who were requested to complement and thank Sir William, in the name of the citizens at large, for his noble and spirited behavior in the cause of Liberty in general, and in favour of the repeal of the American stamp-act in particular." The Bristol celebrations were extended, as three days later "a number of gentlemen spent the evening at the Nag's-head tavern" with their invited guests, Henry Cruger Jr. and another merchant activist, Samuel Sedgley, who were thanked "for their zeal and assiduity in their successful attendance on parliament" to solicit repeal.[71] Bristolians presented Cruger with an elaborate piece of commemorative silver, a hot-water urn now held by the New-York Historical Society.[72] Such celebrations, reported in newspapers around the empire, represented genuine enthusiasm over the act's repeal and fresh performances of political theater aimed at claiming shares of the public credit.

Similar festivities were held in New York. Like the protests of the previous fall, the victory was marked in different registers. The town's sailors and other commonfolk erected a liberty pole on open ground provocatively near the city's barracks. It became a flashpoint in subsequent disputes between British regulars and local radicals.[73] More formally, John Cruger and his fellow New York delegates to the Stamp Act Congress were waited upon by a committee whose creation had been urged by "a great number of your constituents" and whose six members included John Harris Cruger. This committee had been appointed by the "Freeman and Freeholders of the City of New-York, assembled at the Coffee-House the 23d Day of June, 1766," who were "impressed with the deepest Sense of Gratitude to all the Friends of Liberty and America, who exerted themselves in promoting the Repeal of the Stamp Act." John Harris Cruger and his co–committee men were tasked with urging his uncle John Cruger and other leading men in the assembly to introduce a measure directing provincial funds to pay for a statue of William Pitt as "a proper monument, to perpetuate the Memory of so glorious an Event to the latest Posterity."[74] New York's assembly, smoothing ruffled feathers and demonstrating that resistance was not disloyalty, also authorized an equestrian statue of George III. By 1770 both monuments, created by the English sculptor Joseph Wilton, were standing in Manhattan. The statues, like the various addresses of thanks that provincial legislatures sent to Parliament, were formal and no doubt politic ways to mark the colonies' victory. In commemorating their victory, of course, the Crugers and their allies were also providing their fellow New Yorkers with a reminder of their own leadership through the crisis and the benefits that could flow through their preferred channels of transatlantic politics.

The glow from the Stamp Act's repeal prevented most people from seeing it, but trouble loomed. In a symbolic distillation of how the cooperation of 1765 broke down, neither statue erected to commemorate repeal survived the Revolution. Patriots asserted their independence by tearing down the statue of the king in July 1776; a few months later vindicative British soldiers decapitated the Pitt statue after occupying the city.[75] In 1766 neither the Crugers nor many others worried much over the Declaratory Act, but in time it proved poisonous to transatlantic relations. Colonists also drew different conclusions from their victory in the Stamp Act crisis. While the Crugers and their commercially minded collaborators wanted to thank Pitt and congratulate themselves for the repeal of the Stamp Act, most humbler colonists tended to view the victory as *their* own. They—street politicians, sailors, mechanics, servants, shop women—won it with their vigorous, unyielding assertion of their rights. The legacy was that different people around the Atlantic world had different understandings of the political tactics that actually delivered results. Cooperative colonial resistance and the threat of violence had blocked the implementation of the Stamp Act but had not produced the ultimate victory: repeal. The Crugers and their allies could believe that their carefully modulated shuttling between encouraging public protest, coordinating economic pressure, and lobbying behind the scenes provided the best model for truly winning intra-imperial political disputes. In the ensuing decade, they would find that many of their fellow Americans came to think differently.

3. Transatlantic Patriots

The Stamp Act's 1766 repeal was a great victory for the Crugers and their fellow Americans. Many colonists hoped that Parliament's decision was a first step heralding freer trade, more liberty, and greater prosperity. But repeal had not solved some of the most pressing constitutional and political dilemmas facing the British Empire. Several of these issues crystallized in confrontations that occurred in New York between 1766 and 1772. Through them, the Crugers were immersed in political controversies, dominated by colonial responses to the Townshend Acts, that feature in many major accounts of the Revolution's causes.[1]

Between 1766 and 1772 the Crugers were, in both the language of the day and in terms of subsequent histories, colonial patriots. They worked alongside other Americans and British allies to articulate grievances and mobilize resistance. Although the goals of this patriot movement were often framed as a desire to return to a pre-1763 imperial system, the Crugers and their allies had a forward-looking vision encapsulated by the slogan "trade and liberty." They wanted economic and political arrangements that would enable their communities— and themselves—to prosper and develop. As they joined with other colonists in pursuing this vision, they helped foment a series of confrontations with the British government. While initially about commercial regulation and taxation, these conflicts revealed differences over underlying principles that reverberated widely, putting New York at the center of transatlantic debates over the imperial constitution.

These years might be seen as a golden era for the Crugers. Rich, respected, and able to influence events at the local, provincial, and sometimes transatlantic levels, John and Henry of the family's second generation were at the height of their powers, and those of the third generation were increasingly prominent. The Crugers' activities between 1766 and 1772 help show how future nobodyists experienced the British Empire's constitutional crisis and why, in 1775, they believed that there were better options than civil war for resolving it. Moreover, because in these years the Crugers' ideological commitments were far more similar to than different from those of other transatlantic patriots, tracing their involvement in the politics surrounding the Townshend Acts reveals how central contingency and the emergence of revolutionary violence were to their subsequent decision-making.

In May 1765, Parliament passed the American Mutiny Act, known in the colonies as the Quartering Act.[2] While initially overshadowed by the Stamp Act crisis, this new measure became a source of controversy and continuing tensions between soldiers and civilians in New York. In 1766 the New York General Assembly, motivated by principle and public opinion, enacted a provincial billeting law that was deliberately noncompliant with Parliament's new measure. Among its intentional omissions, it did not supply troops with the alcohol rations at local expense that the mutiny act mandated.[3] Various incidents between troops and citizens occurred in the summer and fall of 1766, including a large brawl in August sparked by soldiers cutting down a liberty pole erected to celebrate the Stamp Act's repeal. Following this, local Liberty Boys resolved to isolate the troops further by pressuring townspeople to cease doing business with them.[4] Strong reactions to the American Mutiny Act were not universal. Pennsylvania, where many troops were also posted, obeyed the law until 1774. In fact, British politicians believed that other colonies, such as New Jersey, were following New York's lead in resisting the new law.[5] New York City was attracting wider attention as a center of resistance.

After ten years in office, John Cruger stopped serving as mayor in September 1766.[6] He immediately turned to more vocal politicking on behalf of mercantile New York. In October 1766, he joined leading Liberty Boy Isaac Sears and nine other prominent New York traders in drafting a petition to Parliament laying out the "Grievances attending the Trade of this Colony." The petition was the brainchild of William Kelly, a retired New York merchant who had testified on behalf of North American commercial interests during parliamentary inquiries into the Stamp Act and the depressed state of colonial trade. Kelly was supported by the ambitious British politician Charles Townshend, who generated many ideas about how to reform imperial finances and governance. The petition, it has been argued, attracted little interest until Kelly won the support of one of the Crugers—presumably John—and it then gained wider backing.[7]

New York's merchants, emboldened by the Stamp Act's repeal, may have envisioned wider commercial possibilities because of Parliament's recent passage of a Free Port Act liberalizing some Caribbean trade and because William Pitt, now Lord Chatham, had become prime minister.[8] In their petition Cruger, Sears, and their colleagues reported that they had heard that Parliament was preparing to undertake a major revision of the laws governing transatlantic trade and so wanted to give members of Parliament information on it. New York's merchants approved the petition at a meeting on November 28, 1766, and requested that Governor Moore forward it to London. Building on the previous year's efforts at intercolonial cooperation, the New Yorkers reached out to fellow traders in Massachusetts, encouraging them to likewise petition Parliament. "Silence," Cruger and his colleagues wrote, "at this time would be a crime," but the "concurrent Opinion of the principal Merchants, thro the Continent, all uniting in material points must carry Conviction."[9] To Governor Moore's evident surprise—he subsequently made the laughably improbable claim that he had not read the petition before forwarding it—the document created serious controversy when it arrived in London.

In a lecturing tone, Cruger and his colleagues insisted that their having a free-flowing commerce with the multinational West Indies and continental Europe was essential to their ability to settle accounts with their English correspondents and thus in the best interest of Britain itself. They wanted changes to regulations enacted since 1763, requesting reductions in the duties levied on sugar products and the right to ship foreign West Indian cargoes directly to European ports without first landing them in Great Britain. The New Yorkers also complained that, despite the recent establishment of free ports in Dominica and Jamaica, the terms governing trade with those islands still made it too difficult to exchange North American lumber and provisions for foreign sugars. "Experience has evinced," the New Yorkers wrote, that Parliament's attempts to revive trade had instead "encreased the heavy burthen under which it already laboured."[10] Further liberalizing North American merchants' commerce, they insisted, was in the whole empire's best interest. The historian Lawrence Henry Gipson thought the petition advocated nothing less than "free trade and the virtual scrapping of the navigation and trade system."[11] The progressive vision of empire that the petition advocated was not a return to the 1750s, but one in which growing colonial ports like New York would ascend to new levels of economic prosperity and political influence through an expansion of a particularly commercial conception of liberty.

Seen rightly in Westminster as linked to New York's continued opposition to quartering and a wider colonial resistance movement, the petition angered those it was intended to persuade. London merchants refused to support the petition, which frustrated even those English politicians, including Chatham, who were regarded as friends to America. "A spirit of infatuation has taken possession of New York," Chatham wrote. The province's "disobedience to the mutiny act," he observed "will *justly* create a great ferment here" and "leave no room to any to say a word in their defence." He maintained that "the petition of the merchants of New York is highly improper: in point of time, most absurd; in the extent of their pretensions, most excessive; and in the reasoning, most grossly fallacious and offensive." In sending such petitions, Chatham argued, Cruger and his colleagues were "doing the work of their worst enemies themselves." He warned "they will draw upon their heads national resentment by their ingratitude, and ruin, I fear upon the whole state." The prime minister, concerned that suppressing the petition would do more harm than good, had it laid before the Commons, where it attracted much resentment.[12]

Cruger and his associates wanted less interference from Westminster in New York's affairs. But their petition, combined with the General Assembly's stance on quartering, had the paradoxical effect of putting New York squarely in British politicians' sights. Chatham's ministry was shaky, challenged both by advocates for a firmer American policy and by the Rockinghamites.[13] The king and nearly all British politicians believed that the colonial quartering issue needed to be permanently resolved. Chatham aimed, therefore, to uphold parliamentary prerogatives regarding quartering without stirring up the widespread opposition activated by the Stamp Act. New York, it seemed clear, was the main source of trouble and therefore the place to start. "The controversy," one key account has noted, "was not over whether New York should be coerced, but how."[14] Several different schemes circulated among officials in February and March.

The New York Restraining Act emerged from governmental deliberations. It stipulated that unless New York's assembly passed a quartering bill fully compliant with parliamentary law before October 1, 1767, it would be prohibited from enacting any other legislation. The measure, shepherded through the Commons by Charles Townshend, now chancellor of the exchequer, had from the perspective of British politics the twin merits of sending a broad message to all colonial assemblies while being limited in its punitive effects to one. In supporting the measure, Townshend argued that New York's behaving "boldly and insolently" meant that it should receive "an adequate punishment to deter others."[15] Cruger and his associates in New York's political and commercial leadership were now to be made an example.

The New York Restraining Act was criticized in Parliament as both too harsh and too lenient, but it passed easily. In the same session Parliament enacted several other laws that Townshend advocated, placing duties on enumerated colonial imports and creating a new American board of customs. Townshend, Chatham, and other British politicians simultaneously faced complex issues regarding the East India Company and the large Asian territories it won during the Seven Years' War. Therefore, the measures included a new American import duty on tea as part of a wider reworking of the terms under which the company operated.[16] John Cruger and his fellow New Yorkers hoped that their petition might see imperial regulations adjusted in their favor, but what they got was quite the opposite.

These laws—collectively known as the Townshend Acts—were intricately interlocking. A new American tea duty was imposed, but the taxes the company paid when tea was first landed in Britain from Asia were also adjusted to reduce colonial buyers' final price. Collectively, it was envisioned that these changes would benefit consumers, help the company, and boost government revenues, all while undercutting Dutch interlopers and their American allies in smuggling. Townshend also earmarked the anticipated new American income for paying the salaries of some colonial governors and judges. This made it clear that these duties were directly funding colonial administration and, from the British government's perspective, provided a neat solution to the perpetual problem of provincial legislatures using their control over officials' salaries as a point of leverage. These measures were proposed with an eye to the long term and, within the dynamics of parliamentary politics, were intended as a carefully modulated response to what were seen as colonial provocations and systemic problems. Few in the colonies, however, saw in the acts the "moderation and prudence" that Townshend had urged when putting forward his program.[17] Instead, they were regarded as unacceptable forms of parliamentary taxation and provoked fresh opposition that defeated the hopes for transatlantic détente encouraged by the repeal of the Stamp Act. The Crugers were prominent among a group of New

Yorkers who, by pursuing a vision of trade and liberty that alarmed British leaders, helped push the imperial crisis into a new and dangerous phase.

The New York Restraining Act and the other Townshend Acts meant that local and imperial politics were increasingly entangled for the Crugers and their fellow New Yorkers. Henry Sr., who had served in the General Assembly until 1758, reentered formal politics in 1767 when he became a member of New York's small Provincial Council.[18] His appointment, determined by the Crown, reflected the Crugers' social capital in New York. Henry Cruger Jr.'s increasing prominence in Bristol helped too. According to John Watts, Governor Moore recommended Henry Sr. for the council a year previously, but Cruger's appointment "faultered till his Lordship of Trade discovered that his son was Sheriff of Bristol, then it cut immediately."[19] Cruger attended his first council meeting in November 1767.

Henry's appointment was quickly followed by developments surrounding the New York elections of 1768 and 1769.[20] The last General Assembly election took place in 1761, and in accordance with the province's Septennial Act, in February 1768 Moore announced a general election for early March. The contest pitted the De Lancey faction against the Livingstons in head-to-head fashion. Besides being more nakedly partisan than previous assembly elections, it occurred amid expanding colonial political engagement spurred by the Townshend duties. John Dickinson's influential *Letters from a Farmer in Pennsylvania*, which argued that the Townshend taxes were unconstitutional, began being widely discussed in late 1767. Likewise, merchants in various ports began considering reviving nonimportation agreements. In February 1768, as campaigning began for the New York elections, the Massachusetts House of Representatives repeated the tactics that spawned the Stamp Act Congress and sent a circular letter inviting other colonial legislatures to cooperate in protesting the new duties.[21]

Though the city's leading vote getter in 1761, John Cruger did not stand for reelection in 1768, but the family remained engaged in popular politics. The Sons of Liberty, including the influential Isaac Sears, participated directly in electioneering for the first time in 1768 and supported the De Lanceyites against the Livingstons.[22] One anecdote records that the elder Henry Cruger stationed himself at city hall, the polling place, to make certain that those he knew voted the right way: for De Lanceyites.[23] The final result was a three-to-one De Lanceyite victory, with James De Lancey, Cruger son-in-law Jacob Walton, and their ally James Jauncey winning city seats along with Philip Livingston. In the assembly as a whole, the Livingston faction retained a narrow but reduced majority.

John Cruger's decision not to stand for reelection in 1768 may have been due to his interests in another project. In April 1768, immediately following the assembly elections, he played a leading part in establishing a new civic organization that blended political and economic goals: the New York Chamber of Commerce. His name appears first among the chamber's twenty-four founders in its minutes, and he was unanimously chosen as its first president. Cruger served two annual terms, leaving office in May 1770. Longtime Cruger connections, including Jacob and William Walton, James Jauncey, and Lawrence Kortright, were also founders. John Harris Cruger was now established as a merchant in his own right; in December 1767, for example, he offered a variety of "just imported" blankets, rugs, cloth, nails, shot, pipes, sugar, and Madeira and Teneriffe wines for sale in the city.[24] He was among nineteen additional traders (including Isaac Sears) elected members at the chamber's second official meeting, further underlining the family's influence in its early history.[25]

Although its name might today suggest otherwise, the chamber of commerce was established exclusively by and for maritime traders. Its earliest records also called the group "the said Society of Merchants," and it aimed to aid them in three ways. First, and most straightforwardly, it would work toward "procuring such laws and regulations as may be found necessary for the benefit of trade in general." To that end it engaged in political lobbying, presenting the chamber's preferences on commercial legislation to appointed and elected officials. In this vein it also organized events, including a May 1770 dinner hosted by the chamber to which nearly all of New York's political, administrative, and military officers were invited.[26] Second, the members would implement mutually binding regulations intended to benefit trade in the city. Finally, the chamber would provide a mechanism for the arbitration of merchants' commercial disputes by other experienced traders. These aspects of the chamber's program had significant political implications for controversies that had emerged since the end of the Seven Years' War.

The failure of the New York's merchants' 1767 petition, the threat posed by the New York Restraining Act, and swirling talk about nonimportation framed the chamber's founding too.[27] Together, these developments suggest that the Crugers and other leading traders wanted mechanisms for forging consensus and projecting unity. In October 1767 Boston's merchants had made agreements not to import the Townshend Acts' enumerated items and to encourage domestic manufacturing.[28] In March 1768, Boston merchants proposed reviving nonimportation throughout the colonies. On April 13, just as the chamber of commerce was getting off the ground, a committee of thirteen New York merchants including John Harris Cruger, Isaac Sears, and William Walton responded to Massachusetts' proposal by sending a letter to John Hancock and his colleagues on Boston's nonimportation committee, reporting that New York merchants would prohibit the sale or importation of goods shipped from Britain after October 1, 1768.[29] Philadelphia came into the fold more slowly, but it did so in the spring of 1769 and by the ensuing fall similar but locally determined nonimportation agreements had been put in place in most ports.[30]

The chamber's ties to the nonimportation movement intersected with its commitment to formulating mutually binding regulations on trade. The Crugers and their colleagues chafed at imperial rules they saw as detrimental to their own interests, but they were not doctrinaire believers in an abstract form of laissez-faire economics. "Free trade" was closer to a slogan than a philosophy, and what it often meant in practice was the restructuring—rather than abandonment—of regulation in ways beneficial to particular interest groups.[31] The chamber's members sought early and often to intervene in markets and organize trade as they thought best. In November 1768, for example, the chamber considered "whether the price of flour and bread cask should not be reduced" and a new price set. The chamber unilaterally decided that the proper price was 25 shillings 6 pence per ton and resolved that none of its members would pay more. When this decision was opposed by "a combination among the Bolters, Millers, Bakers, and sellers of flour" who thought that the price should be 28 shillings, the chamber resolved to spend its collective funds—each member was required to contribute £50—to dispatch a representative to Philadelphia to purchase between 1,500 and 2,000 barrels of flour as cheaply as possible, for sale first to chamber members and then on its behalf. The chamber members flexed their collective economic muscles through this exercise in market manipulation. When several suppliers of bread and flour attended a subsequent chamber meeting, they were permitted to speak but failed to get the merchants to set a higher price despite their claims of "flour being rather scarce." The chastened sellers "acquiesced with charging in future no more than 25s. 6d. per ton."[32] The chamber claimed to operate in the collective interest of all New Yorkers: its Latin motto translated as "not for ourselves alone." But it also asserted the primacy of merchants and maritime trade within the political economy of the city.

The chamber's dedication to arbitrating disputes between merchants reveals its members' particularly commercial conception of what liberty meant. As mayor, John Cruger had extensive experience with commercial law in the city through presiding over the Mayor's Court. Managing disputes between New York traders was good for the economic welfare of the port. By agreeing to arbitration, traders could obtain justice more speedily and cheaply than they could through provincial courts, where lawyers dominated, and keep commerce humming. The first dispute settled through chamber arbitration was won by John Harris Cruger, acting for his wife's uncle Moses Franks.[33]

The arbitration program was also politically charged because in creating a means to dispense justice within their own community, New York's traders were abrogating power to themselves at the expense of the king's judicial officers and long-established systems. Disputes like *Forsey v. Cunningham*, over whether the governor and council could overrule a jury's judgment, had roiled provincial politics for several years.[34] The Stamp Act crisis also showed that under royal authority the machinery of justice could be subjected to taxation and other forms of parliamentary and ministerial interference. In the crisis of 1765 the colony's economy had been hurt by the closing of courts and its politics enflamed by debates over reopening them without stamped paper. New Yorkers were increasingly seeing London's power over colonial and admiralty courts as inimical to their welfare and rights, and, in this light, the chamber of commerce's creation of a parallel system for adjudicating commercial disputes amounted to a clever riposte to London's efforts to tighten its grip on the empire. In establishing a mechanism to be judged by their fellow merchants, the members of New York's new chamber of commerce were taking a quiet but significant step to more fully govern themselves.

The Crugers' parts in establishing the chamber and other efforts at promoting commercial development reflected the future they wanted for New York. They did not aim at full political separation, but they envisioned an increasingly strong and locally directed economy giving New Yorkers more and more de facto independence and power. If, in their view, it might be foolish to cut ties with the British Empire, it would be equally foolish to entrust New York's welfare to others' goodwill. In 1776, most members of the family did not favor independence in the way that it came to be defined by some Americans, but they worked for years against abject dependence on Britain and had a different, particularly concrete understanding of what constituted real liberty.

Initially there were hopes that the General Assembly elected in 1768 might have good relations with Governor Moore, in part because he had stretched the truth and informed London in late 1767 that the last assembly had satisfactorily complied with the Quartering Act and that the New York Restraining Act did not need to be implemented.[35] Yet the new assembly proved resolute and even radical in asserting its own power and in raising New York's grievances with imperial governance. This intersected with party politics as the De Lanceyites looked to retain the Sons of Liberty's favor, while the Livingstons sought to win more popular support. With both factions courting public opinion, disputes between the governor and the assembly took on a new resonance.

In April 1768, Secretary of State Lord Hillsborough instructed colonial governors to dissolve any assemblies that took notice of the Massachusetts circular letter proposing collective action on the Townshend Acts. The Massachusetts Assembly refused to rescind its actions, and in June 1768 the colony's governor, Francis Bernard, dissolved it on instructions from London. The ministry, moreover, decided to send troops to Massachusetts, which it regarded as becoming insurrectionary.[36] These measures led popular leaders elsewhere to urge their own people and legislatures to support the Massachusetts Assembly and to stand together as they had in 1765. In New York, street protests in support of Massachusetts began in November 1768. Isaac Sears and other Sons of Liberty advocated issuing fresh instructions to the city's elected representatives calling for New York's assembly to support Massachusetts on the circular letter and to resist parliamentary coercion over quartering.[37]

In the face of such pressures, relations between Moore and the assembly quickly deteriorated.[38] Mindful of growing popular agitation, the assembly refused to approve an annual budget because of a dispute over whether it could issue paper money to alleviate the ongoing economic depression. The defiant assembly issued resolutions on December 31, 1768, calling the unenforced New York Restraining Act illegal and, despite Hillsborough's threats, asserted its right to "correspond and consult with any of the neighboring colonies" if members thought "the rights, liberties, or privileges of the House or its constituents" to be affected. Moore felt obligated to act. On January 2, 1769, he dissolved the assembly and ordered fresh elections.[39]

Factional rivalry and opportunism were part of these maneuvers alongside issues of constitutional principle.[40] Henry Cruger, as a member of the Provincial Council, voted along with three other De Lancey–aligned councilors against endorsing the governor's dissolution of the assembly.[41] This was interpreted in London as evidence of these men's radical sympathies, with Hillsborough urging the king to have Cruger and the others removed from office for their actions. The king evidently approved Hillsborough's plan for retribution, but the distraction of ensuing events prevented it from being put into effect.[42]

Even if they had not wanted the new elections, the Crugers were ready for them. John Cruger returned as a candidate in 1769, running alongside the incumbents, James De Lancey, Jacob Walton, and James Jauncey, on a De Lancey-ite slate that campaigned jointly against Livingston supporters. Their opponents again included the popular incumbent Philip Livingston, and his ally John Morin Scott.[43] Still backed by Sears and many of his supporters, the De Lanceyites portrayed themselves as the friends of commerce, artisans, seamen, and "the real defenders of the constitutional liberties and rights of Americans."[44] De Lanceyite campaign materials also used Cruger's candidacy to appeal to the city's Dutch and German voters.[45] In 1769 the De Lanceyites embraced the idea that "the people" had the right to instruct their representatives, a recurring democratic theme in the Crugers' politics that went to the heart of what constituted representative government. Cruger and all the other De Lanceyite city candidates were elected, and victories elsewhere helped their faction gain control of the assembly. John Cruger became its new Speaker.

The anger over the Townshend Acts also fueled activism surrounding nonimportation. In March 1769, John Harris Cruger, alongside twenty-three other New York merchants including Jacob Walton and Isaac Sears, was named to an extralegal "Committee of Inspection" tasked with enforcing nonimportation.[46] Cruger and fourteen other members of this committee were also in the sixty-three-member chamber of commerce.[47] An account in the transatlantic press shows how nonimportation functioned and the Crugers' part in it. Simeon Cooley, "an English dealer in the hardware-business" violated nonimportation in the summer of 1769 and was brought before New York's Committee of Inspection. When Cooley defied the committee's authority, he was attacked in the press, and handbills circulated calling for New Yorkers to meet at a re-erected liberty pole and, in Cooley's words, "consult what death I should die." Cooley tried to assuage communal anger with his own handbill promising to give up his goods, but at least three particularly hostile members of the committee continued to insist he appear at the liberty pole. He refused and took refuge in the city's fort, but Governor Moore, no doubt anxious to prevent further tensions between the townspeople and the troops, had Cooley told that he "must go to Mr. John [Harris] Cruger's, one of the committee, at whose house I should be safe." Cooley, afraid of exposing himself to mob violence, demurred, but the governor soon ordered him to leave the fort anyway. In the end, Cooley endured the frightening ritual humiliation he had hoped to escape. Several merchants escorted him to the liberty pole, where he "asked pardon of the mobility, and was most ignominiously treated."[48] John Harris Cruger, in a reprise of his uncle's 1765 role, seems to have played a carefully calibrated part in enforcing nonimportation, simultaneously coordinating resistance and acting as someone who could keep popular agitation and the threat of violence within productive channels.

Cooley, like abettors of the Stamp Act, was outmaneuvered by New Yorkers' collective actions, and he was not alone. To be effective, nonimportation required wide cooperation. It needed organization by committeemen like Isaac Sears and John Harris Cruger, merchants' support, and the dedication of ordinary women and men, who did without British goods, and, when necessary, took to the streets to intimidate violators like Cooley.[49] It has been noted that "there is every reason to believe that non-importation was exceedingly well enforced in New York," with reported annual imports from Britain falling from £490,673 in 1768 to £75,930 in 1769, "a record which was not equaled or even approached in any other province."[50] General Thomas Gage observed in December 1769 that "committees of Merchants at Boston, N[ew] York, and Philadelphia contrive to exercise the Government" and wondered that "an illegal Combination of People" could establish "such an Imperium" without "the least Show of Opposition."[51]

While nonimportation took hold, the key questions within New York's 1769 assembly were how to address continuing economic stagnation and the perennial problem of quartering. Parliament's 1764 Currency Act, which limited colonial issuances of paper money, remained on the books and continued, many thought, to harm American economies. The now De Lancey–controlled assembly nevertheless passed a bill for issuing £120,000 in New York bills of credit that would circulate as a paper currency. Moore wrote to London urging the bill's approval, but he died in September 1769 before a response was received, and the aged lieutenant governor, Cadwallader Colden, again stepped in to assume temporary power. With the fate of its paper money bill still uncertain and facing increasing public pressure to stand up to Parliament, the legislature began considering the issue of supplying the troops for the year.[52]

Because of their persistent tensions with British regulars, quartering remained an infuriating issue for the Sons of Liberty and the sailors, mechanics, and other New Yorkers with whom they were connected. Having aided the De Lanceyites in recent elections, Sears and his allies expected the assembly to defend colonial rights, as it did in May 1769 by endorsing a Virginia resolution protesting the Townshend Acts. Yet absolutely refusing to pay for quartering would have been a provocation certain to entail a parliamentary response. The De Lanceyites soon found themselves caught between a rock and a hard place. When John Cruger asked Sears if he would support voting money for the troops in light of the assembly's willingness to again assert provincial rights, Sears said he would not. Instead, he told Speaker Cruger that "I always was averse to granting money to the Troops in Time of profound Peace, and was always against the former assemblies for doing it." In discussions with other De Lanceyites, however, Sears seemed to suggest that his supporters could accept quartering expenditures *if* supplies were purchased for troops through newly issued New York bills of credit.[53] Looking for a way out, the De Lanceyite majority searched for a compromise acceptable to Parliament and the Sons of Liberty. The assembly passed one bill again authorizing the issuance of provincial bills of credit and a second providing quartering funds, with half the needed sum to be drawn from money already in New York's treasury and half to come from the to-be-issued bills of credit. Colden and the council, despite the absence of any reply from Westminster on the acceptability of the previously passed money bill, approved the new measures.[54]

Creative dealmaking like this was a hallmark of John Cruger's career, but in 1769 it came with new costs. The British government eventually disallowed the New York money bill outright, scolding Colden and the council for having approved a clear violation of the 1764 Currency Act. Worse, and more immediately, the Livingston faction, insulated from the need to compromise by their own weakness in the assembly, seized on the passage of the quartering bill as a betrayal of the interests of the province.[55] Personalities mattered too. The man who made the most of the issue, and in doing so became a formidable popular figure in New York politics in the run-up to the Revolution, was Alexander McDougall, a Scottish-born seafarer and the captain of a privateer during the Seven Years' War.[56] In a short piece published anonymously in December 1769 titled "To the Betrayed Inhabitants of the City and Colony of New-York," the Presbyterian and pro-Livingston McDougall flagellated the De Lanceyite majority assembly as corrupt and the De Lancey family as having designs on "the Sovereign

Lordship of this Colony." Signing himself with the pseudonym "A Son of Liberty," McDougall called for a mass meeting to signal popular opposition to the legislature's vote of quartering money.[57] The De Lanceyites regarded McDougall's text as a gross libel but miscalculated how their actions would be received by the influential Isaac Sears. He, it became clear, did not regard the assembly's new measures as an acceptable compromise, especially after McDougall's meeting further enflamed people. That meeting led Sears to believe that hardly any common person in New York City would now support giving "any Money to the Troops, on any Consideration whatsover."[58]

In January 1770 off-duty soldiers repeatedly attacked and finally destroyed another large liberty pole that the Sons of Liberty had erected in the city.[59] On January 19, 1770, brawling over liberty poles culminated in a large-scale riot that saw off-duty British regulars draw their bayonets against civilians, the so-called Battle of Golden Hill. A few weeks later, the Sons of Liberty erected a huge new liberty pole—nearly sixty feet tall, encased in a protective iron cover, and planted twelve feet deep—that remained standing as a symbol of defiance until 1776, when British soldiers then dominating the wartime city felled it. Rather surprisingly, no one on either side was killed during these violent clashes in early 1770. But in the ensuing months New Yorkers' hostility toward the regulars increased when they learned that similar tensions in Massachusetts had led to the Boston Massacre.[60]

New York's liberty pole rioting suggested to some that law and order was breaking down in the city. In this atmosphere, tensions increased between unelected popular leaders and those officeholders responsible for governance. When, in an ill-advised move in February 1770, the De Lancey–controlled assembly under Speaker Cruger ordered McDougall arrested for libel, he portrayed himself as persecuted by provincial authorities now acting as enemies to the very colonial liberties they ought to defend. The case against him was ultimately dismissed, but McDougall spent a total of five months in prison. His supporters characterized him as an American John Wilkes, unjustly jailed for daring to speak truth to power. His opponents regarded him as a demagogue, but their high-handed efforts to punish McDougall angered many in New York including Isaac Sears. The alliance between Sears and the De Lancey faction was breaking down while Sears and the Livingston-supporting McDougall began bringing their followers together.

In March 1770, in a sign of the widening rift, New Yorkers held two separate banquets to commemorate the repeal of the Stamp Act. One was led by

Sears and his new friends, who styled themselves as the "real" Sons of Liberty. Its attendees included John Morin Scott and other Livingston politicians, and among the toasts drunk was one to Alexander McDougall, then still in jail. A rival dinner was attended by 233 people who considered themselves "The Friends of Liberty and Trade" or the "true" Sons of Liberty, including John Cruger, John Harris Cruger, Peter Van Schaack, Jacob Walton, Oliver De Lancey, John De Lancey, and many other longtime associates and De Lanceyites.[61] In the aftermath of these competing celebrations, the groups publicly criticized each other's proceedings, bickered over attendance figures, and trumpeted that they were the colonial cause's genuine supporters.

In adopting the double-barreled name of the "Friends of Liberty and Trade," the Crugers and their allies signaled that they considered individual and communal economic interests on a plane with any desires to defend more abstract rights. In the context of the recent turmoil over compromises regarding paper money and quartering, their point was that they—not people they perceived as rabble-rousers—had the true best interests of New Yorkers at heart. Political and constitutional principles should be defended, but not with a self-defeating single-mindedness as if such principles were the only thing that mattered to individual and collective well-being. In 1769 and 1770, a crack began appearing in New York's resistance movement as factional politics hammered on what liberty really meant.

In April 1770, after months of rumors that it would do so, Parliament repealed the Townshend Acts. Lord North, prime minister from January 1770, was prepared to sacrifice what he regarded as the bad policies of his predecessor—the Townshend Acts raised little money for much trouble—but he, like most British members of Parliament, believed in Parliament's right to issue such laws. Nearly all of the duties on goods enumerated under the Townshend Acts were repealed, but that on tea was left in place. The tax on tea was both the largest revenue generator in the Townshend Acts, and a symbolic assertion of parliamentary authority.[62] For supporters of nonimportation, the repeal of almost all the Townshend duties was a success, but the maintenance of the tea duty made it a bittersweet one that required a choice about what to do next. One option was to claim victory and resume most importation while, in a proportional response, maintaining the boycott on still-taxed tea as a statement of principle. The other option was to keep comprehensive but painful nonimportation agreements in place in pursuit of a final resolution to the underlying constitutional dispute.

Intercolonial dynamics were also a factor. When New Yorkers learned in May 1770 that Rhode Island merchants intended to resume importing, local tensions grew between hardliners, including Sears and his allies, who favored maintaining total nonimportation, and the bulk of New York's trading community, which increasingly favored restarting at least some trade.[63] At the same time, there also remained powerful, shared desires to preserve local and continental cooperation. In response, New York merchants including Sears issued a circular letter calling on other trading towns to send delegates to an intercolonial meeting at which nonimportation could be discussed and a strategy agreed upon. Reflecting the thin documentation on this complex moment, historians have disagreed over the fundamental purpose of this projected 1770 congress: whether it was proposed by those New Yorkers who hoped to maintain or even strengthen the existing nonimportation agreements or by those who wanted to weaken or end them.[64] In any case, Boston's merchant committee quickly rejected the idea of such a meeting, and it was not held. Some claimed that this was because the politically committed Boston traders did not want to participate in any meeting that could lead to the repeal of the existing agreements. The skeptical said it was because the Bostonians wanted to continue their profitable but duplicitous practice of importing while keeping other ports bound to nonimportation.[65] The tree of liberty was becoming a thicket. Unable to convene a wider congress, New Yorkers had to find their own way through it.

Those on either side of altering nonimporation agreements claimed that their position reflected the will of the people. The Crugers were among those for modification.[66] In this they were joined by other De Lanceyite politicians; larger, more established, and wealthier merchants; and a probable majority of the common people of New York City. In June 1770 those who favored modification circulated a subscription list through which city residents were asked to signal their support for resuming imports. The Sons of Liberty at first did not oppose taking the sense of the people in this way but then hurriedly tried circulating their own subscription paper to record the names of those in favor of maintaining full nonimportation. Although the Sons of Liberty subsequently cried foul, the competing lists revealed a large majority for restarting trade.

A few days later, the New York Committee of Inspection, which still included John Harris Cruger and many of the Crugers' friends, sent letters to the merchants of Philadelphia and Boston informing them of the results of the recent canvass. That they took this step, rather than simply starting to import, suggests that they hoped for an orderly and unified transition to a new policy, but it is also clear that some in New York and elsewhere would not follow this course. Philadelphia's merchants, who had been difficult to bring into nonimportation initially, signaled their disapproval of New York's proceedings. Locally, Sears and an ally of his resigned from the Committee of Inspection in light of these developments.[67] Writing to Peter Van Schaack about these "great commotions," Henry Cruger Sr. reported on June 18 that importing would soon resume as "our merchants in general declare openly & publicly they'll be no longer imposed on by the perfidy of Boston & Newport" and that three ships were preparing to sail the next day for London and another, the Crugers' own *Ellin*, was readying for Bristol.[68]

When news arrived in early July that Boston merchants had resolved to retain full nonimportation, New York's Committee of Inspection decided to hold a poll to again assess local sentiments.[69] Merchants' regard for their pocketbooks played a part in these developments, but so too did other factors. Consumers were anxious to resume purchasing "the goods they so dearly loved" once they were freed of troubling taxes.[70] Moreover, it is misleading to assume that all common people were always in favor of the most radical measures. As Michael Hattem has argued, many colonists cared less about "the abstract ideas behind imperial policy and colonial resistance" than their "immediate effects" on people's "daily lives and their immediate prospects for social mobility."[71] Nonimportation was painful for everyone, but poorer New Yorkers were particularly vulnerable and less able to indefinitely continue making economic sacrifices in pursuit of political principles. What opponents of resuming importation called greed, some New Yorkers understood as need. Sailors, artisans, merchants, and all those connected to the maritime economy had strong reasons to want commerce restarted.[72] Alexander Colden claimed in July 1770 that "many families must starve if an importation of goods from Great Britain did not soon take place."[73] The "Friends of Liberty and Trade" could—with considerable reason—argue that ending nonimportation was for New York's common good. Moreover, in late June word arrived that Parliament had granted New York a special exemption to the Currency Act, allowing it to issue bills of credit that would circulate in the province as legal tender. To some it probably seemed wise to offer a reciprocal gesture of goodwill by ending comprehensive nonimportation.[74]

For their part, Sears, McDougall, and their allies held a meeting at which, as McDougall noted, they "resolved not to take the sense of the People" on the resumption of imports but to oppose modification anyway.[75] When, after demonstrations and a street fight between pro- and anti-importers, the poll was held on July 9, the results were striking: 794 people for resuming imports and 465 against.[76] The anti-importers again cried foul, but the Committee of Inspection upheld the outcome. McDougall rued that following these events "DeLancey and Walton headed the importers from the Coffee House."[77] As one historian has observed, "when faced with a choice, the majority chose the merchants over the radicals."[78] In the coming days, the Committee sent dispatches informing Philadelphia of New York's reconfirmed decision to resume imports, and more New York traders sent orders for goods to Britain. Despite their rhetoric, Sears and his local allies quickly sent orders for imports too, and, amid recriminations, traders in other ports followed suit in the coming months.[79]

The Crugers and other advocates for modifying nonimportation, like Sears, McDougall, Scott, and their supporters, embraced the colonial cause in the transatlantic constitutional dispute with Britain. As comprehensive non-importation ended, the two groups that emerged had political disagreements but still more in common. Neither was in favor of expanding the power of the king or Parliament over New York and other colonies. Both thought that parliamentary taxation of the colonies was problematic and opposed the remaining Townshend duty on tea. The people who came to see themselves as the "Friends of Liberty and Trade" had been central to developing and enforcing nonimportation as an extralegal strategy of resistance. They were not timid, indecisive, or much worried about the interests of the Crown or Parliament. They wanted to cooperate with New York's workers. Moreover, the measures they took to secure a modification of the nonimportation agreement—public meetings, subscriptions and polls, supporting an intercolonial conference, open correspondence with merchants and committees elsewhere—all suggest that they were as invested in the maintenance of colonial unity and democratic procedures as strict anti-importers were.[80]

Despite the acrimony of 1770, politics in New York and other colonies were less tumultuous after importing resumed.[81] The tea tax still rankled, but as tempers cooled, it came to seem less important. As one recent account has put it, "for the vast majority of colonists, the remaining tea duty, even to pay colonial officials, was worth neither war nor continuing nonimportation."[82] Tea would later return as a potent symbol, but for a few years the controversies over it went off the boil. Traders elsewhere, including Boston, soon imported and sold duties British tea, and consumer demand remained strong. The two places, in fact, where efforts to shun taxed tea continued were Philadelphia and New York. Between December 1770 and the outbreak of the Revolution, only 874 pounds of taxed "British" tea were imported into New York.[83] This may have reflected public tumults in the middle colonies over the end of nonimportation, but it was also connected to their active trades in smuggled "Dutch" tea.[84] Thomas Hutchinson reported in 1771 that "in New York they import scarce any other than Dutch teas," and that Pennsylvania and, of course, Rhode Island were little better.[85] The Crugers were likely part of New York's wider reliance on "Dutch" middlemen as sources for tea, although in their particular case some of the middlemen might have been at least nominally "Danish" rather than Dutch. In June 1772, Nicholas Cruger, based on St. Croix, wrote guardedly but hardly cryptically to John Harris Cruger and Jacob Walton to inform them that chests of "T" that he had sourced through Copenhagen were being sent to them in New York. Nicholas had previously written to Cruger and Walton about smuggling "R"—rum from St. Croix—so it would seem that he certainly had "developed some proficiency in the field of smuggling."[86] Some New Yorkers may have regarded a thriving local trade in smuggled tea as a better way to assert real colonial autonomy than inflammatory constitutional rhetoric. In a return to something like business as usual, customs inspectors were bribed, importers schemed, and profits and principle jogged along together.

In 1772, presumably on the back of his recent civic involvement, his commercial reputation, and his family's political clout, John Harris Cruger was appointed New York City's chamberlain.[87] As the municipal government's treasurer, the chamberlain collected revenue and made payments on the city's behalf. The post was unsalaried, but the holder was entitled to collect fees and sometimes loaned the city money at interest to enable it to meet its obligations.[88] The office, which blended civic responsibility, the need for business acumen, and the opportunity for profit, was exactly in the family line. As 1772 closed, the Crugers, like other colonists, had reasons to continue worrying over constitutional issues, but the previous five years had underlined the family's positions in New York and in a wider movement that was prepared to defend the intertwined causes of trade and liberty.

Like his brother John Harris, Henry Cruger Jr. in Bristol was increasingly in the public eye. In 1765, amid his Stamp Act activism, Henry Jr. became a member of Bristol's Society of Merchant Venturers, the city's incorporated body of maritime traders. The society, which received a royal charter in the mid-sixteenth century, provided social connections and commercial privileges while acting as a collective voice for Bristol's merchants. It also functioned as a quasi-governmental organization, responsible for maintaining Bristol's navigable waterways and wharves and collecting fees from their users.[89] In 1766, Henry became a member of Bristol's self-perpetuating municipal government, the Common Council, and served as one of the city's sheriffs. By 1768 Henry described himself as having "sufficient Interest amongst the great men here" to assist his New York relatives.[90] That year, although still under age thirty, Henry acted as one of the Society of Merchant Venturers' two wardens, who served under the master as the organization's principal officers.[91] These activities signaled Henry's acceptance by Bristol's commercial elite and his growing public reputation as an advocate for trade in the aftermath of the Stamp Act crisis (fig. 7).

From the 1760s Henry also became part of the influential movement that adopted John Wilkes as its talisman. For nearly twenty years, Wilkes's battles with the Crown and a succession of governments roiled British life and inspired Americans. With an instantly recognizable face and a golden pen, Wilkes created a more populist register for English politics beginning in the 1760s. In long-running fights over his publication of *The North Briton* and his representing Middlesex in Parliament, Wilkes railed against government malfeasance, pushed for parliamentary reform and the expansion of democracy, and championed freedom of speech and the wider rights of Englishmen. His sharp tongue earned him powerful enemies, including George III, but Wilkes's steadfast refusal to be silenced made him the embodiment of the grievances that many nonelite Britons and colonial Americans had with the oligarchic aristocrats who ruled over them.[92] When, in 1770, disputes in New York over ending nonimportation led to rival dinners being held by the "real Friends of Liberty" and the Cruger-supported "Friends of Liberty and Trade," both groups toasted Wilkes during their celebrations.[93]

In March 1769, just after the New York election in which the De Lancey-ites supported issuing popular instructions to assemblymen, radically minded people in Bristol held a meeting that adopted a set of Wilkesite instructions to the city's members of Parliament and called for a more conciliatory policy toward America.[94] Soon thereafter, Cruger and his father-in-law, Samuel Peach, became leaders of an Independent Society formed as a deliberate alternative to politics as usual in Bristol.[95] In July 1769 Cruger chaired a boisterous meeting at the Bristol Guildhall that produced an anti-ministerial petition to the throne presenting Wilkesite grievances and blaming the government for having "alienated the affections of our American brethren." At the meeting Cruger observed that Townshend's duties had badly hurt his trade and, while insisting that he

Figure 7. Henry Cruger Jr. as a Bristol Merchant. This engraving captures the public persona that Cruger cultivated following the Stamp Act crisis. Bristol Archives, ref. 40826.PEO/9. Image from Bristol Archives.

spoke just as a merchant, he shared popular anger over "the numberless Persecutions and Cruelties committed against the Person of Mr. John Wilkes."[96] Cruger was among the delegation that presented the resulting Bristol petition to the king in 1770, a fact noted in the colonial press.[97]

One revealing consequence of Henry Cruger's immersion in Wilkesite politics was that he became business associates and close friends with the Boston-based William Palfrey, who was both a junior partner in John Hancock's business and secretary to Boston's Sons of Liberty. By the late 1760s, Palfrey was corresponding with Wilkes in England, helping to forge ties between the colonial resistance movement and English radicalism. Palfrey visited England in 1771 and met Wilkes personally.[98] Cruger evidently came to know Palfrey during this visit and subsequently did business with Hancock through Palfrey's assistance. Letters later exchanged between Cruger and Palfrey show that their relationship intermingled business, personal friendship, and political sympathy. The friends shipped each other dogs across the Atlantic, and Palfrey was godfather to one of Cruger's children. In 1772, Cruger sent Palfrey a cask of ale with thanks for recent commercial favors and congratulations on Wilkes's recent victory in the Middlesex election dispute.[99] Cruger also developed relationships with other English friends to America in this period, including the future Continental general Horatio Gates—still a British Army officer—and the prominent opposition member of Parliament Isaac Barré, whom Cruger described as a "fine laughing fellow" in 1770."[100]

In January 1772, Cruger, Peach, and several others invited Wilkes and the London radical Frederick Bull to Bristol and hosted a banquet honoring them.[101] Their visit to Bristol and Cruger's role in it were reported in the colonial press, underlining ties between anti-ministerial patriots around the empire.[102] The following month, Cruger cemented his radical credentials by speaking before a Bristol Guildhall meeting on a favorite Wilkesite theme, the "necessity of shortening the duration of Parliaments, in order to put a stop to that unbounded corruption which no other measure could so effectually restrain." Under the leadership of Peach and Cruger, this meeting issued fresh instructions to Bristol's members of Parliament, directing them to support shorter Parliaments.[103] Henry was becoming a prominent spokesperson for an ocean-spanning common cause.

Amid colonial anger over the Townshend Acts, members of the Cruger family were integral to an Anglo-American movement that promoted freer maritime trade, increased practical colonial autonomy, and the more amorphous value of liberty. They operated in these years as a family of transatlantic patriots and engaged in the multivocal urban politics of protest and resistance. There were sometimes disagreements among patriots over who spoke for the people and how best to achieve common aims, and the Crugers were part of these controversies. But they also cooperated with a range of figures who, although they would occupy various positions after 1775, had more in common during these years than they did differences.

The Crugers' collective role in this period's political history defies easy assumptions sometimes made about wartime nobody men. Far from being uninterested in politics or focused exclusively on their private financial concerns, the Crugers were deeply invested in pursuing what they saw as the public good. While, like many people, they could equate what was in their personal best interests with that of the wider communities to which they belonged, they were no more conspicuous in doing so than a range of other people who occupied a variety of political positions once the war started. As they made choices in the late 1760s and early 1770s, they, like others on both sides of the ocean, engaged with a complex set of issues that muddled any simple distinctions between patriotic and unpatriotic positions. Sharing a language of liberty with other Anglo-Americans, the Crugers wanted change, not to preserve the status quo. But, again like many others, they could not foresee how events would unfold.

4. The Center Fails

Between 1772 and 1775, the Crugers joined a failed effort to find a peaceful resolution to the constitutional crisis that roiled the British Empire. There was no referendum on whether the colonies should begin an armed revolt against British rule. Rather, in 1774 and 1775 there was a succession of moments during which people made political choices in the wake of the Boston Tea Party and the Coercive Acts. People picked their way through these events not as solitary individuals but as parts of families, groups, and communities; few knew exactly where they wanted to go and fewer still how to get there. The Crugers were well-established defenders of colonial positions in disputes over taxation, representation, and trade, and there was little difference between the Crugers' views on the transatlantic disagreement and those of other prominent colonial leaders. They remained committed to the goals of the common cause, but they came to believe that some of the tactics employed by their fellow patriots were dangerous and self-defeating, and that reconciliation and compromise were better outcomes than civil war.

By the spring of 1775 this procolonial but antiwar center ground failed in New York and Westminster. The Crugers participated in the prewar crisis in multiple ways, and their collective history reveals the descent into civil war in its local, intracolonial, and imperial contexts, showing how developments in each shaped peoples' subsequent wartime choices. The Crugers did not aim to end up between warring parties, but they made a series of incremental choices that landed them there. Above all, the Crugers' experiences illustrate how it was the turn to violence rather than any prewar ideological distinctiveness on the transatlantic issues ostensibly at stake in the Revolution that finally transformed most of them into nobody men.

After the repeal of the Townshend Acts, adjusting the imperial constitution remained a goal for almost all colonial patriots, but rending it was not. Cautious optimism about the direction of events was buttressed by the appointment of Lord Dartmouth, widely seen as sympathetic to the colonies, as secretary of state for America in August 1772.[1] Because of this, the Crugers and others continued making choices premised on New York developing within the empire. In late 1772, John Harris Cruger became, alongside William Walton, one of the "lieutenant colonels" in the Governor's Guard, a new unit created as part of an expanded provincial militia. His father-in-law, Oliver De Lancey, a member of the Provincial Council since 1760, became commander of the militia in southern New York.[2] William Smith, also a councilor but a strong partisan of the Livingston faction, thought John Harris's new post proved the Cruger family's "rage for offices."[3]

John Harris Cruger succeeded his father, Henry, on the Provincial Council in 1773. This Crown appointment was the culmination of transatlantic politicking, as Henry Sr. had proposed the idea to Governor Tryon at least a year previously. Henry Cruger Jr. lobbied in England, and Speaker John Cruger even solicited Edmund Burke, with whom he was in correspondence because of Burke's role as the New York assembly's agent, for help that would "Gratify my Brother, my Nephew & My Self."[4] Notice of John Harris Cruger's appointment to the council arrived in New York in August 1773.[5] With the speakership and a continuing place on the council, the Crugers' long-term political prospects in New York seemed secure.

Trading and professional life continued too, with John Harris preparing ships like the *Phila*, his mother-in-law's namesake, to sail from Cruger's Wharf to Bristol in August 1773.[6] He advertised, worked to recover commercial debts, and otherwise acted as the rising leader of his family's business interests in New York.[7] Like other prominent New Yorkers, the Crugers were also interested in the legal and political disputes over what became Vermont. John Harris Cruger led a consortium that obtained New York title to a large tract of land in 1767 and was in partnerships that obtained other large grants in the region in 1771 and 1772.[8] In 1772 and 1773, Peter Van Schaack compiled the statute law of colonial New York at the behest of the self-consciously independent General Assembly, an undertaking imbued with provincial patriotism while also premised on the idea that this explicitly *colonial* form of law would matter in the future.[9] In 1773, Nicholas's talented teenaged clerk, Alexander Hamilton, arrived in British North America from St. Croix to pursue his education.[10] That same year, Henry Cruger Jr. also traveled to America to strengthen business ties and try to collect on his correspondents' debts. In all these spheres of life there was little sign that the Crugers anticipated the coming rupture.

As the Crugers' affairs showed, New York and other North American colonies were becoming more, rather than less, integrated into the global British Empire, which is why it was Parliament's 1773 Tea Act that spawned the tempest that ended in war. Another attempt to address the East India Company's difficulties, the law lowered the total duties on tea legally exported to the colonies with the aim of making it more competitive with smuggled alternatives. But it left in place a small duty on tea payable in America that would continue to fund the payment of some officeholders.[11] In August 1773 the buoyed company made plans to ship nearly 600,000 pounds of tea to colonial ports including New York, Philadelphia, and Boston. Colonists, however, were enraged by the Tea Act, seeing it as renewing Parliament's efforts to tax them without their consent.[12]

What first unfolded in New York, much like what had happened during the Stamp Act crisis, was a modulated resistance that encompassed common people, popular leaders, merchants, and elected and appointed politicians like the Crugers. Even some of the city's most confrontational patriots, like Isaac Sears and Alexander McDougall, aimed "not to overthrow an allegedly 'unstable' old order in the province but to unite all New Yorkers, regardless of political affiliation, in a crusade against British imperialism."[13] Therefore the tactics of 1765 were redeployed. Newspapers attacked the Tea Act, and threatening handbills warned would-be handlers of dutied tea that they faced public wrath. On November 24, 1773, the three New York traders appointed as the company's local agents were pressured into pledging that they would not accept its tea. In a plan supported by Livingstons, De Lanceyites, and popular leaders including McDougall, the Provincial Council agreed that when the company's tea arrived, it would be stored in New York's fort and not allowed to be sold.[14] A similar process played out in Philadelphia, where public pressure, including a mass meeting, convinced the company's local consignees to resign by early December.[15]

What continued adherence to the tactics of 1765 might have meant for New Yorkers and subsequent Anglo-American relations is impossible to say because resistance to the Tea Act unfolded differently in Massachusetts. Boston patriots failed to intimidate the company's local agents into resigning or to force the ships carrying tea back to England when they arrived in late November. Facing the imminent possibility of the company's tea being unloaded, and perhaps having "internalized the accusatory rhetoric from New York City and Philadelphia" questioning their commitment to the colonial cause, a group of Bostonians made a momentous choice.[16] On December 16, 1773, a party of thinly disguised men boarded the *Dartmouth* and her sisters and dumped 90,000 pounds of tea into the harbor.[17] In the wake of Boston's Tea Party, Philadelphians and New Yorkers, deploying less obviously illegal and escalatory tactics, forced the ships carrying company tea to their ports to return to England with their cargoes still aboard.[18]

When it learned of the Boston Tea Party, the British cabinet quickly decided that "in consequence of the present disorders in America, effectual steps be taken to secure the dependence of the colonies on the mother country."[19] The resulting Boston Port Act, a calculated exercise in collective punishment, closed Boston to nearly all maritime commerce as of June 1, 1774, and until the company was reimbursed "by or on behalf of the inhabitants."[20] With Boston chastised, the ministry turned to other measures designed to address what many in British politics understood to be the Tea Party's underlying causes. The resulting legislation, the Coercive or Intolerable Acts, aimed to bring Massachusetts, increasingly seen as the font of continental disorder, under firmer imperial control. The Massachusetts Government Act unilaterally altered the province's charter to give more power to its royal governor, and the Administration of Justice Act allowed him to send defendants to England for trial. A new Quartering Act allowed all colonial governors to house soldiers in unoccupied buildings if they deemed it necessary.[21] Finally, the Quebec Act created a new, larger Province of Quebec, legalized Catholicism there, and vested power in a royally appointed governor and council without an elected legislature.[22] Together, these laws appeared to many in America to mark a far-reaching ministerial assault on fundamental colonial rights.

On May 11, 1774, the inaptly named *Concord* delivered news of the Boston Port Act to New York.[23] There were near-universal expressions of anger and concern. Oliver De Lancey said he "would rather spend every shilling of his Fortune" than see "the Boston Port Bill be complied with."[24] The Livingstonian William Smith observed "a General Consternation and Disgust."[25] Provincial Council president John Watts called the king a "Huckster."[26] The extended Cruger family shared the consternation. "The measures of government," Peter Van Schaack wrote on May 13, "so strongly indicating a determination to establish the supremacy of Parliament over these colonies, are truly alarming." With fundamental constitutional issues now openly at stake, he thought the situation was extremely dangerous. "An absolute exemption from Parliamentary taxation in every case whatever, is what the colonies will never recede from." If, he continued "that is not their *right*, they do not enjoy the privileges of British subjects" but this was "a concession we cannot expect from England until necessity shall compel them to it." Just two days after the news of the Boston Port Act arrived in New York, Van Schaack feared that "an appeal to the sword" was "inevitable."[27]

The Boston Port Act prompted fresh activism in New York. Factional antipathy and tensions between popular and more elite leaders again arose in subsequent events, but near-universal anger over Parliament's actions meant that there was still much common ground.[28] Because effective resistance required coordination, many New Yorkers supported forming a committee to correspond with other colonies and develop a strategy. Bostonians were reviving nonimportation and wanted support; on May 15 Sears and McDougall wrote to them proposing an intercolonial meeting. The next day, some three hundred New Yorkers attended a meeting to organize local resistance in New York and "those present proved how deeply the controversy had penetrated into all social ranks."[29] Members of the city's leading merchant families were there, including the Crugers, Waltons, Beekmans, Ludlows, and Livingstons. Five members of the council attended, as did assembly members, lawyers, and many clerks and mechanics. The deliberately inclusive body that emerged, called the Committee of Fifty-One for its number of members, encompassed street politicians like Sears and McDougall, allies of both the De Lancey and Livingston factions, and many merchants.[30] Isaac Low, a De Lanceyite trader, one of the chamber of commerce's founders, and a key figure in nonimportation, became its chairman.[31]

British politicians failed to predict the extent to which the Coercive Acts would bring the colonies together, but "because it was so malleable and useful, the rhetoric of 'common cause' became almost hegemonic by 1774."[32] Like many other New Yorkers, the Crugers supported the common cause and worked to have their views and interests represented within it. Most important, Peter Van Schaack was on the Committee of Fifty-One.[33] In a sign of his embrace of the politics of resistance, Peter joined fellow lawyers John Jay and James Duane on a subcommittee tasked with drawing up a set of regulations for the Fifty-One's proceedings. Van Schaack also helped spread resistance, serving on another subcommittee with Jay, McDougall, and two others that wrote other New

96   "CRUGER AND LIBERTY!"

York counties about city developments and encouraged them to form their own corresponding committees.[34]

Many New Yorkers and the Committee of Fifty-One supported holding an intercolonial meeting to decide on collective action.[35] Boston patriots, supported by local figures like Sears and McDougall, wanted New York and other ports to back them by reviving total nonimportation, but other New Yorkers were skeptical about this course. Therefore, as John Jay put it, the Committee of Fifty-One "agreed to attempt a Congress of Deputies from all the Colonies, as the most probable Means of effecting a general Union and Consistency of Councils."[36] The calling of what subsequently became known as the First Continental Congress received widespread backing in other colonies too. There were factional tensions in New York, but ultimately the poll for electing delegates to this congress was open to all taxpayers and jointly overseen by a remarkable conglomeration of the city's interest groups: the Common Council, church vestrymen, the Liberty Boys, and the Committee of Fifty-One. The Committee of Fifty-One also removed a major source of tension between more and less militant New Yorkers when it agreed on July 26, 1774, that it would back a general nonimportation agreement if one was recommended by the continental congress. The final poll saw five candidates originally nominated by the Committee of Fifty-One, now endorsed by the Sons of Liberty, all elected. Philip Livingston, Isaac Low, John Alsop, James Duane, and John Jay would represent the city.[37] The subsequent loyalist Thomas Jones observed that New York's delegates had been "chosen by the people at large, with little or no opposition, all parties, denominations and religions, apprehending at the time, that the Colonies laboured under grievances which wanted redressing."[38]

The First Continental Congress sat in Philadelphia in September and October 1774. Van Schaack dined with John Adams as he traveled to it and corresponded with Duane and Jay as it met.[39] Revealingly, while Van Schaack remained immersed in the politics of resistance, other New Yorkers, most notably Church of England clergymen including Samuel Seabury and Charles Inglis, began articulating a critique of the congress as illegal, illegitimate, and aimed at nothing less than colonial independence. Between the meeting of the First Continental Congress and April 1775, these writers "produced perhaps the most voluminous literature in favor of Great Britain during the entire conflict."[40] Their critiques of congress were a far cry from Van Schaack's commitment to the common cause and to the wider Cruger family's established place in colonial politics. In ideological terms, the future nobodyman Van Schaack and others in the Cruger clan continued to have more in common with the patriot leadership than they did with emerging opponents to it.

The First Continental Congress's most concrete outcome was the Continental Association, which put in place a nonimportation agreement effective December 1, mandated the nonconsumption of tea, and stated that unless Parliament repealed offensive laws, the colonies would implement nonexportation in September 1775. Moreover, the association created a system of committees, to be formed in "every county, city, and town" to attentively observe the people in their district and publicize any violations so that adherents to the association could "break off all dealings with him or her."[41] The Fifty-One had already indicated its willingness to support nonimportation if the congress agreed to it, but many people also expected the delegates meeting in Philadelphia to develop strategies for constructively reforming the imperial relationship. As Thomas Jones put it later, some New Yorkers thought the congress would redress colonial grievances and work to "form a happy, perpetual, and lasting, alliance, between Great Britain and America."[42] What they envisioned was resistance modulated with forward-looking measures for promoting reconciliation.

This was why two other interlinked congressional actions were as important as the Continental Association for future nobody men like the Crugers. In mid-September, the congress adopted Massachusetts' Suffolk Resolves as its own. The resolves called on citizens to "use their utmost Diligence to acquaint themselves with the Art of War as soon as possible" and to train weekly under arms. When congressmen endorsed this language with little debate, they sanctioned organizing militarized resistance and further widened the gulf between the colonies and Britain.[43] Congressmen also rejected and tried to bury the most carefully worked-out set of ideas for reworking the imperial constitution brought to Philadelphia: Joseph Galloway's "Plan of Union." What Galloway proposed was a nonviolent revolution: a radical transformation of the fundamental structures of imperial governance via a royally appointed colonial "President General" and a legislative "grand Council" made of up of delegates selected by colonial assemblies. Galloway's plan intrigued many congressmen, and it got particularly strong support from the New York delegation, which seconded Galloway's motion proposing it.[44] William Franklin reported that Galloway's proposal was "greatly approved of by some of the most sensible men" in New York.[45] However, opponents in the congress defeated Galloway's plan by getting it tabled and then, according to James Duane, it was "rejected and ordered to be left out of the minutes," deliberately preventing the plan from being considered by the wider public.[46] Galloway's plan may have been unworkable, but the congress's smothering of it signaled that patriots seeking compromise faced organized opposition from more hard-line militants. The First Continental Congress adjourned in late October with a plan for another congress to be held in 1775 if the Coercive Acts were not repealed.

In late November 1774 New York's Committee of Fifty-One was dissolved and replaced by the Committee of Sixty, a new extralegal body explicitly empowered to enforce the Continental Association citywide. These developments have been interpreted as an important power shift, as the city's popular politicians, Liberty Boys, and common people steered events in a more radical direction while traditional elites lost power. This may have been true, but a wide spectrum of New Yorkers continued supporting the common cause. The new body included all five congressional delegates, Sears and McDougall, other Livingston supporters, John De Lancey, two Waltons, and Peter Van Schaack, who was among the twenty-nine men from the Fifty-One who also joined the Sixty. As Van Schaack's son summarized his actions during this period, "he is known to have been friendly to the measures of non-importation, and non-consumption, and he was in favor of all peaceful remedies to procure a redress of grievances."[47] A cross section of New York's politically active population, including future nobody men like Peter Van Schaack, supported the Committee of Sixty because they shared its aims even as they did not know where expanded resistance would lead as 1775 dawned.[48]

Henry Cruger Jr. spent nearly a year in America in 1773/74, witnessing the widespread opposition to the Tea Act. He knew many politically prominent New Yorkers and traveled widely on business, meeting with people in Philadelphia and New England. Cruger visited his friend, the Son of Liberty William Palfrey in Boston in 1773 and was in America when the Boston Tea Party occurred. He departed America in the spring of 1774, likely just before news of the Boston Port Act broke, with experiences that gave him a rare perspective within British politics.[49]

Cruger arrived in Bristol in July 1774, returning to a British political scene that was also in flux. The last general election for Parliament had been held in 1768, and in the intervening years the two issues with which Henry was most was closely connected—democratic political reform and the American situation—had become increasingly important in national politics. It was during the final session of the Parliament elected in 1768 that the North administration passed the Coercive Acts. Under British law, a general election did not have to occur until March 1775, so the ministry's surprise decision to call the election early, announced on September 30, left many of North's opponents scrambling.[50]

Bristol's radicals, however, had already decided that Cruger would be their candidate.[51] Organized Whigs and Tories in Bristol had long operated under an agreement that saw each group return one member to Parliament, but by 1774 many local Whigs had grown disenchanted with both this arrangement and the holder of "their" seat, the ministry supporter Robert Nugent (Viscount Clare). Cruger, in fact, knew while still in America in March 1774 that he would be a candidate, writing Palfrey "in confidence" that "my friends are making a strong party in Bristol to put me in nomination next General Election."[52] This timing means Cruger had ample time to discuss his English political plans in person with his New York relatives and that his run for Parliament reflected both developments in Bristol and the American crisis over the Tea Act. Cruger's willingness to confide his plans to Boston's Palfrey, who was at the leading edge of the colonial resistance movement, is also an indication of the circles in which Cruger was moving when he decided to seek a parliamentary seat.[53]

Cruger's Bristol friends, led by Samuel Peach, may have initially envisioned merely challenging the Tory member of Parliament Matthew Brickdale, but Edmund Burke's entry into the race complicated matters. The incumbents both had the ministry's support. Cruger and Burke ran as oppositional Whigs—but not as real allies—in a multisided contest. As one commentator saw it, "the Patriots with the almighty mob" were "determined to turn out the old Members."[54] After twenty-three days of voting, Cruger was elected, finishing first in the poll by a considerable margin, with the second-place Burke also winning a seat.[55] Nugent returned to Parliament nonetheless as member for a pocket borough he controlled. He would be a stalwart supporter of the North administration and someone with whom Cruger would have many future clashes.[56] On November 3, 1774, the victorious Cruger and Burke were chaired by their Bristol backers.[57]

The result was a major achievement. Bristol was England's third-largest urban constituency. It had over five thousand voters, and obtaining enough support to win was expensive and complex. Peach contributed much of the £10,000 probably spent on Cruger's election, accomplished largely through the support of tradesmen and other middling and poorer voters. Over two thousand new freemen entitled to vote were enrolled in Bristol Corporation's books during the hard-fought campaign. The requisite enrollment fees for most of these men were paid by the candidates' agents, who also expended large sums on transporting nonresident voters to the city and on providing the thinly disguised payments for votes that many electors expected.[58]

While they both opposed North's American policies, Cruger and Burke drew on different circles of support in Bristol, and their personal and political relations were poor. In a difference that resonated with transatlantic debates over the fraying imperial constitution, Burke and Cruger disagreed about what it meant to be an elected representative. In 1774, Burke was already well known in Parliament, serving as member for a borough controlled by an ally of his patron the Marquess of Rockingham. He viewed sitting for a large and prominent constituency like Bristol as politically useful for himself and the Rockinghamites, but he had little interest in the specific concerns of the city's voters and less taste for its boisterous politics. Burke hardly ever visited the city and disliked mundane constituency work on behalf of Bristolians, later admitting he thought "their local agency is vexatious and sometimes humiliating."[59] In contrast, Cruger, with a rakish and convivial reputation, was popular, active in Bristol's many civic societies, and engaged in the homegrown radical movement that asserted citizens' right to instruct their members of Parliament. Once elected, Cruger was much more assiduous in serving as the Bristol voters' *representative*—what Burke derisively called "their special agent"—and saw himself fundamentally as a spokesman for their interests. Cruger was Bristol's man; Burke was not and did not want to be.

The two men clarified their dramatically different conceptions of a member of Parliament's role in speeches they gave when Bristol's election results were announced. Cruger, because he had received the most votes, spoke first and asserted, "It has ever been my opinion that the electors have a right to instruct their members. For my part, I shall always think it my duty in Parliament to be guided by your counsels and instructions. I shall consider myself the servant of my constituents, not their master. Subservient to their will, not superior to it."[60] Burke followed with a speech that became celebrated as an expression of a core tenet of his political philosophy. He denied that electors had a right to instruct their representatives, which arose, he said, from a "fundamental mistake of the whole order and tenor of our constitution." "Parliament," Burke argued, "is not a congress of Ambassadors from different and hostile interests [but] a deliberative assembly of one nation, with one interest, that of the whole; where not local purposes, not local prejudices ought to guide but the general good, resulting from the general reason of the whole."[61] In Burke's view, the legislator primarily served the nation, not his constituents, and had to exercise his private judgment in the service of his public duty.

These philosophical differences were compounded by both men's ties to New York. Cruger knew New York's politics, people, and commercial interests intimately. Burke, recognized since the Stamp Act crisis as sympathetic to colonial grievances, served as the New York assembly's salaried London agent between 1771 and 1776. Speaker John Cruger was part of the group that offered him the position.[62] Despite these connections, the situation of Bristol's new members of Parliament in relation to New York was strange. Burke was poorly suited to serving as the New York assembly's London mouthpiece. Moreover, he had helped pass the Rockingham administration's Declaratory Act, which was increasingly resented in America. When Henry Jr. returned to England in 1774, he carried letters from New York's assembly to Burke, one of which asked him to arrange a meeting between Cruger and "Lord Dartmouth, or such other noble personage as you may conceive would like to have a full, precise & faithful communication of the general sentiments & wishes of the people of this Colony."[63] The vision seems to have been that Burke would use his English connections to let someone who actually knew about New York do the talking. Yet before and after he became a member of Parliament, Cruger lacked any official standing vis-à-vis New York.

Cruger came to think that Burke served New York's interests poorly. In May 1775, as the war began, Cruger frankly warned Peter Van Schaack about Burke, whom he adjudged "so cursed crafty and selfish" that "no one can possibly receive the least benefit from a connection with him." As to Burke's American policy and New York's interests, Cruger wrote, "He will always be at liberty to take whichever side best serves his own immediate interest. Today, he shall be the first great Promoter of a Declaratory Bill. Tomorrow he shall insinuate the Parliament have not a right to bind the Americans in all cases—and yet, put him in power, and the third day you shall find him asserting the supremacy of this country with a vengeance."[64] Cruger believed that Burke's allegiance to the Rockinghamites would always trump his responsibilities to New York, but Cruger's own status in regard to his birthplace was also uncertain.

After his election, Henry was a prominent critic of the British policies that outraged the colonies. There were only six months between Cruger's election and the first shots at Lexington and Concord, so he was finding his feet in Parliament as the imperial emergency became acute. Advocates for America were never in lockstep about goals or tactics, but Cruger's experiences show how connected he was to other patriot leaders in England in 1774 and 1775 and how "a complete lack of structure" hampered Anglo-American attempts to prevent war.[65] No one in England could really speak for "America" as a whole, partly because the North administration rejected both the First and Second Continental Congresses' legitimacy. As a result, Cruger and many other people operated in a context in which the pro-America movement in England had members, but no clear leaders.

Parliament convened for the first time after Cruger's election on November 29, 1774. Cruger regarded the ministry-penned King's Speech that opened the term as "flaming" for characterizing recent resistance in Massachusetts as criminal violence.[66] Cruger feared that North had been wrongly led to believe "I am all gunpowder," and he hoped that a moderate and independent stance would enable him to contribute to solving the transatlantic crisis.[67] "I will," he told Peter Van Schaack, "connect myself with none of the violent parties, but endeavor to temper my fire with prudence."[68] While Cruger was an independent within parliamentary party politics, more broadly he cultivated associations with members of loose-knit and overlapping interest groups that reflected his background and ideological commitments: merchants and other advocates for trade, "Americans" of various descriptions, British reconciliationists, and Wilkesite radicals. Colonists regarded Cruger's election as good news for the common cause. Josiah Quincy, one of Boston's leading Sons of Liberty and in England as an unofficial emissary of Massachusetts patriots, met with Cruger in Bristol in January 1775.[69] In February 1775, John Adams, writing as "Novanglus," characterized Cruger's victory as evidence that not all Britons supported the ministry. Cruger, Adams claimed, was nothing less than "one attached to us by principle, birth, and the most ardent affection."[70]

In his maiden speech before Parliament on December 16, 1774, Cruger called himself "an American," thereby claiming a right and duty to speak on the damage North's policies were causing.[71] He described ministerial attempts to coerce the colonies as inhumane and contrary to British interests, and urged reconciliation and negotiation. His maiden speech was reprinted in New York alongside others "in favour of the rights of America."[72] However, because he aimed at calming tensions, Cruger was more personally charitable toward North than some of his fellow pro-Americans. Cruger also addressed a more fundamental point that suggested future difficulties: parliamentary supremacy. What was needed, he concluded, was not more failed coercion but "a different plan of conduct," the creation of "some firm and liberal constitution adopted by the wisdom of this House, which may secure the colonists in their liberties, while it maintains the just supremacy of Parliament."[73] This was a call for change and compromise, but it also put him on the record on what was becoming a key point of colonial principle.

In the first months following his election, Cruger hoped to use his transatlantic ties and his seat in Parliament to help broker a settlement. As a result, he initially aimed to develop working relationships with supporters of North's government. As he later recounted, "during the sessions of Parliament, I now and then contrived to get amongst some of them in hopes of at length being able, by repeated conversations, to abate their rigour."[74] In 1774 these hopes were naive, but Cruger was soon disabused of them by the intransigence of North's government, which had a solid majority in the Commons in favor of a rigorous American policy and enjoyed the support of the king. Moreover, Cruger's residence in England and his position as member of Parliament meant that it was easy for space to grow between him, American patriot leadership, and colonial public opinion. This dynamic became stronger later, but there were prewar hints of it. For example, in a report published in Pennsylvania on Parliament's first session, a correspondent observed that Cruger, "as a young member, gave his opinion on the state of the colonies with great becoming diffidence" and was "heard with a considerable deal of attention." The writer noted that Cruger "recommended conciliatory measures," but also thought he "rather went a little out of his way to compliment the minister."[75] It was an early sign of the difficulty Cruger faced in trying to remain a voice for compromise as polarization increased. Yet, as long as he remained in Parliament, Cruger never abandoned his willingness to work with anyone whom he thought might be able to secure peace between the colonies and Britain (fig. 8).

As Henry's parliamentary career began, his New York relatives continued participating in the colonial resistance movement. Thanks to broad support from the city's maritime community, the Continental Association was "rigorously enforced" in New York City.[76] However support for the association's ban on importing was decidedly weaker in rural New York counties. The New York General Assembly, which had been prorogued since March 1774, was scheduled to meet again beginning in mid-January 1775. In late 1774, politically engaged New Yorkers, including Livingstonians and De Lanceyites, began planning for the upcoming legislative session. The province's internal politics again intersected

Figure 8. George Romney, *Henry Cruger (1739–1827)*, c. 1775–90. Oil on linen. Gift of Mr. T. Oakley Rhinelander, New-York Historical Society, 1976.68. Photography © New-York Historical Society.

with transatlantic issues as the two parties maneuvered to maintain popular support and to shape resistance tactics while the most militant patriots were increasingly committed to extralegal bodies and the congress. It was also significant that "everywhere in the colonies moderates looked to New York and its Assembly to find a way toward peaceful reconciliation with England," in part because many were concerned by inflammatory rhetoric that came out of Philadelphia, the First Continental Congress's failure to offer concrete proposals for imperial reform, and Parliament's unwillingness to negotiate with what it considered a constitutionally unacceptable body.[77]

New York's General Assembly convened on January 10, 1775. On January

26, with John Cruger as speaker, it voted 11–10 not to formally take up consideration of the proceedings of the First Continental Congress, defeating a motion made by the Livingston-supporting Philip Schuyler. This meant that the assembly, the embodiment of the province's democratic traditions, would not follow other colonial legislatures in ratifying the actions that the intercolonial congress had already taken. In the coming weeks New York's factional politics and the imperial crisis became more entangled as the De Lanceyite–controlled assembly voted down further efforts promoted by Livingstonian members and their out-of-doors allies, including McDougall, to record support for the congress. Instead, in an echo of the procedures used in 1765, the assembly named a committee to draft its own petitions to the king and Parliament and to prepare a list of New York's grievances. The complaints in those petitions echoed those articulated by the congress, emphasizing that much of the dispute was about tactics. These disputes culminated in a vote in late February by which the assembly declined to select delegates to an anticipated second continental congress, which was expected to begin meeting in May.[78]

Members of the Cruger family and their circles were intensely involved in these developments, and the growing possibility of violence weighed heavily on their minds. Henry Van Schaack, Peter's brother, wrote him in January 1775 that "the dispute with the Mother Country is carried on with too much acrimony" and worried that "the Proceedings of the Congress have left no back door open for a reconciliation."[79] Just over a month later, after the assembly declined ratifying the first congress's proceedings, Peter replied that he thought it was "impossible to conceive what will be the end of the present troubles." If, he said, Britain should now "fail in asserting her supremacy, this colony will be eternally odious" and yet he thought "it is impossible that we can unite in the violent measures of our neighbors on either side of us." He had not broken with the idea of nonviolently resisting the Coercive Acts and thought many New Yorkers "of the moderate party" would continue to support the congress's Continental Association as "a non-importation and a non-consumption are what we expected they would agree to. It is a peaceable mode of obtaining redress." Yet he saw danger in being identified as insufficiently zealous, and he was worried about reports of preparations for war, telling his brother that "in some of the Southern colonies, they are raising money and levying troops, with a design, as they say, to defend themselves." He regarded this as "just the cant of the republicans in the last century" and thought "all the present manœuvres have a tendency to the same unhappy catastrophe."[80] Both Van Schaacks feared a slide toward civil war.

As the Crugers and their allies tried to use the provincial assembly to de-escalate the crisis, in Britain opposition members of Parliament and pro-Americans also tried to change the direction of events. On January 19, 1775, Parliament reconvened after its holiday recess. The next day Chatham made a motion in the House of Lords calling for the immediate withdrawal of troops from Boston, which was widely recognized as on the cusp of violence. Chatham's speech was a stirring piece or oratory: full of praise and sympathy for the colonists and condemnation for the behavior of the ministry. A "glorious spirit of Whiggism animates three millions in America," Chatham declared, "who prefer poverty with liberty, to gilded chains and sordid affluence; and who will die in defence of their rights."[81] In 1778, when the war was in a particularly dark phase and Chatham was near death, Henry Cruger paid to have this 1775 speech reprinted for distribution in Bristol.[82] Cruger shared Chatham's sentiments, but Chatham's call for withdrawing British regulars before it was too late was overwhelmingly defeated in the Lords.

Cruger also marshaled commercial opposition to the government's management of the crisis. On January 23, merchants from London, Bristol, Glasgow, and other ports, aided by parliamentary allies including Burke and Cruger, presented petitions against coercing Boston and urging reconciliation. In another repeat of the tactics of 1765, these petitions focused on Britain's economic self-interest rather than inflammatory questions of constitutional principle. The Bristol petition that Cruger presented highlighted the Continental Association's impact on Britons and blamed the "stagnation of trade at present subsisting" on ministerial policies. Rather than seriously consider these petitions, North and his supporters used their majority to bury them in what Burke sardonically called a "Committee of Oblivion." Merchant and opposition hopes were quietly suffocated.[83]

Having previously implemented the Coercive Acts and dispatched General Thomas Gage and more troops to Boston, the North administration floated a small concession in late February 1775. If a colony passed acceptable laws providing revenues for imperial defense and provincial governance, then the British government would not levy taxes on the colony while those revenues continued. Rather than reach a grand constitutional bargain, the ministry's goal was to use "force and limited concessions to stop colonial resistance short of war."[84] Critics in England and America, including Burke, quickly pointed out the offer gave the colonies little of substance and failed to address underlying questions about the distribution of power within the empire.[85] North's measure also envisioned no role for any intercolonial congress, instead calling for each colony to deal with Parliament individually.[86] Some pro-Americans in England, however, hoped that the proposal "might mark the beginning of a more substantial peace initiative from the North administration" and signal that de-escalation through diplomacy remained possible.[87]

The news that New York's assembly had voted against endorsing the congress's proceedings reached London on February 28. On that same day, the Commons considered the government's New England Trade and Fishery Bill, which aimed to further punish Massachusetts, New Hampshire, Connecticut, and Rhode Island until good order was restored by banning their vessels from trading outside the empire and from the Grand Banks fishery. This coincidence led some observers to believe that events in New York played a part in what they interpreted as the North administration's decision to abandon a short-lived flirtation with conciliation for a return to coercion. The North administration, however, was already settled on offering a limited conciliatory gesture while punishing Massachusetts and other openly rebellious colonies and upholding parliamentary supremacy by war if necessary.[88] What some wrongly interpreted as the North administration tacking between peacemaking and coercion in response to news from America was in fact a single, albeit ultimately disastrous, two-pronged strategy for quelling unrest.[89]

The ministry, however, was interested in trying to isolate Massachusetts and circumvent the congress. In mid-January, Dartmouth had proposed that any colonies that decided to "vacate the (Continental) Association" should be exempted from punitive measures.[90] Then, on March 7, as the New England Trade and Fishery Bill went to the House of Lords, the government introduced another bill stopping the non-British trade of five more named colonies—New Jersey, Pennsylvania, Maryland, Virginia, and South Carolina—because their legislatures had approved the congress's Continental Association. Because the operating principle was that the government was responding to specific acts of dangerous illegality, other colonies remained unmentioned in either of these two laws, which came to be known jointly as the Restraining Acts. The unmentioned colonies included the various Caribbean and northern North American colonies not represented at the congress and four of the thirteen mainland colonies that would eventually rebel: Delaware, North Carolina, Georgia, and, most significantly, New York. By this point it was known that the New York assembly had declined to recognize the congress's measures.[91]

Compromise was not easy in the febrile politics of the moment, and those emerging as nobodyists increasingly had their motives questioned. A broadside, which presumably appeared in the colonies very near to the moment war broke out, made the inflammatory charge that the New York assembly's break with the congress was not the product of sincere differences among patriots over the way forward, but the poisonous fruit of transatlantic corruption. It carried the lurid title of "The Plot Discovered" and claimed that New York was "designedly left out" of the recently introduced second Restraining Act "in hopes of making that colony secede from the general American system of opposition, and secure it to assist in the abominable ministerial measures." The broadside's charges of conspiracy rested on the claim that "several of the majority in the Assembly" of New York had "actually received a bribe, in money, £1000 sterling a man" to vote as they had when the body had voted not to formally recognize the proceedings of the congress. The "Delanceys, Watts, Coldens, and the leaders of the party" were "to be rewarded much higher" with "honour, profit, and pensions," lands, and offices. "Cruger [was] to be of the Council, also a young Colden, McEvers, and some of the Watts's." The broadside's rhetoric culminated in a terrorizing question: "Is it just and proper, good heaven" that "such parricides should live?"[92] The threat was unmistakable and demonstrated the dangers of being in the middle as war approached.

The broadside was likely based on information sent to America by the London-based Arthur and William Lee. Its charges, advanced by patriots who were overly optimistic that an American show of unity would force the ministry to back down, were partly attempts to claim the moral high ground for their own preferred tactical approaches to resolving the constitutional crisis.[93] The mixture of fact, suspicion, and innuendo in "The Plot Discovered" was powerful, but the bribery charges at its core seem to be the product more of paranoia or policy than real knowledge.[94] There is no apparent direct evidence that any such bribes were paid to the Crugers or their New York allies. Moreover, some of the broadside's other charges make little sense. For example, it suggested that a Cruger would receive a seat on New York's Provincial Council for participating in the conspiracy, but through John Harris Cruger, the family already held one. Charges of bribery were so emotive because they implied that people were acting against what they knew to be the common good in pursuit of their own sordid interests.[95] This too seems like a poor fit with the Crugers' collective and individual behavior because they repeatedly publicly and privately advocated for a negotiated settlement: there was no switch in their political position that

THE CENTER FAILS 109

bribery might help explain. What is much clearer is that rhetoric was becoming increasingly charged and that the center ground for compromise was failing.

As these events unfolded, Henry Cruger Jr. grew increasingly pessimistic that military conflict would be averted. In the aftermath of North's Conciliatory Proposal, he told another member of England's pro-American network, the South Carolina–born Ralph Izard, that he was tired of the ever-changing arguments made by both the ministry and the organized opposition to justify their latest views on whether and how Parliament might tax America.[96] Similarly, in a letter containing pointed criticism of Burke in particular, Cruger warned Peter Van Schaack that "the *Opposition* in the House of Commons flatter themselves that the confusion in *your* country will overthrow the Ministry in this." The reality, he warned, was that "let them come in when they will, they must adopt, and they know it, *nearly* the same measures that have been pursued by the present administration, or they cannot hold their places [for] a single session. To get in is what we all want, and *patriots* in one station are great tyrants in another. America has long been made a cat's paw."[97] The more he learned about how things stood in Parliament, the more profound his pessimism. A "dreadful crisis" loomed for America; "the flattering prospect of soon conciliating the unnatural breach, is vanished, and it is much to be feared that some events are not far distant, which will render *this* one of the most important eras in the history of our native country."[98] Cruger increasingly doubted there was a way out.

Cruger also criticized what he saw as self-destructive mutual intransigence. "The leaders, on both sides," he told Izard, "are too vindictive," focused on the pain they could inflict on the other side rather than the benefits that would flow from their own positions. The result, he concluded, was that "the breach daily grows wider, and God only knows, what events are to terminate the unhappy contest."[99] Regardless of whether one side or the other should have made concessions in early 1775, Cruger was right that their mutual unwillingness to do so would lead to war. The Restraining Acts that caused such controversy in March became law in April 1775, but it mattered little. The outbreak of fighting at Lexington and Concord occurred before the news of their passage reached the colonies. Having failed to prevent bloodshed, both sides would find it even harder to staunch it.

For patriots becoming nobody men, there was a final, painful coda to this prewar maneuvering. On March 6, 1775, the Committee of Sixty, supported by influential Livingstonians and local Liberty Boys, decided to hold a public meeting in New York City on whether the colony should send delegates to the upcoming Second Continental Congress despite the assembly's refusal to endorse doing so. Although the De Lanceyites had determined the assembly's stance, they continued engaging in extralegal politics too. Peter Van Schaack remained one of the Committee of Sixty, and members of New York's General Assembly and Provincial Council, likely including members of the Cruger family, also participated in the extralegal March 6 meeting. What happened on the day is contested and uncertain; Thomas Jones claimed that the Sons of Liberty and the Livingstons carried clubs to the meeting and intimidated anyone who wanted to oppose New York's sending delegates to Philadelphia. It was a tumultuous affair, but what emerged from March 6 and subsequent meetings of the Committee of Sixty was a plan to hold an election to select city delegates for a Provincial Convention—the body that subsequently became New York's revolutionary Provincial Congress—that would in turn select delegates for the Second Continental Congress.[100]

Even as the Committee of Sixty took these further extralegal steps, the General Assembly, also meeting in New York City, completed its work on its petitions. On March 24, 1775, more than three weeks before Lexington and Concord, New York's assembly finally approved the documents on which those most focused on reconciliation had pinned so many of their hopes: a "petition" to the king, a "representation and remonstrance" to the House of Commons, and a "memorial" to the House of Lords. They asserted colonial rights and grievances, but these complaints were deliberately framed as traditional and valid modes of communicating with the British government, serving as "an expression of moderate colonial opinion" that was "clearly meant to pave the way for an alternative means of resolving differences which would lead away from violence."[101] The documents were quickly dispatched to Edmund Burke, still the assembly's London agent, for presentation.

New York's Provincial Convention to select delegates for the Second Continental Congress met on April 20, just before the news that fighting had broken out in Massachusetts reached the city. All five New Yorkers sent to the First Continental Congress were reselected, and five more were added as part of a deliberately diverse delegation. The ship carrying New York's petitions was at sea when the fighting began, and Burke received them on May 4. After having first privately shared the petitions with the ministry, Burke formally presented the one to the Commons on May 15, before reports of Lexington and Concord reached England at month's end.[102]

The North ministry had some initial differences over how to respond to this overture from New York.[103] The documents were scrupulously correct in form and constitutionally legitimate in ways that communications from a congress were not. They also acknowledged Parliament as the ultimate authority within the empire, recognized its right to regulate trade, and professed the colony's attachment to Britain. Moreover, as the remonstrance to the House of Commons put it, they expressed "disapprobation of the violent measures that have been pursed in some of the colonies" as tending "to increase our misfortunes, and to prevent our obtaining redress." But they included language that challenged Parliament's authority over the colonies, asserting that New Yorkers had "undoubted and unalienable rights, as Englishmen" to be exempted from internal taxes levied by Parliament and the "exclusive right" to control the purse strings for their own courts and government. They also objected to the Declaratory Act, infringements on the right to trial by jury, the imposition of quartering, the limitations placed on colonial currency, and the Quebec Act.[104]

The petitions claimed that all that was sought was "a restoration of those rights which we enjoyed by general consent before the close of the last war." However, the New Yorkers' insistence that Parliament had limited authority over the colonies was unacceptable to some supporters of the government, including the attorney-general, Edward Thurlow, and the solicitor-general, Alexander Wedderburn. By May 10, the forewarned ministry had decided to block officially receiving the New York petitions. When Burke introduced the Commons petition, he encouraged members of Parliament to only take up New Yorkers' local grievances and ignore their objection to the Declaratory Act. For his part, North "spoke greatly in favour of New York, and said that he would gladly do every thing in his power to shew his regard to the good behaviour of that colony," but he insisted that "the honour of parliament required, that no paper should be presented to that House, which tended to call in question the unlimited rights of parliament."[105] Charles Jenkinson, a government supporter who had the king's ear, "reprobated every part of the Remonstrance, and therefore was not for suffering so disrespectful a paper to be brought up."[106]

Henry Cruger, silent in the recent debates on North's Conciliatory Proposal and the Restraining Acts, spoke in Parliament on May 15, rising immediately after North. Given North's stance, Cruger must have realized that the New

York petition was a dead letter. His speech had a ring of pitiable desperation to it, one that captured the essence of his position but underlined the failure of those who sought to find a way out of the crisis. He avowed that "I pant after peace between this country and its colonies, and will gladly join my feeble voice to any proposal or overture that tends to an amicable settlement of the dispute." The New York assembly, he said, had "endeavoured to put a truce to resentment and tumult, and, while the other colonies (in the frenzy of riot, commotion, and despair) have nearly annihilated the powers of their legislatures, and rush on to civil war, they dutifully submit their complaints to the clemency of the mother country." If New York's petitions were simply cast aside, Cruger warned, "the colonies will be discouraged from such attempts, and the assembly of New York [will] be driven into the common stream of opposition, to escape the charge of ineffectual and imprudent singularity." The New Yorkers, Cruger pointed out, did "particularly disclaim all intentions and desire of independence" and even confessed "the necessity of a superintending power in parliament." What more, Cruger wondered, could "Englishmen ask from Englishmen and the sons of Englishmen?"[107] It was a speech redolent of pathos and defeat. New York's Commons petition was preemptively rejected by a large margin. The memorial to the House of Lords was similarly blocked three days later.[108] On May 5, in a last grab for peace after the fighting began, John Cruger, Jacob Walton, and twelve other members of the now recessed New York General Assembly— unaware as yet of the fate of their petitions—wrote General Thomas Gage a letter asking him to "immediately order a cessation of further hostilities" to prevent a "further effusion of blood" and allow for "a negotiation to take place."[109] It too failed.

The North ministry's abrupt dismissal of the New York petitions was a crushing blow for the Crugers on both sides of the Atlantic. John Cruger, in his capacity as speaker, had literally signed his name to all three documents, and the New York assembly's decision to try to act independently of the congress in the hopes of promoting reconciliation had exposed the De Lanceyites, including the Crugers, to great political risk at home. Popularly discredited and supplanted by newly-created bodies controlled by militarizing patriots, the colonial New York General Assembly never undertook substantive business after April 1775.[110] These failed attempts in early 1775 to prevent violence proved crucial to the Cruger's journey to nobodyism. Like those who subsequently led the American war effort, the Crugers believed that the colonies were right in their economic and constitutional dispute with the British government, thought the colonies should engage in resistance, and agreed that Americans should create extralegal associations intended to wrest power away from the British government. Despite all this common ground, the Crugers and like-minded people who emerged as nobodyists departed from those who became militant revolutionaries on a significantly narrower but ultimately crucial question: Was waging civil war in defense of colonial rights sensible and just?

PART TWO

"Some Middle Way Should Be Found Out"

1775–1783

5. Whigs Killing for the King

The electric news from Lexington and Concord reached New York on April 23, 1775. That day, the city was in a tumult. Members of the Sons of Liberty, parading with flags and martial music, called on the inhabitants to arm themselves. A crowd forcibly unloaded two ships carrying supplies intended for General Gage's troops in Boston. After nightfall, patriot militants broke into city hall to seize gunpowder and five hundred muskets. The disorder continued for a week as patriot vigilantes forced New York's custom collector to shut its port. Parties drilled in preparation for their own battle with the British Army, and groups of armed men roamed the streets intimidating those they perceived as tories or just insufficiently zealous.[1]

Since they do not start with diplomatic formalities or frontier-crossing military offensives, civil wars often have beginnings that are apparent only in retrospect. While people around the Atlantic recognized events in Massachusetts as momentous, what would ensue was uncertain. It was unclear whether citizens elsewhere would join New England's rebels. Like others in his family, John Harris Cruger had helped organize resistance during the previous decade. By 1775, however, like many New Yorkers, he was suspicious of both more militant patriots and the British government. As what had been a political crisis became a shooting war, many of the province's prewar leaders, including John Harris, hoped to contain revolutionary violence even as they continued identifying with colonial grievances. John Harris Cruger's efforts to steer this course failed as more militant patriots categorized him as a dangerous opponent. In time, the war in fact made him one.

John Harris Cruger was not a nobodyist across the Revolution; he became an active and militant loyalist. Anne De Lancey Cruger, his wife, also saw firsthand the panoply of violence unleashed in April 1775. John Harris's political principles differed little if at all from those of his Cruger relatives, but he finally chose to fight for the Crown although none of the others did. His path to loyalism was shaped not primarily by ideology but by a combination of factors: his physical presence in New York City at a moment of intense crisis, his position as a member of the late colonial Provincial Council, his treatment at the hands of insurgents, and, especially, the ties of interdependence that connected him to his more militant loyalist in-laws the De Lanceys. An officer in a British provincial regiment from the summer of 1776, John Harris saw long, hard, and brutal service. For Anne too the war was terrible and transformative. Their linked experiences are important to considering the histories of nobody men and nobody women because they reveal how some people became enmeshed in the violence of civil war even as others, including most of the Crugers, managed to keep it at arms' length.

Local contexts—the microdynamics of civil war—shaped how people traversed the Revolution. Anne De Lancey Cruger's family proved critical to how she and her husband experienced the conflict. Her father, Oliver De Lancey, was a powerful figure, and several of her relatives, including an uncle, a brother, and a brother-in-law, were career British military officers.[2] These ties framed the couple's wartime choices. Far from being authoritarian royalists, however, the De Lanceys and some of their allies, including John Harris Cruger, are best understood ideologically as whigs who became loyalists in the changing contexts of 1775 and 1776.[3]

Throughout 1775 New York was neither fully in nor fully out of the burgeoning conflict. While patriot militants wanted citizens to mobilize and support the New Englanders, wider opinion about the best way forward was deeply divided. Real and imagined plots multiplied while New Yorkers knew that the city's harbor and strategic location made it a military target for both sides. Their office holding, commitment to the New York assembly's petitions, and rumors like those in "The Plot Discovered" broadside made the Crugers, the De Lanceys, and others suspect in the eyes of increasingly anxious militants. In early June 1775, Philip Skene, a British-born former army officer and ambitious landholder in upstate New York, arrived in Philadelphia after spending a year in London. "The Plot Discovered" had warned that he was a conspirator, and he bore commissions appointing him the British lieutenant governor of the forts at Crown Point and Ticonderoga. Prior to Skene's landing in Philadelphia, however, the forts were captured by patriot militia and their cannons hauled off to aid in the siege of Boston. The Second Continental Congress therefore viewed Skene's arrival as a threat. Based on letters confiscated from Skene and reports from London, influential patriots believed that Skene was a spy aiming to subvert their movement.[4] Among the letters Skene carried was an introduction he had solicited from Henry Cruger Jr. in Bristol to Henry Sr. in New York, and this led to the Crugers' entanglement in the affair. Whether Skene was up to something "else"—whether he had intentions beyond his publicly stated ones to promote reconciliation and take up his official but now moot appointments—remains unknown. Based on their private correspondence and public denials, however, it does not appear that the Crugers were conspiring with Skene.

Nevertheless, in June 1775 a correspondent, seemingly the congressman James Duane, reported an alarming story to John Harris Cruger. Skene, Cruger learned, was claiming that before he left England, Henry Cruger Jr. had employed him as an agent to Lord North to secure a contract for the New York–based Henry & John Cruger to provision British troops in America. These were inflammatory, insulting, and no doubt frightening charges, especially because the skirmishing in New England became much bloodier following the Battle of Bunker Hill on June 17, 1775. The story again suggested that the Crugers were too self-interested and insufficiently patriotic, and it emerged at a moment of intense anxiety about the conflict's future course.

Conspiracy theories are hard to counter today; they were in 1775 too. In consequence, John Harris Cruger wrote a lengthy, explicit refutation of the rumors on July 13, 1775. He had, he reported, shown Duane's letter to his uncle John, who insisted "he does not know any thing more of the matter than you do"; that he had not "directly or indirectly apply'd for a contract" through Henry Cruger Jr. or anyone else; that he did not "believe there is a word of truth in what Skene has reported"; that he never heard Henry Cruger Sr. mention anything of the kind; and that his family neither "desired, or ever wo[ul]d accept of any Commission whatsoever, in the least degree, incompatible with the Liberties of their Country." John Harris's exasperation at the charge comes through even centuries later. "In justice to our family," Cruger insisted, "who are as much attach'd to the Liberties & prosperity of America as any family on the Continent," Duane could "shew this Letter to any body." As for himself, John Harris Cruger was clear about where his loyalties lay. He appreciated, he said, Duane's regard for "my sentiments & principles in regard to the Liberties of our oppressed & much injured Country" and said that if Duane would "continue to think me a <u>warm</u> & <u>sincere friend</u> to the Liberties of all America" then "you will do me justice."[5] John Harris's political ideology remained unchanged, but it was being scrutinized by others in changing circumstances.

Henry Cruger Jr. likewise insisted that he was no plotter. He wrote confidentially to his father in May 1775, before Skene's arrival, to tell him Skene was "by no Means the very great and consequential Man he will endevour to make all believe."[6] Henry clearly, however, did not envision his letter for Skene being pored over by anxious congressmen. He wrote Van Schaack that although he had said "many *fulsome*, perhaps *ironical*, things in favor of a vain, weak man, who out of his own mouth, requested me to write the nonsense I did," he was not part of any conspiracy. Henry believed that the suspicions the affair raised were a product of the times. "I am sorry for the frenzy of my countrymen," he noted, but "to wrest and torture the only construction that could be put upon my letter per Col. Skene into any sense inimical to the liberties of America, is strange indeed!"[7] The incident demonstrated that the Crugers' transatlantic family ties now entailed new dangers.

As the conflict in Massachusetts deepened, New Yorkers became increasingly divided.[8] John Harris would later characterize his actions in this period as early manifestations of a steadfast commitment to the loyalist cause, but this was a case of the retrospective oversimplification common in civil wars. In the 1784 account he produced for Britain's Loyalist Claims Commission, he wrote "that altho after Hostilitys were commenced in 1775 the proceedings against the Kings friends became more and more threatening yet your Memorialist remained in the City of New York" in the hope he might "counteract the designs of the factious by his influence as an Officer of Government and that he might be ready to seize any occasion that should offer to make himself useful."[9] Yet John Harris was not prominent or outspoken as one of the king's friends in 1775/76.[10] He neither cited any specific actions he took to quell the burgeoning revolution, nor does he feature significantly in historians' accounts of political developments in the city during the war's first year. In fact, even after the war began, John Harris remained much more emotionally and ideologically aligned with the patriot cause.

On June 27, 1775, for example, John Harris wrote a short letter to Peter Van Schaack, noting the extraordinary events of the previous Sunday, when New York's royal governor, William Tryon, had coincidentally returned to the city after a year's absence in England on the same day that the newly appointed Continental generals George Washington, Philip Schuyler, and Charles Lee passed through New York City while traveling to their commands. John Harris noted the "rattling of Drums, & display of Colours" that accompanied Tryon's landing. Washington and his fellow Continental generals, he observed more favorably, "moved off with a pomp, magnificence, & grandeur becoming the importance of the Cause in which for the Liberties of America they are embark'd." Given his place on New York's Provincial Council, it was a remarkable statement, portraying the patriot generals as defenders of his own rights rather than as traitors. Yet he was not anxious to see the war widen. He closed with a sentiment that encapsulated his wider family's hopes: "God grant us peace, a restoration of our Liberties, & a good Constitution."[11] In 1775 John Harris tried, like other moderate patriots, to walk a narrowing line between actively supporting armed rebellion—the goals of which remained uncertain—and renouncing deeply held procolonial political beliefs.

John Harris had reason to be wary of ultras on both sides. As war began, the British government embarked on an intelligence campaign: the mass interception of letters between colonists and British correspondents. Letters exchanged by the Crugers, including some to and from Henry Jr., a sitting member of Parliament, were among those swept up in this operation. These letters were opened, examined, and copied for use by the British ministry before being sent on to their intended recipients.[12] In one such letter, John Harris wrote frankly to Henry about the situation in New York in November 1775. New England, at least, was now in open revolt. A new and growing army surrounded Boston, and congressional troops had invaded Quebec. Governor Tryon had recently taken refuge aboard a warship anchored in New York harbor. Fearing for the city that had long been at the center of his family's life, John Harris wrote "poor New York! With what envy and malice art thou persecuted, if you escape the Storm we will set it down amongst miracles." In the letter John Harris mocked his family's old rivals among the Livingstons for currying favor with the radicals, but nothing in it amounted to a renunciation of the colonial cause nor an embrace of active loyalism. Patriot militants came to see John Harris as a danger, but the British spymasters reading his letters would have had little reason to regard him as a friend.

John Harris continued identifying strongly with the American cause and hoping for reconciliation. He wished, in particular, that the "Olive Branch Petition" adopted by the Second Continental Congress in July 1775 might lead the king and Parliament, including his brother, to de-escalate the crisis. He wrote to Henry Jr.:

> God grant [the Congress's petition] may promote a treaty or negociation,
> for when once that's begun I do not doubt of accomplishing the great work
> of accommodation. <u>Declare you will not tax us</u>. I know you don't mean it,
> and don't be too tenacious of Words, to wit, a Supremacy of Parliament
> in all cases; and the work will soon be done. [. . .] Then sheathe the sword
> and trust to American Generosity. We will be faithfull, we will be loyal, and
> we will be just. Pardon worthy member the Dictates of an anxious breast.[13]

Far from being prepared to embrace violence to maintain royal authority, John Harris remained first and foremost a patriotic colonist. While hoping to find a road to peace, in framing the constitutional crisis in terms of "you" and "us," he signaled his loyalties.

Although John Harris did not know it, George III had already summarily rejected the Olive Branch Petition and proclaimed his ministry's intention to put down the rebellion by force. In the absence of a viable negotiation process, the men of the sword and gun increasingly dominated. On November 23, 1775, Isaac Sears and a troop of mounted patriot vigilantes from Connecticut attacked the New York printing press of James Rivington, who had published a wide variety of opinions on the crisis, including loyalist ones. Rivington's press was silenced for more than a year, resuming operations only after he returned from an extended visit to England. Patriots elsewhere likewise looked to suppress public dissent.[14]

Sears's raid raised an alarming possibility for reconciliationists: if New Yorkers refused to embrace the patriot cause zealously enough on their own, then outsiders might enter the city to bring liberty by force. As the siege of Boston neared its conclusion in the winter of 1775/76, patriot leaders feared that the British army there would be evacuated to New York City. The congress however, had been unwilling to prepare for New York's defense without the support of local patriot leadership. General Charles Lee, whose firebrand radicalism endeared him to other uncompromising patriots, had earlier advocated for destroying New York if strategically necessary. He now urged George Washington to peremptorily order the city's occupation and fortification without prior civilian approval. Lee, moreover, offered himself as the man for the job, which he argued could be accomplished by raising militiamen in more politically reliable Connecticut. Washington could then present New York's military occupation by New England soldiers as a fait accompli—a development Lee asserted most delegates would welcome—and obtain retroactive congressional dispensation for what he had done. Washington saw the military expediency of Lee's suggestion but was wary of exceeding his authority until John Adams, then absent from the congress, was consulted and quietly gave his support, and thereby political cover, to the generals' scheme. Washington ordered Lee to execute the plan.

As Lee gathered troops in Connecticut, New York's Committee of Public Safety, then the province's highest patriot authority, learned of his plans and were "almost horrified by the news of his approach."[15] The committee, fearing that Lee's movement might lead to a disastrous British attack on New York, urged Lee to remain at the Connecticut border until they could confer. Nevertheless, in early February 1776 Lee, abetted by a three-man visiting committee from the Continental Congress, marched into New York at the head of a substantial body of Connecticut militia. As Lee predicted, New York's patriot civilian authorities subsequently accepted his actions.[16] It was a canny, profoundly undemocratic, and crucial moment of revolutionary chicanery.

Appointing the longtime Son of Liberty Isaac Sears as a lieutenant colonel under his command, Lee began a campaign to strengthen the political power of New York militants and force people into the insurgents' camp.[17] Yet, even after Lee's arrival, John Harris continued identifying with patriot grievances rather than militant loyalism. In March 1776 he told Peter Van Schaack, "I have seen no occasion, as yet, to quit the town, nor do I believe there will be any, unless troops arrive here from England, which, with me, yet remains a doubtful case." Besides implying British regulars were the greatest threat to New York, he also wrote approvingly of efforts to erect military defenses on Lee's orders. Cruger wrote that if British troops "do come they will meet with a warm reception; as we are preparing batteries in several places," including one on the strategically located Manhattan property of his sister Mary and her husband, Jacob Walton. Its construction resulted in "the entire ruin and destruction of every thing" with the Waltons' "house being common barracks for between two and three hundred men." The Waltons moved to Long Island, but while John Harris thought their situation "truly hard," he regarded it more as an unfortunate consequence of the circumstances than as a political injustice.[18]

While John Harris favored reconciliation and regarded some of the local patriot leadership skeptically, even after nearly a year of fighting, there was no clear indication that he would take up arms in defense of royal authority. However, his March 1776 letter to Peter Van Schaack closed with a casual but portentous notice. "I have this morning," he wrote, "bought you 'Common Sense' and send it herewith." Peter was in Kinderhook, and John Harris did not want to miss getting his letter conveyed upriver, so he simply noted that "it is the first time I have seen the pamphlet, and I have not time now to read it."[19] Perhaps he later regretted distributing the most incendiary document of the Revolution. By convincing many that the colonies' future lay in republicanism and independence, Thomas Paine's work struck another blow against the hopes of moderates and reconciliationists on both sides of the Atlantic. If Paine's reasoning persuaded some colonists to support independence, it also helped other Americans realize they no longer shared the insurgents' aims.

In New York, Lee dispatched Sears and a body of troops to Long Island to administer patriot oaths to the reluctant civilian population. Lee had already ordered the imposition of oaths in the similarly politically divided town of Newport, Rhode Island, in 1775.[20] If, as seems likely, the form of the oath that Lee deployed there was repeated in New York, it was an onerous one. It required people to swear not to aid the king's forces and to inform on anyone providing them with intelligence. Even more tellingly, Lee's oath concluded by forcing people to choose sides. It required sworn agreement that "neutrality is not less base and criminal than open and avowed hostility" and a promise, if called upon, to "take up arms and subject myself to military discipline in defence of the common rights and liberties of America. So help me God."[21] Those refusing the oath faced arrest and imprisonment.

New York's Provincial Congress, organized in May 1775 to replace the colonial legislature, objected to Lee's oaths and the treatment of Long Islanders, raising provocative questions about who spoke for New Yorkers and what was being done in their names. The Provincial Congress protested Lee's and Sears's actions and instructed New York's delegates to raise the matter in the Continental Congress, which resolved that no military officers under its command should impose such test oaths on civilians.[22] Lee was temporarily embarrassed, but soldiers on both sides continued deploying oaths as the conflict expanded. In March 1776, Lee left New York for a command in the South. When the British army evacuated Boston on March 17, it defied popular expectations and sailed for Halifax. Washington, however, still anticipating a British descent on New York, marched the bulk of the patriot army there anyway in early April. Once arrived, he continued Lee's political and military efforts to put the city into a defensible condition. With the clouds of war gathering over the city's streets and docks, patriot leaders' fears, anger, and suspicions intensified.[23]

This was the critical moment for John Harris and Anne. On the morning of June 5, 1776, the New York Provincial Congress, sitting in the city, adopted resolutions "relative to persons dangerous and disaffected to the American cause, and to persons of equivocal character." These measures criminalized insufficient zeal and neutrality and sanctioned peoples' arrests based on unspecified others' mere suspicions. Among those the body focused upon were

> divers persons who, by reason of their holding offices from the King of Great Britain, from their having neglected or refused to associate with their fellow-citizens for the defence of their common rights, from their having never manifested by their conduct a zeal for and attachment to the American cause, or from having maintained an equivocal neutrality, have been considered by their countrymen in a suspicious light, whereby it hath become necessary [to summon them], as well for the safety as for the satisfaction of the people, who in times so dangerous and critical, are naturally led to consider those as their enemies who withhold from them their aid and influence.

Those subsequently named were required to appear before the Provincial Congress and—in a telling inversion of the presumption of innocence—to provide evidence as to "why they should be considered as friends to the American cause." If any of them failed to appear, then they were to be arrested by the militia. The Crugers and their relatives and friends made up a large portion of the twenty-two inhabitants of New York City and county named in these resolutions. John Harris was named, as was his uncle John, his father-in-law, Oliver, and his two brothers-in-law, Peter Van Schaack and Jacob Walton. The elder John Cruger and Peter were no longer in the city, but John Harris, Oliver, and Jacob now had to appear before the Provincial Congress, go into hiding, or face arrest.[24]

Behind these formal pronouncements lay the power of revolutionary violence, and those named by the Provincial Congress soon witnessed what their fates might be. According to Thomas Jones, in mid-June 1776 New York radicals raised a mob to root out remaining local tories. It "searched the whole town" and "found and dragged several from their lurking holes." These unfortunate, unnamed men were placed upon "sharp rails with one leg on each side" and then paraded painfully through the streets. According to Jones, the raucous processions stopped before the buildings housing the Provincial Congress, the Committee of Public Safety, and Washington's headquarters, and received "the sanction of them all" when the leaders within appeared at windows to doff their caps and signal their approbation for the vigilantism without.[25]

Facing arrest and with the wider pressure on the "disaffected" intensifying, John Harris Cruger fled the city at some point in June 1776 and spent much of the ensuing summer on the run. He later said that he remained in New York "untill all Government, and order were totally subverted and his person in imminent danger" and he was "compelled to fly to Long Island."[26] Fearing capture by patriot patrols, he was "obliged to take to refuge in woods and swamps where he suffered extreme hardships."[27] At some point in this ordeal he met up with his brother-in-law Jacob Walton, also a fugitive fearing arrest. According to Jones, John Harris and Jacob were together "concealed for three weeks in the sultry heat of summer, upon a mow in a farmer's barn, and supplied by the owner, a loyal old Quaker, with whatever they wanted."[28] Both men were now publicly marked as enemies of the Revolution.

Patriot fears that the British were coming lay behind the anti-tory furor that ensnared John Harris. They finally arrived on July 3, 1776, when a huge Royal Navy fleet began putting a heavy force ashore on Staten Island. As the congress enacted the Declaration of Independence in Philadelphia, in New York the British initiated operations to restore the colonies to imperial control. Many British politicians and military commanders were confident this impressive army of 32,000 professional and well-equipped soldiers could quickly destroy patriot resistance. Many in the colonies—whatever their political preferences—believed the same. On August 22, General William Howe started landing troops on Long Island. Sometime in August, John Harris took refuge with British troops and offered Howe his services. This was a moment of choice and likely a decision made in consultation with Anne and their De Lancey relatives. Oliver De Lancey, who had also resisted the June efforts to round up the insufficiently zealous, likewise decided to take refuge with the British Army. Despite his years of advocacy for American grievances, John Harris was now willing to fight to end the rebellion. On September 15, following their victory at the Battle of Long Island, British troops marched into New York City. They remained for seven years.[29]

John Harris Cruger became clearly identifiable as an opponent of the Revolution only after it had declared him as an enemy. Had he been less prominent in the prewar period, less closely tied to the De Lancey family, or treated differently by patriot authorities, he might have had a very different war. But from August 1776 John Harris Cruger chose to be a militant loyalist, and he maintained this alignment for the rest of the Revolution. Following the British army's arrival in New York, anti-rebellion Americans created many new military units in the region. In September 1776 Oliver De Lancey offered to raise a brigade of Americans for Crown service. Howe accepted and De Lancey was commissioned a brigadier general, making him the senior loyalist officer in all America. John Harris and Stephen De Lancey, Oliver's son, were commissioned lieutenant colonels in the new unit. These choices enlisted John Harris and Anne in what was effectively a family firm for waging counterrevolution.

Now embarked on establishing what came to be called De Lancey's Brigade, Cruger signaled a sharp set of new political commitments. In October 1776 he and Jacob Walton signed a loyal address directed to Admiral Richard Howe and General William Howe; other members of the Cruger clan did not.[30] John Harris Cruger's name appears second on this so-called Loyalist Declaration of Dependence, signed by 547 New Yorkers in late November 1776 as a "Testimony of our Zeal to preserve and support the Constitutional Supremacy of Great Britain over the Colonies."[31] His winding journey from whig patriot to loyalist warrior was complete.

For most of the Revolutionary War, the British Army was on the offensive, looking to advance and extinguish the rebellion. De Lancey's Brigade, however, was raised specifically "for the defence of Long Island, and other exigencies" and for two years John Harris's military service centered on holding New York for the Crown against patriot invasion from New England rather than subjugating other colonies.[32] In the winter of 1776/77 De Lancey's Brigade was posted to Long Island's northern shore. After then being stationed for a few months in 1777 at Kingsbridge, in what is today the Bronx, Cruger and his men returned to Long Island. Tasked with the construction of a new fort at Huntington, they worked there until the spring of 1778.[33]

With patriots in control of much of northern New York State, especially after the battles of Saratoga in September and October 1777, and with the British secure in the city, the farms and villages of southern New York became the frontlines. The fighting in the space between the main armies, known as New York's "neutral ground," was intensely bitter and personal. Civilians were victimized by both sides, neighbors settled old scores, and violence begat violence in a cycle of raids and reprisals.[34] Civil war such as this rarely announces itself with martial pomp before arriving on people's doorsteps. Anne experienced this first-hand. Oliver De Lancey owned a substantial farm with a large country house at Bloomingdale, which is today part of urban Manhattan's Upper West Side. On the night of November 26, 1777, with John Harris and Oliver away on duty, Anne was staying there with her mother, Phila; her sister Charlotte, age about sixteen; a family friend, Elizabeth Floyd; an infant child of Anne's absent brother Stephen; and an unknown number of servants. While the inhabitants slept, a patriot contingent rowed across the Hudson River and captured a small guard before attacking the De Lancey house. The raiders stripped the house of its contents, taking not just smaller valuables and money but also larger items including furniture. According to outraged loyalists' accounts, the attackers then set the house on fire while Anne and the other women were still inside, forcing them to flee, barefoot and in their nightgowns, into the night. In his postwar loyalist claim, John Harris reported that he and Anne had previously moved all of their possessions—clothing, furniture, and business records—out of their own New York townhouse and stored them at Bloomingdale. All of these things, and likely many personal papers, were taken or destroyed in the attack.[35]

The raid had little in common with the punctilios of formal warfare associated with the eighteenth century. Loyalist historian Thomas Jones recorded that one of the patriot raiding party tried to throw a flaming bedsheet over Elizabeth Floyd as she fled downstairs. Charlotte was said to have been hit several times by a patriot soldier with his rifle butt before rescuing her infant nephew and escaping. While Phila hid under the stoop of the house, the other women, acting on the advice of one of the raiding party "of more humanity than the rest," scattered into the surrounding countryside as the building went up in flames. Elizabeth and Charlotte, still carrying the baby, fled into a swamp, where they remained throughout the night before being found in the morning and carried to a nearby home.[36]

Anne Cruger had her own terrifying experience. Alone and shaken after escaping the burning house, she tried reaching a British post two miles away but became disoriented in the cold November darkness. She spent the night wandering the countryside, sometimes looping back on her own tracks, and becoming more and more lost. When daylight finally broke, she found a farmhouse, whose inhabitants took her in. She had traveled more than seven miles from her parents' home. Jones recounted these events in detail, he said, because "the rebels during the whole of the war represented the British as the most inhuman, barbarous set of butchers that the world ever produced, and themselves as the most humane, kind, and generous enemies upon the globe." He, however, defied supporters of the Revolution "to produce such an act of inhumanity committed by the British during all the war."[37] There were strong elements of loyalist propaganda in such lurid, gendered, and class-inflected stories of the burning of the

De Lanceys' house. They emphasized patriot assaults on wealthy white women as particularly heinous; many incidents of violence that traumatized poorer and nonwhite women and men were not so fully recounted. Yet Anne's experiences that night showed the harrowing reality of civil war and its capacity to traumatize civilians far from better-known battlefields.

In the summer of 1778, John Harris and Anne got a final indication their former lives were over. Wartime New York City, crowded with wooden buildings, was acutely vulnerable to fire. The Great Fire of late September 1776, which blazed within a week of the British army's arrival, began on the city's west side. Among the hundreds of buildings it consumed was Trinity Church, where the Anglican Crugers worshipped and where Elizabeth Harris Cruger was buried.[38] Believing that patriots had set it, British authorities investigated, but no clear culprits were ever identified.[39] Two years later, on the night of August 3, 1778, another major fire struck the city. This one began in a building on Cruger's Wharf, and it destroyed more than sixty homes and commercial buildings and several docked ships (fig. 9).[40] The British officer John Montresor, one of the many who lost property in the blaze, estimated its total damage at £250,000.[41] David Matthews, New York's loyalist wartime mayor, was wounded by a falling timber as sailors, soldiers, and townspeople all rallied to contain the "great conflagration."[42] Eight buildings owned by Henry Cruger Sr. were consumed by the flames, as were those of many other longtime Cruger associates. Although its cause remained disputed, in a postwar request for British compensation Henry Cruger Jr. said the fire was purposely set "by the Rebells."[43] Cruger's Wharf—the symbolic center of the family's prewar wealth and power—was in ruins. As John Harris and Anne's war turned in a violent new direction in late 1778, the Crugers' pre-revolutionary world lay in ashes.

The second phase of the couple's revolution was defined by what occurred in the South, where British commanders hoped a new strategy would win the war. John Harris and Anne spent several years in the region, immersed in a particularly violent theater of civil war (fig. 10). In November 1778, John Harris and two battalions of De Lancey's Brigade left their Long Island posts and boarded ships as part of a three thousand–man force under Sir Henry Clinton bound for Savannah, Georgia. The ensuing battle for Savannah proved a rout for the British, who captured the city and held it for nearly four years. In the following months, John Harris commanded detachments trying to secure Georgia for the

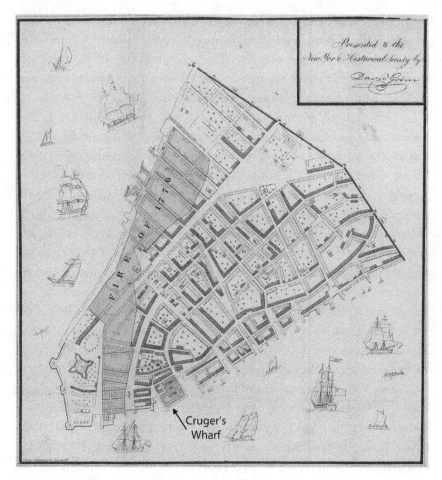

Figure 9. Cruger's Wharf and the Fires of 1776 and 1778. Lightly shaded areas mark the destruction wrought by the Great Fire of 1776 and the 1778 fire that struck Cruger's Wharf. Courtesy of Princeton University Library, Princeton, NJ.

Crown. He was briefly a prisoner of war, captured with a party celebrating the king's birthday at a plantation near Belfast, Georgia, on June 4, 1779, but was soon exchanged for a similarly ranked officer, John McIntosh.[44] Inspired by Savannah's seizure, the British government encouraged Georgia loyalists to return home. In June 1779, the province's royal governor, Sir James Wright, exiled since 1776, formally reestablished his government, making Georgia the only colony returned to prewar civilian authority during the conflict.

In the fall of 1779 John Harris and his men played a prominent part in the defense of British-controlled Savannah against a combined Franco-American

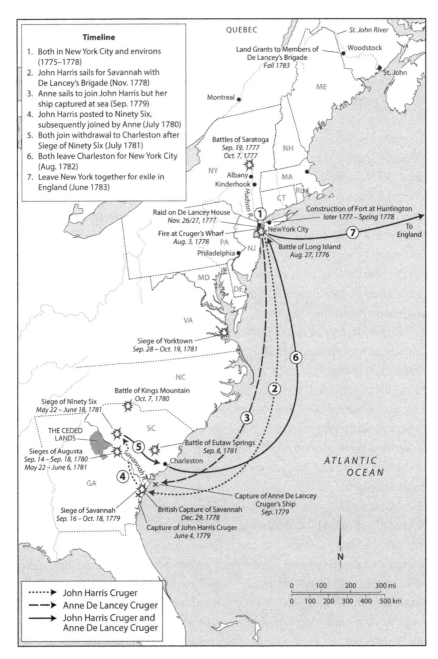

Figure 10. John Harris Cruger and Anne De Lancey Cruger at War, 1777–83.

siege. In September, a French fleet landed some four thousand soldiers commanded by the Comte D'Estaing near the town. Augmented by a thousand patriot troops under General Benjamin Lincoln, D'Estaing confronted approximately thirty-two hundred British, German, and loyalist defenders. After several weeks of preparation, the French began a week-long cannonade on October 3. The bombardment was horrific for trapped civilians but did comparatively little damage to the fortifications ringing the town. With the garrison showing no signs of surrendering, D'Estaing decided to attempt a direct assault on October 9. D'Estaing himself was wounded twice, and the French and their American allies sustained some seven hundred and fifty casualties in an hour as British defenders repulsed desperate attacks on a key redoubt in their line. John Harris, who wrote his father and brother an extensive account of the siege, said "The Lord fought on our side, & totally defeated the blood thirsty purposes of the Enemy, who talk'd of nothing but putting all to the Sword." In the ensuing days the defeated French returned to their ships, and on October 19 the last American besiegers withdrew.[45]

John Harris was in the thick of these events. De Lancey's first battalion held one of the principal British earthworks, and in the early stages of the siege, Cruger and his men were active in dangerous sorties against the attackers' trenches. As the battle unfolded, they held and repaired their bastion under the Franco-American bombardment and, during D'Estaing's final assault, repulsed a diversionary American attack (fig. 11). As John Harris later put it, he "for the whole of the siege was honor'd by the Commanding Officer with a very important post in the line."[46] He and his men took pride in having played an active part in a major victory.

Anne had her own remarkable experience at Savannah. In the fall of 1779, before D'Estaing's attack, she decided to join John Harris in the South. The Crugers were childless, so Anne was comparatively mobile, but she was not unique: women—elite and working class—regularly joined eighteenth-century armies on campaign, and female labor was integral to their ability to wage war. Unbeknownst to the Crugers, Anne's voyage from New York aboard a Georgia-bound supply convoy coincided with the French fleet's movement toward Savannah. A storm scattered the convoy, and Anne's vessel nearly foundered. She told her father that she "was for some time in expectation of being drowned."[47] Her battered ship was captured by one of D'Estaing's warships and she remained a captive throughout the French attempt to take Savannah. John Harris reported

Figure 11. A Plan of the Siege of Savannah, 1779. John Harris Cruger and his troops defended a redoubt on the left side of the British line throughout the siege of Savannah. Courtesy of the Library of Congress.

she had "suffer'd on her passage exceedingly by a most violent storm & being detain'd a prisoner a month on board the French fleet."[48] Anne said that she was "treated with the utmost attention & politeness," which probably owed much to her wealth and status.[49] In what must have been an emotionally excruciating experience, she was said to have stood on the deck of a French warship as the besiegers bombarded Savannah and her own husband. After D'Estaing's failed assault, Anne was put ashore and reunited with John Harris. These events are easily romanticized, but they conjure the feelings of fear and powerlessness noncombatants confronted during the Revolution.[50]

Although it was subsequently obscured by the wider course of events, many who supported the Crown celebrated Savannah's defense as crucial.[51] It helped British people, and perhaps especially anti-revolutionary Americans like John Harris and Anne, fit the war more comfortably into long-standing mindsets.[52] Savannah was broadly seen as a victory over the French rather than the rebellious Americans, which made it a more noteworthy triumph and frameable as a defense of British territory against an old imperial rival bent on conquest. The civil war's internationalization proved essential to the United States' ultimate victory, but fighting the French also made the conflict ideologically simpler for many opponents of independence.

If Savannah's defense provided John Harris and Anne with any moral clarity, in its immediate aftermath they were reminded of their choices' costs. On October 22, 1779, New York's patriot legislature passed an act attainting fifty-nine named individuals, including John Harris Cruger and Oliver De Lancey, as traitors for having "adhered to the enemies of this state." The Forfeiture or Confiscation Act, as it became variously known, subjected all the personal property and real estate of those named to seizure by the state government. The new law also said that those named in it were hereby "adjudged and declared guilty of [a] felony" without trial, and if subsequently "found in any part of this State," they could "suffer death as in cases of felony, without Benefit of Clergy."[53] Cruger and De Lancey were probably named in the act because of their high military ranks and prewar status. All of the other surviving members of the old Provincial Council still in British-occupied New York were also attainted.[54] This measure outraged loyalists and troubled even some patriots because of its harshness and disregard for fundamental legal rights. John Jay, in Spain as Congress's ambassador, thought that the measure meant "New York is disgraced by injustice too palpable to admit even of palliation."[55] In the Revolution's aftermath, partly because of these proceedings, similar bills of attainder were prohibited by the Constitution. If Savannah enabled John Harris and Anne to envision final victory, the Forfeiture Act made the prospect of defeat all the more terrible.

Following Savannah, De Lancey's Brigade took up garrison duties in Georgia, while, in May 1780, other British units won another major victory by taking Charleston, South Carolina, and capturing more than five thousand patriot troops. In the ensuing months, with no substantial congressional army left in the region, a brutal and intimate war of small-scale raid and counter-raid by soldiers and partisans occurred as British commanders tried to "pacify" the lower South.[56] In June 1780, before turning regional command over to Charles Cornwallis, Henry Clinton issued proclamations requiring civilians and former patriot fighters to swear loyalty oaths and join loyalist militias. Clinton's proclamations were widely seen in retrospect as mistakes, pushing some from inaction into direct participation in armed resistance.[57] Moreover, many people who took these oaths regarded them as extorted and therefore did not feel themselves subsequently bound by them.

In July 1780, Cornwallis sent John Harris and his men into this maelstrom by posting them to Ninety Six, a South Carolina backcountry station about one hundred and fifty miles northwest of Charleston. As Cornwallis wrote in instructions to Cruger in early August 1780, "keeping possession of the backcountry is of utmost importance, indeed the Success of the War in the Southern District depends totally upon it," and Ninety Six was one of a string of strongpoints through which British commanders planned to control the region.[58] Cruger's command, all Americans drawn from De Lancey's Brigade, the New Jersey Volunteers, and South Carolina's loyalist militia, undertook the construction of an improved stockade, blockhouses, and defensive ditches. Some two hundred enslaved people from the surrounding area performed significant labor. Cornwallis's chief engineer, Henry Haldane, visited in November 1780, and subsequently a large star-shaped earthwork was added to the growing fortifications.

John Harris and his men waged war out of Ninety Six for more than a year. Memories of this period were long divided and depended largely on one's postwar political position. Cruger stated in 1784 that he and his men had operated "with such good effect as to establish the tranquility of the country."[59] Such guarded generalizations, both self-effacing and sanitizing, mask the awful reality of the backcountry struggle. In September 1780, the patriot partisan Elijah Clarke assembled some five hundred fighters in northern Georgia for a surprise attack on Augusta, another link in Britain's chain of backcountry strongpoints and a site for trade and diplomacy with Native Americans. Augusta's besieged commander, the Georgia loyalist Thomas Brown, dispatched messengers to Ninety Six, and Cruger led his provincials through forced marches to Augusta's relief. Brown's small force, augmented by several hundred Native allies, held out for five excruciating days until Cruger arrived. Brown was shot with a ball that passed through both thighs; his second-in-command was killed.[60] When Cruger's relief column appeared, the attackers fled in disorder. Clarke and some of his men escaped westward, but others were captured or killed by pursuing Muscogee and Cherokee warriors and British troops. Cruger sent out mounted patrols to bring in as many "the traitorous Rebels of this Neighborhood" as he could.[61]

British commanders in the region were vexed to find themselves fighting repeatedly against men who had signed loyalty oaths or whom they had previously captured and paroled on promises to stay out of the war. When either side gained even temporary control over an area, they engaged in a new round of threats and intimidation surrounding the administration of oaths. According to one careful assessment, residents of western Georgia were probably pressured to change their allegiances seven times between January 1779 and October 1780.[62]

There was a blend of high-mindedness, piety, cruelty, and naivete in this shared Anglo-American culture of pledging allegiance. Men of violence on both sides extracted promises at the barrel of the gun and then claimed to be outraged when the vulnerable, terrified, or duplicitous reneged. Nevertheless, terrible consequences could accompany perceived violations of expected norms.

When Brown's men first occupied Augusta in June 1780, they accepted the surrenders of hundreds of backcountry patriot fighters and paroled them, while other people in the region subsequently made oaths of allegiance. However, in a trenchant example of the dilemmas of civil war, when Elijah Clarke was assembling men for his attack on Augusta, he threatened to kill any erstwhile patriot who refused to join his force on account of having previously given the British a parole.[63] While most patriot fighters captured during Augusta's relief were released after more oaths, an unlucky thirteen were determined by their captors to have previously given their paroles. These men were summarily hanged on orders from either Brown, Cruger, or both. On the day after Augusta's relief, John Harris wrote to a fellow officer with blasé callousness that the prisoners "will be roughly handled, some very probably suspended for their good deeds."[64] According to patriot tradition, Brown was largely responsible for these executions and took vindictive pleasure in watching them.

According to Brown's modern biographer, however, the responsibility for these summary executions rested primarily with Cruger, as the senior officer on the spot, and ultimately with Cornwallis.[65] Indeed, in August 1780 Cornwallis had directly ordered Cruger that any captured militiamen who had borne arms for the British and then joined the rebels "should be immediately hanged."[66] Among those executed was the patriot captain Henry Duke. A British press report noted with satisfaction that "Col. Cruger found a rascal amongst the rebel prisoners (one Duke, who after having submitted to the government, and taking the oaths, was found in arms at Augusta) whom he ordered to be hanged."[67] The metastasizing hatred produced by the backcountry war spread elsewhere as patriots publicized these executions as part of their growing list of grievances.[68]

The ensuing events were similarly grim. Clarke and his surviving men fled back toward what settlers called the Ceded Lands, territory northwest of Augusta that Georgians had taken from Muscogee and Cherokee people in 1773.[69] Cruger and his soldiers marched in pursuit, and although they never caught Clarke, they laid waste to the Ceded Lands, which were considered the wellspring of his attack. Cruger's men burned farms and homes, seized livestock, rounded up suspected rebels, and drove off the wives and children of men believed to have escaped with Clarke. John Harris told Cornwallis that the "most notorious Villains" were "paying the price of their treachery." There was little glory to be had in such warfare. While he punished the families of Clarke's most committed fighters, Cruger thought most of the men his troops actually captured were just "poor Wretches, who were carried down by force and threats from Clark and his adherents." According to Wright, Cruger's men destroyed approximately one hundred homesteads.[70] Cruger and his men returned to Ninety Six in late September 1780.

The British army was on the offensive in the backcountry, and more southerners were taking oaths of allegiance and joining loyalist militias, but this proved the highwater mark for the royal cause in the region. On October 7, 1780, at the Battle of Kings Mountain near the South Carolina/North Carolina border, a patriot force consisting largely of "overmountain men" from settlements beyond the Appalachians surrounded and destroyed a contingent of loyalist militia. Britons and loyalists subsequently charged the patriots with postbattle atrocities including massacres of the wounded, summary executions, and desecrations of the dead.[71] In the battle's aftermath, the microdynamics of civil war changed in the backcountry. Regional patriots were emboldened, while loyalists and neutrals increasingly lost faith in the ability of the British to hold territory and protect them. Cornwallis grew more pessimistic about loyalist militias, while, on the patriot side, Nathanael Greene was appointed to replace Horatio Gates in December 1780. Greene proved an able and elusive commander, frustrating British efforts to win a decisive victory while sapping their strength. As patriot influence grew, Ninety Six and other British outposts began to look less like bases for launching offensive pacification operations and more like dangerously isolated targets.

In late 1780 John Harris temporarily entrusted Ninety Six to a subordinate and traveled to Charleston to meet Anne, who had moved there when De Lancey's Brigade shifted from Georgia to South Carolina. The couple then returned to Ninety Six, where, according to Thomas Jones, Anne lived for several months "in the garrison, fared as the people did, was beloved by the privates, and caressed, esteemed, and almost adored, by the officers, for her kindness and hospitalities upon all occasions."[72] Such romanticization aside, Anne was by now an experienced campaigner. In entering the backcountry, she voluntarily ran considerable risks to support her husband and his troops as they waged war.

Many of Cruger's men were ill in the winter of 1780/81, and he was increasingly concerned over Ninety Six's defenses as the insurgent threat in the backcountry grew.

In April 1781 Cornwallis took the bulk of his army into Virginia with the aim of securing that influential province; it was the start of the campaign that culminated in his defeat at Yorktown. Cornwallis left his subordinate, Lord Rawdon, and a small number of dispersed British troops to oppose Greene in the lower South. In early May 1781, Rawdon instructed several of his western contingents to abandon their posts to give him a larger, consolidated, and more mobile force. On May 8, he dispatched orders directing Cruger to raze Ninety Six's fortifications and march its garrison to Augusta, but the patriot militia now dominating the countryside intercepted Rawdon's messengers. Greene's forces soon captured several other British forts and invested Augusta, leaving Ninety Six as the last British outpost in the backcountry. Cut off and unaware of Rawdon's order to withdraw, Cruger's people continued preparing for an attack that seemed imminent.

On May 21, Greene arrived near Ninety Six with a force of just under one thousand men. Cruger commanded about five hundred and fifty provincials and militia, about one hundred loyalist civilians sheltering in the fort, and perhaps fifty or so enslaved people. As the patriot army approached, Anne Cruger left the fortifications and was taken into the home of a nearby family. According to Jones, this family was that of a "loyal Presbyterian parson," while other sources claimed that Anne took refuge with a local patriot. As Greene's army approached Ninety Six, Anne, with a veteran's guile, reportedly gathered up the hard money that she had and sewed "her guineas in girdles or belts, for the purpose of securing them about her person." When Greene learned of Anne's presence, he dispatched a guard to the house.[73] Anne remained in these circumstances of polite but close confinement throughout the ensuing struggle. Once again, she found herself in the anxious position of being entirely in an enemy's power as they attacked her husband and his men.

Patriot troops surrounded Ninety Six on May 22. After a hasty attempt to storm the post failed, Greene set about a more systematic siege, and his men began digging a series of approach trenches and earthwork batteries. Cruger's defenders fought to disrupt the work parties with gun and cannon fire and occasional nighttime sorties, while laboring continuously to repair damage caused by patriot artillery. Greene knew that Rawdon would eventually learn of the siege and grew increasingly concerned with its slow progress. On June 7, Rawdon and a column that grew to over two thousand troops began marching to Ninety Six. The next day, Greene's besiegers were augmented by troops under Colonel Henry Lee fresh from capturing Augusta, and the pressure on Cruger's garrison became relentless. Between June 12 and June 14, Cruger received the welcome news that Rawdon was on his way and used it to rally his hard-pressed men. Greene also learned of the British column's approach and concluded that, even with Lee's reinforcements, he could not complete the siege before it arrived.

Retreat might have been prudent, but Greene decided to order a final all-out assault on June 18. At the crucial star redoubt, Cruger's men unleashed a deadly fusillade of cannon and musket fire. The patriot advance stalled in the ditch surrounding the redoubt, and two groups of defenders sallied out from the fort's rear and launched bayonet charges against their enemy's flanks. A second simultaneous attack led by Lee against a part of the stockade surrounding several buildings had more initial success. Lee's troops advanced into that part of the fortifications, but Cruger's men withdrew into the town's brick jailhouse, which presented a formidable new obstacle. Blocked by Cruger's carefully coordinated defense, Greene called the attack off after an hour and retreated the next day. Cruger's force had won a stubborn victory against long odds.

While Cruger's post had been preserved, Britain's fundamental problems in the backcountry remained. Ninety Six was more isolated than ever, and its fortifications were badly damaged, so Rawdon reissued his order that it be abandoned. John Harris was given responsibility for a bittersweet task: the destruction of Ninety Six's defenses to prevent them from being taken over by the patriots. His men labored for several days to level Ninety Six's stockade and earthworks, and then burned down its remaining buildings.[74] Anne, allowed to remain when Greene retreated, presumably joined Cruger's column and its train of backcountry refugees when they marched east in July. For loyalists like John Harris and Anne, it was becoming hard to distinguish victories from defeats.

At Eutaw Springs in September 1781, the Crugers were part of a fittingly inconclusive final large battle in South Carolina. Greene's advancing army surprised foragers from a force of two thousand British troops, including Cruger and his New York veterans. An unexpected, see-sawing battle ensued. According to his postwar loyalist claim, John Harris was second-in-command of the British army at Eutaw Springs, to the "success of which day he presumes to think he had some share in contributing."[75] Anne, still traveling with the army, hurriedly left the British camp and took refuge in a house only about half a mile from the battlefield, where she heard "every cannon" and "every musket" that was fired.[76]

As Greene's troops attacked, Cruger's men were in the center of a hurriedly drawn up British line. There were multiple rounds of intense hand-to-hand combat, many prisoners were taken, and Cruger and his men both delivered and received bayonet charges. Patriot troops nearly overwhelmed the British, pushing them backward through their camp. With a collapse looming, Cruger helped rally the retreating and disorganized soldiers around a brick house. The patriots proved unable to storm the stoutly defended building, and Greene ordered a withdrawal. Cornwallis later said that John Harris "particularly distinguished himself" on the day, while Sir Guy Carleton noted Eutaw Springs as another example of Cruger's "prudence and gallantry."[77] John Harris escaped uninjured, but combined the opposing forces had more than twelve hundred soldiers killed, wounded, or missing in a few hours of fighting.[78]

Both sides claimed victory, but it proved a moot point. After Eutaw Springs the British were increasingly confined to the coastal low country. More important, in the following month, Cornwallis's attempts to subdue Virginia ended in disaster for the British and loyalist cause. Besieged by Franco-American forces at Yorktown and waiting in vain for naval aid, Cornwallis was forced to surrender his entire army on October 19, 1781. The year began with the British envisioning a Virginia campaign to end the rebellion, but it closed with the patriots triumphant. John Harris and Anne had been part of victories that, it turned out, mattered very little.

Following Yorktown, people like John Harris and Anne were in limbo. In April 1782, news reached New York that the British government had declared a cessation to offensive military activities in North America.[79] The war kept claiming casualties as it limped toward a conclusion. Mary Cruger Walton and her husband, Jacob, remained living around crowded British-controlled New York City. The Waltons' eldest daughter, Polly, had died of an infectious disease in August 1781.[80] Then, in August 1782, Mary and Jacob died of disease within weeks of each other, leaving behind three children under age sixteen as orphans. Jacob's will named John Harris Cruger and Peter Van Schaack as among the children's guardians, and caring for them concerned the wider family in the years to come.[81]

In South Carolina, British troops including Cruger's battalion remained garrisoned around Charleston, under arms but without a clear goal. For a period, John Harris represented the army on the military/civilian board that governed British-controlled Charleston.[82] In July 1782, the British evacuated Savannah, and Charleston was clearly next. That summer, after nearly four years' service in the south, John Harris received leave to travel to New York on account of illness, arriving home in mid-August.[83] Anne, if she hadn't already sailed for New York, presumably accompanied him. On his departure, the "Inhabitants of Charlestown" issued an address praising Cruger for his part in "the many brilliant actions that have so eminently distinguished the British arms in the Southern Colonies, which, had they been aided by a proper system of policy, would have effected the establishment of peace." His response drew a veil over the brutal realities of what he had seen and done in the backcountry, while reflecting a sense of loss. He observed that Charleston's address "greatly compensates for my utmost services, which have, and ever shall be, exerted in that just cause, in which we are jointly embarked."[84] The remnants of De Lancey's Brigade sailed for New York with the final evacuation of Charleston in December 1782.

A copy of the provisional peace treaty arrived in New York on April 5, 1783, and four days later John Harris wrote to Peter Van Schaack in terms capturing the disillusionment that loyalists felt as they reckoned with defeat.[85] Profoundly pessimistic about his prospects, he reported that "as soon as I can get a passage for <u>nothing</u> I shall embark with Mrs. Cruger to beg my bread in England."[86] Over the next several months John Harris and Anne did what they could to tie up the loose ends of their former lives. On June 5, in a stinging moment, their remaining "household and kitchen furniture" was auctioned off at their Hanover Square house.[87] Amid the wider loyalist exodus, John Harris and Anne left for England aboard the ship *Adamant* in the early summer of 1783.[88] Neither would ever return.

As they sailed eastward, a tumultuous phase of John Harris and Anne's lives closed, but the Revolution's repercussions traveled with them. Once in England, they settled alongside Oliver, Phila, and other De Lanceys. John Harris's political opinions differed little from those of his nobodyist Cruger kin, yet he took up arms while they did not. Ultimately, the intensely violent nature of his and Anne's revolution owed more to the microdynamics of civil war in New York City in 1776 and their particular set of community and family relationships than to ideology. Until 1776, John Harris Cruger identified with the patriot cause, but the subsequent years of violence changed him into someone who, at war's end, defined himself as a forever loyalist.

6. The Price of Neutrality

Peter Van Schaack, his wife, Elizabeth, and their family paid a heavy price for his following his conscience during the American Revolution. Seeing the conflict as an unnatural civil war, Van Schaack never took up arms for either side and wanted peace above all else. Nevertheless, the conflict was intensely difficult for him. Elizabeth and several of their children died, victims of the epidemics that ravaged revolutionary America. He was banished by the revolutionary government of New York, spent years in exile, and endured severe vision problems that threatened total blindness. Yet, like others in his circle, Van Schaack remained emotionally tied to New York and invested in its future. During the last years of the war, unhappy in England, Van Schaack began planning a way to return home.[1]

While not all nobodyists made decisions in accordance with fully thought-out political and moral positions, Van Schaack's neutrality was a carefully developed and ideologically informed choice that he maintained at great personal cost. While the term "conscientious objector" postdates the American Revolution, it captures the morally inflected and self-determined nature of Van Schaack's wartime stance.[2] Van Schaack was not a pacifist opposed to all wars, but he did reject and resist participating in the revolutionary era's violence himself. His experiences illustrate that nobodyism could be based on principle as well as fear, irresolution, or dishonesty. They also show that, paradoxically, sometimes an avowedly antiwar stance made it harder to keep the conflict at arm's length.

Like John Harris Cruger, Van Schaack has sometimes been described as a Whig-Loyalist, but in Peter's case this label fits poorly.[3] While certainly whiggish in his political philosophy—he held John Locke in particular esteem—Van Schaack never identified himself clearly as a loyalist as his brother-in-law did. Rather, Van Schaack wanted, desperately at times, to be neutral. Like other members of the Cruger family, his primary prewar allegiances were local: he wanted his family, community, and New York to thrive and grow. As the war unfolded, Van Schaack came to disagree with more militant New Yorkers, but he was only a loyalist if one accepts the rigid dichotomies pushed by patriot leaders. Looking back at the 1770s and the circumstances that led to Van Schaack's exile, his friend John Jay wrote to him in 1782 that "as an independent American, I considered all who were not for us, and you among the rest, as against us."[4] This deliberate political dualism may have made sense to patriot leaders like Jay once they were set on American independence, but histories of the Revolution should not remain captive to the reductive categorizations deployed as weapons by the conflict's combatants. The Van Schaacks' experiences as nobodyists offer better and more subtle ways to understand the dynamics of the revolutionary conflict.

In late April 1775, as the patriot siege of Boston began, Van Schaack remained immersed in New York's resistance movement. He, along with John Jay and James Duane, wrote a new "Association" in response to the outbreak of fighting. Subscribers resolved "never to become slaves" and to "associate, under all the ties of religion, honor, and love to our Country, to adopt and to endeavour to carry into execution whatever measures may be recommended by the Continental Congress, or resolved upon by our Provincial Convention" until a "reconciliation" was effected.[5] It was a statement full of fury and righteous anger that blamed the British government and military for the bloodshed in Massachusetts. While this might have been an attempt by moderates including Jay, Duane, and Van Schaack to "contain the violence" of New York's Liberty Boys, the acerbic Thomas Jones later wrote that its real aim was "to strengthen and cement the solemn league and covenant, which had only been privately entered into by the heads of the faction before." As a loyalist, Jones disparaged Van Schaack for his role in this association, considering him "a lad of great duplicity" who furthered the developing Revolution at a crucial moment.[6]

Yet Peter was downcast by the news from Massachusetts and mindful of the forces being unleashed. He reported in May 1775 that "my mind is distresed with the gloomy prospect of my country. Such a spirit of anarchy and disregard of the powers of government may prevail, as may prevent us from soon returning to the old channel, and that affection which is the bond of our common union with the mother country, may perhaps forever be destroyed."[7] Despite Van Schaack's role in writing the new association, at least two members of the extended Cruger family, the elder John Cruger and Jacob Walton, refused to sign it. In publicly explaining their actions, they declared their "approbation of any Association for preserving the peace" and belief that the British constitution "gives us a right to an absolute exemption from Parliamentary taxation," but said they believed signing the new association was inconsistent with their ability to act freely as members of New York's assembly, which had recently sent its petitions to the king and Parliament.[8]

Colonial cities were hothouses of partisanship, and they became more unsettled after the outbreak of fighting, so many people sought to leave them. This might or might not signal a particular ideological commitment. One option, especially for those with wealth and transatlantic connections, was to go to England. James De Lancey, the key leader of the De Lanceyite faction, did so in April 1775.[9] Henry Cruger Sr. left New York in May 1775 and resided for several years with his son Henry in Bristol. Retreat to the countryside was another strategy. Kinderhook, where Peter's family was from, contained many reconciliationists. As Peter's brother, David Van Schaack, wrote him during this period, "If anywhere, we shall preserve peace here. We are, and have been, very circumspect for a long while."[10]

The Van Schaacks left New York City too, and their movements illustrate how the personal was frequently inseparable from the political in interdependent people's wartime decision-making. Elizabeth and Peter had seven children between 1765 and 1774, with two more born after the war began. High childhood mortality rates had claimed four of these children by 1774, and just as news of Lexington and Concord reached New York City, the Van Schaacks' eldest surviving child, Cornelius, became dangerously ill. Fears for his health added to Peter and Elizabeth's anxiety over the radicalizing situation, and, on the advice of friends and family, they went to Kinderhook in May 1775.[11] John Harris Cruger, whose decision to remain in New York had major consequences for his wartime experiences, noted in June that "the timid, the cautious, the judicious, or the prudent, call them by which name you will, are removing their effects again out of town."[12] The ex-speaker John Cruger, withdrawing from active politics, followed the Van Schaacks to Kinderhook that fall.[13] While John subsequently had some uncomfortable dealings with patriot authorities, he was able—perhaps due to his age and prewar reputation—to avoid the worst wartime turmoil through quiet retirement.

Despite the move to the Kinderhook, young Cornelius Van Schaack died in July 1775, and then in a crushing double blow, Peter and Elizabeth's youngest son, an infant, died two days later. In a short, profoundly sad letter that Elizabeth Van Schaack wrote Henry Sr. in July 1775, she hoped for peace and for some deeper meaning in the family's trials: "may the Lord soon restore peace in our Land! and may the present distress be the means of humbling us all."[14] Peter too sought consolation in faith, writing a pious personal reflection titled "Upon the death of two of my children within two days of each other."[15] Whether the young Van Schaacks' deaths were related to the increasing movement of people and pathogens sparked by the start of the war is not clear, but more than a hundred thousand died from smallpox alone in North America between 1775 and 1782.[16] Like many American families, the Van Schaacks endured civil war, disease, and dislocation as entangled, fatal calamities in the 1770s.

As revolutionary turmoil deepened, Peter worried constantly over the health of his diminished family. Elizabeth became unwell in 1775, and she gradually deteriorated further in Kinderhook. Nevertheless, she had a son, christened Cornelius after his deceased brother and nicknamed Buck, in Kinderhook in April 1776, and another daughter, named Elizabeth and called Betsey, was born in June 1777.[17] Van Schaack also had serious health concerns of his own. Cataracts in both eyes, the onset of which he attributed to his compiling New York's laws in 1773, grew increasingly serious.[18] He had lost all sight in his right eye by the spring of 1776—when he was still only twenty-nine years old—while worsening vision in his left threatened him with total blindness.[19] Van Schaack was rarely explicit about how his family tragedies shaped his wartime decision-making, but the juxtaposition of the personal and the political in his letters makes it clear that he navigated the Revolution as father, husband, and citizen simultaneously.

Personality and character also affected choices. As Peter noted in an intimate 1779 letter to his son, "how strange is it, that men of equal degrees of understanding, of equally enlarged and liberal minds, who have been educated in the same schools, and in the same general principles of government, whose characters were equally fair and unblemished, and who had actually the same identical interest and the same object, the welfare of their country,—that men so situated, and moreover intimately connected by the strongest bonds of friendship, should have taken opposite sides in this great cause!" In Van Schaack's case, he preferred approaching problems as a detached observer and, as far as possible, arriving at deliberate decisions on how to act. He encouraged his son, for example, to observe the historic events unfolding around him "dispassionately, like a philosopher," and reminded him that "you have only your own *opinion* that you are right; this indeed is the strongest guide for *your own* conduct, but not for others."[20] This conscientious commitment to deliberative private judgment played a major part in how Peter experienced the conflict.

As a well-educated lawyer who had invested much in compiling New York's statutes, he also seems to have had a deep respect for law *qua* law. This made the inherent illegality of revolutionary violence hard for him to accept.[21] He was much more bookish than most of his relatives. As a young man he called history the "grand fountain of instruction" and recommended Cicero and Samuel von Pufendorf.[22] While particularly versed in history, political philosophy, and law, Peter also extracted what he saw as wisdom from fiction, poetry, and other genres. He praised and recommended works by Samuel Richardson, Shakespeare, Greek and Latin poets, and many other writers. Van Schaack's commitments to the rule of law and the instructive power of history and literature were his guiding lights, but in the storm of revolutionary passions they often led him into trouble.

Van Schaack's character provides the best explanation for his repeated difficulties with oaths. As Peter pointed out in some of his dealings with patriot committees, oaths were unlikely to trouble the wicked but could put terrible pressure on a good man who would be torn "between duty to God" and "affection to an innocent family," which might be ruined if he refused to swear one.[23] Van Schaack also took the precise wording of oaths seriously and quite separately from whatever larger political judgments or preferences the oath signaled. In his view, a person of integrity could not swear a badly framed oath in the service of even a good cause. It was a principled, rigorous stance that was difficult to maintain in his tumultuous times.[24] The line between moral courage and self-destructive fastidiousness was not always easy to discern then or now. Even some of Van Schaack's friends seem to have regarded his character with a mixture of admiration and bewilderment. It did not make his revolution easier (fig. 12).

Peter and Elizabeth's decision to leave New York City in the spring of 1775 did not signal a decisive break with the colonial cause, but Peter was moving apart from some of his longtime friends and political allies. In the same month the Van Schaacks left for Kinderhook, John Jay, a confidant of Peter's since their days together at King's College, went to Philadelphia as a New York delegate to the Second Continental Congress.[25] Jay and Van Schaack had cooperated closely in

Figure 12. Peter Van Schaack. Frontispiece from Henry C. Van Schaack, *Life of Peter Van Schaack*, LL. D. [...] (New York: D. Appleton, 1842). Courtesy of HathiTrust.

the prewar protest movement, but this was probably the moment when their paths began diverging. After Van Schaack retreated to Kinderhook, he sought to make sense of political events by intensively studying political philosophy, including works by Cesare Beccaria, Hugo Grotius, John Locke, Montesquieu, Samuel von Pufendorf, Emer de Vattel, and others, on which he made substantial notes. In January 1776, following this intense period of study and reflection,

Van Schaack set down, in a closely reasoned, extended memo to himself, his views on the widening civil war.

Van Schaack's document was steeped in the self-consciously Enlightened and whiggish arguments of the eighteenth-century Anglo-American world. It is most revealing as an expression of an ideological neutrality, one based on a systematic, carefully worked-out set of political ideas. Unlike the war's most famous group of "conscientious objectors," the Quakers, Van Schaack arrived at his neutrality outside of the long-established religious and communal norms of the Friends. Christian principles infused his reflections, but these were of a broadly Protestant sort and intertwined with secular rationales. In his January 1776 document, he cited Locke twice in support of his arguments, took as a given the contractual nature of government, and insisted that "at this enlightened day" there could be no doubt about the lawfulness of resistance in the face of "gross and palpable infractions on the part of the governing power." Rather than finding support within a proudly and self-consciously distinctive minority tradition, Van Schaack spoke the language of his patriot neighbors.

The central political question, he thought, was "the *degree* of subordination we owed to the British Parliament," and there were three possible answers: colonists owed no obedience to any acts of Parliament, colonists were bound by any acts passed by Parliament that would also bind people in Great Britain if passed in respect to them, and colonists were bound only to some acts that would be valid if passed in respect to subjects in Great Britain. The first possibility Van Schaack dismissed out of hand, for "I consider the Colonies as members of the British empire, and subordinate to the Parliament." While he identified strongly with New York and with the colonial cause, Van Schaack was no advocate for a separate American nationality in early 1776. Choosing between the other two possibilities was much harder, however, because of the "necessity of a supreme power in every state" on the one hand, and the "destructive consequence of a right in Parliament to bind us in all cases whatsoever" on the other. The best resolution would be that "some middle way should be found out," a compromise—the bedeviling specific terms of which he did not spell out—that secured "to the Americans, the essential rights of Britons, but so modified as shall best consist with the general benefit of the *whole*." This hoped-for compromise through constitutional reform informed many people's nobodyism in the war's first year.

Van Schaack also resisted the temptation to see various bad British policies as part of a conspiratorial plot. In reviewing the events of the past decade,

Van Schaack believed that several acts had exceeded "those bounds, which, of right, ought to circumscribe the Parliament," but that "taking the whole of the acts complained of together, they do not, I think, manifest a system of slavery, but may fairly be imputed to human frailty, and the difficulty of the subject." Likewise he noted that some recent parliamentary measures that were rightly objected to were nevertheless "precisely of the nature of other acts made before the commencement of his present Majesty's reign, which is the era when the supposed design of subjugating the colonies began."[26] In one of the most influential interpretations of the Revolution's origins, Bernard Bailyn argued that "the colonists believed they saw emerging from the welter of events during the decade after the Stamp Act a pattern whose meaning was unmistakable." They "saw about them, with increasingly clarity, not merely mistaken, or even evil, policies violating the principles upon which freedom rested, but what appeared to be evidence of nothing less than a deliberate assault launched surreptitiously by plotters against liberty both in England and in America." It was this belief "above all else that in the end propelled them into Revolution."[27] If the ideological origins of the American Revolution rested on such a conspiracy theory, then it is notable that Van Schaack departed from more militant patriots by refusing to countenance such arguments because of an instinctive belief in widespread human decency and a commitment to reasoned analysis in the face of paranoia.[28] "In short," Van Schaack concluded, "I think those acts may have been passed without a preconcerted plan of enslaving us, and it appears to me that the more favorable construction ought ever to be put on the conduct of our rulers." It was a characteristic blend of optimism and level-headedness, admirable but isolating in intemperate times.

Van Schaack also believed that the colonies had benefited and would continue to benefit from their relationship with Britain because "without such a controlling common umpire, the colonies must become independent states, which would be introductive of anarchy and confusion among ourselves." Because he thought that "some kind of dependence" on Parliament was "necessary for our own happiness," he thought that the colonies should concede this point. Unless they did so, and such a concession was rejected by Britain, Van Schaack wrote, "I cannot see any principle of regard for my country, which will authorize me in taking up arms, as absolute *dependence* and *independence* are two extremes which I would avoid." There were, he claimed, also "many very weighty reasons besides the above, to restrain a man from taking up arms, but some of them are of too delicate a nature to be put upon paper." What these were—religious beliefs, fears for his family, or something else—Van Shaack did not specify. He did note that he was not opposed to taking up arms himself because of the "consequences should America be subdued," the "hopes of any favor from government," or, most important, from any "disparagement of the cause my countrymen are engaged in, or a desire of obstructing the present measures." In Van Schaack's view, wanting a given political outcome and being personally willing to engage in violence to obtain it were not the same thing.

Van Schaack argued that every person had to exercise their own judgment in what was "a question of morality and religion, in which a man cannot conscientiously take an active part, without being convinced in his own mind of the justice of the cause." Aware that these sentiments would expose him to danger, he nonetheless concluded "whatever disagreeable consequences may follow from dissenting from the general voice, yet I cannot but remember that I am to render an account of my conduct before a more awful tribunal, where no man can be justified, who stands accused by his own conscience of taking part in measures, which, through the distress and bloodshed of his fellow-creatures, may precipitate his country into ruin."[29] Van Schaack does not seem to have intended this document for any readers beyond himself, and he does not seem to have shared it with others. Rather, such exercises seem to have been a habit with Van Schaack: a way of taking stock and marshaling his own thoughts in moments of crisis.

Peter's reflections put the problem of violence at the heart of his reckoning with the Revolution.[30] The primary issue for Van Schaack was not whether monarchy or republicanism was preferable as a system of government, or whether empire or independence best promoted American welfare and liberty. Rather the central question he grappled with was whether what had occurred since 1765 justified *his* use of violence and provided moral sanction for *him* to attempt to kill others. "Upon the whole," he later told John Jay in explaining his wartime decisions, "even in a doubtful case, I would rather be the patient sufferer, than run the risk of being the active aggressor," and "I concluded, rather than to support a cause I could not approve, to bear every distress that might result from the part I took."[31] It was not the legitimacy of resistance in general that most troubled him but whether or not he could, in accordance with his conscience, participate personally in his society's civil war.

Van Schaack became unfortunately prominent in his neutrality, but he was perceived as dangerous because he was not alone. Many of his neighbors had sim-

THE PRICE OF NEUTRALITY 151

ilar doubts about the increasingly violent turn of events even as they resented British measures. Collapsing this position into a "loyalist" one is again to fundamentally misunderstand it. Rather, it is a testament to Van Schaack's continued attachment to the patriot cause that in May 1776 electors in the Kinderhook district chose Van Schaack as one of four representatives to the "Committee of safety, correspondence, and protection" for Albany County. One way to understand such actions is to see in them an effort by "conservatives" or even "tories" to block "patriots," but that ignores the fact that this committee was a new, elective, and extralegal wartime emergency body. Participating in it at all meant continuing to acknowledge the legitimacy of the colonial common cause. Van Schaack took up his seat when this committee first sat in late May.

In retrospect, accepting this office proved a dangerous step for Van Schaack. At the first meeting of the new committee in Albany, Van Schaack and other Kinderhook representatives complained on behalf of their constituents against "bodies of armed men from Claverack and Kings district" and from Massachusetts who had "invaded" Kinderhook district and "disarmed, dragooned, and ill treated the inhabitants." However, the bulk of the Albany County Committee was of no mind to sanction any complaints against the armed resistance movement. Instead, the committee immediately adopted a resolution requiring that all its members subscribe to the "general association" recently produced by the province's Committee of Safety that included a pledge to "to defend by arms the United American Colonies against the hostile attempts of the British fleets and armies."[32] Van Schaack and the other Kinderhook delegates refused to sign the new association, and they were expelled from the Albany County Committee, while the more violent patriot partisans who had seized property and harassed persons in Kinderhook remained uncensured. In his son's view, it was from this point forward that "probably, he ceased to act with the friends of the Revolution."[33] Following these events, Peter and Speaker John Cruger, were named in the June 5, 1776, resolutions of the Provincial Congress on "persons dangerous and disaffected to the American cause" that ensnared other members of their extended family. Yet, while John Harris Cruger, Jacob Walton, and others resident in the city at this moment were forced to flee or face arrest, Peter and the elder John, living in Kinderhook, remained at home and appear to have escaped further consequences from this particular resolution.

Like members of the extended Cruger family, Peter's older brothers, David and Henry Van Schaack, were also considered of doubtful loyalties by more militant patriots. Kinderhook voters had repeatedly chosen Henry Van Schaack to represent them in extralegal committees before and after Lexington and Concord, but he had challenged patriot militancy on several occasions and sought to promote reconciliation.[34] In June 1776, he and sixteen other Kinderhook men were summarily arrested by Albany County's Committee of Safety and jailed for seventeen days until it was decided that "the charge against them was not of sufficient weight to require defense." In July, Henry Van Schaack was again imprisoned in Albany for more than a week and then banished to Hartford, Connecticut, where he spent several months before being allowed to return to Kinderhook on parole.[35]

While Peter was quiet on the Declaration of Independence in the summer of 1776, he probably found it an unwelcome development. In November 1776 someone denounced Peter as one of a group of "persons disaffected to the cause of American liberty" to the New York Committee of Safety.[36] As scholarship on civil wars has noted, "denunciation is central" and "it is common" rather than a "particular twist" in such conflicts. Who informed on Van Schaack was not recorded. This too is typical in civil wars because people who denounce others, regardless of their motives, often violate community norms and are driven "to keep it concealed."[37] Despite this, the wider context surrounding Van Schaack's denunciation is revealing.

The winter of 1776/77 was an anguished period for committed patriots. After being forced out of New York City by Britain's expeditionary force, Washington's army retreated to Pennsylvania, and some feared the rebellion would collapse. Many New Yorkers were declaring themselves loyalists and joining counterrevolutionary military units. The first issue of Thomas Paine's *American Crisis*, published in December 1776, captured the desperate dynamics of the moment as "the times that try men's souls" and called for new patriot volunteers. The threat posed by the British army forced New York's Provincial Congress to move its meeting place repeatedly. New York's patriot leaders were simultaneously operating without a clear democratic mandate or set of constitutional arrangements and afraid that an imminent British offensive could result in their province's complete occupation and their personal arrest.

Van Schaack was caught up in these panic-inducing microdynamics. In late December, Albany County's Committee to Detect Conspiracies, taking up the previous report that Van Schaack was disaffected, further reported that "this committee have been credibly informed, and have good reason to believe" that David and Peter Van Schaack and two other named men had "long maintained an equivocal neutrality in the present struggles." The men, the committee continued, were "in general supposed unfriendly to the American cause, and from their influence are enabled to do it essential injury."[38] Peter was not present at this meeting, and, again, he was not charged with having done anything specific to oppose the rebellion. Rather, it was claimed that he showed an insufficient zeal, which led to "general" fears exacerbated by perceptions of his influence.

The Albany committee ordered Van Schaack to appear before it in January 1777. At that meeting, he refused to take an "Oath of Allegiance directed by the said Committee to be taken by those who Consider themselves Subjects of the State of New York." In addition to his wider concerns about oaths, he found this one legally absurd. The State of New York, the polity that the oath required the taker to subject himself to, did not formally come into being until the adoption of the first state constitution in April 1777, so Peter was being required to swear loyalty to a state that did not yet legally exist and whose constitution was undefined.[39] Van Schaack refused the oath, and the committee ordered him to leave New York within ten days and to reside in Massachusetts or face imprisonment.

He appealed this banishment in a carefully argued letter to the then sitting New York Convention, in the process of drafting a new constitution for the state, which he pointedly called "the representatives of a free people" and whose ranks included some longtime friends and collaborators in resistance—John Jay among them.[40] It was a learned and carefully aimed appeal, one that drew both on his expertise in New York law and on principles that patriot insurgents claimed as their own justifications for rebellion and independence. Van Schaack also retained the support of many Kinderhookers, ninety-eight of whom signed a petition to the convention asking that Van Schaack and two other banished men be allowed to return home.

Lines of authority and rules for procedure were not clear amid the revolutionary ferment. Van Schaack's petition resulted in the New York Convention passing an order granting him a hearing in person, but by the time Van Schaack was informed of this, he had already left for Massachusetts in accordance with the orders of the Albany County Committee. Van Schaack traveled as required to Boston, and after some uncertainty and debate among patriots there about what to do with him, he was sent to the town of Leominster. He remained there for several months, telling Elizabeth, still in Kinderhook, that "we have been treated here with a civility and hospitality that are very flattering to us." Van Schaack also suggested a contrast between Massachusetts and New York, adding that "we see here nothing but candor and humanity, and no man here is punished, as far as I can find out, who has committed no crime."[41] Finally learning through Elizabeth that the New York Convention had granted him a hearing, Van Schaack returned and appeared before it in Kingston on April 4, 1777. Perhaps Van Schaack envisioned impressing the delegates with a learned defense, but the day proved a damp squib. Rather than allow Van Schaack to present his case, the Convention ordered in deflating officialese that because "many important affairs highly interesting to the public, at present so engross the attention of this house," it did not have time to consider Van Schaack's appeal. Instead, the convention simply ordered him to return under parole to his "usual place of abode" in Kinderhook. In the meantime, he was "neither to do or say any thing to the prejudice of the American cause." Following this, he was able to live in quiet seclusion in Kinderhook for more than a year.[42]

In the wake of these developments, Van Schaack wrote another of his characteristic reflections in August 1777 on what could and could not be demanded of people living through civil war. Beginning with a quotation from Horace's *Epistles* translated as "I am not bound to swear an oath to any master," Van Schaack observed that "civil wars arise from a difference of opinion between members of the same political community, respecting the extent of the reciprocal rights and duties of the sovereign power, and its subjects." People had to make private judgments about whether to participate, and while these could be mistaken, people of honor and goodwill could be on both sides of such a conflict. As Van Schaack wrote, "we may think our opponents wrong, and be justifiable in thinking them so, but it is uncharitable to charge them with want of principle for their difference in opinion from us." On the basis of this understanding of the inherent moral complexity of a civil war, Van Schaack argued that the two sides had somewhat different rights to restrain the actions of individuals, with the existing government entitled to go farther than the purely "voluntary association" of those insurgents who rebelled against it. Yet neither side had the right to punish people solely for their opinions, because only God could fully judge motives.[43] Van Schaack seems to have put considerable store in these reflections, revisiting them in the ensuing years to annotate them in the margins with relevant Latin and English quotations. Thinkers such as Erasmus, Alexander Pope, and Lord Bolingbroke, his notes suggest, all reinforced Van Schaack's continuing belief in his arguments.

In the summer and fall of 1777 northern New York became the key theater in the war, and the events that unfolded around Van Schaack as he articulated his thoughts on civil war affected the Revolution as a whole. Now controlling

New York City and Long Island, the British plan that developed in the winter of 1776/77 called for the large number of royal troops amassed in North America to go on the offensive during the campaign season of 1777. It was decided in London, principally by Lord George Germain and General John Burgoyne, to launch a multipronged attack that would converge on Albany, cut New England off from the other colonies, and thereby end the rebellion.

The strongest force, under Burgoyne himself, was to move south from Quebec down Lake Champlain, while a second attack was to move eastward from Lake Ontario through the Mohawk Valley. Troops from New York City were to move north along the Hudson River, a path that would have taken them through Kinderhook. Burgoyne's column began moving south in June 1777 and had several initial successes, including the easy recapture of Fort Ticonderoga. As the summer wore on, however, the British plan began to unravel. In August 1777, the contingent from Lake Ontario was stopped when it failed to capture Fort Stanwix. The movement northward from New York City proved even more problematic because British leaders disagreed about priorities. Howe, commanding in New York, preferred to attack Philadelphia, so the coordinated advance up the Hudson envisioned by Burgoyne and Germain did not occur in the summer of 1777. As Burgoyne's main army moved south, its supply lines became dangerously stretched and subject to attacks by militiamen arriving from New England. Burgoyne's provisions began running low, and a growing patriot army entrenched itself near the modern town of Saratoga—about forty miles up the Hudson from Kinderhook—in order to block any further advance to Albany. A force under General Henry Clinton was finally dispatched from New York City to Burgoyne's aid in early October, but it proved too late.

The end to Britain's offensive came through two battles fought on the same ground. In the First Battle of Saratoga, fought on September 19, 1777, the British won a narrow tactical victory, but the rebels prevented Burgoyne's army from flanking their position and continuing its advance. As it became clear that relief from New York City would not arrive in time, Burgoyne's supply problems forced him to either begin a long retreat north or try to force a way past the American army blocking his way south. He opted to attack on October 7, 1777, beginning the decisive Second Battle of Saratoga. In the first day of fighting, the British were unable to break through and retreated to fortified positions. Over the next week the colonial army, continually reinforced by arriving militia, encircled the British, and Burgoyne surrendered his entire army on October 17, 1777.

156   "SOME MIDDLE WAY SHOULD BE FOUND OUT"

These events ratcheted up the pressure on the residents of upstate New York: nobodyist, loyalist, and patriot alike. Notably, Van Schaack neither took up arms nor otherwise acted to support the British during their offensive into northern New York. In fact, as Burgoyne advanced southward, Van Schaack's family took in a patriot refugee: Hester Gansevoort, the wife of one of Albany's leading militant patriots and Peter's former law clerk, Leonard Gansevoort.[44] Hester was a Cuyler by birth and therefore a somewhat distant relative of Elizabeth Van Schaack and her Cruger kin. Like other refugees, Hester fled from Albany as the British advanced, and the Van Schaacks sheltered her, another indication that prewar bonds of interdependence remained powerful in people's decision-making.

Burgoyne's surrender shocked British partisans and gave the rebels a new hope. It also led some waverers to more firmly support Congress and independence. Nevertheless, having not aided Burgoyne, Van Schaack maintained his strict neutrality in the ensuing months. He did so even as patriot friends like John Jay wrongly predicted that their remarkable provincial victory might lead to a quick end to the war. Van Schaack himself may have thought that the patriot star was now ascendant. According to family history, he is said to have told the man who brought him the news of Burgoyone's surrender, "if this be true, I pronounce you an independent nation."[45] That distancing "you"—rather than an adhering "us"—was likely the sort of comment to give his militantly patriot friends and neighbors pause.

The terms of Burgoyne's capitulation required his army to march into captivity in Massachusetts, and its route went through Kinderhook. Several thousand prisoners of war camped for several days in the village. On their arrival, Burgoyne, some of his officers, and their American escort dined at the house of David Van Schaack. Peter, and probably Elizabeth, met the gathered soldiers there that evening. Burgoyne would later state that the hospitality the Van Schaacks showed this day was "evidence of loyalty" that "gave great jealousy & umbrage" to the patriot soldiers guarding them. Yet, what this gentlemanly provision of hospitality to men on both sides meant was largely in the eye of the beholder. Burgoyne later claimed David Van Schaack was "very respectable, & marked with the strongest attachment to the King's cause" but described Peter—rather more circumspectly—as "affluent & happy."[46]

One of the many ironies of Van Schaack's revolution is that after weathering the time of maximum military danger for northern New York, his own situation became much worse when the center of the armed struggle shifted elsewhere.[47] In March 1778, Elizabeth Van Schaack, long unwell, became dangerously ill. She likely suffered from tuberculosis. Her serious decline began in August 1776 with a "dreadful vomiting of blood, which produced a weakness in the lungs," and Peter observed that in the early spring of 1778 she experienced "violent cough, slow fever, and other consumptive symptoms."[48] A letter to a friend suggests Elizabeth was increasingly despondent over the toll the war had taken on her family. "How suddenly were my hopes blasted! Deprived at one stroke of almost every earthly comfort! My church! My friends! My children! My native place and little family!"[49] As her condition worsened, Elizabeth wanted to return to British-occupied New York City in the hope that a change of environment and access to doctors and medicine there would restore her health.

In this period, an achingly painful one for the family, Van Schaack wrote several letters to New York's new patriot governor, George Clinton, and Clinton's newly appointed secretary, John Jay. These letters asked Clinton to permit Elizabeth, to be accompanied at her request by Peter, to pass between the armies and return to New York City. While Clinton and Jay's replies were courteous and even friendly, the Van Schaacks' requests were denied. Patriot leaders also refused to allow a well-regarded doctor who was part of Burgoyne's army to come to Kinderhook and treat her.[50] Officially, Clinton and Jay's position was that they could not consistent with their public duty permit any intercourse with the enemy, but it may be that the Van Schaacks' family connections and prominence made it harder for patriot leaders to grant their request.

Unable to stop the course of her disease, Elizabeth Cruger Van Schaack died in Kinderhook in April 1778. According to Peter, on her deathbed Elizabeth "wished me to convince" John Jay that "she harbored no resentment for the refusal of her request" to return to New York City. When asked whether she also forgave the patriot committee that prevented a British army doctor from seeing her, Elizabeth said "Yes, she forgave them and every body." Peter preserved this story as a signal example of Elizabeth's Christian charity.[51] Elizabeth's death was noted in James Rivington's *New York Gazette*, which deemed her "a Lady greatly esteemed and respected by all who had the Pleasure of her Acquaintance."[52] She was only thirty years old. While her personal political views beyond her wishes for peace remain unknowable, she was a casualty of the conflict.

In the wake of Elizabeth's death, Peter continued aspiring to complete neutrality, but maintaining such a position became harder. At some point while trying to live quietly in Kinderhook, probably in the first half of 1778, Van Schaack was subjected to a court-martial for refusing to bear arms as part of the

New York militia.[53] His deteriorating vision also made him increasingly fearful of becoming totally blind. In June 1778, amid this grief, concern for his own health, and continuing political pressure, Peter requested and received permission from Governor Clinton to travel to England to obtain treatment for his worsening vision when military conditions allowed.

Despite this development, in July 1778, Peter, still in Kinderhook, was summoned to Albany to appear before the state's new "Commissioners for Detecting and Defeating Conspiracies," one of whom was his old friend Jay. They instructed Peter to take a new oath to the State of New York stipulated by the Banishment Act, a recently passed law written to ferret out "all persons of neutral and equivocal characters who have influence sufficient to do mischief." Van Schaack's son would later observe that the act was not applied to him out of maliciousness on the part of the committee members, several of whom knew and liked Peter, but because it was not thought proper to exempt him from the law when he clearly fell within its letter.[54]

Peter refused this oath, and, in accordance with the law and the treatment of others who refused it, he was held in anticipation of being sent behind British lines and banished from New York State. According to the law, his exile would be permanent. The property of banished persons was to be subject to "double taxation," and if he returned to New York, Van Schaack could be charged with treason and thereby subject to execution. Van Schaack saw his banishment as extraordinarily harsh, the law that mandated it as unjust, and the proceedings of the board that imposed it as illegal even under the terms of New York's new state constitution.[55] In a painful twist of fate, Leonard Gansevoort, whose wife the Van Schaacks had sheltered during Burgoyne's advance, signed the letter notifying Peter of his banishment. Peter is said to have told him, "Leonard! You have signed my death-warrant; but I appreciate your motives."[56] On August 15, 1778, Peter departed Kinderhook for British-held New York City. He left his three young children—two sons and a daughter—behind in his family's care. His children, he noted with melancholy to his sympathetic patriot friend Theodore Sedgwick, had already seen their mother die and would now be deprived of their father's presence "not indeed for his crimes, nor even indiscretion, but because he dares *think* for himself."[57]

Van Schaack insisted that he had done nothing to oppose the rebellion, and "whatever the policy may be of banishing me from my native country, I dare confidently say that my political principles are not incompatible, either with the just rights of government, or the liberties of a free people." Peter told Jay that if he read Montesquieu, Beccaria, and Locke "with the same temper you used [to]," he would find that Britain was not the only side that had "trampled upon the rights of mankind" in the ongoing conflict.[58] Both Jay and Clinton wrote him supportive letters after the committee ordered his banishment. At a last-minute meeting in Poughkeepsie held as Van Schaack traveled to New York City, Clinton claimed that Peter should not have been compelled to appear before the committee in the first place because "his conduct had been different from that which was the object of the act; that his character was not equivocal, or suspicious, but well understood." At this meeting Clinton, in a tactic seemingly intended as either a last-gasp attempt to exempt Van Schaack from the Banishment Act or to facilitate his eventual return, issued Van Schaack a letter stating that he gave him permission to travel to England "on account of a cataract in one of his eyes, and for the purpose of having an operation performed upon it by an oculist." Nevertheless, Van Schaack's banishment was now deemed officially enacted, and he was escorted across British lines.[59] Van Schaack stayed for a few months in New York City, leaving for London aboard the ship *Rachel* with a large convoy in mid-October. He arrived in December 1778 after a frightening passage in which his ship was nearly sunk in a gale and stopped at Cork for emergency repairs.[60] He remained in England for the next six years.

Van Schaack's transatlantic voyage transformed his experience of the remainder of the Revolution. Arriving in England made behaving as a neutral simpler in some ways. Britain was a country at war in the colonies but at peace in the metropole, a dynamic that helped the conflict last as long as it did. Few people in England worried much about the nuanced intricacies of Van Schaack's personal politics after his arrival. Van Schaack was not subjected to any oaths or called upon to perform military or political service, but his exile also created new dilemmas. He did not abandon his carefully worked-out principles, but being neutral in England was different because compliance and interacting with the British government might be read as supporting its actions in North America. Like many other nobodyists who, through choice or coercion, emigrated from areas of revolutionary conflict, Van Schaack was quite powerless in Britain. In New York, he had received a great deal of attention from patriot authorities because people cared about what he said, did, and thought. In exile he was just one more refugee.

Despite Elizabeth's death, Peter remained on close terms with the Crugers. He visited Henry Junior and Senior in Bristol immediately following his arrival in England, but then settled in London. Freed from having his movements monitored, he looked at art, attended the theater, observed the courts, and often listened to parliamentary debates. Van Schaack also traveled, seeing Bath, Oxford, Stonehenge, Salisbury Cathedral, and many other sites. Van Schaack, like other exiles, visited the studios of Benjamin West in London's Newman Street, viewing "a great variety of exquisite paintings, and sketches of that eminent artist." In the company of Henry Cruger Jr., he saw Stourhead, the estate of the immensely rich banker Henry "the Magnificent" Hoare, and observed that "the most luxurious description would fall short of the beautiful scenes this place affords."[61] For a provincial, seeing England for the first time was a heady experience, even given the catastrophes that spawned his travel.

Van Schaack's vision continued to trouble him in exile. He consulted with several of London's most celebrated doctors, including the surgeon John Hunter and the "royal oculist," Baron Michael de Wenzel. Van Schaack considered undergoing the latter's pioneering but risky cataract procedure before ultimately opting against it.[62] Van Schaack also worried incessantly over his children, who lived with his mother, sister Jane, and her patriot husband, Peter Silvester, in Kinderhook. "The dear little pledges I have left behind," Van Schaack told his father-in-law in 1779, "continuously haunt my imagination, and urge my return."[63] He monitored their education under a tutor and wrote many letters to his eldest son, Henry Cruger Van Schaack. Harry, as Peter called him, was twelve years old when Peter left New York, and he grew from a boy into a young man during his father's six years in exile. Besides experiencing adolescence and going to school amid the tumults of the Revolution, Harry helped raise his younger siblings in their father's absence.

Peter's long letters to Harry offered guidance, suggestions for reading, and good wishes. Feelings of powerlessness are a hallmark of exile, and a painful desperation underpins Peter's correspondence with his son: a desire to try and do something—even if it was just sending long didactic letters—to remain an influence in his children's lives. His children's welfare, Peter told Harry in 1779, was "now the great, almost the only view I have in the world."[64] Later in his exile, Van Schaack also took a close interest in his nephew and ward, Henry Walton, who was in school in England after the deaths of his parents.

Another challenge that exiles faced, regardless of their politics, was how to support themselves as strangers in new communities. Van Schaack was much less wealthy than his Cruger in-laws and arrived in England without a way to meet future living expenses. In his biography of his late father, Van Schaack's son claimed that Peter "never made any application to the British government for renumeration for his own losses and sufferings in the American war."[65] This was not the whole story. Van Schaack applied for "temporary support" from the British government—that is, an annual grant to give him an income—by June 1779, within about six months of his arriving in exile. He filed other documents with the British government in ensuing years in pursuit of financial aid.[66]

Peter's initial petition said he was "not only deprived of the Exercise of his Profession, but at various Times abridged of his personal Liberty and subjected to Fines and Penalties for not taking up Arms against his Majesty." He had then been banished from his home, he related, for "having refused to comply with the Terms of a Provincial Law, in taking the Oath of Allegiance to the Congress and abjuring his Fealty to his Majesty." He had since traveled to England "by Reason of a very serious Complaint, which made it necessary for him to take the Opinions of Physicians of the greatest Eminence."[67] It was a characteristically precise document. It spelled out what happened to Van Schaack at the hands of New York's patriot committees, but he also made no false claims that he had done anything to actively support royal authority or the British army. It also, however, could create the impression that Van Schaack's suffering was due to a straightforward commitment to the king's cause, and it neither detailed the grounds on which he had refused oaths, mentioned his role in prewar resistance, nor discussed the many dealings he had with patriot militants. In some of those interactions, Van Schaack had implicitly acknowledged the legitimacy of some of the nascent New York government's actions and railed against the very readings of political preferences into his silences that his deliberately oversimplified petition now seemed to encourage.

Van Schaack's 1779 petition for financial support also contained the revealing detail that in late 1778, when he was briefly in British-controlled New York City prior to embarking for England, he "waited on his Majesty's Commissioners in the Beginning of September and stated the Hardship of his Situation."[68] These were the members of the Carlisle Peace Commission, a diplomatic effort to negotiate with the Continental Congress launched by the North administration in the aftermath of Burgoyne's surrender.[69] Van Schaack's affinity for the Carlisle Commission's reconciliationist aims probably explains why its members—the members of Parliament William Eden and George Johnstone and Lord Carlisle—found him a sympathetic figure. Peter evidently solicited support from Eden and Johnstone, back in London after their mission's failure, for his 1779 request for financial assistance. In July 1779, Van Schaack told Henry

Cruger Sr. that Eden's "Friendship exceeds my warmest Expectations."[70] Van Schaack heard nothing, positive or negative, from the Treasury for several months. When he asked Eden in September 1779 for assistance in gaining any sort of response from the Treasury, Eden forwarded it but only added a jot observing, "I am sorry for the poor gentleman."[71] Johnstone was more effusive, endorsing Van Schaack's initial petition and later writing a longer letter to Lord George Germain, the powerful secretary of state, praising Van Schaack as "a man of Singular Genius & great Worth & Modesty, labouring under Misfortunes."[72] Johnstone's letter also suggests that he lobbied for Van Schaack behind the scenes.

Van Schaack's request languished for nearly two years before being considered by Treasury officials for the first time in May 1781. After finally reading Van Schaack's file, they granted him an annual stipend of £100, made retroactive to January 1780.[73] Peter, however, was not notified of this decision and so remained trapped in a bureaucratic no-man's-land. He may also have pursued his claim less aggressively thanks to a financial lifeline. When Henry Cruger Sr. died in Bristol in 1780, he left his descendants, including Peter's children, substantial property. Peter cooperated with his Cruger brothers-in-law to secure and distribute this family wealth amid the transatlantic tumults. Peter subsequently reported to officials that he supported himself in England "by the interest of some money of which he is a trustee," that is, by managing his children's inheritances.[74]

Still unaware of his previous award, in late 1782 Van Schaack secured an in-person hearing with the two men now responsible for refugees' petitions, the members of Parliament John Wilmot and Daniel Parker Coke. Both had opposed the North administration, and now, under the new government of the pro-peace Lord Shelburne, they were plowing through a backlog of cases. While sympathetic to Americans' sufferings, Wilmot and Coke were operating in a new reality. As Peter knew all too well, British aid had been distributed in an ad hoc and inconsistent fashion since 1775. Now, however, the war's end was in the offing. As they addressed outstanding claims for short-term relief like Peter's, Wilmot, Coke, and others knew that whatever they did could set precedents for future and potentially massive loyalist claims for lost property.[75] Civil war had ruined many. Wilmot and Coke were operating in a moment when who deserved what and why was becoming an issue in the spotlight.

When Peter finally appeared before the commissioners, he learned that he had previously been granted a stipend for which the Treasury now owed him £300 in arrears. Yet, Wilmot and Coke also posed some uncomfortable questions.

While their exact queries are not preserved, Peter's subsequent correspondence suggests they asked about his precise loyalties and whether his prewar wealth really entitled him to the £100 annual stipend he had been granted. Van Schaack subsequently wrote the pair a defensive letter stating that "after saying so much of myself, as in answer to your Questions I did, it became a Point of Honor with me to substantiate what I had alledged."[76] To support his testimony he solicited and forwarded new letters of recommendation from New York's former governor, William Tryon, and from General John Burgoyne and British officers who had served under him in the Saratoga campaign.[77]

All of these letter writers sympathized with Van Schaack, but none could document any active loyalism on his part. Tryon, for example, went so far as to assert that "I have been well informed" that Van Schaack had been "uniformly steady in his Loyalty & Attachment to His Majesty and His Government" and suffered for it, but offered no specific examples of Van Schaack doing anything on behalf of the king's cause.[78] Moreover, Peter truthfully told the commissioners that he hoped to return to New York when able. Wilmot and Coke, having piqued Peter's sense of honor, also reduced his future stipend to £60 per year.[79] Van Schaack's experience was not unique; Wilmot and Coke managed to work through the backlog in claims for emergency relief while reducing the Treasury's total commitments by one-third.[80]

Van Schaack's views on the conflict also changed as he observed British politics up close. North's ministry and other British leaders, he thought, had come to recognize that America was lost but continued waging terrible, increasingly pointless war anyway. He regarded their position as abhorrent and considered his own duties in light of this assessment. As he wrote from London in January 1780, "I do not think an American bound to promote the views of Great Britain, when they are directed only to weaken, to cripple America, and not to recover her; or when that recovery is only hoped for, from the ruin and destruction, by conflagration, pestilence and famine, of America."[81] These observations led Van Schaack, claiming to maintain his Lockean principles, to conclude that the social contract that had previously prevented him from actively supporting the rebellion was broken after all. "Under these circumstances," he wrote, "I find my mind totally absolved from all ideas of duty" to Britain. He now considered himself "a citizen of the world, and to my native country am I determined to return, as the country of all others the dearest to me."[82] He continued to rue the conflict's costs. "A civil war," he reminded his brother Henry Van Schaack in 1783, "is an epitome of all human wretchedness."[83]

Tellingly, as the war's end neared, Van Schaack also articulated his distinctiveness from the growing loyalist community in England. Van Schaack had ties to many militant loyalist refugees—and used his legal training to help some of them obtain British financial aid—but he did not include himself among them. In 1782 he wrote his brother Henry Van Schaack, still in New York, with the welcome news that Shelburne's ministry was prepared to recognize American independence to obtain peace. "The United States," he told his brother, "are now independent, and from the bottom of my heart I rejoice at it; but this joy you will easily suppose is not unmingled with distress." He felt for "the sufferings of the unhappy loyalists," who were "unfortunate men" in "pursuit of a vain shadow" because "they have been contending for a government which had no existence, and have sacrificed their lives and fortunes to an object merely ideal."[84] The loyalists were to be pitied, but Van Schaack saw his own situation as distinct from theirs because of fundamentally different past choices.

Given his rocky revolution, as peace dawned Van Schaack made the deliberate choice to focus on the future. "I dread," he wrote in the summer of 1783, "any discussions that have a retrospect to the past. Oblivion is what I wish."[85] Crucially for his prospects, Van Schaack did nothing in exile to make himself odious to New York's new leaders. John Jay, in particular, remained a friend to Van Schaack and facilitated his return to America. Jay arrived in Paris in 1782, one of the five Americans appointed peace negotiators after Yorktown. Van Schaack wrote Jay a tentative letter in August 1782 asking whether they might renew their old friendship in some fashion, and Jay sent a warm and magnanimous reply.[86] Van Schaack used this opening to carefully and tactfully raise the possibility of a return to New York and to apprise Jay of where he now stood. He wrote Jay in August 1783 that "I freely declare to you what I profess in all companies, that I consider myself a citizen of the United States, *de jure* at least, whether I become so *de facto* or not. In this I feel no sense of humiliation, and I conceive I am warranted in the declaration by established principles, and a perfect consistency of character. I would not obtain my most favorite object by a dishonorable concession, but I will not be restrained by false shame, or mean pride, from avowing my principles and opinions."[87]

When diplomats signed the Treaty of Paris in September 1783, Van Schaack welcomed it. Many loyalists were furious over the lack of detailed protections for them in the agreement and understandably fearful for the future. Van Schaack's response, however, was fittingly different, and he was in no mood to quibble. He thought "it is sufficient that it *is* peace."[88] Peter had paid an extraordinarily heavy price for refusing to personally take up arms to establish the United States, but he regarded it as *his* country. The question for Van Schaack in the coming years was not whether he would accept the new republic's legitimacy, but whether the United States would accept him.

7. The Search for Peace

When the fighting started in Massachusetts, Henry Cruger Jr. believed that Parliament's cruel and misguided drive to humble the colonies had produced disaster. As he told Peter Van Schaack in June 1775, he had "talked, and reasoned and prayed—prophesied, deprecated, and rued; but all to no purpose." Yet "I shall remain," he insisted, "to my dying day, America's fast and unalterable friend."[1] When the war began, Cruger was an independent-minded member of Parliament whose primary loyalties to Bristol, New York, trade, and Wilkesite patriotism were clear and consistent. He was also an established opponent of the ministry's American policies, but his ties with some patriots had been strained by the New York assembly's failed petitioning effort. Believing civil war disastrous for both sides, after fighting began Henry remained dedicated above all to ending the military conflict.

Because finding a speedy route out of the war was Cruger's focus, between 1775 and 1783 he associated with people holding a variety of political opinions and engaged in activities not easily categorizable as either patriot or loyalist. While he had long supported the causes of trade and liberty and was invested in the constitutional, economic, and other structures that might follow an end to the armed conflict, his nobodyism rested on a belief that any practicable postwar arrangements were better than continued fighting. Therefore he was consistently willing to support any proposal that might lead to a ceasefire. Cruger may or may not have been correct in his political assessments. Nor was he a consistent exemplar of virtue. But partly because his political career entailed a revealing series of choices as the war unfolded, his experiences capture

THE SEARCH FOR PEACE

some of the little-understood principles, dilemmas, and compromises that were integral to the transatlantic history of a "peace first" nobodyism.

In the first year of the war, Henry, his father, and like-minded others in England hoped to get both sides to pull back from hostilities before the situation became irredeemable. Henry Sr. arrived in Bristol from New York City in June 1775.[2] By some accounts, he went to England because of his failing health—and he was unwell in the coming years—but this alone seems an insufficient explanation.[3] He may have feared what would happen if he stayed in New York; perhaps he wanted to help effect reconciliation. Henry Jr. was relieved that his father joined him in England as the turmoil in America intensified. Expressing the emotional bonds that underlay the Crugers' family life, he told Peter Van Schaack that his father's presence in Bristol would "yield me infinite happiness" and that he would do "every thing that a son can or ought to do, to make a father comfortable."[4] As with other New Yorkers, a combination of factors probably informed Henry Sr.'s decision to leave the city.

Initially, the English-resident Crugers' hopes for peace, like John Harris's in New York, centered on the Second Continental Congress's Olive Branch Petition. In late August 1775, Henry Sr. met Edmund Burke for the first time, and the Olive Branch Petition was Cruger's focus. Given the recent turmoil in New York, the exchange underlined that the Crugers' real commitment was to peace by whatever means possible rather than doctrinaire opposition to congress. In response to Cruger's questioning, Burke acknowledged that he, like other colonial agents, had received congress's petition, but demurred that he had not presented it because without explicit instructions from the now moribund New York General Assembly, he "thought himself not authorized to do so." The elder Cruger told Burke, however, "that I conceived it the duty of all Colony agents to Deliver the petition and that in so interesting an affair to America all punctillioes sh[oul]d be waived." Although Henry Sr. evidently did not yet know it, hopes for the Olive Branch Petition were collapsing. The king, consulting with the Privy Council, refused to receive congress's petition and instead, on August 23, proclaimed some colonists to be "in open and avowed Rebellion" and called for the loyal to aid in suppressing "all traitorous Conspiracies."[5] These developments meant that the Crown was now openly at war with its own subjects when, in October 1775, Parliament reconvened for the first time since hostilities began.

Despite the king's bellicose language, some, including the Crugers, hoped that transatlantic negotiations might remain possible. Rumors swirled that the administration was considering sending some sort of delegation to North America.[6] Pro-Americans distrusted North's government, but the ministry's secure parliamentary majority meant that only it actually had the power to end the fighting quickly. This was the context in which Henry Cruger Sr. had a personal meeting with North "at his house in Downing Street" brokered by the member of Parliament Sir William Meredith on November 3, 1775. In reply to hopeful, leading questioning from North, Cruger reported bluntly that the government should not expect New Yorkers to welcome any British troops sent to their city, instead warning presciently that inhabitants "intended to set fire to the town to prevent the Soldiers having the use of the houses" and that regulars "would meet with opposition on Landing."

Henry Sr. was also cautious in handling what seems to have been the main reason for the meeting. Meredith, Cruger recorded, then asked "what I thought of the American Gentlemen now in London going over to Endeavor to settle matters." Whether Meredith or North had the Crugers or any other "American Gentleman" specifically in mind as possible emissaries is unclear, but instead the elder Cruger advocated sending disinterested but respected Britons, "Gentlemen of Dignified Characters that had no Connection in that Country" who had not "distinguished themselves for their warmth against the Colonies." Cruger also told North he "most heartily wished" a delegation would be sent, "as I Verily believed it would be opening a door for a Reconciliation." North was characteristically noncommittal. Tellingly, Cruger told North that the Olive Branch Petition was "Conceived in very decent humiliating terms" and "much more moderate than the productions of the first Gen[era]l Congress." It indicated, Cruger thought, "a wish for a negotiation on the important subject of American Disputes." North had already rejected the Olive Branch Petition, however, and had no intention of revisiting it. The meeting broke up with North asking deflective questions about prominent New Yorkers rather than discussing the congressional overture.[7]

To the distress of reconciliationists, the cabinet soon threatened expanded war. On November 20, North introduced new legislation, the Prohibitory Act, that outlawed "all manner of trade and commerce" in the colonies. Extending the more specifically targeted prewar Restraining Acts, the Prohibitory Act made normal maritime commerce in all thirteen colonies illegal under British law. It made all colonial shipping—save that specifically licensed by military authorities to supply British troops or "the inhabitants of any town or place garrisoned or possessed by any of his Majesty's troops"—subject to capture by the Royal

Navy and forfeiture as a lawful prize. Any sailors on board captured colonial vessels were explicitly subjected to impressment. Together, these provisions amounted to a blockade of the thirteen colonies' trade and made clear that Britain was prepared to treat its erstwhile American subjects as foreign enemies.

The Prohibitory Act's penultimate clause, and it alone, offered a reference to reconciliation through sending delegates to America. It stipulated that to encourage "all well-affected persons" to aid the Crown and to "afford a speedy protection" to those who would "return to their duty," the king could appoint people with the authority "to grant a pardon or pardons" to individuals. These appointees could also proclaim "any colony or province" or "any county, town port, district or place" to be "at the peace of his Majesty," which would allow normal trade to resume. The Prohibitory Act, coming on the heels of the rejection of the Olive Branch Petition, revealed the government's position that the road to peace lay through colonial submission rather than negotiation.[8]

The Prohibitory Act became law in late December 1775, with its provisions phased in by March 1776. Henry Cruger was silent in Parliament on the measure, but it struck the Crugers and other nobodyists in multiple ways. The law divided the population of a vast expanse of territory from modern Maine to Georgia into two and only two categories: the great bulk of the population, which was now by default deemed outside the empire and the king's protection, and a very small subset of the population formally recognized by officials as being constantly loyal or repentant. The law required people to prove their allegiance to the Crown rather than assuming it to be widespread, and equated loyalty with actively aiding the British war effort. Contrary to prewar efforts to distinguish disloyal colonies from loyal ones, the Prohibitory Act operated on the presumption of wholesale rebelliousness. New York and Massachusetts were now in the same boat, and it lay under the Royal Navy's guns.

The Prohibitory Act also hurt the Crugers' trade. One of Henry and John Cruger's ships, the *George*, was captured by a Royal Navy cruiser in February 1776 and subsequently condemned as a prize in a Caribbean vice-admiralty court. The family long blamed the Prohibitory Act for it.[9] The act strangled Henry Cruger Jr.'s business by ending traditional commerce between Bristol and British America and making collecting debts harder. In March 1776, the New York merchant Peter Curtenius told Cruger that he would be sending him no more remittances because all trade and communication had been halted "by the Pirate Act which your bloody King and Parliament have lately made."[10] For colonials across the political spectrum, the Prohibitory Act signaled that the British government would no longer countenance a "loyal opposition" in America and made dissenting from congress's growing war effort harder.

John Adams gave the most trenchant assessment of the Prohibitory Act. News of the law reached the colonies in February 1776. Adams, already personally committed to independence and strategizing about how to get others in the congress on board, saw in the law an opportunity. In March, Adams told Horatio Gates, that while some might call it "the prohibitory Act, or piratical Act, or plundering Act," he thought the best name for it was "the Act of Independency" because through it the king and Parliament "united in Sundering this Country and that I think forever." It was, he said, "a compleat Dismemberment of the British Empire" that "throws thirteen Colonies out of the Royal Protection, levels all Distinctions and makes us independent in Spight of all our supplications and Entreaties." Mindful of still-divided colonial opinion, he noted that "it may be fortunate that the Act of Independency should come from the British Parliament, rather than the American Congress."[11] The law's measures, Adams thought, were so onerous, far-reaching, and hostile that they made making the case for total separation easier.

On February 20, 1776, on the cusp of the Prohibitory Act coming into effect, the parliamentary opposition again challenged North's American policy. Charles Fox called for an inquiry to understand who was responsible for "all the disgraces the British arms had suffered" in the American conflict. Framed to appeal to members who were "unconnected with the ministry, and at the same time wished success [in] the American war," the proposed inquiry aimed to peel away government votes by attacking North without openly supporting the rebels.[12] In response to Fox's motion, Henry Cruger delivered an extended speech that illustrated the increasing precariousness of his position.

Cruger offered a stridently antigovernment reading of recent history but also revealed the emerging transatlantic gulf over reconciliation as a goal. Cruger's speech was dominated by sympathy for the Americans, who held their liberties "dearer to them than their lives," and relentless criticism of North's record as productive of "miscarriages and evils." Running through it was also a claim that the ministry had repeatedly sabotaged peace and mistreated its advocates. It was "unjust" and "impolitic," he said, "to reduce men to the miserable alternative of being branded with the epithet of cowards, or taking up arms to vindicate their injured honour and liberties." Moreover, Cruger argued, when some members had suggested exempting colonial "friends of government" from the Prohibitory Act's provisions, the "administration suddenly changed its voice" and held that now "no distinction could be made" between outright rebels and those that "preserved at best 'a shameful neutrality,'" and therefore "deserved to be subject to the common calamity of their country." When Cruger observed bitterly that "this was the liberal reward bestowed on men who espoused their cause from principle," and in the face of threats to their "fortunes, families, and lives," it was obvious that his grievances were personal.

This was made even clearer when Cruger took the emotional and impolitic decision to explicitly address New York. "I cannot forbear saying," he continued, that "the friends of peace and good order in the province of New-York, did not deserve to be reproached with a shameful neutrality." New Yorkers had "in a dutiful manner" submitted "their grievances to the clemency of this House, and the justice of their sovereign." Yet "their zealous advances to a reconciliation were rejected" with contempt. Those who now complained of New Yorkers' "ignominious neutrality" should remember that North's government "neglected to aid them with a force sufficient to maintain their opposition against the zealots in their own province" and preserve "order, and the freedom and impartiality of public proceedings." This, Cruger said, had exposed New York to "incursions" from outsiders, forced many into exile, and left more waiting for the "vigorous protection of Great Britain." North's mismanagement, Cruger argued, had crippled New York moderates and its democratic traditions. Cruger held, however, that "the breach" between Britain and the colonies was "not yet irreparable." He claimed that "liberal and explicit terms of reconciliation with a full and firm security against an oppressive exercise of parliamentary taxation" would, if offered soon, "lead instantly to a settlement."[13]

Cruger's arguments suited Fox's parliamentary tactics and may have resonated with some in Britain, but they highlighted his growing distance from old patriot allies who were now moving toward independence. Subsequent newspaper accounts focused on his remarks regarding New York—the very part of his speech most likely to alienate rebellious Americans—rather than on his repeated criticism of ministerial policy more generally. The *Pennsylvania Packet*, for example, printed an account of Cruger's speech that was then republished in other colonial newspapers in the spring of 1776. It observed that "Cruger called the attention of the house particularly to the conduct of the administration respecting the province of New York" and asked "why that colony had been so long left neglected and unsupported, and the friends of government there given up to the resentment of their enemies, when by timely aid that province might have been secured to the interests of government, and the chain of American union broken."[14] The *Pennsylvania Packet's* report, and some of its colonial reprintings, had a telling editorial appendage: "Is it thus, traitor, thou shewest thy regard for thy native country? Had it not been for such ingrates, America had still been happy."[15] The account of Cruger's speech presented in Philadelphia was not a whole-cloth fabrication, but it offered a partial and reductive reading that stripped his arguments of their main thrust—their sympathy for the colonies and hopes for an end to the war—in a way that reflected reconciliationists' increasing isolation.[16]

The growing divide was widened by other political and military developments. On March 23 congress approved a new measure authorizing American privateers to operate against all British shipping in a tit-for-tat reply to the Prohibitory Act. When independence was first mooted in congress on May 15—less than a month after Cruger's speech on Fox's motion—three primary charges were brought against the king: the Prohibitory Act, his refusal to answer American petitions, and the decision to employ German "mercenaries."[17] Moreover, when North's much delayed peace commissioners were finally named, the constrained powers that the Prohibitory Act provided were entrusted to military men, General Sir William Howe and Admiral Richard Howe, who also led the expeditionary force sent to America in the summer of 1776.[18] While the Howes were personally sympathetic toward the colonies, their joint military and diplomatic appointments never led to genuine negotiations.

For the Crugers and others who prioritized ending the fighting, the companion measure to the Prohibitory Act was the Declaration of Independence. Working from opposite ends, both shrank the space for compromise. The declaration fundamentally changed the stakes of the conflict, exploding oft-repeated patriot claims that the colonial opposition was fundamentally loyal and aimed at a return to the imperial constitution of 1763. In Britain, where skeptical hardliners had long insisted that American resistance *really* reflected a bid for independence, the declaration compelled many people to rethink where they stood. In America, the Declaration of Independence reframed the rhetoric surrounding moderation and reconciliation. After it, considering anything less than independence, regardless of its price, smacked of treason. For the Crugers and other nobodyists, it marked the start of a testing new phase of the conflict.

Whatever lofty hopes for the future the declaration inspired in some, it more immediately meant that there would be no speedy negotiated end to the war. Because the United States were now committed to permanent separation and the British government was unwilling to concede it, the declaration guaranteed many more casualties in an expanded and ideologically intensified conflict. With Britain's build-up of forces in the colonies and its seizure of New York City, it seemed to many that the quickest remaining plausible path to peace was a decisive British military victory. Alternatively, it was clear that American independence, whether desired or not, could only be achieved through a longer struggle.

These dynamics contextualize the decisions that Henry Cruger and some other nobodyists made in the declaration's wake. It has been noted that "there is some ambiguity about Cruger's political attitude" in Parliament.[19] But, his political attitudes, especially after 1776, become clearer through recognizing that he prioritized ending the war as quickly as possible over loyalty to any parliamentary faction or any specific postwar constitutional arrangements. Cruger's decisions, like those of many others, were also based on a continuing dialogue between what he viewed as the perfect, the possible, and the probable as events unfolded. In late 1776 and 1777, he likely forecast the restoration of British supremacy as more probable than the securing of American independence.

Cruger's residence in Britain rather than America and his role as member of Parliament for Bristol—part of the microdynamics of his civil war—also affected his response to the declaration. The war wrecked Bristol's economy, leading to more than five hundred bankruptcies in the city.[20] Many Bristolians sympathized with America, but they did not want to see their shipping destroyed by rebel privateers. As normal trade declined, many of the city's people, regardless of what they thought about the war's origins, were increasingly economically entangled in privateering, maritime warfare, and transatlantic military supply.[21] Cruger's core Bristol constituents remained critical of the ministry, but as the war changed, many Britons rallied to the banners of "King and Country." When news reached Bristol in October 1776 that New York had been occupied by Howe's forces, people celebrated with "great rejoicings" that included a bonfire, gun salutes, singing "God Save the King," and torturing Washington in effigy.[22] Burke later remembered this as when "the phrensy of the American war broke in upon us like a deluge" and "all men who wished for peace, or retained any sentiments of moderation, were overborne or silenced."[23]

Cruger experienced these dynamics as both a politician and a merchant. The large debts that American correspondents owed Cruger encouraged him to keep his hand in trade as best he could, and he was heir to an ethos that commerce should carry on even in wartime. The partial records that exist for Bristol's exports and imports show Cruger to have done relatively little wartime business, especially after 1776, with most trading done with a small set of destinations within the empire, including St. Christopher's, Jamaica, Tortola, Dublin, and Halifax. They also record a venture in which Cruger and Mallard dispatched a cargo of beer, salt, and wheat to British-controlled New York in February 1778, but that vessel, the *Swift*, was captured by the *Tyrranicide*, a Massachusetts privateer.[24] The complications and risks of even limited wartime business were brought home to Cruger in other ways too. In September 1778, Isaac Collins's pro-patriot *New-Jersey Gazette* published extracts from several letters sent in March and April 1778 by the firm of Cruger and Mallard to John Perry, a trader who kept a store on Little Dock Street in what was now British-controlled New York City.[25] The letters had been taken out of a Bristol ship, the hopefully named *Love and Unity*, captured at sea by a Connecticut privateer and brought into a New Jersey harbor.[26] Cruger and Mallard's letters lamented the poor state of trade, including the high costs of insurance, the recent bankruptcies of some significant British merchants, and the breakdown of credit networks. Like so many of Cruger and Mallard's correspondents, Perry was in arrears, and they urged him to quickly "close the sales of all our effects in your hands," and "remit all you can, as soon as you can."[27] Collins's *New-Jersey Gazette* published the captured correspondence to expose and embarrass the parties involved, insisting that real patriots should not do business with British New York. A brief introduction that accompanied the printed extracts labeled Cruger in strikingly oversimplified terms as "a Member of Parliament for Bristol, a MINISTERIAL Gentleman."[28] The incident emphasized how widening gulfs threatened long-standing relationships. Hobbled by their inability to collect American debts, Cruger and Mallard dissolved their partnership in June 1778, and Mallard subsequently declared bankruptcy.[29]

The complexities of loyalty for British-based pro-Americans in the aftermath of the Declaration of Independence are part of the backdrop to a correspondence that developed by the spring of 1777 between Henry Cruger and an influential government figure, Charles Jenkinson. Jenkinson, later in life made Baron Hawkesbury and then Earl of Liverpool, was a North supporter, a career ministerialist, and "a born bureaucrat, of restricted sympathies." He had spoken in 1775 against Parliament receiving the New York assembly's petitions, and multiple observers, including Burke, maintained that Jenkinson had "an influence at court and in Administration beyond that to which he was entitled by office."[30] There was significant conspiracy-mongering in some of this, but Jenkinson, like his friend and ally John Robinson, made himself indispensable to

THE SEARCH FOR PEACE   175

the king and ministry by mastering the intricacies of practical governance.[31] In December 1778, Jenkinson stepped out of the shadows and became secretary at war, serving until 1782.[32]

When and how the pair came into contact is unclear, but by May 1777 Cruger was writing Jenkinson to pass on information that he was receiving from connections in New York. In the first preserved letter, Cruger told Jenkinson that various letters recently arrived from New York seemed "to be of one accord" that the war "is not so near an end as we could wish." Much would depend, he thought, on what happened in New England, where "the poor deluded inhabitants are anxiously & seriously looking for large supplies of men & money from the French & other foreign Powers."[33] Sometime after October 1777, Cruger shared with Jenkinson a letter written by an unnamed source that detailed congress's issuances of paper money and estimated how much in total had been printed.[34] It was a technical piece of analytic intelligence suggesting that the dramatic depreciation of Continental currency would hurt congress's standing with the public. A few other letters from Cruger to Jenkinson over the ensuing years are preserved, and they suggest that there were other letters between the two that do not survive.

Cruger closed his first surviving letter to Jenkinson by thanking him for having been "peculiarly obliging to me" and with assurances of gratitude. There are no clear indications of what Jenkinson did to earn them. Perhaps Jenkinson had used his influence to do something financial or otherwise for Henry, a relation, or another ally. As discussed below, Cruger seems to have been awarded a Crown pension by 1779, although details about this are scant. Later, in 1781, Henry unsuccessfully asked Jenkinson to intercede with the king for some reward for John Harris Cruger's service at Savannah and Ninety Six.[35] While it is unclear what Jenkinson did for Cruger, it is clearer what Cruger provided: information from his correspondents on developments in New York. Given that he remained publicly opposed to North's program in Parliament, Cruger evidently did not regard sharing reports on New York with Jenkinson as the equivalent of adhering politically to the ministry.

Another example of this complexity is the deteriorating relations between Cruger and Burke. As the war dragged on, and especially following the shocking news of Burgoyne's surrender at Saratoga in mid-October 1777, some observers thought that North's ministry could be forced out of office. Politicians aspiring to government, like Burke's Rockinghamites, hoped that responsibility would soon be in their hands. For independents, however, the resulting parliamentary maneuvering for factional advantage was a distraction from the real issues. In December 1777, Wilkes moved to repeal the Declaratory Act, calling it "the fountain, from which not only waters of bitterness, but rivers of blood, have flowed" and arguing that as long as it remained in force "you never can think of any negociation with the Congress." This move, Wilkes knew, put the focus on the Rockingham ministry that had passed the Declaratory Act. Tellingly, the Rockinghamites joined pro-government members of Parliament in opposing Wilkes's discomfiting motion.[36]

Cruger, however, supported Wilkes in the debate. This was the first time he had spoken in Parliament since his personally damaging intervention on behalf of Fox's February 1776 call for a parliamentary inquiry; it was also his first speech since the Declaration of Independence. Cruger reminded his listeners that New York's 1775 petition, which had "contained the most explicit acknowledgement of the supremacy" of Parliament, had been rejected and "the pride of conquest preferred to the humanity of reconciliation." Given what had transpired, Cruger argued, repealing the Declaratory Act was now necessary because regaining "the confidence and affection which we have lost" required giving Americans "the most undeniable proofs that you wish not to oppress them." Wilkes criticized the Declaratory Act largely on principle, as an attack on English liberties writ large. Cruger argued on practical grounds. "I wa[i]ve all question of your authority and right," he told his fellow members of Parliament. "Peace ought now to be our object, and it is a sufficient reason for an immediate repeal." Cruger also claimed that "from my connections in America," he had "reason to believe that independency is not yet the great object of the majority of the people."[37] Wilkes's motion to repeal the Declaratory Act was defeated by the crushing margin of 160–10, with Cruger supporting the tiny minority alongside a handful of Britain's best-known radical members of Parliament.[38]

By the end of 1777, Britons feared France's entry into the conflict. The presence of Franklin, Silas Deane, and other American diplomats in Paris was known, and reports of French preparations for war were frequent. In response, North's government adopted a new two-track strategy aimed at creating the grounds for negotiations with America, undercutting the parliamentary opposition, and outflanking the ongoing Franco-American talks. William Eden, the key figure in developing this strategy, was, like Jenkinson, known as an effective behind-the-scenes operator, and his ministerial portfolio included managing intelligence operations.[39] Despite the governmental opposition to Wilkes's recent motion, the first part of this new strategy was to be the parliamentary repeal of the laws central to American grievances at the war's outset. The second was to be the sending of a new British commission to America with far-reaching authority to negotiate a settlement.[40]

Having secured reluctant cabinet approval for this new strategy, North introduced the government's plans in the House of Commons on February 17. One motion introduced "an act for removing all doubts and apprehensions concerning taxation by the parliament of Great Britain in any of the colonies" and specifically proposed repealing the disastrous Tea Act of 1773. A second called for creating a delegation, subsequently known as the Carlisle Commission, to be sent to America with powers to negotiate with congress and even halt British military operations. North had previously hinted about conciliatory measures, but his apparent U-turn on fundamental constitutional questions over Parliament's taxation powers and conditions surrounding negotiations stunned government and opposition supporters alike.[41] Some members of Parliament carped, but North's two measures sailed through Parliament. Cruger, alongside other opposition members, seems to have voted for them.[42] Soon after these developments, the feared news of the Franco-American treaty of alliance became public.

North's apparent newfound willingness to negotiate, coupled with expectations of imminent war with France, posed fresh conundrums for those who prioritized Anglo-American peace. In March 1778, Cruger published in Bristol Chatham's celebrated January 1775 speech urging the North administration to withdraw British troops from Boston before it was too late. In a preface, Cruger's handbill observed that had Chatham's "wisdom" been heeded "we should have been a united—a happy people," but "unfortunately for the nation, it was rejected with insolent contempt." Chatham, who had a reputation as both pro-American and resolutely anti-French, was gravely ill in March 1778, so the reprinting of his speech saluted a man that the Crugers and their allies had long admired. Chatham's "prophetic speech," Cruger's handbill observed, was being republished "not so much in accusation of the present Ministry and their deluded adherents, as in justification of the conduct of that part of the nation who have been uniform advocates of Liberty and Peace."[43] Cruger would support the government's surprising peace initiatives, but he wanted to remind Bristolians of the ministry's responsibility for the present calamities.

Cruger's signaling of affinity with Chatham in March 1778 was also significant because the parliamentary opposition was fracturing over recognizing American independence. In the debates spawned by North's conciliatory measures, Rockingham and the Duke of Richmond argued that the last, best hope for preventing war with France was recognizing American independence. From this point forward, the Rockinghamites, including Burke, held that independence should be conceded as the only way to end the war. Other opposition figures, however, including the infirm Chatham and his small coterie of followers, stopped short of this emergent Rockinghamite position while remaining hostile to the government. For example, the Earl of Shelburne, Chatham's key follower, excoriated North's record but supported the new conciliatory bills and called for better management of the war effort to try to salvage the situation. Given that this was the moment that Cruger chose to trumpet his own affinity for Chatam, Cruger was likely signaling his support for an antigovernment position that stopped short of conceding the necessity of independence. Cruger eventually supported recognizing independence, but that position only emerged clearly in 1780 and in light of subsequent military and political developments. The events of 1778 culminated on April 7—a few weeks after Cruger published Chatham's 1775 speech—when Chatham collapsed in the House of Lords after an oration criticizing Richmond and insisting that Britain should not give up America. Chatham died soon after, leaving Shelburne as the key oppositional advocate for the idea that reconciliation without independence was still an achievable goal.[44] Any very faint hopes for preventing Anglo-French war died too in the spring of 1778, and there was fighting at sea by June, with formal declarations of war coming the following month.[45]

The Carlisle Commission's efforts at peace also failed. The commissioners—the Earl of Carlisle, William Eden, and George Johnstone—sailed for America in mid-April 1778. Cruger did not speak in Parliament during the run-up to their departure, but he likely backed the mission because of his consistent support for any attempts at peace. According to the postwar claim that Cruger filed with the British government, he also provided Eden, the commission's key figure, with information at some point; it may have been in connection with this prominent attempt to end the war.[46] The concessions that North offered were by design essentially public knowledge before the commissioners arrived in America. Printing presses in then British-controlled New York and Philadelphia issued pieces intended to prepare the commissioners' way. This advance notice, however, enabled those patriots who prioritized independence to mobilize against the peace initiative before it gained any traction.[47] Fundamentally, pro-independence congressional leaders feared what many reconciliationists of various stripes hoped: that the Carlisle Commission's offer of a speedy end to the war and the reintegration of the colonies into a constitutionally modified empire might prove attractive to significant numbers of Americans. In late April, before the commissioners arrived, congress unanimously declared that it would not meet with them "unless they shall, as a preliminary thereto, either withdraw their fleets and armies, or else, in positive and express terms, acknowledge the independence of the said states." This preemptive demand deliberately blocked talks, while the congress also warned that anyone treating with the commissioners on their own would be considered "open and avowed enemies of these United States."[48] Soon after this, in early May, congress received the Franco-American treaty and ratified it. Further hurting the prospects for negotiations, loyalists feared that the Carlisle Commission signaled that the ministry was preparing to abandon them. Henry forwarded Jenkinson a May 1778 letter from New York that reported that the loyalist and former president of the chamber of commerce, Elias DeBrosses, had died by suicide on hearing of North's new policy and that "madness" had "seiz'd half the town."[49]

When Carlisle, Eden, and Johnstone landed in America in early June, they were unable to resurrect the prospects for peace. The commissioners took up residence in New York City—Peter Van Schaack met them there in September 1778—but congress's stance prevented them from even opening talks. The frustrated British envoys accused congress of "fraudulent domination" and tried appealing directly to the American people, but this only further poisoned the atmosphere.[50] In a final failed gambit to spur negotiations, the commissioners issued threats. Their October 1778 "Manifesto and Proclamation" contrasted the blessings that would accompany peace with warnings that congress's French alliance could unleash total war because Britain's survival would now be at stake.[51] By November 1778, the commission's effort was over, and the prospects for Anglo-American peace were more remote than ever.

The Franco-American alliance fused the imperial civil war with a traditional but more dangerous interstate war for Britons, changing the dynamics for Henry Cruger and other British reconciliationists. Most important, it made continuing to defend the colonists, now allied with Britain's hereditary enemies, increasingly difficult. Wilkesite radicalism had long tapped streams of populist, anti-Catholic, English xenophobia. Defending the Americans as mistreated Englishmen deprived of their patrimonial rights had been natural for independent radicals like Cruger and many of his supporters, but the United States' alliance with France scrambled these affinities.

Henry Cruger faced these British "domestic" consequences of the conflict in ways that nobodyists elsewhere did not. The most telling example is Cruger's place in debates over liberalizing Irish trade with Great Britain and the rest of the British Empire in 1778 and 1779, which caused splits among typical government and opposition supporters in Parliament. Cruger, in keeping with his commitment to his constituents, prominently opposed these measures, which many Bristolians regarded as threatening their port's prosperity, and made several impassioned speeches on the topic. Despite Bristolians' views, Burke was a key supporter of Irish reform, which he saw as inherently right and in the national interest because it promoted imperial stability in the face of Ireland's increasingly powerful Volunteer movement. To the disappointment of Bristol and other western ports, measures for liberalizing Irish trade were passed in December 1779.[52]

Cruger did not speak in Parliament on American issues between December 1777 and May 1780, the period when the ministry's apparent interest in negotiations and France's entry into the conflict complicated the politics of peace.[53] Cruger's personal finances, like those of many other Bristol merchants, were worsening. In 1780, Burke told a confidant that Cruger was "now not worth a Shilling."[54] This unstable landscape provides the backdrop to Cruger's muddy connections to figures within North's government during this period.

Cruger seems, at some point by 1779, to have received a £500 pension from the king like those most commonly given to government supporters.[55] However, when and what exactly Cruger received and why he got it are poorly documented, and the pension was discontinued by 1780. Cruger provided the government member Charles Jenkinson with information from New York from at least May 1777 to 1781. He may have had similar contact with others including William Eden and perhaps even North himself. The evidence about these connections is thin and fragmentary, but it indicates that Cruger had some ties to government that likely centered on providing information on New York, but that these did not extend to supporting it in Parliament, where he continued voting against North's policies.[56] In 1780, when Cruger ran for reelection, the ministry classed him as an opponent and spent thousands of pounds to defeat him.[57]

Ultimately it seems unknowable whether whatever Cruger did to receive money from the Crown was consistent or inconsistent with his public record on American issues. Either way, if Cruger received a pension from the government before 1780, his Bristol constituents evidently did not know about it. Given Cruger's own independent stance as a member of Parliament and the theme of parliamentary corruption as a touchstone of oppositional politics, secretly receiving such a pension seems an abdication of Cruger's own stated principles. Even if Cruger was able to justify a pension to himself or others, he would have known how such a payment would have struck independent-minded voters. When in 1780 opposition figures including Burke made an ideologically charged effort to challenge the Crown's political expenditures and influence over Parliament, Cruger voted in favor of reform.[58]

Cruger's only personal comment on his wartime ties to government ministers comes from a much later source, a 1789 application for financial compensation he made to Britain's Loyalist Claims Commission.[59] Cruger made his claim after the legal deadline for filing, and it was dismissed on that account. Nevertheless, his submission underlines the complexities of loyalty, history, and memory in regard to civil war. In his initial 1789 petition Cruger recounted the damage the war had done to his trade and, as one of Henry Cruger Sr.'s heirs, the damages that his father had suffered through the 1776 loss of his ship *George* and the 1778 fire at Cruger's Wharf. He made no mention in this claim of having ever received a government pension. Appended to the first document was a two-page supplement headed "Loyalty & Services" that Cruger submitted after learning such "Proofs" were "material & usually given in." The fact that it was prepared in 1789 requires caution in considering it an accurate guide to Cruger's wartime decision-making, partly since ideological motivations for actions in civil wars are commonly made to seem more important in retrospect than they were at the time of events.[60] Moreover, these claims were made in an application for financial assistance from the British state in a postwar context in which such aid was tied to having actively supported the Crown during the conflict. Together, these factors suggest that Cruger's slim account should be seen as the maximal case that he could reasonably make for himself as a "loyalist" as that concept was understood several years after the war ended.

In this light, the sentence with which Cruger opened his "Loyalty & Services" statement is revealing. "During the American War," he wrote, "I omitted no opportunity of promoting a Reconciliation between the two Countries, and to aid Administration by procuring Intelligence, some times at great Expence, and injury to my Parliamentary Interest." He mentioned two types of "service." First, and most specifically, he noted that in 1775 he had "promoted greatly by my Letters to New York the separation of that Colony from the others, by procuring, thro' the medium of my family & friends there, a Petition from their

Assembly to Parliament for a Repeal of the Tea Act." Obtaining this prewar petition, Cruger noted, "was urged by Government as a very material object, as they meant by repealing the Act with respect to New York, to shew the other Colonies what they might expect from a constitutional application, instead of thro' Congress." His family connections—including his father, uncle, and "my Brother in Law (Mr. Walton) member of the Assembly at New York, and at the head of the Loyal Party there"—gave Cruger "great influence in that Province," which members of the North administration "well know I applied in their Service." He also noted that "I spoke on the Occasion in the House more than once warmly recommending the Petition & applauding the loyal Conduct of the New York Assembly." This public advocacy for the petition, Cruger claimed, "gave great offence to the violent in America" and "was the Cause of many not paying me who were partial & punctual before."[61] In trying, in 1789, to depict himself as having been an aid to the administration, Cruger was conspicuously silent on the fact that the ministry peremptorily dismissed New York 1775's petitions and then pursued a military solution that Cruger had vehemently opposed. Moreover, rather notably, this one specific "service" was provided in early 1775, and Cruger had nothing specific to offer about his subsequent actions during the long war.

Cruger said little about the second category of service he mentioned to bolster his 1789 claim. "With respect to secret Services, by procuring Intelligence," Cruger wrote, "it is a subject of too delicate a Nature to be very particular." While giving no details about the timing or content of the intelligence he provided, Cruger said he could "appeal" to Jenkinson, Eden, and North "for Proofs of my readiness to furnish them with Information, and often of a very important Nature."[62] The letters connected to Cruger preserved in Jenkinson's papers include economic and political assessments unfavorable toward congress but also very critical of North's policies. Complicating things further, Eden helped superintend the government's overall intelligence gathering, but he also led the North administration's 1778 conciliatory effort, and Cruger consistently prioritized peace.[63] Much about what Cruger told the British government, when he told it, and why he did so remains obscure. Given these complexities, Cruger's unsuccessful 1789 claim underlines how poorly his actions and explanations map onto simple binaries of loyalty. Militant advocates of American independence would have been hostile to Cruger's provision of any information to any supporters of the North administration. Yet it seems unlikely that British hardliners or American loyalists who took up arms would have been impressed by Cruger's description of his "services," especially when set against his other wartime actions.

Fittingly, Cruger's final notable speeches as a wartime member of Parliament came in the form of weary, disappointed support for late and failed conciliation efforts. In early May 1780, General Henry Conway made another proposal in the House of Commons for ending the American war. He claimed that Americans were "naturally adverse to the French," and that recent events, including Britain's victory at Savannah and the depreciation of Continental dollars, left "the majority" of Americans "ardently wishing for a restoration of the old form of government." Conway therefore called for dispatching fresh peace commissioners to settle differences with America, allowing Britain to concentrate on fighting France and Spain. Neither opposition nor government supporters were much impressed.[64]

Cruger's "very long speech" on Conway's proposal reflected Parliament's general lack of enthusiasm. He claimed that "the bill by no means went far enough, that it would do no good in America, and would be no more use than a piece of waste paper."[65] The war, Cruger insisted, was "the real source of all our distresses and burthens" and it *should* be ended, but to do this "independency must be allowed, and the Thirteen Provinces treated as Free States." This was Cruger's first recorded public declaration in favor of recognizing American independence. Despite his doubts about Conway's bill, Cruger emphasized his prioritization of peace by noting that he would not oppose it because "he had uniformly voted in favour of every proposition of that tendency." He had, Cruger concluded with a glance toward the recent past, "been much blamed for voting for Lord North's conciliatory bill," but "he should pursue the same line nevertheless," and "since persons without doors could not be in his bosom and know what passed there," he would continue supporting peace initiatives.[66]

Later that month, Cruger also spoke on Thomas Pownall's effort to authorize the king to make "a peace, truce, or convention with America." Cruger, in what seems to have been a brief, angry speech, agreed with other speakers that ending the war required recognizing American independence, but said he would nevertheless support the motion because "it aimed at peace." He concluded bitterly, however, that since it seemed that the intractable government remained "determined not to treat with America, on the only *terms practicable*" then "let them go on, and *say* no more about the quarrel but *fight* it out like men."[67] Cruger seems to have concluded that as long as North remained in power, the American conflict could only be settled on the battlefield. Cruger was among a small minority that supported Pownall's bill, which the government easily quashed. He had held out hopes for a negotiated peace longer than most others on both sides of the conflict, but by the spring of 1780, even Cruger seems to have given up the ghost.

The political turbulence caused by what was now a war against France, Spain, and America culminated in the North administration calling an early general election in fall 1780. Cruger was a candidate again, but he and Burke both lost their Bristol seats.[68] Their replacements, Matthew Brickdale and Henry Lippincott, were merchants with strong local connections, and both ran as supporters of the ministry.[69] While Cruger and Burke recognized that pro-government sentiment was much stronger in Bristol in 1780 than it had been in 1774, their unwillingness to cooperate and their supporters' mutual antagonism were also significant factors in their defeats. Cruger himself thought he "was turned out because of his attachment to the Americans during the war."[70] His opponents successfully linked Cruger to an unsigned letter "from a Gentleman in Bristol" that had been excerpted in the *Pennsylvania Packet* in October 1774 that urged the colonists to resist the government and called people in England "knaves, scoundrels, and spiritless slaves."[71] North's government also spent money defeating Cruger and Burke.[72] For Burke, the loss in Bristol was an embarrassing inconvenience rather than a calamity. He was immediately returned to Parliament anyway for Yorkshire's Malton, a Rockingham pocket borough. Cruger lacked similarly influential backers outside Bristol, so there was no return to Parliament for him through a Whig aristocrat. Cruger nonetheless remained politically ambitious and retained significant local support.

This set the stage for another bruising Bristol election. Lippincott died unexpectedly, and a by-election occurred in early 1781. Cruger, with Samuel Peach's backing, instantly declared himself a candidate. His strongest support again came from Bristol's non-elite voters. More than a thousand journeymen and freemen subscribed their names to a pledge to vote for him soon after he declared his candidacy.[73] His rival this time was George Daubeny, a Bristol merchant who had emerged as a leading figure in "King and Country" politicking. Daubeny was a strong candidate in his own right, the ministry contributed over £5,000 to back him, and he defeated Cruger by less than four hundred votes.[74] Like many losing candidates in parliamentary elections, Cruger petitioned to the House of Commons against his defeat, but like most others, this appeal failed, and Daubeny was duly seated.[75]

Campaign rhetoric in 1780 and 1781 repeatedly emphasized Cruger as the candidate for Bristol's proudly independent middling and lower-class voters.[76]

"A Freeman" told voters in 1781 that they should refuse to "be bought and sold like Cattle in Smithfield Market" and "let Cruger be the Man of your Choice, he who is the Tradesman's Friend and Support." An author writing as a "Journeyman Cooper" noted how working-class voters had been threatened with being turned out of their jobs if they voted for Cruger in 1780, but urged his "Friends and Fellow-Labourers" to remain with Cruger in 1781 because "we can better do without our Masters, than they can without us." Resolutions at a meeting nominating Cruger in 1781 complained that "it is highly unreasonable and oppressive for any Man, or Set of Men, to avail themselves of their Riches, either to bias or prevent a free Election." In a 1781 speech of his own, Cruger described himself as "zealous in your service, and unshaken in the cause of liberty," while trying to turn his own financial distress into a point of connection with Bristol's people. "I am confident," he claimed, "that the share which I have had in public misfort[u]nes, can never alienate me from the affections of the wise and virtuous" for "nothing can be more absurd, than to measure the abilities and integrity of men by their wealth and luxury."[77]

Cruger's opponents also emphasized his American birth and sympathies and cast his politics and supporters as dangerously revolutionary. A 1781 anti-Cruger pamphlet argued that "in such times as these we ought to prefer a man born amongst us, and whom we know to be a true friend to his King and Country," and its author observed that "I would as soon vote for a Frenchman, a Spaniard, or even a Dutchman, as I would for an American at present." Another anti-Cruger writer made the link to rebel America too, noting that Cruger's supporters were "enemies to obedience, good sense, and good order" and warning that "these liberty-boys argue best with a clinched fist or a short stick." A more imaginative anti-Cruger writer composed a satirical letter in which Cruger, called "Yankee Doodle," tells Bristol's voters that "I am determined to support the independency of the thirteen stripes in opposition to the Royal Standard of Old England, and to vote for the establishment of *republicanism*, in opposition to your constitution in Church and State."[78]

Striking visual material likewise emphasized Cruger's "Americanness," which was contrasted with the "Englishness" of his opponents. An elaborate and bellicose election card prepared on behalf of Cruger's opponents in 1780 features the pithy slogan "Brickdale and Lippincott Englishmen" (fig. 13). In the foreground, Liberty personified spears a wild child representing the upstart colonies. In the background, a devil carries an American-inspired striped flag reading "Cr-ger & Rebellion" and threatens that the pro-American arsonist John the

Figure 13. Bristol Election Card, 1780. This piece of election propaganda attacked Henry Cruger Jr. and supported his opponents in the 1780 Bristol parliamentary election. © The Trustees of the British Museum.

Figure 14. Bristol Election Card, 1781. This election card linked Henry Cruger Jr.'s opponent in Bristol's 1781 parliamentary election with images of British nationalism and royalism to draw a contrast with Cruger's pro-American politics. © The Trustees of the British Museum.

Painter will burn the city. The text at the card's bottom links Cruger with the anti-English sentiments from the *Pennsylvania Packet* in 1774 that were attributed to him. The message was that Cruger was not a patriotic Englishman but something else now legible as dangerous and foreign: a revolutionary American.[79] A 1781 card also highlights the contrast between Cruger's dubious loyalties and the unalloyed patriotism of his opponent, George Daubeny, who amid nationalist imagery reminds voters that he is "an Enemy to anarchy & REBELLION" (fig. 14).

Political cartoons offered similar messages. "Liberty Enlightned" from 1781 depicts Samuel Peach carrying a sick Cruger as a group of watching "Yankeys" mourn and a bird-footed American Indian bids "Farewell, Independency" (fig. 15). While a banner in the cartoon's background connects Daubeny with the reassuringly loyal slogan of "Everlasting Prosperity to our Church and King," Cruger carries a striped American flag, and one of his backers is labeled as a "Supporter of Rebellion" and linked with Oliver Cromwell and rioting. Another 1781 cartoon has Cruger declaring, "I come to Establish America's Independence," while those pulling his cart trample the Crown and the scales of justice (fig. 16). By the time of these elections, Cruger was too British for many American patriots and too American for many Bristol voters.

Figure 15. "Liberty Enlightned," 1781. An elaborate anti-Cruger political cartoon from 1781, this image features an ailing Henry Cruger Jr. holding an American-inspired striped flag, being carried by his father-in-law, Samuel Peach, and surrounded by disconsolate supporters. Courtesy of the John Carter Brown Library, Providence, RI.

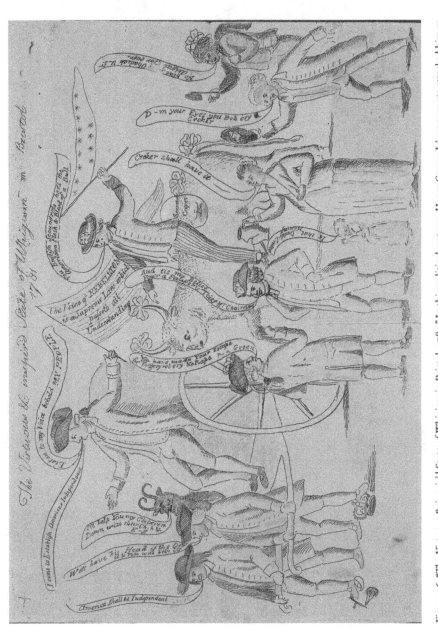

Figure 16. "The Virtuous & inspir'd State of Whigism in Bristol, 1781." In this political cartoon, Henry Cruger Jr.'s opponents attacked him as an immoral supporter of rebellion. © The Trustees of the British Museum.

Figure 17. Gilbert Stuart. *Henry Cruger of New York, Mayor of Bristol and Master of the Merchant Venturers,* 1781. Oil on canvas. © Bristol Museums, Galleries & Archives/ Purchased with the Wills Fund, 1943, acc. no. K1524/Bridgeman Images.

Even after these failed parliamentary campaigns, Cruger still had an appetite for politics. The municipal corporation named Cruger as mayor of Bristol for 1781, an appointment reflecting his continued standing with local merchants and civic leaders.[80] Cruger also remained opposed to the ministry's American policies, participating in a meeting in Bristol in 1782 that produced a petition to Parliament "against the further prosecution of the war in America" and that advised "a total change of the unhappy system that has involved the Nation in such complicated misfortunes."[81] A striking portrait of Cruger by Gilbert Stuart, painted many years later, underlines his close and continuing identification with Bristol by portraying him in his mayoral robes (fig. 17).[82]

Although he had wanted to remain in Parliament, Cruger's electoral losses insulated him from some of the British political turmoil that accompanied the war's end. Cornwallis's surrender at Yorktown in October 1781 proved too catastrophic for even the resilient North ministry to endure. On March 20, 1782, facing the prospect of losing a confidence vote, North finally persuaded the king to let him resign. As Burke, Fox, and other Rockinghamites had long hoped, the king entrusted them with the government after North's fall. The new administration lasted only four months, however, collapsing when Rockingham died on July 1, 1782. Lord Shelburne became prime minister, but some prominent Rockinghamites including Burke and Fox refused to serve under him and resigned.[83]

It fell to Shelburne's ministry and its chief representative, the merchant Richard Oswald, to negotiate an end to the American war. Oswald's view "that America's commercial dependence on Britain was the critical issue, and that political dependence meant comparatively little" was certainly a position that Cruger could support, especially because the resulting treaty was widely considered generous toward the United States.[84] In June 1783, even before peace was formally concluded, Henry Cruger sailed to New York in the hope of finally addressing his financial problems.[85] He was in America rather than England when the Treaty of Paris was finally signed. Cruger was anxious to reconnect ties broken by war, but after a decade of prioritizing Anglo-American peace, he was still dogged by questions over his true loyalties.

8. Friend of Washington?

Navigating the Revolution was partly about managing your reputation. Nicholas Cruger spent most of the war years on St. Croix, a place affected by the conflict but not directly fought over. No battles occurred on the island; it was never occupied by troops from either army. Its residents, shielded by their status as Danish subjects, did not have to take loyalty oaths to congress or the British king. The war—especially fighting at sea—had major implications for islanders, but Crucians could maintain the sort of neutrality to which many on the North American continent aspired. Despite the opportunity he had to stay out of the conflict, Nicholas came to have a reputation as the warmest patriot in the family, in part because of his encounters with the British military during the war. Nicholas's experiences illuminate how the Revolution radiated into the Caribbean. They also underline the power of factors other than ideology in shaping wartime decisions, demonstrate the pliability of national identity during the era, and challenge the assumptions that frequently underlie subsequent assessments of people's wartime loyalties.

Nicholas Cruger's revolution was complex, even mysterious. But from the nineteenth century most later American writers and readers believed Nicholas had a good war, one in which he stood on the right side of history. In part this was because of his relationship with the Caribbean-born Alexander Hamilton, who as a boy in the late 1760s began his working life as a clerk in Nicholas's St. Croix counting house. When Hamilton was consecrated as a Founding Father, Nicholas's memory was burnished by the reflected glory. Henry Cruger Van Schaack, the extended Cruger family's first and most prolific chronicler, lauded

Nicholas in 1859 as "the friend of Washington as well as the patron of Hamilton" and portrayed him as the most committed patriot in the family.[1] Such assessments, based on thin documentation, made their way into nineteenth- and early twentieth-century histories that celebrated the still wealthy and socially prominent Crugers as one of New York's "great families." With time, accounts of Nicholas's wartime allegiance to the patriot cause became more expansive and categorical. One such 1902 account called Nicholas Cruger the "warm friend" of Hamilton and "Washington and the great Revolutionary leaders" and claimed that "in the war he contributed generously to the colonial cause" and was "twice arrested and imprisoned for being a rebel."[2]

Nicholas's contemporaries were not, however, so sure where his real loyalties lay. Some appear to have thought he was a rebel, others a loyalist, and some feared he was a spy. At one point he protested his attachment to the patriot cause in a letter to George Washington, and at another he insisted on his status as a Danish subject to an American court. Was Nicholas a "patriot"? It is possible that he consistently was or that he became one over the course of the war, but other readings of his story are also plausible. Much of Nicholas's life is well documented, yet there are other aspects of it that defy discovery. His actions during the Revolution are so enveloped in ambiguities that the haze surrounding them often seems deliberately created. Nobodyism could be strategic. If it is impossible to be certain of which side—if either—Nicholas was on during the conflict, it may well be because that is what he wanted. Framed this way, Nicholas's history is a reminder that many people buffeted by the Revolution were more interested in getting through it than they were in changing the course of events. Patriots, loyalists, and nobodyists all wanted to preserve their own lives and pursue their own happiness. These goals, rather than the more abstract ones emphasized by the political leaders of both sides, were often the key to wartime decision-making.

Nicholas settled in St. Croix by 1766, the year in which he turned twenty-three. His move likely followed several years of practical mercantile training. In 1765, he was entrusted to serve as supercargo on board Henry and John Cruger's vessel the *Bumper* on a voyage to Jamaica, where his brother John Harris was based.[3] The completion of this voyage may have marked the moment when he was deemed ready to set out on his own. In St. Croix Nicholas initially partnered with another New Yorker, David Beekman, but their firm was dissolved by 1769. Thereafter Cruger operated primarily on his own account, although sometimes he traded in partnership with Cornelius Kortright, also from a long-established New York mercantile family.[4]

The Cruger clan had multigenerational experience in the plantation trade, and in the 1760s and early 1770s St. Croix had much in common with the other sugar-producing islands of the Caribbean. There were also aspects of its development that set it apart, and these shaped Nicholas's wartime experiences. First and foremost, the island was a Danish colony, part of a small but valuable presence that Denmark carved out for itself between the larger Spanish, French, and British empires. St. Croix's colonial history dates back to the earliest European incursions into the Americas—Columbus is traditionally thought to have landed there on his second voyage in 1493—but by the mid-eighteenth century it still was not as fully integrated into the world economy as other Caribbean spaces. Originally lightly settled by French colonists, in 1733 St. Croix was purchased from France by the Danish West India and Guinea Company. Nearly twice the combined area of the older nearby Danish colonies of St. Thomas and St. John, St. Croix was more suited to plantation agriculture, and the company saw an opportunity to develop a larger market for the enslaved people that it acquired in West Africa and to profit from strong Danish demand for tropical commodities. Denmark—in a political union with Norway that lasted until 1814—also saw such expansion as aiding its claims to be a great power. While the company and Danish government tried to manage St. Croix's trade to their benefit, the island was open to private traders and dependent on North America for provisions, lumber, and other goods.

In 1754, with the company in considerable debt, the Danish government took direct control of its Caribbean territories. Because it had long been sparsely inhabited, St. Croix's soil was not as depleted as that of other more intensively exploited islands. The initial laying out of sugar estates, their sale to investors, and the expansion of slavery on the island began during the company's rule and continued after the assertion of royal Danish control, with increasing exports producing large profits for the island's emerging planter class and the merchants who serviced them. Denmark also managed to maintain its neutrality in the Seven Years' War, preserving its West Indian possessions even as the boundaries of other empires were being redrawn.[5]

As a result, the second half of the eighteenth century was a prosperous time for St. Croix's white elite, who built fortunes through the toil of approximately sixty thousand enslaved people who were forcibly transported to the island between 1747 and 1803.[6] Christiansted developed into a thriving port, its increasingly substantial and even opulent buildings reflecting the island's new-found wealth. Outside Christiansted and the island's other main settlement, Frederiksted, large plantation houses set among cane and cotton fields dominated St. Croix's landscape. Nicholas Cruger was part of and profited from these developments, as the Crugers and other New York–based merchant families helped New York City become "the outstanding port" for St. Croix's trade with North America on the eve of the Revolution.[7]

Denmark wanted its Caribbean colonies to produce profits, but it had neither a large, ready supply of willing emigrants nor many nationals with expertise in plantation agriculture.[8] As a result, St. Croix became home to a conspicuously multinational white population in the mid-eighteenth century.[9] Members of planter families with capital to invest emigrated from other Caribbean islands. They were joined by others from continental Europe, the British Isles, and North America. Authorities encouraged these white settlers by naturalizing them as Danish subjects, giving them confidence in their property rights and enabling them to participate in civic associations and governance. St. Croix's trade was further promoted by the liberalizing of Danish mercantile regulations in April 1764. Nicholas Cruger and other voluntary migrants lived among a larger, rapidly growing population of enslaved people. By 1770, St. Croix's population consisted of about fifteen hundred white settlers and nearly nineteen thousand Black people.[10]

While St. Croix's Euro-American population had multinational origins, English-speaking immigrants probably formed a majority of the island's white inhabitants in the years before the Revolution.[11] Their economic power translated into cultural influence. Danish was the language of governance, but Christiansted's newspaper, the *Royal Danish American Gazette*, which began publication in 1770, was published primarily in English and carried reports from London and New York in addition to news from Copenhagen.[12] By the late eighteenth century, a commentator noted that in contrast to Danish St. Thomas, where a Dutch-based creole developed among the island's Black population, on St. Croix an English-based creole emerged.[13]

Nicholas became a successful merchant partly because trade flowed out in many directions from St. Croix. There was some trade with Copenhagen and other northern European ports, but like the Dutch Caribbean colonies, St. Croix and the other Danish Virgin Islands profited from their liminal position between the larger and more intensively regulated Spanish, French, and British empires. Merchants imported and exported on behalf of Crucians, and they used the island and Danish flag to trade across imperial borders in both peace and war. During the Seven Years' War, for example, St. Croix served as a node for exchanges between the sugar-rich but provision-poor French Caribbean and British North America.[14] Family support and patterns of interdependence helped Nicholas too. For example, in 1766, Henry & John Cruger in New York directed a ship of theirs to call first on Nicholas in St. Croix and then Telemon in Curaçao in order "to give all our friends a chance to partake of our little commiss[ions]."[15]

Nicholas was soon doing well enough to take on a clerk. Sometime between 1766 and 1768, Alexander Hamilton, then between eleven and thirteen years old, began his career by working in Cruger's St. Croix countinghouse. Hamilton's mother ran a small store in Christiansted, which she stocked in part with goods imported by Beekman and Cruger, and this probably led to Hamilton's employment. Intelligent, self-confident, and a quick study, Hamilton continued to work for Cruger after his partnership with Beekman ended and played an increasingly active and valuable part in administering Nicholas's trading. This work brought Hamilton into contact with members of the wider Cruger family, with whom he frequently corresponded on business matters.[16]

Hamilton's talents soon became apparent to his young employer and others in St. Croix. After several years in Cruger's employ, the precocious Hamilton emigrated to British North America in 1773 with the support of the Presbyterian minister Hugh Knox, Nicholas, and others on the island. In 1774, Hamilton entered New York's King's College, with which the Cruger family had been closely connected since its founding. Nicholas maintained evidently good relations with Hamilton in ensuing decades as Hamilton rose to prominence in the Continental Army and then in New York and national politics. Working for Nicholas gave young Hamilton firsthand experience with international trade and also saw him witness plantation slavery and the slave trade up close. In his later years, Hamilton spoke of his time as Cruger's clerk as "the most useful part of his education."[17]

Nicholas kept a store in Christiansted and operated as a general merchant, albeit at a growing scale over time. Basic foodstuffs were Nicholas's main imports, which he sold or traded for exportable plantation commodities. A representative 1773 advertisement listing what Cruger had in stock notes "superfine and common" flour imported from Philadelphia and New York, rye flour, "Indian meal," ship's bread in barrels, herring, butter, ham, and beef.[18] He also imported an array of building and maritime products such as lumber, pitch, sailcloth, lime, nails, and hinges. Working animals were valuable on the island, and Cruger sometimes imported mules and cattle from Puerto Rico and the mainland.[19] Nicholas also transshipped continental foodstuffs and other goods through St. Croix for sale elsewhere.

Nicholas supplemented these basics with an array of minor luxuries such as tobacco, "Bohea and Congo tea in chests and cannisters," and Madeira wine.[20] Occasionally he would sell other higher-value items, such as the Windsor chairs and the "excellent chaise with brass worms and steel springs" that he offered for sale in 1774.[21] And, as noted earlier, on at least two occasions in 1771 and 1772, he was involved in the large-scale transport and sale of hundreds of enslaved people. Together, Nicholas's business activities meant he may have been "the most active [merchant] on St. Croix with respect to North American trade" in the decade before 1775.[22]

In 1771, an ill Nicholas Cruger left his business largely in young Alexander Hamilton's hands for several months while he recuperated in New York. Hamilton, writing to Nicholas to keep him abreast of affairs, reported that he had corresponded on trade with members of the Cruger family in England, New York, and elsewhere in the Caribbean. One voyage that Hamilton documented is especially revealing of how Nicholas and his relatives approached trade in the 1770s. The small sloop *Thunderbolt* was jointly owned by Nicholas Cruger and a partnership between John Harris Cruger and Jacob Walton. In mid-November 1771, it arrived in St. Croix, probably after a stop in Jamaica, carrying a cargo that included lumber, flour, bread, apples, and onions. After unloading some of this cargo for sale in St. Croix, Hamilton had other goods put aboard the sloop and dispatched it to Telemon Cruger's care in Curaçao. Telemon was to sell the *Thunderbolt*'s cargo, help the ship's captain to arm the vessel, and then dispatch it for the "Spanish main" to obtain a parcel of mules. The sloop returned to St. Croix with the mules in late January 1772. The *Thunderbolt*'s return passage was slow, and the mules were sickly, so this voyage was not very profitable, but such setbacks happened and trade went on. As Hamilton noted, "we must try a second time." The sloop soon returned to Curaçao laden with codfish, rum, and bread. Telemon was to sell these goods before directing the sloop to Spanish America for another cargo of mules.[23] In three months, the little *Thunderbolt* loaded or landed goods in ports belonging to four European empires—the British, Danish, Dutch, and Spanish—in the intertwined interests of three Cruger brothers and their brother-in-law.

The Crugers' ships carried intelligence to each other as well as goods. Traders valued information on prices, competitors, arrivals and departures, and much else. The mercantilist regulations of competing empires were seen primarily as business problems to be solved. Hamilton warned Telemon, for example, that the talk in St. Croix was that Spanish customs officers had been working to suppress illegal foreign trade, a concern because the Crugers wanted to purchase mules from Spanish sources. "Reports here," Hamilton wrote, "represent matters in a very disagreeable light with regard to the Guarda Costo's which are said to swarm upon the Coast." He repeatedly urged Telemon Cruger and the *Thunderbolt*'s captain to make sure that ship was armed before it sailed into Spanish waters.[24] The laws of supply and demand, rather than those of kings or legislatures, determined the contours of Nicholas's trade.

This commerce made Nicholas wealthy and well established by the eve of the Revolution. In April 1772, soon after returning from New York, Nicholas married Anna de Nully in St. Croix's Dutch Reformed Church. Anna's mother, born Catherine Heyliger, was the granddaughter of a governor of Dutch St. Eustatius. Members of her family—already wealthy on St. Eustatius and with experience in sugar and slavery—were among the first planters who settled on St. Croix in the aftermath of the Danish takeover in 1733, and the Heyligers became among the largest landholders on the island.[25] Anna's father, Bertram Pieter de Nully, was descended from a Huguenot refugee family that had initially settled in Holland and then moved to the Dutch Caribbean. The de Nullys owned large tracts of valuable sugar land on St. Croix, including the neighboring estates a few miles southwest of Christiansted eventually known as Peter's Rest, Catherine's Rest, and Anna's Hope. Bertram de Nully died around the time of his daughter Anna's wedding to Nicholas; she brought substantial property including the Anna's Hope plantation to the marriage.[26] This marriage likely cemented Nicholas's ties to St. Croix, his local influence, and his identification with the island. In 1773, Nicholas was nominated, although not selected by St. Croix's governor general, for service on the island's main representative body, the Burgher Council.[27] He would insist on his status as a Danish subject in the coming tumultuous years.

Nicholas Cruger's revolution, shaped by his pre-1775 life as a St. Croix trader, shows how some nobodyists approached the conflict more as a set of current problems to be overcome than as a battle for the future. Because of St. Croix's strong ties to British North America, the building constitutional crisis there received major attention on the island. Crucians were quite sympathetic to American grievances, and the island's planters and merchants also hoped to profit from any relaxation of British regulations on trade. According to a January 1775 report, the "inhabitants of St. Croix" were preparing to send 130 hogsheads of sugar to occupied Boston "as a present."[28] Political news from England and British America featured frequently in the *Royal Danish American Gazette*, usually with a pro-patriot subtext. Probably because of Nicholas's prominence on St. Croix, and perhaps through his offices, the April 19, 1775, issue of the newspaper printed in its entirety Henry Cruger Jr.'s debut December 1774 speech in Parliament, which focused on American grievances and the need for compromise.[29] Although the paper's St. Croix readers could not have known, on the very morning that they were reading of Henry's attempts to effect reconciliation in London, war was beginning in Massachusetts.

Danish St. Croix occupied a profitable but precarious and changing place during the ensuing struggle. In the American war's first phase, as congress and the colonies mounted an expanding military effort, patriot leaders needed material and moral aid from European powers, and Caribbean ports were essential sites for exchange. According to one estimate, as much as 90 percent of the gunpowder that insurgent patriot forces used in the first two years of fighting came through the Dutch, Danish, and then still officially neutral French islands of the Caribbean, as did many weapons.[30] It is indicative of the sympathies of the island that in October 1776, to the consternation of a British observer, an American-flagged ship received a salute from the guns of the Danish fort at Christiansted, marking what in patriotic lore is sometimes said to be the first ever acknowledgment of the American flag by a foreign power.[31]

Wartime trade with rebellious North America was profitable for Crucians, but it was also risky and diplomatically dangerous for Denmark. In October 1775 the Danish Crown—anxious like other smaller powers to avoid crossing Britain too openly and becoming entangled in the fighting—prohibited its subjects from exporting war materials to the colonies and enjoined them to maintain strict neutrality in the conflict under penalty of confiscation of property.[32] Yet many Crucians had, in addition to their sympathy with and ties to North America, a history of resisting metropolitan Danish regulations alongside French, Spanish and British ones. Nicholas Cruger, for example, was among eleven island-based merchants who in 1774 had protested against special commercial protections and privileges that metropolitan Danish ship captains enjoyed on St. Croix.[33]

As the war deepened, and especially after the Prohibitory Act unleashed the Royal Navy and British-flagged privateers, the diplomatic dangers it posed for Denmark and the financial risks it posed for St. Croix's traders increased. Congress and the patriot state governments also increasingly intervened in the operation of markets as they attempted to direct the colonial economy in the service of their political and military goals. Caribbean merchants could be as reluctant to accept these American attempts to regulate their trade as they were European ones. These dynamics meant "legality" was "a constantly varying phenomenon" for those looking to do business between St. Croix and North America as the military, political, and diplomatic situation evolved.[34] One consequence of constantly changing regulations and the war's jurisdictional complexity was that much of St. Croix's commerce went underground, hidden not just from the British but also from Danish and patriot authorities as "illegal trade dominated the commerce between North America and the Danish West Indies" during the years of fighting.[35]

When France and Spain entered the conflict in 1778 and 1779, the American rebellion became a world war, transforming the diplomatic situation in Europe and the Caribbean. Initially smaller powers including the Netherlands, Denmark, and others tried to remain neutral. In 1780, in response to overtures from Russia, Denmark joined the first League of Armed Neutrality, an alliance of smaller European powers that, while carefully not declaring war against Britain, banded together to protect their right to trade with all belligerent nations in any goods other than war material. In theory, these smaller powers were prepared to defend their oceangoing trade by force against any navies that sought to interdict it. The United States, Spain, and France all quickly recognized the league's assertion of their right to carry on a free neutral commerce, but Britain, against which the league was aimed, did not. In fact, Britain's fears that the Netherlands would join the league and thereby greatly strengthen it, led directly to its declaration of war on the Dutch Republic in late 1780.[36]

This further internationalization of the conflict had immediate effects in the Caribbean. In February 1781, Dutch St. Eustatius was easily captured by the British. The island and more than a hundred merchant ships taken as prizes in its waters were plundered by the British attackers, who seized more than three million pounds sterling in property.[37] Nicholas Cruger was among the sufferers when bills of exchange belonging to him were taken from aboard a Dutch-flagged ship.[38] A French surprise attack recaptured St. Eustatius later in the year, but Britain's assault on the island had complex implications for the Danish Virgin Islands. On the one hand, St. Eustatius's fate was a lesson in the dangers of warring with the Royal Navy. On the other hand, Danish St. Croix and St.

Thomas, now the key neutral islands left in the Caribbean, temporarily became centers for some of the trade with North America previously channeled through St. Eustatius. Indeed, to the consternation of the French, after the British defeat at Yorktown, this trade came to include British merchants taking on Danish flags at St. Thomas in order to restart commerce with Virginia correspondents.[39] Traders in the Danish West Indies therefore played a dangerous game after the internationalization of the American war, one in which there were profits to be made but missteps could entangle them with the militaries of several belligerent powers. Keeping commerce flowing in these circumstances required skill, knowledge, and daring. In some measure, trading with the infant United States was an inherently political act whatever one's motives, but the tradition of maintaining international trade regardless of war or peace was also powerful.

Despite the inherent dangers, Nicholas Cruger kept trading between the Caribbean and North America throughout the war. In July 1775 Nicholas offered an assortment of goods for sale in Christiansted that included "North America" beef and butter, "Connecticut pork" and an array of other foodstuffs and building supplies likely also from the thirteen colonies. This trade continued after Parliament passed the Prohibitory Act and congress passed the Declaration of Independence. In July 1776 Cruger reported he had "just imported" an array of goods including "superfine Philadelphia flour," other provisions and building materials.[40]

Nicholas's wartime business activities included investing in voyages between St. Croix and the continent alongside the partnership of John Willcocks of Philadelphia and Nicholas Low, originally of New York. After a period of British military occupation that ended in June 1778, Philadelphia was back under patriot control when in December 1778, Cruger advised Willcocks to send him "your best superfine flour," as that commodity "never fails" on St. Croix.[41] This relationship was at times contentious—both Cruger and Willcocks and Low objected to investments the other party made on their collective behalf—but Nicholas continued doing business with mainland correspondents as the war deepened. Several of Nicholas's American associates also seem to have supported the American cause during the period when Nicholas traded with them. Like many other merchants, John Willcocks invested, sometimes with Nicholas Low, in patriot privateers from at least 1779.[42] Yet the Philadelphian Tench Coxe, another of Nicholas's American wartime correspondents, began the conflict as a neutral. Coxe went to British-controlled New York in late 1776—at about the time he and Nicholas began doing business—and then profited heavily after returning to Philadelphia while it was occupied by the British. Coxe narrowly avoided being attainted for treason by Pennsylvania's government in 1778 before swearing allegiance to the patriot side. Coxe's cause was likely helped by his deliberate destruction of records documenting his trade out of British-occupied Philadelphia, so whether Nicholas was among his correspondents in this period is unknown.[43]

While Cruger continued trading, he was mindful of the period's increased risks, insisting to Willcocks that any vessel in which he invested be provided with several real cannons and some wooden dummies to make its armament seem more formidable.[44] Such dangers were underlined in 1778, when the *Nancy*, co-owned by Nicholas, Daniel Conant, and Benjamin Yard, was captured by British privateers operating out of Tortola and St. Christopher just as it arrived at St. Croix. Cruger and his partners protested the seizure of their vessel and its cargo—flour, hams, tobacco, and some livestock—with a deposition complaining to British officials that they were "Burghers and Residents" of St. Croix and that their ship was taken on the very beach of their Danish island.[45] The provisions and tobacco aboard the *Nancy* suggest that it likely was trading with the rebellious colonies; there is notably no mention of where the *Nancy* sailed from in the deposition its owners filed with British authorities. Given the dynamics of the moment, perhaps Nicholas regarded the *Nancy*'s ill-fated voyage as intended to benefit the American cause. Yet Nicholas, whatever his preferences in regard to America's constitutional status, appears to have insisted upon his Danish identity and pursued compensation through British systems and networks even as the war continued. In 1780, Nicholas thanked Peter Van Schaack, then in England, for his "kind and polite attention to my brig Nancy's business" and noted that he was also "obliged to our brother Harry on this score."[46] Moreover, he seems to have taken advantage of his Danish subjecthood to continue trading with British ports. In April 1779, for example, Christiansted port records note his involvement in a trading voyage with St. Christopher.[47] Moving between national identities was a feature of Cruger's wartime experiences.

Nicholas Cruger's involvement in the salt trade similarly reveals the complex methods and meanings of wartime commerce. The Crugers had imported salt from the Caribbean in the 1760s, and Nicholas engaged in such ventures during the war.[48] In his December 1778 letter to the Philadelphian John Willcocks, Cruger reported that he had recently sent a Bermuda sloop that he owned in partnership with the vessel's captain, Thomas Guion, from St. Croix to the mainland with a cargo of 1,020 bushels of the commodity. More than a seasoning, salt was required in large quantities to preserve meat and fish and therefore essential to the colonial food supply. It was also used to tan leather, make medicines, and in many other applications. In the prewar period, mainland American production never equaled demand, and salt was imported from Europe and the Caribbean. As Britain's naval attacks on American shipping ramped up, "salt quickly emerged as the Achilles' heel of North America's agricultural economy."[49] Despite congressional and state attention in 1775 and 1776, salt shortages continued to pose a political, economic, and strategic danger to the Revolution.[50]

Despite the war, British Caribbean islands remained valuable and comparatively accessible sources of salt, so traders risked capture by the Royal Navy and privateers to bring it to mainland markets. The thinly settled Turks islands, including uninhabited Salt Cay, were particularly involved in the trade. Bermudian white settlers and enslaved people developed production there, and during the war, the continuation of the Turks' salt trade was important to locals and others.[51] Daring Bermudians shipped salt to the mainland themselves; American-based vessels went to load salt directly when they could elude British ships; and British salt was traded to the rebellious colonies through neutral Caribbean ports such as St. Eustatius and St. Croix.

The subterfuges employed in this trade were legion. In 1777, a British privateer seized a salt-laden vessel belonging to Cornelius Durant, who was born in British North America but lived on St. Croix for many years. A Danish official protested the seizure on Durant's behalf, insisted that he was a Danish subject, and, rather more improbably, claimed that the salt his ship carried was destined not for the nearby American mainland but for Norway and its herring industry.[52] In 1781, in another example, Thomas Shirley, governor of Britain's Leeward Islands, reported to London that he had learned that it was "very common for American vessels to avail themselves of Papers, surreptitiously procured from [British-occupied] New York, and under the cover of them to carry on a trade for salt with the several Islands yielding that commodity."[53] Salt beef and pork were crucial to armies, and Shirley alerted naval commanders to the illicit trade in the hopes of depriving the rebels of "an Article the want whereof alone may reduce them to every imaginable distress in carrying on their military operations."[54] In 1778, one member of the Continental Army reported that "salt was as valuable as gold with the soldiers."[55] In shipping salt to North America, Cruger might be seen to have been supporting the American cause. In this respect, it is notable that Cruger instructed his Philadelphia correspondent to invest any profits earned through his 1778 salt trading voyage in the "public funds," likely a reference to either state- or congressionally issued bonds whose long-term value depended on an American victory in the war.

Yet it is also possible that Nicholas is better understood as like those whom James Fenimore Cooper called in his novel *The Spy* the "patriots by profession."[56] The trade in salt was not only important to the American war effort but also extremely lucrative. As one account has noted, "salt was a prime item of interest to speculators and one which could be hoarded in ways that defied all methods of control."[57] In May 1776, the congress condemned the "avaricious and ill-designing men" who charged an "exorbitant price for salt," but patriot efforts to encourage domestic salt production and regulate salt's price and availability repeatedly failed.[58] Merchants like the Crugers were already well versed in navigating different legal and regulatory systems, and they found ways to adapt to new realities, especially when crossing borders created opportunities for profit.

According to one estimate, salt from the Turks Islands, which may be where Nicholas secured the cargo he dispatched in 1778, consistently traded at fifteen to twenty times its prewar price in wartime Philadelphia.[59] The most searching attempt to create a price series for salt in wartime Philadelphia notes explosive overall price increases, punctuated by dramatic short-term fluctuations and periods when the commodity was almost unobtainable at any price.[60] Between April 1776, when prices began to rise seriously, and the end of 1777, salt went from 2 shillings 9 pence per bushel to perhaps as high as 150 shillings per bushel.[61] Prices stabilized somewhat at these very high levels in 1778 but then resumed their rise in later 1779. Exacerbated by the collapsing purchasing power of Continental currency, salt spiked to a short-term high of £75 (1,500 shillings) per bushel at the end of 1779.[62] A large importation in early 1780 caused prices to improve and further cargoes, especially from St. Eustatius, helped too. News of the British declaration of war on the Dutch, however, caused prices to spike again before they stabilized in the summer of 1781 at about 33 shillings per bushel, around nineteen times salt's prewar price.[63] Tellingly, salt prices collapsed after hostilities ended in 1783.[64]

There is no evidence that Nicholas's salt trading fell afoul of patriot laws, but he was attuned to the variability of prices and markets for salt and in search of profits. Given tenuous supplies and varied demand, there were many geographic fluctuations in salt prices over the course of the war, and sellers focused on profits worked hard to time markets correctly. Nicholas sent an earlier load of salt to the mainland in November 1778; he told Willcocks that he hoped it had gone "to a good Markett." He also told Willcocks that he expected his latest shipment of salt to be sold "to the Eastward" rather than in Philadelphia, suggesting that his vessels' captains were expected to find the best market they could for their cargoes.[65] It is possible that Nicholas Cruger engaged in the trade in salt and other goods for primarily patriotic reasons or because such trading represented a fusion of his political and personal interests, but the wider history of salt trading reveals how difficult it is to apply motivations to his behavior with confidence. The line between "patriot" and "profiteer" could be a thin one, and much depended on managing one's reputation.

Nicholas Cruger's wartime movements also reveal important aspects of his nobodyism (fig. 18). In approximately late 1779, Nicholas decided to travel from neutral St. Croix to war-torn British North America. This was not a permanent move, and he returned to St. Croix before the war was over. His wife, Anna, and their family remained on the island, where children of the couple were baptized in July 1779, May 1781, and September 1782. This trip into the war zone, as subsequent events were to prove, entailed considerable personal risk, and the reasons for it are not fully clear. He may have traveled out of the tropics in the hopes of improving his health, but this does not explain all his subsequent movements.[66]

Nicholas's voyage to the continent produced several encounters with the British and patriot militaries. Accounts suggest that Nicholas was, over the course of the war, captured twice at sea by British ships and brought to New York as a prisoner at least once and perhaps twice.[67] He may also have had an additional near escape from being made a British prisoner. A striking feature of Nicholas's story in these years is how he was able to move between British and American zones of military control. Nicholas's movements reveal that he maintained contacts with high-ranking patriots; British and loyalist leaders; North American, Caribbean, and British merchants; and other correspondents. Most of them appear to have regarded him as someone with whom they could do business.

While it seems certain that Nicholas was captured at least once by the British, what exactly happened is muddy, and it is difficult to fully reconstruct Nicholas's movements in wartime North America. There is little contemporaneous evidence documenting them, and the most detailed accounts of what happened to Nicholas while he was on the mainland date to 1784 and later. They come from *after* the war had ended in American victory and the British had

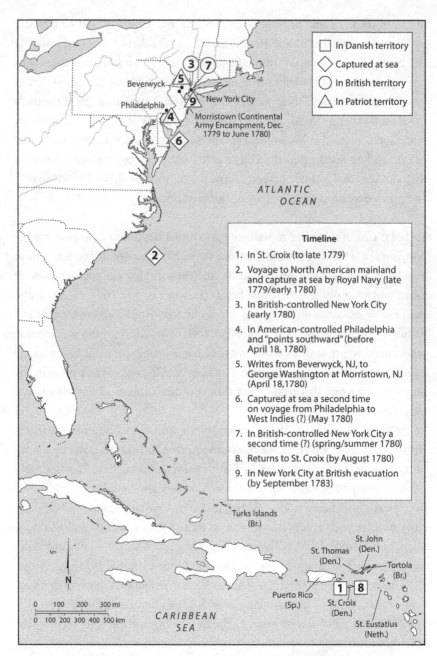

Figure 18. Nicholas Cruger's Border-Crossing War, 1779–83. Nicholas Cruger moved repeatedly between Danish, patriot, and British territory as he continued trading during the Revolutionary War.

evacuated New York and, as we will see, from a period during which Nicholas worked to establish himself as having been a patriotic American. In the few wartime family letters that survive, there is little detailed discussion of Nicholas being a British prisoner, perhaps because of desires to be discreet in dangerous times, or perhaps because these incidents were not as traumatic or significant as they were made to be in later histories. Considering accounts of Nicholas's captures by the British reveals how the outcome of the conflict immediately began shaping memories and narratives of it. In some hands, such as those of family historians in the nineteenth century, Nicholas's captures were recounted—and probably embellished—to emphasize his fidelity to the American cause, but other readings are possible.

According to an account that Jacob Walton sent to Peter Van Schaack, in late October 1779 Nicholas was a passenger bound for Boston aboard a Danish-flagged sloop that was seized by two Royal Navy vessels. The warships had sent the sloop, which New York Vice-Admiralty Court records show was the *Adriane*, into British New York, and legal proceedings were begun to enable its captors to profit from its seizure. The captured sloop was owned by the St. Croix merchant Pieter Heyliger Abrahamson, however, and he was tied to the transnational and well-connected family of Dutch/Danish/North American merchants to which Nicholas's wife, Anna, was also related. Nicholas, the *Adriane*'s captain told the New York court, was traveling with a servant and a few other passengers to Boston to recover his health, and the vessel sailed under a flag of truce granted by St. Croix's Danish governor. When the captured vessel, which carried no cargo, arrived in New York, Jacob Walton was entrusted to act on behalf of the ship's owners. Walton, helping the ship's owners but also a loyalist in good standing, challenged efforts to have the vessel declared a lawful prize and then began legal action against its captors for damages, a proceeding that Walton asked Peter Van Schaack to assist with in England.[68] Neither court records nor Walton's account, however, make clear whether Nicholas was personally regarded by the sloop's British captors as a neutral Dane, a rebellious American, or a loyal Briton.

However Nicholas was classified in New York, this incident shows that, by sailing in a Danish-flagged vessel, Nicholas was ready and able to use the legal frameworks that circumscribed maritime warfare during the Revolution to facilitate his own movement and further his own interests. As one account has put it, "the major contribution of the Danes in the carriage of products to and from their Caribbean possessions and North America lay in supplying Danish papers to merchant, vessel and cargo, United States and British, alike."[69] In this environment, neutrality was neither a state of mind nor an abstraction. Rather it was something of concrete value: a legal status that could be used by those like Nicholas who had the savvy and willingness to make the most of it.

By the late winter or early spring of 1780, Nicholas was *outside* of British-controlled New York City and in patriot-held territory in New Jersey. According to a short item that appeared in the Philadelphia press in early February 1780, "Richard Cruger, Esquire, a gentleman of eminence, and a zealous Advocate for the rights and independence of America" had recently "arrived at Morris Town, from St. Croix (via N. York)."[70] If this was a botched reference to Nicholas Cruger, as seems likely, someone was touting his American bona fides in early 1780. When and why Nicholas crossed between the armies is not well documented, but his own correspondence reveals that he did so with British permission. In April 1780 Nicholas sent, through Alexander Hamilton, a letter to George Washington, who was encamped with the Continental Army in Morristown, New Jersey. In this letter, dispatched from Beverwyck, near Morristown, Nicholas recounted that he had recently been in New York and granted a pass to travel through British lines to Philadelphia and points southward in return for a promise that he would return to New York City if instructed to do so by its British military commandant, General James Pattison. Nicholas reported that other people in New York—Jacob Walton seems a likely candidate—had also made pledges to Pattison to help secure him a pass. Now Pattison had sent word through these friends that he wanted Nicholas to return to British-occupied New York. Nicholas had been intending to sail from Philadelphia, perhaps back to St. Croix, but "knowing the Situation of my Friends" and "fearing they might Suffer & being bound by every Tie of Honor & Affection, I Determin'd to Comply with the Request & go into N[ew] York."

The problem, Nicholas told Washington, was that supporters of the Revolution had now become suspicious of his movements. He reported being "inform'd by some of my Friends that illgrounded Suspitions have allready Takeing Place in the Breasts of some infamous suspicious Charactors to my Prejudice & that insinuations have been and wou'd, Continue to be Thrown out that I had Come into the Country to serve the Purposes of the Enemy Shou'd, I Return to N[ew]York." These fears that he was a British spy, Nicholas told Washington, were unjust. They were not, however, unreasonable, as New York was a hotbed of espionage by both sides. "I would wish," Nicholas wrote, "the Good People of this Country to entertain that Opinion of me to which I think the Rectitude of my Conduct from the Earliest Period of this Controversy to the Present day entitles me." Cruger wanted simultaneously to protect his "friends" in New York, stay out of the British-controlled city, and preserve his reputation among patriotic Americans.

He wrote to Washington seeking a way out of this dilemma, and what he requested was a revealingly cunning expedient. Cruger asked Washington to refuse in writing his own formal—but in fact entirely insincere—request for permission to pass through the American lines and go into British New York. By staying out of British New York, Cruger hoped that there "may be no Possible Doubt Left (with any) of my Attachment to the Interest of the States," while Washington's written refusal to grant him a pass through American lines would "Serve to exculpate my Friend in N[ew] York, and be a justification to me."[71] He planned, he told Washington, to sail from Philadelphia in a few days.

Despite its rather extraordinary nature, Washington complied with Cruger's request, writing shortly thereafter in punctilious fashion: "I have considered the request You were pleased to make for permission to return to New York and beg leave to inform You – that I do not think myself authorized to grant it. I hope this will not be attended with any personal inconveniences to Yourself or with any embarrassments to your friends in New York."[72] Here again, questions multiply. Washington's willingness to participate in Cruger's plan might be read as an indication of Cruger's patriot bona fides; perhaps Washington believed Cruger had or would render valuable service to the patriot cause.[73] The event might also be read as reflecting Nicholas's ability to leverage relationships with influential figures on both sides of the conflict. Most clearly, it suggests the subtle, even slippery, methods by which Nicholas made his way through the Revolution.

If the subterfuge abetted by Washington allowed Nicholas to escape a tight spot in April, he seems to have soon found himself in more difficulty. Another run-in with British military officialdom is attested to in a newspaper published in New York in May 1780, although Nicholas's personal connection to these events was not clear in the initial published account of what happened. In this case, a vessel leaving Philadelphia and bound for the West Indies was captured by the Royal Navy frigate HMS *Iris*. The likeliest scenario given the timing of these events is that soon after his correspondence with Washington, Nicholas traveled to Philadelphia in order to sail for St. Croix and that the vessel on which he then left was captured by the *Iris*. After the *Iris*'s seizure of the West Indies–bound vessel, perhaps the *Active* of Philadelphia that was sailing to St. Eustatius under the command of Thomas Mesnard, its passengers and its cargo were brought up on deck. According to the account published by the New York loyalist printer James Rivington on May 31, 1780, as the *Iris*'s crew assessed their capture, a portrait of George Washington intended "to *illuminate* the parlour of a zealot" who was one of the "passengers to the West Indies," was among the items brought up on deck.[74] Rivington did not name this "zealot" in his 1780 newspaper article.

In 1784, however, soon after the British army left New York, Nicholas was named in print as the passenger associated with the Washington portrait, and more details of the story emerged. It was claimed that after its capture by the *Iris*, Cruger's vessel was sent as a prize to British-occupied New York. There, Rivington denounced Nicholas to British military authorities as a "dangerous rebel" who "ought to be taken great care of" and urged his close confinement in jail or aboard a prison ship. Had the British put Cruger on a prison ship, he may well have died, as did many other patriot prisoners held in horrific conditions in New York. In urging Cruger's confinement, Rivington reportedly told British authorities that Nicholas lived on "a neutral island in the West-Indies, from whence he supplied the rebels; that he was returning thither for no other purpose; and that if it had not been for the supplies which such damn'd rascals constantly furnished, the rebellion would long since have been ended." Nicholas had returned "home" to New York once again, but he had landed in a situation in which his allegiance could be interrogated.

Whatever his politics, however, Nicholas Cruger still had powerful friends in British-occupied New York. According to postwar accounts, Nicholas was warned of Rivington's denunciation by a sympathetic British officer and again aided by his loyalist brother-in-law, Jacob Walton, "whose exertions with the Commander in Chief and other officers, ultimately prevailed."[75] Rather than being confined aboard a prison ship, Nicholas was allowed to give his parole and live comfortably in his sister Mary and Jacob's house. As he later told Peter Van Schaack, "the civilitys and many good offices I rec[eive]d from our estimed friend J.W." would "ever be most greatfully remembered & acknowledg'd."[76] Once again, it was Nicholas's connections to influential loyalists that proved his salvation.

Throughout the story of Nicholas's revolution, private and family interests intertwined with political developments. While in British-controlled New York at some point in 1780, Nicholas learned that his father, Henry Cruger Sr., had died in England in February.[77] In the midst of the war, and against the backdrop of his own retreat to England, the wealthy Henry had written a will designed to secure legacies for his children, grandchildren, and other relatives whatever the conflict's outcome. In it, Henry distinguished between property that he owned in England, North America, and the West Indies and named different executors and beneficiaries for these different parts of his estate. John Harris Cruger, having been attainted by New York State, was left nothing in North America but was bequeathed all of Henry's property in Jamaica and the West Indies, which could not be touched by patriot authorities. All of Henry's surviving children, except for Telemon of Curaçao, who was not mentioned in the will, and Henry's Van Schaack grandchildren stood to gain sizable legacies. Nicholas stood to inherit a quarter of his father's North American property.

Nicholas, Jacob Walton, and Peter Van Schaack were named as executors for the North American portion of the elder Cruger's estate. Its settlement was complicated by Henry's ownership of real estate in both British-occupied New York City and in patriot-controlled New York State. Moreover, one of the executors, Peter Van Schaack, was in exile in England, while Walton was in good standing in wartime New York City but unable to travel outside British lines. Delay increased the risks that political and military developments might prevent Henry's heirs from securing their legacies. If Nicholas was forced to return to the city in 1780, therefore, the timing was rather auspicious. On learning of Henry Cruger's death, Nicholas and Jacob Walton took advantage of being together on the spot and worked to sell off Henry Sr.'s substantial New York City holdings.[78] Nicholas subsequently gave Jacob power of attorney to act regarding the estate in his name, as did Peter Van Schaack in letters from England. As he worked to help settle this important family business, and as he had various run-ins with the Royal Navy, Nicholas was able to call on powerful friends to aid his movements in wartime America.

By August 1780, Nicholas was back in St. Croix.[79] Once again, how or why Nicholas was allowed by British authorities to leave New York and return to St. Croix following Rivington's denunciation is mysterious. Nicholas was presumably regarded as a civilian, New York was overcrowded, and Nicholas had both wealth and connections. It also seems possible that he made the most of his status as a Danish subject. Perhaps after a time the terms of Nicholas's parole were extended to allow him to return to neutral St. Croix. Crucially, many of the details surrounding these events—the identification of Nicholas with the passenger who had a portrait of Washington, the account of Rivington's unsuccessful efforts to have him jailed, and his being allowed to live in the Waltons' house—all made their way into print only *after* the war, when they emerged in the context of Nicholas's efforts to resettle himself permanently in the newly independent United States. Then, like other nobody men, Nicholas would have been anxious to put his wartime choices in the best political light possible.

These may not have been Nicholas's only encounters with the Royal Navy. In another incident, according to a colorful but unsourced family story, a vessel on which Nicholas was a passenger was captured by a Royal Navy ship. After Cruger's vessel was boarded, the British commander interrogated Nicholas. On learning Nicholas's name, the British officer asked him whether he was related to Colonel (John Harris) Cruger, who was mentioned for the defense of Ninety Six in the military dispatches that the British vessel was carrying to Halifax. Nicholas affirmed that John Harris was his brother, and then, whether in an act of kindness, because of a presumption that Nicholas shared his brother's loyalties, or because of a subterfuge on Nicholas's part, the Royal Navy officer let Nicholas go. In this episode, which must have taken place after June 1781 if it occurred, Nicholas appeared willing to take advantage of his brother's loyalties when it suited him to do so.[80]

Nicholas's encounters with the Revolution's contending militaries do not appear to have damaged his finances; he prospered during the war. In 1780, Nicholas purchased 104 enslaved people from Denmark's slave trading company, evidently for the purpose of resale on the island.[81] He purchased more property in Christiansted in 1781.[82] In August 1780, after his return to St. Croix, Nicholas offered revealing advice to Peter Van Schaack, then in England, on how he might return to then British-controlled New York when he wanted to do so and stay clear of both patriot and British warships. "Permitt me," Nicholas wrote his brother-in-law, "to point out a safe way [to go] as it's warr time & going from England you may be captured." Nicholas suggested sailing "via Copenhagen or via Amsterdam in a Deans [Danish] or Dutch Vessel" to St. Croix and then travelling on to British "Tortola [which] is in sight of this island" and "from whence you can take passage to New York."[83] Throughout the war, Nicholas was able to call on his professional knowledge and networks to steer through revolutionary dangers that wrecked the lives of others.

Fighting on the North American mainland was greatly reduced after the American victory at Yorktown, but the war at sea and in the Caribbean continued. It was against this backdrop that another ship carrying cargo owned by Nicholas Cruger was seized in September 1782. Nicholas's previous—and more often subsequently recounted—dealings with belligerent forces had involved the Royal Navy, but on this occasion his interests fell afoul of a patriot vessel when the brig *Cumberland* was captured by a privateer out of New London, Connecticut. The *Harmony* was a recently commissioned eight-gun sloop with a crew of twenty-five under the command of Thomas Hopkins, and its owner, the merchant John Deshon, was an influential patriot who served as a civilian official for both the Continental Navy and the Connecticut state navy.[84]

The *Cumberland* was sailing from Tortola to Glasgow when it was taken. The *Harmony* attacked the brig about three hundred miles south of Bermuda and seized it after a violent encounter subsequently euphemized as a "spirited engagement." The *Cumberland*'s cargo included fifty bales of cotton belonging to Cruger being sent to the Scottish merchant John Morrice and fifty-five hogsheads of sugar owned by Cruger's sometimes St. Croix business associate, David McFarlane, and consigned to another Scottish trading house.[85] The *Cumberland* itself, according to subsequently submitted legal documents, was owned by merchants from the northwestern English port of Whitehaven, and British merchants also presumably owned other parts of the vessel's cargo.

Nicholas's involvement in this British-flagged venture undermines any easy assumptions that his wartime trading was undertaken consistently in the service of the American cause. Tortola was a British possession whose aggressive privateers frequently attacked American shipping and harassed Danish-flagged vessels that they believed were supporting the rebels. Moreover, from a patriot perspective, Cruger and McFarlane were engaging in wartime trade in a British ship between two British ports. In this venture Nicholas, who had previously advised Peter Van Schaack on Tortola's utility for wartime border crossing, was drawing on his knowledge of the transnational gray trading networks that crisscrossed the Caribbean to gain access to British markets. Nor does the voyage of the *Cumberland* appear to have been the only investment that Nicholas made in wartime trading between the Caribbean and Britain. In 1782, the New York–connected Bristol merchant Thomas Hayes wrote to Peter Van Schaack referencing business that he had done with Nicholas Cruger and Nicholas's orders that he pay money to the London merchant Alexander Grant. Nicholas remained involved in trading with British ports and correspondents even after insisting on his patriot credentials to Washington in 1780.[86]

After capturing the *Cumberland*, the *Harmony*'s captain sent the ship and its cargo into New Haven, where it was condemned as a lawful prize at a session of a revolutionary maritime court sitting there in November 1782.[87] Cruger and

McFarlane seem not to have challenged these initial proceedings—they may not have known yet of the *Cumberland*'s fate—but eventually Nicholas learned of what happened to the ship and his cotton. Others without the legal and political resources of the Cruger family might have let the matter drop, but Nicholas did not. He evidently believed that his property should not have been condemned by the Connecticut court. In 1783, with the fighting drawing to a close but Britain and the United States still formally at war, Nicholas launched an effort to recover his property. In April 1783, Cruger and MacFarlane were granted a hearing to petition for a new trial by the Connecticut maritime court that had condemned the *Cumberland* and her cargo as lawful prizes.[88] This hearing failed to lead to the return of their property, but Nicholas persisted in his efforts to win restitution for the seizure of the *Cumberland* in the postwar period. Through it all, Nicholas continued to trade. He joined other St. Croix merchants in channeling some trade in North American tobacco and provisions in exchange for European manufactures through the Danish island of St. Thomas during the war's closing stages.[89] More broadly, Danish authorities on St. Croix issued passes authorizing Nicholas's ships to make twenty-four voyages between December 1782 and September 1784, and they went to a telling array of ports: New York, Philadelphia, and "Carolina" in the United States, Montreal in British North America, and a host of harbors in the multinational Caribbean including Puerto Rico, Havana, the Bay of Honduras, St. Martin, Curaçao, and Tortuga.[90]

Nicholas Cruger's war illustrates the reality of historical uncertainty as a feature of the nobody men's history. It is possible that some as-yet undiscovered document might be a Rosetta Stone to Nicholas's war, a key to the decoding of all his actions. It seems more likely that Nicholas would never have allowed such a document to survive. If definitive answers about Nicholas's motivations are unlikely, his actions are revealing. Nicholas responded to the Revolution much like he and other members of the Cruger family did to wars during the colonial period: with one eye on the dangers and the other on the opportunities that the storm created. He may have had political preferences, but these preferences did not necessarily outweigh other more mundane priorities. Rather, insulated to some extent by his Danish subjecthood, he spent much of the war pursuing his own interests, financial and otherwise, and doing mutually beneficial business with like-minded others.

Nicholas Cruger approached the war as a logistical problem to be overcome rather than as a referendum on his political philosophy. In this, Nicholas was like many other people affected by the conflict in North America, the Caribbean, and elsewhere. The Revolution is frequently sanitized into a battle of ideas, as if the opposing armies were firing quotations from John Locke and Magna Carta rather than musket shot and cannonballs, but the conflict killed, traumatized, and impoverished many caught up in it. Understandably, many people endeavored to keep the pain and misery it caused from darkening their doors. If ways of getting around the war rather than going through it could be found, they were often taken. When the conflict ended, Nicholas was able to return to New York City with his reputation, health, and fortune intact. Had the British won the war, he might well have been able to do the same thing. Many revolutionary-era people would have seen such an outcome as nothing less than a victory.

PART THREE

"My Heart Still Cleaves to New York"

1783–1800

9. Subjects and Citizens

In the wake of the 1783 Treaty of Paris, the Crugers were on the move, criss-crossing the Atlantic to refit their families, commerce, and politics to match new realities. When the war finally ended, the Crugers' primary reaction was relief. The treaty's generous terms toward the United States, which almost certainly exceeded what family members had imagined as winnable in 1775, made the end of the fighting even sweeter. Like other survivors of the war's tumults, how-ever, they found that peace was no panacea. The years of violence had a long tail, and the challenges posed by the Revolution did not end when the last British fleet departed New York harbor.

All the Crugers had to negotiate the legacies of their wartime choices. They went in various directions, literal and figurative, after the war, but the family's interdependence endured. Between 1783 and 1788, like others affected by the conflict, the Crugers adapted to an uncertain world, one in which the meaning and consequences of new borders, new politics, and new economic conditions had to be confronted (fig. 19). As Henry Cruger put it in 1784, "the times, though tranquil, are rather agitating."[1] While the postwar years were difficult, most of the Crugers gradually found their feet. Collectively, the family's history in these years shows how the Treaty of Paris began a prolonged and multisided process through which a transnational revolutionary generation adjusted to a remade and—whatever its other promises—more fragmented world.

In some ways, John Harris and Anne De Lancey Cruger's postwar choices were the simplest. Having decisively cast their lot with the Crown, remaining in New

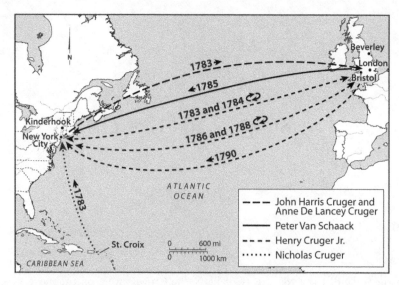

Figure 19. The Crugers' Post-Revolutionary Migrations, 1783–90.

York was effectively impossible, and they sailed for England in 1783. The couple's ties to their De Lancey relatives—central to their way into participation in violent civil war—were crucial to their route out. Oliver and Phila De Lancey and much of their extended family joined some sixty thousand other loyalists (and fifteen thousand enslaved people owned by them) who left America following the British defeat. Approximately seven thousand of them, including many of the wealthier and better-connected loyalists like the De Lanceys, landed in Britain.[2] London became the capital of the loyalist diaspora and, as John Harris observed to a fellow officer in 1784, "this hug[e] unwieldy Town swarms with Americans grumbling and discontented."[3] Others, however, were drawn to smaller places.[4] The De Lanceys settled in Beverley, a relatively small market town in Yorkshire's East Riding. Why they chose Beverley remains obscure, but like other "people with independent means" the De Lanceys probably appreciated "its polite and cultivated life and the availability of elegant but comparatively cheap houses."[5] John Harris and Anne joined what became a small loyalist colony there. Peter Van Schaack made the two-hundred-mile trip north from London to Beverley in the fall of 1784 and stayed for several months in what he deemed a "remote place."[6]

Oliver De Lancey Sr. did not long outlive his cause, dying in Beverley in October 1785. John Harris and Anne continued living there among other relatives and associates, including Anne's brother, Oliver De Lancey Jr. (1749–1822), whose militant loyalism also made him a postwar exile. The younger Oliver had obtained a regular commission in the British army in 1766 and continued his military career long after 1783, which shaped John Harris's future. Collectively, the De Lanceys maintained their connections to the British army for decades. A nephew of Oliver Sr. became an aide to the duke of Wellington and died on the field at Waterloo. Oliver Jr.'s son, another Oliver (1805–1837), died following the family trade while leading volunteers in Spain's first Carlist civil war.[7] While her father's time in exile was short, Anne's mother, Phila, resided in England for nearly three decades, dying in 1811. It was as part of this increasingly anglicized army family that John Harris and Anne spent the rest of their lives.

Like other officers, John Harris felt a continuing responsibility to the men who had served under him. Before leaving America, he lobbied for the survivors of De Lancey's Brigade to be resettled on good land in Nova Scotia.[8] They received grants around what became the town of Woodstock in newly created New Brunswick, less than fifteen miles from the current US/Canada border. While this proffered a fresh start for some of Cruger's comrades, resettlement brought new tragedy when a transport ship from New York, the *Martha*, loaded with refugees including men and families from the brigade's second battalion, was wrecked off St. John in September 1783. Fishing boats rescued seventy-five survivors, who were now without the few possessions that they had carried into exile. Ninety-nine of the *Martha's* passengers perished.[9]

John Harris Cruger, Oliver De Lancey, and others in their families filed claims with the Loyalist Claims Commission established by the British government in June 1783. Britain paid out more than £3 million to loyalists in a process that stretched over six years. While this was only approximately a third of the compensation requested, it was an unprecedented assumption of government responsibility for civil war's consequences.[10] Because of their high military ranks, prewar wealth and status, and because they had been named in punitive American legislation, Oliver and John Harris, both already placed on half pay by the army, were better placed than most loyalists to obtain substantial compensation. Oliver claimed that his prewar estate had been worth some £100,000 and that he had lost over £78,000 through the Revolution; the commission awarded him £23,446. The commission also awarded Anne's mother, Phila, £200 per year and her sister Charlotte an annual stipend of £100 in recognition of her courage during the 1777 attack on the family's Bloomingdale house.[11]

Even for powerful loyalists, dealing with the claims commission was difficult and frequently dispiriting. In his February 1784 claim, John Harris calculated that he had lost over £2,100 New York currency between the seizure of his Manhattan house and the destruction of nearly all his and Anne's movable property at Bloomingdale. He also claimed that New York City's municipal corporation owed him a prewar debt of £1,100 plus nearly £400 in interest for money he advanced it as chamberlain, but which it now refused to repay. He had lost title to two tracts totaling eight thousand acres in what had been Charlotte County, New York. Calculating the value of such unimproved land was difficult, and the best Cruger could do was to note that he had turned down a prewar offer to sell one of his parcels for ten shillings an acre and that the second parcel was of equal value. That suggests that he thought the land was worth no less than £4,000; like the many Americans who speculated in land, he probably envisioned it being worth far more someday.

The Revolution had also destroyed Cruger's career. It cost him his trading business, which he estimated had brought in £600 to £700 per year, and the office of chamberlain in New York, worth another £300 to £400 annually. Last, he noted the existence of debts owed by prewar trading partners but did not try to estimate them beyond observing that his business had "been extensive."[12] Article 4 of the Treaty of Paris had blithely stated in just one sentence that "creditors on either side shall meet with no lawful impediment to the recovery of the full value in sterling money of all bona fide debts heretofore contracted." But it stipulated no mechanisms for such recoveries from American citizens and left British merchants and loyalist exiles with few options other than repeatedly asking for repayment. In a 1788 letter to the commissioners, John Harris observed with some exasperation that on their instructions, he had tried to ascertain exactly what he owed to "subjects of the United States" from his trading before 1775. Because of the passage of time and the destruction of his papers at Bloomingdale, he was unable to precisely document his prewar liabilities, but swore they totaled less than £500 New York currency. More important, he thought, these debts were "very small and very few in comparison to what the subjects of the United States owe me."[13] Over time, he experienced being dunned by long-lost trading partners for old debts even as he could not collect his own.

As Cruger's claim inched forward, he received support from Peter Van Schaack, the exiled former New York alderman and trader William Waddell, and more powerful figures including Lord North and Sir Guy Carleton. Charles Cornwallis testified in June 1785 that John Harris had "conducted himself in a manner highly for the good of the country" and "rendered very essential services to the British Government."[14] Nevertheless, John Harris faced the situation common to all claimants: there were many worthy cases, the commission was overtaxed, and bureaucracy moved slowly. In 1786 he was still working to obtain proof that his New York property had been seized and sold in accordance with the 1779 Forfeiture Act, a process that made him, like other claimants, oddly reliant on patriot officials to document his losses. His New York townhouse, it emerged, had been legally seized and then sold off in 1784.[15] The purchaser, Malachi Treat, had been a doctor in the Continental Army. While Cruger and his supporters valued the house as worth at least £1,200 New York money, Treat had paid just £800 for it.[16]

The commission determined that Cruger had a claim for just under £3,473 in lost property. It awarded him, as a final settlement, £928 in restitution and a yearly stipend of £180 to replace his lost income. According to even his incomplete estimates, he received compensation amounting to only perhaps one-quarter of his prewar personal wealth and could expect an annual income of about one-fifth what he earned in 1775. John Harris probably had other financial resources—his father had left him unspecified property in Jamaica—and he and Anne were better off than many loyalists, but the war caused a dramatic deterioration in their position and prospects. John Harris appears to have never worked as a large-scale merchant again. He and Anne had found a haven in Beverley, but on dark Yorkshire nights they likely lingered over the memories of brighter New York days.

The end of the war set the loyalist diaspora in motion, but it also launched other sorts of voyages. Several Crugers sailed west after 1783, joining a stream of America-bound migrants who saw the war's end as an opening rather than a closing. Approximately fifty-two thousand people from the United Kingdom emigrated to the United States between 1783 and 1789, a counterflow to the loyalist exodus that started when the Treaty of Paris "released a valve long held shut."[17] Most British emigrants were Irish Protestants, but English and Scottish people went to the new United States too, and they were joined by others from continental Europe and the Caribbean, including Nicholas Cruger. Before the Revolution, it seemed that as a younger son, Nicholas's future lay in St. Croix, but his father's death and eldest brother's exile created space in the city of his birth. Between 1783 and 1788 Nicholas established himself more definitively as an American and became the head of his family's interests in New York.

In this process, Nicholas worked to redefine his past to suit a changing world. Implementing peace was not simple, and Nicholas's movements in 1783 were products of the uncertainty and instability that accompanied translating diplomatic agreements into on-the-ground realities. American and British negotiators in Paris signed preliminary peace terms in late November 1782. George III's public declaration of a cessation of hostilities in America was subsequently issued on February 14, 1783. It made its way across the Atlantic and was read at New York's city hall in early April, where assembled loyalist crowds responded with "groans and hisses" and "bitter reproaches and curses upon their king, for having deserted them in the midst of their calamities."[18] Although a final peace treaty was not signed until September 1783, the announcement of provisional peace terms set in motion a months-long withdrawal during which the British military held on to New York City as a last bastion in the United States.

Much was up for grabs in what was simultaneously an imperial twilight and a national dawn. New York saw "a continuous parade of loyalist departures, and some patriot returns" in the summer of 1783.[19] Among those entering the city were people who had left when the British army arrived in 1776 but were now anxious to reclaim houses and other properties.[20] While loyalists preparing to leave New York sold their property for cash that they could carry into exile, others intending to stay or to stake a claim saw remarkable opportunities. Henry Cruger was in New York by August 1783 to promote his business interests, and Nicholas was there by September. Nicholas was openly doing business in America before the Treaty of Paris became official.[21]

On November 25, 1783, the last elements of the British army boarded their ships, and George Washington led the victorious Continental Army into New York City. Commemorated for generations as Evacuation Day, the moment was replete with symbolism as the multiyear local dominance of the British and American loyalists was overthrown. New York's patriots were, at long last, ascendant, and some of them had scores to settle. In some later accounts, Nicholas Cruger is said to have been in the entourage that accompanied Washington on his triumphal entrance into the city, but other accounts do not mention him, and the story may reflect later attempts to burnish his image.[22]

Whether or not he rode in with Washington, in January 1784 Nicholas had an encounter in New York City that illustrates the complexities of reputation in the postwar period. To the surprise of many, the printer James Rivington, an object of public patriot scorn because of his highly visible support for the British cause, remained in New York after the evacuation. Nicholas encountered

Rivington in the street and attacked him, perhaps after Rivington attempted to shake his hand or greet him. In the words of one early report, Nicholas "disciplined him very handsomely for some of his meritorious actions in the reign of George III."[23] Nicholas's assault on Rivington, whom the Crugers had known for many years, captured public attention. Robert R. Livingston, son to the delegate to the Stamp Act Congress, recorded that "Rivington has been beat by N. Cruger and intimidated by the Committee of Mechanicks so as to be induced to stop his press."[24] The incident led to the publication of a lengthy letter, signed "Vindicator," which acknowledged that Nicholas had knocked Rivington down in the street and given him "a kick or two."[25] Nicholas's grievance, the January 1784 letter claimed, was that in 1780 Rivington had denounced him to British authorities as a dangerous patriot when his ship was captured and brought in to New York. Indeed, it is primarily from this 1784 letter that the details of what may have happened to Cruger in 1780 are known.[26]

Parsing what transpired between Cruger and Rivington in 1780 and 1784 is complicated by a fact unknown to most people in revolutionary New York: the apparent loyalist Rivington was a patriot spy who provided Washington timely intelligence from within the British-controlled city.[27] Some people noted with surprise that Rivington remained in New York after the British evacuated. According to one newspaper account, "as soon as our troops entered the city, Rivington was "protected in person and property by a guard" and would "be allowed to reside in the country, for reasons best known to the great men at the helm."[28] Yet Rivington was more generally reviled by many of his patriot contemporaries, who, labeling him an arch-tory and an inveterate liar, could not forgive him for openly supporting the British regime in wartime New York. Both Cruger and Rivington made revolutionary choices that remain difficult to decipher. Rivington publicly denied the charges "Vindicator" made with the "firmest confidence" and called for his antagonist to produce evidence.[29] The events that "Vindicator" recounted in his 1784 letter—in which the angry "patriot" Cruger assaulted the "loyalist" Rivington—may well have occurred, but neither Cruger nor Rivington may have been exactly what he seemed to his contemporaries in this postwar hall of mirrors.

What is clearer is that Cruger's 1784 attack on the deeply unpopular Rivington and the ensuing reports justifying it combined to position Nicholas publicly on the right side of recent history. Because the war was now over, how people wanted to talk about it changed. For former patriots, loyalists, and nobodyists alike, controlling narratives about the past was important to people's future prospects. Cruger may have wanted to assert his patriot credentials at a liminal moment because people had so evidently doubted them in previous years. Beating the hated James Rivington was one way for Nicholas Cruger to pledge allegiance in newly American New York.[30]

Nicholas retained property on St. Croix and visited and kept up his connections with the island, but from 1784 his interests increasingly centered on New York City. He likely sensed commercial opportunities in postwar New York, but other factors probably shaped this decision-making. Anna de Nully Cruger died on St. Croix in November 1784, which may have made it easier for Nicholas to emigrate permanently. In November 1785, the recently widowed Nicholas married Ann Markoe in Philadelphia's Episcopal Christ Church parish. About twenty at the time of her marriage—less than half Nicholas's age—Ann was the daughter of Elizabeth and Isaac Markoe (1736?–1777).[31] The young bride, like Nicholas, was from a transnational family with members and property in the Caribbean and North America. Descended from Dutch settlers on St. Eustatius, the Markoes had become St. Croix planters. Isaac moved to Philadelphia in the pre-revolutionary period, perhaps along with or following his older brother Abraham, who arrived there in 1770 and became conspicuous in the prewar patriot movement despite his Danish subjecthood. Given the small size of the St. Croix elite, it seems likely that Nicholas had known Ann's family for many years prior to their marriage. Nicholas's second marriage strengthened his economic and political connections in St. Croix and the United States while underlining his patriotic credentials in a time of change.

Nicholas's reputation affected his business prospects in the postwar United States. Cruger had failed in April 1783 to have a Connecticut court overturn the seizure of his goods aboard the *Cumberland*, which had been captured by patriot privateers in 1782 while trading between Tortola and Glasgow. In late 1783 or early 1784, Cruger reopened the matter with new proceedings before the Court of Appeals in Cases of Capture, created by congress in 1780 as the first federal appeals court.[32] In a signed petition, Cruger described himself as now "of New York" but insisted that "long before and during the whole of the late war between the King of Great Britain and the United States of America" he was a "burgher and Inhabitant of the said Island of St. Croix within the dominions and jurisdictions of the King of Denmark and a subject of the said King." As a Danish subject, Cruger argued, he had been legally entitled to trade with Great Britain in 1782. Since the United States and Denmark were not at war at the time of the *Cumberland*'s capture, he held, his property was not a lawful prize and should be returned to him.[33] In these proceedings at least, the New York–born Nicholas wanted to be considered by nascent American institutions as having been neither a patriot nor a loyalist but a Dane during the war.

Even as he made such arguments, Cruger was becoming more and more certainly an American. By late 1785, he offered goods for sale including "choice muscovado sugars, rum, Carolina indigo, tobacco, and turpentine" from a New York store at 16 Duke Street.[34] His ships continued trading in the Caribbean, but he was managing his affairs from New York. He and Ann began socializing with prominent patriots such as Samuel B. Webb, one of Washington's wartime aides, and Sarah and John Jay.[35] Cruger's profitable trading enabled him to acquire considerable real estate in greater New York City, some of which he used and more of which he rented out. This property came to include a well-known gentleman's farm, Rose Hill, on land today part of the neighborhood named for it on Manhattan's East Side. Before the Revolution, Rose Hill had been owned by John Watts. He was attainted as a loyalist, but Watts's sons repurchased it and other family holdings from New York State in 1784. When Nicholas bought Rose Hill in 1786, it reflected the Crugers' return to prominence in New York while indicating his own commitment to the post-revolutionary order.[36] General Horatio Gates, Henry Cruger's old friend from Bristol, leased the farm from Nicholas for many years.

Against the backdrop of Nicholas's increasingly visible presence in New York, his lawsuit over the *Cumberland* ended. The court dismissed the case in May 1787 because neither side appeared before it.[37] Nicholas presumably had let the matter drop, possibly because he decided that he was unlikely to win or because pursuing it was too troublesome or expensive. It may also be that he, by then resident in New York and invested in having a reputation as a patriot, decided that he would rather not continue insisting upon his previous Danish subjecthood. It ill suited a "friend of Washington" to defend trading with the British during the war through the technicalities of international maritime law. Nicholas had previously found his Danish subjecthood an asset, but after the war he may have recognized that reminding people of his recent neutrality was a liability. Not all of the nobody men wanted to be remembered as such.

Although still in English exile, Peter Van Schaack was elated by the war's end. In early 1783 he told his nephew, the orphaned Henry Walton, that he had sent a set of books to Kinderhook as a prize for the local schoolboy who composed "the best exercise upon the blessings of *peace*, either in prose or poetry." Young

Walton, Van Schaack urged, should likewise encourage his classmates at the English school he was now attending to write "an ode to peace."[38] The Walton children, like Van Schaack's own, had not had a say in their parents' wartime choices, but they had to live with their consequences. Peter wanted people, especially the young, to put recent animosities behind them. In November 1784, Peter wrote his son Harry Van Schaack that "to pour balm into the yet bleeding wounds of our country, should be the object of every good citizen, of whatever party he *may have been.*"[39] It was time, he believed, for forgiveness and for looking forward on both sides of the Atlantic.

Capturing the continuing dangers that recent nobodyists faced and some of their strategies for dealing with them, Peter also gave his son advice on how to behave in public. "I hope," he wrote, "you will not get into any warm arguments on political subjects." Harry, it seems, was anxious to defend his father from critics, but Peter urged him to bite his tongue. "If you should hear me, or any of your other friends censured," Peter continued, "evade any altercation by saying it is a delicate subject as it affects your feelings, and too complicated a one for you to comprehend it." Reply, Peter advised, "that you can only answer for the integrity of your friends, but if they have not been blessed with abilities equal to those who censure them, it was their misfortune, not their fault."[40] This was asking much of a sixteen-year-old whose childhood had been blighted by the death of his mother and his father's absence, but Peter's advice was born of an assessment that silence was probably the best way to transcend history. Keeping quiet was a deliberate postwar strategy for reintegration.

Peter himself paired public reserve with careful private diplomacy. Besides reaching out to John Jay in 1783, Van Schaack reestablished connections with other old friends and influential figures in America. These included Egbert Benson and Gouverneur Morris, the latter of whom Van Schaack told in 1784 that "oblivion and conciliation are the great objects of my incessant, most fervent wish."[41] He particularly appreciated support from Theodore Sedgwick, an influential western Massachusetts patriot who served in the Continental Army and in 1780 entered the Continental Congress. Despite their wartime differences, Sedgwick became a firm friend to the extended Van Schaack family, and as Peter planned his return home, he told his brothers that Sedgwick had been so "uniformly friendly" that he could not "express myself with sufficient energy respecting him."[42] As such examples show, the nobodyists had some influential postwar American allies in their efforts to focus on the future.

Yet Van Schaack's experiences also highlight the political tensions, frequent arbitrariness, and legal uncertainties that shaded nobodyists' postwar lives. Peter was increasingly anxious to return to New York, and his children wanted him home immediately, but his politically-minded American friends urged patience until tensions eased. As Jay counseled from Paris in 1783, when it came to exiles like Van Schaack "the discussions of questions *de jure* require dispassionate and calm reflection, and that season must arrive before speculative principles can acquire sufficient force to produce fruit *de facto.*"[43] While the Treaty of Paris that Jay helped negotiate brought a welcome end to hostilities, the transnational legal position of many classes of people, including American-born European exiles like Van Schaack, remained unclear.

Peter considered himself an American citizen, but his lawyerly mind and firsthand experience of the capriciousness of revolutionary-era politics led him to proceed carefully. Understandably, he was particularly concerned about his children's futures in the United States, encouraging his eldest son to cultivate a personal relationship with Jay and worrying over the bequests that Henry Cruger Sr. left them in 1780. As Van Schaack knew, the loose terms of the American union meant that the individual states held the real practical power over nobodyists' futures. "I am exceedingly anxious," he wrote his brothers in February 1783, "to know what sort of maxims the States will adopt in this time of peace; the wisdom of them must determine what degree of happiness the country is to expect, at least in our time."[44] Deciding when and how to return required assessing risk.

Much of Van Schaack's strategizing remained out of the written record. In October 1783, with the peace negotiations in Paris concluded, Jay traveled to England. He and Van Schaack met and presumably discussed Peter's situation with much greater frankness than they were prepared to commit to letters. They spoke, Peter recorded, "with all the cordiality of old friends, who had long been absent, without the least retrospect to the cause of that absence."[45] Jay was in London for three months and Van Schaack reported that "he and I were often together." Rather than "wasting our time in unavailing recriminations," Peter said, "the present and future happiness of our common country, and the means conducive to it, afforded ample subjects for conversation."[46] Peter's subsequent confidence that Jay and other allies would help him get back to New York proved well placed.

Most people in Britain and Europe understood the preliminary terms of the peace as extremely favorable toward the United States. However, in America, and especially in New York, some patriots, seeing the issue in national and class terms, were enraged that loyalists might recover property and collect on debts. Skeptical of the elite patriots directing peace negotiations and mindful of their own wartime sacrifices, some in the new United States regarded anyone who had not fought for the Revolution as an inveterate enemy to American freedom. One significant expression of this popular anti-loyalist sentiment, the May 1783 Worcester Resolves, characterized those who had left the Massachusetts town during the war rather than take up arms on behalf of the patriot cause as "conspirators" who had engaged in "traitorous conduct." This meant they should forfeit their "civil and political relation to their injured and betrayed country" and be permanently classed as "enemies and aliens."[47] Van Schaack, weighing his future, followed these developments closely, recording that the Worcester Resolves tried "imperfect beings by rules of perfection, the resolvers being themselves the judges of what truth is."[48] As the resolves captured, significant numbers of victorious patriots were in little mood to compromise with loyalists.

Retribution-minded patriots tried to pass anti-loyalist laws in New York and elsewhere in late 1783 and early 1784.[49] There were also counter-efforts to block such legislation and tamp down anti-loyalist fury. Van Schaack's friend Gouverneur Morris, who had helped write New York's state constitution and subsequently drafted the preamble to the federal constitution, was among those who wanted as many exiles as possible to return home and participate in building the new nation. He told Peter in 1784 that "with a very few exceptions" of "old and powerful enemies, I would open wide the doors" and "not exclude those, who first drew the vital air, and first saw the light in America."[50] Jay was also part of this counter-effort, as was Hamilton, who published two letters as "Phocion" in early 1784 that condemned continuing efforts to punish or expel supposed loyalists as unjust, a violation of the Treaty of Paris, and ultimately self-defeating.[51] Henry Cruger revealed to Van Schaack that Hamilton was believed to be "Phocion" and praised him for it as "a brave, good, sensible man."[52]

Across 1784 it was uncertain whether proponents of reconciliation or reprisal would win out. Henry Cruger dismissively claimed that it was only "the Eructations of patriotic Mechanicks, whose stomachs are fuller of flatulent Liberty, than solid food" that alarmed "the unfortunate Loyalists," but he underestimated the depth of lingering animosities.[53] In May 1784, New York passed a new law intended "to preserve the freedom and independence of this state." A striking expression of postwar anti-loyalist sentiment, the measure formally disenfranchised and banished from the state not only those who had taken up arms for the Crown or held civilian offices under its authority after July 1776, but also anyone who had "gone over to, joined, or put himself or themselves under the Power and Protection of the Fleets or Armies of the King of Great-Britain," even if they had done nothing else to aid the British war effort. The law made having chosen to live behind British lines a crime for New Yorkers, one that permanently disqualified them from being citizens. It was a measure, like the Worcester Resolves, that retroactively cast forms of wartime nobodyism as loyalism.

While many thousands of people fell within the law's scope, its final section expressly exempted only twenty-seven named persons from its provisions because "a very respectable number of Citizens of this State, well attached to the Freedom and Independence thereof, have intreated the Legislature to extend Mercy to Persons herein after mentioned, and to restore them to their Country."[54] Among this small exempted group were Peter's brothers, Henry and David Van Schaack. Both men had reconciliationist inclinations during the war and had fallen repeatedly afoul of suspicious upstate patriots. They spent the later part of the conflict banished behind British lines around New York City after refusing to take the same oath to New York State that led to Peter's exile. But despite many hardships, they rode out the fighting without taking up arms for either side or going abroad. Henry Van Schaack had already settled in western Massachusetts with the help of Theodore Sedgwick by the time the New York law was passed, but David remained in New York, and his rehabilitation was welcome news.[55]

Unlike his brothers, Peter was not exempted by name from the harsh provisions of this May 1784 New York law. Peter thought this might be because Governor Clinton believed he was already legally permitted to return home. Henry Cruger, then visiting New York, had written to Van Schaack in February 1784 to tell him that he had dined at the governor's house in the company of a large party of influential men and that he had discussed Peter's desire to return with Clinton, who said "he did not know what was to hinder your returning to your family here when ever you thought proper."[56] Given the moment's animosities and uncertainties, however, the new risk was that Peter might fall afoul of the very law that had rehabilitated his brothers.[57]

Peter and his American friends therefore continued laying the groundwork for his return. Jay obtained Clinton's written statement that "it would be peculiarly hard" if Peter was prosecuted upon returning home and then advised Van Schaack in November 1784 to "return to this country as soon as you conveniently can." Then, Jay said, "such further steps may be taken as circumstances may render expedient."[58] With this encouragement from Jay and others, Peter began readying to leave England. Passions were cooling, but those in favor of reintegrating absentees and loyalists did not have things entirely in their favor. In October 1779 the New York legislature had made it illegal for any lawyers licensed before April 1777, as Peter had been, to continue practicing in New York's courts unless a jury found that the applicant was "a good and zealous friend to the American cause." In March 1785, as Van Schaack was making final preparations to sail home, an effort was made to repeal this law as well as to mitigate some of the harsher aspects of the May 1784 law that had defined loyalism so broadly. However, these legislative attempts failed and, as Jay had predicted, Van Schaack's full reincorporation had to follow his arrival back on American soil. As Van Schaack's departure neared, he remained hopeful about resettling in New York but was also aware that anti-loyalist sentiment there remained especially potent. His plan was to sail to New York and "upon my arrival in the harbor" to write to the governor about whether he could legally land. If, he said, "the answer I receive is not satisfactory, I shall go up the Sound and through Connecticut into Berkshire county." Residing in western Massachusetts, where his brother was making a new start, was Peter's backup plan if New York rejected him.[59]

As he prepared to leave England, Peter also settled his accounts with the Loyalist Claims Commission. In a hearing, Van Schaack frankly told the commissioners that he intended "to return to America but not immediately to the State of New York," probably reflecting the idea that he might join his brother in Massachusetts. In the language of postwar loyalist politics, the record of his appearance also observed that "Mr. Van Schaack has no particular Services to state"; he had done nothing to aid the British war effort. In May 1785 the commissioners wrapped up Van Schaack's case, taking away the £60 per year relief pension that he had previously been granted. Instead they awarded him a small lump sum, £30, as final compensation for his sufferings and closed his claim permanently.[60]

With this door shut, Van Schaack left for America in June 1785. Despite the previous decade's many tribulations, Van Schaack was still under forty years old and fully committed to a future in the United States. On his arrival in New York, Van Schaack got the welcome he had worked for. In a carefully choreographed display of acceptance and reintegration by New York's coalescing political elite, Jay personally came aboard Van Schaack's ship after it anchored on July 20, 1785, and escorted him to meetings with Clinton and New York Chief Justice Richard Morris. Peter's son Harry, "my dear boy," also met him in the city.

Seeing Harry reminded Peter "how thankful I ought to be, and instead of repining at my not being still more happy, my heart should overflow with gratitude for what I do enjoy." There was sadness, though, because Peter learned that his mother, who had been unwell for several years and much affected by her family's wartime sufferings, had died in Kinderhook shortly before his landing. Van Schaack had hoped to see her before she died, so this marked a tragic coda to his banishment.[61] On the advice of "friends," Peter spent ten days in New York City as "a matter of prudence, which will contribute to my peaceable establishment in future," before traveling north to Kinderhook.[62] Like Nicholas Cruger—albeit in a different register—Peter found ways to publicly pledge his allegiance.

Van Schaack first lived in some political and professional limbo, but the 1786 session of the New York state legislature was more willing than the previous one to relax anti-loyalist measures. It undid the wartime measure preventing insufficiently zealous lawyers from practicing, requiring only "evidence of good moral character, and an oath of abjuration and allegiance, and for the faithful execution of their offices." This was likely the moment when Peter swore loyalty to New York State because, in April 1786, he was readmitted to the New York bar at a session of the state supreme court. In May 1786, the assembly removed any final doubts about Van Schaack's status when it passed a law restoring citizenship to Peter and other named persons if they were prepared to take a loyalty oath.[63]

Perhaps because of his lifetime knack for friendship, Van Schaack's social reintegration was relatively smooth. He chose to reside in the quieter confines of Kinderhook rather than New York City. Most of his neighbors seem to have been happy to welcome him back; many people in the Hudson River Valley had harbored similar, albeit less intently scrutinized, doubts about the war. He became a figure in real estate law, with special expertise in cases involving old Dutch titles. The continuing turmoil over land claims kept him well supplied with business, and he was consulted by people resident in both the United States and Britain. In 1786 Peter began running a small law school out of his Kinderhook home and trained young lawyers for decades thereafter.[64] His son Harry, whose future had preoccupied Peter in exile, enrolled at his father's alma mater, rechristened as Columbia College to suit the new order; in 1787 Harry was valedictorian of his class.[65] Peter had negotiated the postwar crisis and won a future in his "native country."

Immediately after the preliminary peace proposals became known in 1783, Henry Cruger Jr. sailed to New York to wring payments out of old correspondents and secure new orders for goods. He arrived in New York City in August 1783, before the final conclusion of the peace and as the British Army and loyalists continued their evacuation. His very public arrival—in his own ship *Cruger* no less—was reported in multiple newspapers.[66] He traveled between United States territory and still-British New York during his visit. The North Carolinian Thomas Blount reported in September 1783 that Cruger was in Philadelphia and "solliciting orders from the Merchants to send them Goods."[67] Remarkably, the former member of Parliament was in New York City when the British completed their evacuation in November 1783. In its aftermath, he wrote Peter Van Schaack a largely hopeful letter observing that despite people's fears, "everything remains peaceable and quiet" after the British withdrawal. He celebrated that "Freedom, Generosity and America have shook hands."[68]

Henry was relieved that mob violence did not accompany the transfer of power in New York, but reestablishing his transatlantic business was a politically delicate and commercially uncertain prospect. Cruger's partnership with John Mallard had failed during the war, and Mallard had gone bankrupt. As peace neared, Cruger created a fresh Bristol-based partnership and a new firm with a London office with his longtime friend and political ally Thomas Mullett and a third partner, Thomas Lediard.[69] Mullett also traveled to America in 1783 and worked to renew economic and political ties between Britain's radicals and transatlantic merchants and their old allies there. On his 1783 trip, Mullett carried a letter from John Wilkes introducing him to John Hancock, then governor of Massachusetts, and he managed to meet personally with George Washington at Mount Vernon during his travels.[70]

The wider economic situation proved challenging. Henry Cruger and Company, as his Bristol firm was now known, faced stiff competition as Anglo-American merchants rushed European goods to American ports to capitalize on pent-up consumer demand. Many American importers, planning to pay for these imports through the sale of commodities like wheat and tobacco, defaulted on their debts when postwar international demand for American produce proved softer than they had hoped, in part because Britain restricted American access to its West Indian islands. Those with goods and capital in Britain and America became increasingly unwilling to extend much credit. Adding to the difficulty were serious problems in relation to government finance. States carried substantial wartime debt, and the tax revenues servicing it, mainly import duties, were undermined by the commercial downturn. Moreover, bankruptcies, land seizures, and other legal proceedings spawned by economic difficulty taxed fragile court systems, leaving creditors frustrated and debtors desperate. These difficulties intersected with profound uncertainty about the relationship between state governments and economies and the weak national government operating under the Articles of Confederation.[71]

Hoping to secure and capitalize on a reputation as a steadfast friend to America, Henry worked to flatten his complex wartime peace-first politics and convince old and prospective customers in the now independent United States that they had been on the same side all along. He wrote John Hancock in March 1783 to celebrate "the Channels of our Intercourse again being opened" and declare his plans to "repair the ravages" the war made "on my fortune, because of the steady principles which so strongly attach'd me to the just cause of America & Mankind."[72] A printed circular letter that Cruger and Mullett distributed in the fall of 1783 assured old and potential new American correspondents that "uniting in sentiment, as we uniformly have, with the Citizens of these States, political events have not in the least diminished our confidence in their integrity." While other British merchants, the letter suggested, would now offer American customers credit only on more cautious and expensive terms, because of their political sentiments Cruger and his partners would "transact all business with which we may be favored, on the terms and credit usually given previous to the late war." Another of Cruger's flyers, printed in Philadelphia in this period and sent to Nicholas Brown of Providence, listed more than thirty types of goods he was prepared to ship from Bristol to US correspondents with peace in the offing.[73]

Henry Cruger was better positioned than most people to see and understand the interlocking conditions that roiled the transatlantic economy after the Treaty of Paris. Most people—sailors, small American farmers, English artisans, local retailers—affected by the downturn in trade and the increase in debt at all levels of American society after 1783 lacked Cruger's commercial experience and access to information. Postwar economic difficulties fueled political turbulence, most notably in Shays's Rebellion in 1786/87. Henry Van Schaack, living in Pittsfield, Massachusetts, was at the epicenter of the growing unrest and a strong "government man" in opposition to Shays's supporters. In March 1787 he reported that Theodore Sedgwick, also a prominent government backer, had narrowly escaped assassination by Shaysites. Tensions in the borderlands between the two states were high, much as they had been during the Revolution,

236 "MY HEART STILL CLEAVES TO NEW YORK"

as some of Shays's supporters sought allies and refuge in northeastern New York. Henry Van Schaack warned Peter that "the people here will not be insulted at home nor from abroad" and hoped "we may not get to quarreling with your state."[74] The turmoil raised the specter of renewed civil war.

Henry Cruger felt the effects of the wider crisis of the mid-1780s quickly. To his disappointment, the end of the war did not end his financial difficulties. While he resumed trading, he continued finding it easier to attract customers than payers. Moreover, the operations of his Bristol-based house, under the care of clerks while he and Mullett were in America, fell into disarray in 1784 when it accepted far larger orders from American correspondents than it could fulfill.[75] The Bristol-based partnership with Lediard and Mullett was dissolved by mutual consent in January 1785.[76] Soon after, enough "malicious and injurious reports" circulated in America that Cruger's London partnership had gone bankrupt that a rebuttal—complete with an affidavit signed by representatives of other British trading houses—was inserted in the New York press. Rumored insolvency could easily lead to actual failure, and similar items defending Cruger's ability to continue paying his debts appeared in Baltimore and Philadelphia.[77] By October 1785, Cruger told Peter Van Schaack that his financial situation was "much the same—rather mended than otherwise," but this was "thanks to the Creditor's Pity more than the Debtor's punctuality."[78] Henry again managed to stave off bankruptcy, but the situation remained dire. One merchant claimed that Cruger was owed £200,000 by citizens of the United States in 1785, twice what correspondents owed him in 1772.[79]

Besides trying to reenergize his trade, Henry also reentered politics by running again to represent Bristol in Parliament in 1784. He was in America when the election was announced and remained there during the entire campaign. Samuel Peach served again as Cruger's principal agent and likely provided financial backing.[80] Cruger's American birth and ties resurfaced in this election, but the context had changed. In 1774 New York was still part of the British Empire, and in 1780/81, while congress had declared American independence, Britain did not recognize it. By 1784, Britain had done so, yet the Treaty of Paris contained no specific language for determining whether an individual was a British subject or an American citizen. Between 1776 and 1790, when the Naturalization Act clarified US law, the issue remained vexed and largely within the purview of the individual American states. English law was long even less clear on how US citizens should be differentiated from British subjects.

Parliamentary politics had also changed. When first a member of Parliament, Cruger had stressed his independence from factional politics. In 1784, however, he was aligned with William Pitt the younger, whose government's continuation versus a return of the Fox-North coalition was the election's central national issue. Cruger won a hard-fought contest after five weeks of polling, beating his old rival George Daubeny by just sixty-eight votes. The Cruger family's continuing interdependence was underlined as John Harris Cruger, now resident in England, stood in for Henry, absent in America, during the campaign. Ultimately, it was the loyalist exile, John Harris, whom Bristolians chaired through the streets to celebrate his pro-American brother's 1784 election.[81]

Losers of parliamentary elections often contested the results, and Daubeny petitioned the House of Commons to overturn the 1784 poll. Charges of corruption and the violation of election laws were common in such petitions, and Daubeny made them. His petition also argued that Cruger, whose financial problems were well known, no longer owned the amount of English property required to hold a parliamentary seat. With more novelty, Daubeny also challenged the poll results by claiming that Cruger had become an American citizen. Cruger, Daubeny's petition asserted, was "a native of one of the United States of America, and was at the time of the said election resident within the territories of one of the said States." Moreover, Daubeny claimed, Cruger had taken "an oath or oaths of allegiance to the said United States, or to one or more of them" and did thereby "renounce his allegiance to his Majesty and this country and the government thereof."[82] The origins of these revealing charges were probably pseudonymous letters that appeared in the Bristol press during the election centering on what Cruger had done in America in late 1783 during the transitional period between war and peace. Most significantly, they accused Cruger of swearing allegiance to the United States in New York shortly after its evacuation by the British and, more vividly and symbolically, of his "tearing down at New York the Royal Standard of poor Old England, with his own hands and with the same erecting the Thirteen Stripes." Cruger took these oaths, these letters claimed, because of his political principles and from a desire to preserve property in now American New York.[83]

These charges were probably spurious, but Cruger's having taken an oath of allegiance to New York or the United States was hardly impossible. Cruger's trip to America in 1783 was motivated by concerns for his business, and he likely wanted to help secure inherited family real estate and other property in New York State. The Treaty of Paris stipulated a twelve-month window for those displaced by the conflict to return to the United States and claim property. Given percolating American hostility to loyalists and uncertainty about who would be deemed one, there were good reasons to be concerned about Henry Sr.'s valuable legacy. Moreover, John Harris Cruger had been banished by New York and his property seized. If his military service had made him an enemy of the United States, might not Henry Cruger's continuing membership in the Parliament that authorized and directed the British war effort have done the same? At least one 1780 English newspaper report had claimed that "Henry Cruger"— whether father or son was not noted—had been formally declared a forfeit traitor by New York, while another printed in Bristol in 1783 listed an unspecified "Cruger" as declared a traitor by New York.[84] Most concretely, Peter Van Schaack mistakenly believed in 1783 that Henry Sr.'s New York property had been declared forfeit.[85] These reports were ultimately incorrect, but they were credible and consequential enough to seriously concern the entire family.

If Henry Cruger Jr. *did* swear allegiance in New York in 1783, he would have joined the many people of his era who defended their own interests by telling partisans on both sides what they wanted to hear. Nevertheless, John Harris Cruger and Henry's other supporters in Bristol denied these scandalous rumors in print and challenged the improbable particulars of the most specific version of the tale that his opponents circulated.[86] Tellingly, these accusations mirrored the rhetoric of disloyalty that Cruger's opponents had long deployed against him. Cartoons and election cards had associated Cruger with the "Thirteen Stripes" since 1780, while his British political opponents had long draped themselves in the Union Jack. The war was over, but its legacy remained central to Henry's future.

Despite these attacks, it is less clear how Cruger himself understood his status in relation to the infant North American republics or their union in this period. However, Henry's lawyer, Mannaseh Dawes, shared his client's American sympathies and radical politics and in 1784 Dawes published a pamphlet defending Cruger's election victory against Daubeny's charges. The pamphlet likely had Cruger's blessing, and on the crucial question of whether Henry had taken an oath of allegiance in the United States, Dawes stated clearly that he had not.[87] More interesting and surprising is that Dawes also engaged in an extended discussion of what it would mean if Cruger had taken such an oath. These arguments offer a glimpse of how Cruger and some other former nobodyists likely viewed the transatlantic dynamics surrounding subjecthood and citizenship in the immediate postwar period.

Dawes expressed the profound uncertainty that many people reasonably had about the United States' future in the years after 1783. Considering what it would mean if Cruger had taken an oath of allegiance in New York, Dawes wrote "the separation of a dependent territory on Britain" was "a new case in politicks." Although the United States was "now acknowledged to be independent," it was "a country like unto our own, peopled as it were by our fellow countrymen, who speak our language, bear our names, profess our religion, and are governed in a like way." As a result, he continued, it would be difficult to prove that a man's taking an oath there to preserve his landed property "amounts to his renunciation of his allegiance as an Englishman." This was especially the case because there was no reason to believe that the United States' separation from Britain by "mutual consent" via a peace treaty meant that "she is to become, like France or Spain, a natural enemy in spirit, genius and disposition—in laws, religion, constitution, and views." Rather, Dawes claimed, it was more likely that the United States would eventually "become a co-operating friend, under the cement of a fœderal union." Given this, Dawes concluded rhetorically, "is it to be inferred then in such a case, new as it is in the annals of this country, that an Englishman's taking an oath to Congress would be a renunciation of his allegiance in England?"[88] In Dawes's view, the constitutional settlement of 1783 was novel and likely to evolve. The ties of culture and interest that bound North America to Britain, however, were deep and enduring. In this context, even after 1783, affinity for America was no crime and allegiance was no simple matter.

Cruger took up his parliamentary seat in 1784 but, after repeated delays, Daubeny's petition was finally considered by a select committee of the House of Commons in March 1786.[89] British and American newspapers carried a report stating that one of the "principal questions to be determined in the Bristol election, is of a new and curious nature." The issue was that "Mr. Cruger, one of the sitting members (being an American) is said to have taken the oaths of allegiance to the United States, and of course became *bona fide* a liege subject of those States." But Cruger was "before this circumstance, a British subject, and had sat in Parliament." The report concluded that "the determination of this singular question, will be the first of its kind ever tried before a committee of the British Commons."[90] By the time this assessment appeared in the American press, the saga of the 1784 election was over. On March 24, 1786, the select committee reported, in standard language and without explanation, its determination that Cruger was duly elected and eligible to represent Bristol.[91] A New York newspaper subsequently carried the news that when a hearing on his petition was finally held, Daubeny's council abandoned the charges of Cruger having

240 "MY HEART STILL CLEAVES TO NEW YORK"

taken a disqualifying oath of allegiance in America because "they had not legal evidence to support them."[92]

Cruger continued acting as a friend to America, maritime trade, and Bristol's commercial interests after returning to Westminster. In a 1785 debate he urged Parliament to promote trade with the United States and insisted, no doubt with his opponents' accusations in mind, that he spoke "as a merchant, whose attachment was to Great Britain alone, and who regarded her prosperity as superior to every other consideration."[93] Cruger likewise represented both the interests of his urban constituents and those of overseas merchants by opposing British Corn Laws, tariffs that kept the price of imported grain high to the benefit of English landowners and the detriment of commercial interests and the urban poor.[94] This record led John Frederick Bryant, a tobacco-pipe maker and working-class poet, to celebrate Cruger as "the hero of Bristolia's choice/the man who claims the people's voice" in his 1787 book of verse.[95] Cruger remained popular with many middling and poorer people in Bristol as someone who spoke for them.

The 1784 election seemingly settled Henry Cruger's place in the postwar world by validating him as British, but the period's economic difficulties prevented him from fully regaining his earlier status. Despite the political controversy that his 1783 trip to the United States generated, he traveled there again in 1786 to dun his customers. He also joined the revived New York Chamber of Commerce even as he remained a member of Parliament.[96] While Daubeny failed to prove that Cruger had taken an oath of allegiance in the United States, he was not wrong that Cruger continued trying to straddle the Atlantic. By 1788 other members of the Cruger family bowed to the realities created by the Treaty of Paris and decisively committed their futures to either the United States or Britain, but in Henry's case this process took longer. It was only after 1789, when further changes in Britain and America spurred him to reevaluate his postwar choices, that Henry Cruger finally gave up on reconstructing the world he had lost.

Many people welcomed peace, but whether the United States would survive infancy was questionable. As the Crugers' history makes clear, the political choices that people in the Anglo-American world had to make did not end in July 1776 or even when the last British troops left New York in November 1783. The issues surrounding citizenship, property, reputation, and contested memory that recur in the Crugers' stories were not unique to them but reflected wider experiences in the war's wake. Most of the Crugers managed the turmoil and found relatively stable places in the new order. Just as important, the fragile peace of 1783 held; there was no immediate large-scale return to civil war or international conflict. But all of the Crugers had to struggle for what they gained and ended up with postwar lives that were very different from their prewar plans. In the ensuing years, more confident and secure than they were immediately following the peace, they looked to reenter New York politics and join in shaping the future of the United States.

10. Oblivion and Conciliation

Though having made his home in England for more than thirty years, in 1788 Henry Cruger told Peter Van Schaack that "my heart still cleaves to New York."[1] After twice visiting America in the 1780s, in 1790 Henry emigrated permanently, casting his lot once and for all with the United States. He joined his brother Nicholas and Peter in New York, and together they embraced its political, economic, and social opportunities. In the process, they became finally reconciled to the Revolution. The Crugers' lives were irrevocably transformed by wartime experiences of family deaths, dislocation, and exile. But having spent the first years of peace finding their footing, in the decade after 1787 they shed their nobodyist pasts and committed themselves to the new republic.

As a family, the Crugers supported the Constitution and the developing Federalist Party. They joined in the street and committee politics of the early republic with skill and commitment. Wartime militants—especially patriots—had looked to quash dissent and enforce unanimity, but this did not happen in the 1790s. While intense, the early republic's partisanship facilitated peaceful modes of political contestation within the emerging civic order of the United States. Over time, the involvement of former nobodyists like the Crugers in economic development and electoral politics incorporated them into a wider Federalist movement that transcended some revolutionary divisions even as it contributed to new ones in the early republic.

As they did during the war years, in the 1790s the Crugers promoted Anglo-American peace. The emergence of party politics in the early republic—intertwined with disputes over the French Revolution and American foreign relations—has often been read as the product of competing visions for the young nation's economic and political future. Centering former nobodyists in the history of the 1790s adds to this picture. The Crugers' story shows that some Federalists' concerns for stability and security were not only manifestations of incipient class or geographical conflict but also products of difficult wartime experiences. Within Federalist efforts to prevent war with Britain in the 1790s lay the revolutionary-era histories of people like the Crugers, and their long-standing arguments that peace, trade, and liberty were connected.

Peter Van Schaack and Nicholas Cruger, like nearly everyone else in their circles, were strong "federal men" and supporters of the Constitution in 1787 and 1788. Like many others of their class, the Crugers likely saw a stronger national government as a means to secure property and create future economic conditions from which they could profit. Yet historians of Federalists have also argued that there was an affective element to their politics and "that these currents of feeling had little reference in any primary way to private interests. They arose out of deep anxieties as to the very character the new republic was to assume, the moral direction it would take, and the sorts of men who would give it its predominant tone."[2] Typically, the Crugers' collective support for the Constitution was the product of multiple factors. It involved personal relationships and patterns of interdependence, understandings of self-interest and the common good, and more abstract political principles. Their engagement with what was becoming Federalism reflected their prewar connections, wartime experiences, and postwar hopes.

Although he remarried in 1789, Peter Van Schaack and the Crugers continued regarding each other as family and stayed connected with a circle of other New Yorkers across the tumultuous 1790s. Moreover, the support several of these associates gave to Peter and other members of the family as they resettled in New York after 1783 inspired abiding loyalty and obligation. In 1785, Henry Cruger told Peter that John Jay's aid "must make him your great Apollo," and supporting Jay became Van Schaack's most intense political commitment.[3] His Cruger in-laws supported Jay too, and for reasons that touched but transcended self-interest, the extended family backed Alexander Hamilton's ambitious political and financial projects. Theodore Sedgwick was also a strong federal man. In 1783, still in England, Van Schaack described Sedgwick as "a man near my heart" and thought "our minds have a near alliance." This led Peter to lament their wartime differences: "What good could we have done if we had both been on one side!"[4] By 1787 they were. After years of isolating exile, engaging again in a common cause with like-minded, influential men must have been a welcome change for Van Schaack. For former nobodyists, the early republic's party politics could be a way back home.

But entering the political fray was risky. The Crugers knew that some New Yorkers resented the return of people with wartime histories like theirs. In 1783, Van Schaack told his brother that "a life of *retirement*, study and reflection is my object."[5] Keeping quiet was safer, and many former nobodyists probably continued to do so in the debates surrounding the Constitution. Despite such inclinations, Van Schaack ran to represent Columbia County at the 1788 New York State ratification convention because, as he later explained to his son, it was a "peculiar case and justified by the *occasion*."[6] Nicholas Cruger too was mooted as a candidate, but he does not appear to have run.[7] Van Schaack was no natural campaigner, but he "mounted the rostrum several times, and harangued the multitude on law, government and politics."[8] He also published some unidentified pseudonymous essays supporting the Constitution.[9] Peter and the other pro-Constitution candidates for Columbia County all lost because "the popular tide was against us," meaning "against what was *right* and *good*."[10] More important to Van Schaack than his personal defeat was that New York ratified the Constitution and that it came into effect. By February 1789, Van Schaack looked "forward to the important event of the organization of the Federal Government, with sincere pleasure, and unless I egregiously mistake my own heart, it is a pleasure derived from the love of my country."[11]

Across 1788, many Americans celebrated their state's ratification of the Constitution with increasingly elaborate and symbolic parades and public ceremonies. These events, growing to encompass thousands of participants, featured grand floats and other imagery depicting commerce, agriculture, and the arts flourishing under the new Constitution. They also lionized Washington and other statesmen as national heroes and encouraged holdout states to ratify. Because of their size, novelty, and cultural power, these "Federal Processions" were important sites for expressing new forms of social, cultural, and national identity.[12]

New York's contentious ratification convention stretched into late July 1788, and state federal men decided to hold their own parade in Manhattan on July 23, hoping that a mass pro-Constitution demonstration would encourage the delegates in Poughkeepsie to finally ratify.[13] Nicholas Cruger was prominent in these symbolically potent proceedings. Marching in the parade's first division, he was dressed as a farmer and conducted "a plough drawn by six oxen" while supporting "the farmers' arms." Cruger was followed by two unnamed men sowing grain and then the scion of another family dislocated by the Revolution, John Watts, also dressed as a farmer and steering a harrow pulled by two horses and two oxen. The symbols of agriculture were followed by a soldier, mounted on a "beautifully caparisoned" horse, carrying "the United States' arms" and "supported by the Cincinnati."[14] It was a strikingly prominent part for Nicholas given the Crugers' wartime history, and his proximity to the patriot veterans of the Society of the Cincinnati spoke to the political and cultural coalition-making on display. Those watching the parade, marching behind Nicholas, or reading the many newspaper accounts of the day would have been in no doubt: the Crugers were going to be part of the new order created by the Constitution.

While Henry Cruger's New York relatives worked for the Constitution, he was back in Parliament. His 1784 reelection was a personal triumph, but the accompanying debates over his citizenship revealed continuing uncertainty about America's place in the postwar world. Henry's second term in Parliament was quieter than his first. Moreover, as the United States moved through the adoption of the Constitution, Henry's own sense of where his future lay changed. Between 1787 and 1790 he gradually gave up on his previous attempts to restore his prewar position and then, emigrating to New York, fashioned himself into an American.

During his second parliamentary term, Henry focused on the interests of Bristol's merchants, maritime workers, and artisans. Cruger was elected as a supporter of William Pitt's administration, but his deeper loyalties made him an unreliable vote. Reflecting his Wilkesite history, he voted for Pitt's failed 1785 proposals for parliamentary reform, one of the first serious attempts to make representation in the Commons more democratic.[15] Cruger, however, then opposed Pitt's 1785 efforts to liberalize Anglo-Irish trade as part of a "final settlement" between Britain and Ireland, remaining resolutely—myopically—his constituents' representative.[16] Much of Cruger's other politicking, like his efforts to help small traders hurt by Pitt's controversial Shop Tax or to have a Bristol bridge rebuilt, similarly reflected his second term's focus on local issues.[17]

Although a sitting member of Parliament, Cruger returned to America in the summer of 1786 to again address his business and stayed for nearly two years, through the Constitution's drafting and many debates over ratification. Cruger's continuing efforts to collect old debts saw him initiate legal proceedings against correspondents like South Carolina's John Jacob Sluyter and New York's Christopher Bancker.[18] A mangled account book for Henry Cruger & Company from the period documents hard but frequently unsuccessful dunning by his partner Thomas Mullett up and down the Atlantic seaboard.[19] Cruger had thus far staved off bankruptcy, but he remained under intense financial pressure. In 1787, he was trying from America to renegotiate terms with his English creditors, and while the "gentlemen in London & Bristol" were amenable, the "Manchester men mean to obdurate," and he was anxiously awaiting news. "At such a Crisis," he told Van Schaack, "Suspence is Torture."[20] The remaining London partnership of Cruger, Lediard, and Mullett was legally dissolved in March 1788.[21] Henry arrived back in England by August 1788.[22]

After returning to Britain, Cruger engaged in his final parliamentary business. In May 1789 Cruger honored his enduring ties to Bristol's dissenters by voting for repealing the Test and Corporation Acts, which restricted public office holding to members of the Church of England. In supporting this failed measure, Cruger again voted against Pitt, now on an issue fundamental to Britain's eighteenth-century constitution.[23] If support for religious liberty was one side of Henry Cruger's populist commitment to Bristol, another was far uglier: his defense of the transatlantic slave trade against the first national campaigns organized by British abolitionists.

In 1789, Cruger was an active part of the "West India interest," which "was essentially an amalgamation of locally based groups, coming together from time to time for national campaigns."[24] To counteract abolitionist petitions, proslavery groups organized their own emphasizing the slave trade's economic significance; Cruger worked on Bristol's.[25] On May 12, 1789, William Wilberforce delivered a landmark parliamentary speech urging abolition.[26] That same day, Cruger presented "six different petitions from various descriptions of inhabitants of Bristol," defending the slave trade.[27] Cruger then participated in a May 18 meeting of the West Indian Committee that decided upon a strategy of delay, hoping to blunt the impact of Wilberforce's powerful speech by arguing that the House of Commons needed more evidence before voting on abolition.[28]

Cruger spoke when the Commons resumed debating abolition on May 21.[29] He claimed that he opposed "every species of oppression" but argued that if Parliament was "at all hazards" determined to support abolition, then it should compensate planters and merchants and "must think of raising a fund of at least sixty or seventy millions sterling" to do so. Cruger held that it would be "infinitely more prudent, instead of precipitately amputating the trade, to try to remedy the abuses" and then "gradually to abolish it." Whether Cruger sincerely believed in gradual abolition or not, the point was to dissuade the Commons from voting for immediate abolition. Cruger concluded by insisting "he conceived it his duty, as the representative of a great commercial city" to vote against Wilberforce's measure.[30] Edmund Burke in an answering speech described the slave trade as "absolute robbery" and said that its victims had "a claim on our humanity which could not be resisted, whatever might have been advanced" by Cruger "in defense of the property of the planters." Cruger replied that "justice ought not be sacrificed to humanity."[31] The echoes of Cruger's old disagreement with Burke over what it meant to be a member of Parliament were unmistakable. So too was the fact that Cruger's commitment to defending Bristol's trade meant that his conceptions of neither liberty nor justice extended to the rights of enslaved people. The delaying tactics adopted by the West India lobby were largely successful. Immediate abolition was not passed in 1789, debate continued, and it was nearly twenty years before Britain ended its slave trade.

This was Cruger's last substantive intervention in parliamentary politics. Emigration had been on his mind for some time. In a July 1787 letter to Van Schaack, written while he was in New York but his family remained in Bristol, Henry wished "Would to God my Wife and Children were now Here!!"[32] Returning permanently to New York was attractive partly because it placed him nearer to those who owed him money, and he knew of American hopes that a new federal government would revive the national economy. Leaving England might have also been appealing if he feared bankruptcy or lawsuits there. Cruger's attempt in January 1789 to obtain compensation from Britain's Loyalist Claims Commission reflected his continuing financial desperation. In September 1789, Cruger asked Pitt to appoint him to a consular position in the United States, "which would tend to rescue me and a large family from great difficulties."[33] These requests failed, but even as Cruger contemplated moving to the United States, he considered remaining a British subject.

Wider family dynamics also mattered. Henry's father-in-law, Samuel Peach, his key political backer long after the 1767 death of Ellin Peach Cruger, died in May 1785.[34] Peach's will named his grandson Samuel Peach Cruger—Henry and Ellin's only child—as primary heir to his large fortune, including an estate at Tockington outside Bristol, on the condition that Samuel adopt the last name Peach. Samuel, about nineteen when his grandfather died, petitioned and was granted permission to "use and continue the surname of Peach only, and also to bear the Arms of Peach" in May 1788.[35] In August 1788, soon after Henry returned from America, the freshly renamed Samuel Peach Peach married Clara Partridge, the daughter of a Bristol merchant.[36] These arrangements rather spectacularly settled the social and financial position of the young Peaches, but they addressed neither Henry's personal finances nor the futures of the five younger children he had with his second wife, Elizabeth Blair Cruger.[37] So, in 1790 Henry Cruger's transatlantic family tree split into two branches mirroring postwar divisions. The sweetly situated Samuel Peach Peach and his descendants would remain English; Henry, Elizabeth, and their children would become transplanted Americans.

In March 1790, Henry announced in Bristol he would not stand for reelection. In a farewell address, Cruger said he had "been uniformly an advocate for those measures which promised an advancement of the general liberty and happiness and a warm opposer of those claims and proceedings which have in the event proved so unfortunate and fatal to millions." A popular politician to the end, he noted the honor of "representing a body of independent men, *whose unshaken friendship*, no reverse of fortune could change, and no influence of titles, grandeur, or party, destroy."[38] Although Parliament was still sitting, the Crugers left Bristol in early April, reportedly carrying with them a set of glasses inscribed "Cruger, Trade and Liberty." They arrived in New York in June 1790 and settled near Nicholas in Hanover Square.[39]

Against the backdrop of the Constitution's ratification, the New York Crugers engaged in business that mixed older practices with politically potent innovations. After immigrating, Henry "did not engage extensively in business," but according to a family account, "he suffered very heavy pecuniary losses arising from misplaced confidence; for a confiding disposition formed a prominent part of his generous character."[40] Much of his attention probably remained focused on old debts.[41] When he had goods for sale, they included the window glass, English porter, "good Russia Hemp," and gunpowder he advertised in 1792 and the "Jamaica Spirits" and grindstones that he offered in 1793.[42] In December 1800 Henry Cruger acted as the New York consignee for four hogsheads of rum, a transaction that might have occurred at almost any point in a previous century of family history.[43]

Nicholas's trade was larger and much more successful. He regularly sold cargoes of sugar and rum imported from St. Croix or other islands. He sometimes offered other Atlantic goods for sale, such as the "Barcelona hides" imported via Curaçao and window glass advertised in 1788; the coffee, pimento, and flour he had in 1795; and the "London particular Madeira wine" he imported in 1797.[44] In these activities, Nicholas Cruger remained an Atlantic trader much like his father and grandfather had been, but he invested his profits in many other ventures. He kept buying real estate in and around New York City, owning twenty-nine urban properties and three farms and a lot in the nearby countryside by the time of his death. He also had some holdings in upstate New York, but rather than putting substantial capital into undeveloped acreage Nicholas linked his own finances closely with urban New York's growth.[45]

Nicholas's participation in the United States' new trade with Asia encapsulated how his business and political interests converged in these years. Cruger co-owned the ship *Jenny* that departed New York for Canton (Guangzhou) in February 1788. The early republic's China trade conjured visions of wealth and appealed to citizens as a means of actualizing national independence.[46] The *Jenny*'s voyage was organized by the New York partnership of Dominick Lynch and Thomas Stoughton, and Nicholas helped assemble her outbound cargo by purchasing ginseng, one of the few North American products that appealed to Chinese correspondents. More important, he brought hard cash to the table, which was essential to obtaining the tea, silks, porcelain, and other Asian products American consumers craved. According to one report, the *Jenny* carried 68,000 pounds of ginseng in its hold and some 60,000 Spanish silver dollars.[47] Per Lynch and Stoughton's accounts, Cruger owned 13/37 of the venture.[48]

The *Jenny* departed as the Crugers and their associates were campaigning for the Constitution's ratification, and the ship fired a symbolic thirteen-gun salute as it left New York harbor.[49] British officials, worried about American competition in Asia, took note of the *Jenny* and its backers too.[50] Britain's East India Company tried to interdict British interlopers in its Asian trade, so Americans looked to establish that their vessels were the property of United States citizens. In February 1788, Cruger and his partners petitioned Congress for documentation that the *Jenny* was "owned entirely by citizens of the United States and manned for the most part with citizens of the said states."[51] In this process, Nicholas left his nobodyist claims to Danish subjecthood further behind to seize new political and economic opportunities.

The *Jenny*'s first voyage failed to produce windfall profits, but Nicholas continued believing in the economic and political project that the China trade represented.[52] Cruger invested in subsequent Asian voyages organized by the firm of Gouverneur and Kemble, including the voyage of the *America* in 1795.[53]

Nicholas also began advertising Asian goods for sale like "the fresh hyson, hyson skin, young hyson, and souchong teas" he offered in 1793.[54] Cruger sold silks, sugar, nankeens, rhubarb, and porcelain imported from Asia too.[55] Sons of both Nicholas and Henry helped launch their own mercantile careers by making Asian voyages in the mid-1790s.[56] As one recent history has noted, "among an influential group of American leaders, the China trade seemed to offer a particularly useful instrument for expanding economic power and buttressing the infant republic's independence within a republican ideological framework."[57] By investing the profits from his established Atlantic business into the emerging Pacific trade, Nicholas linked his fortune with this wider nation-building project.

Other investments by Nicholas blended economic and political aims. New York merchants founded the Bank of New York in 1784 to promote commercial lending and revive trade following the British evacuation.[58] Hamilton steered the bank in its early years, while Alexander McDougall, who had helped bring the Revolution to New York, acted as its president. The bank's establishment was premised on New York and the United States building upon, rather than abandoning, older connections to transnational trade. It brought together men who shared a common commercial outlook despite past differences.[59] In a postwar New York roiled by disputes over the return of loyalists and other exiles, the bank's founding by wealthy merchants has also been seen as a "major way of gaining control over society."[60] When Nicholas started investing in the Bank of New York is uncertain, partly because ownership shares quickly became marketable securities, but in 1800 he owned thirty-six shares valued at over $24,000. Like other traders, he also used the bank's services; Cruger had nearly $65,000 deposited in it when he died.[61]

Alexander Hamilton's appointment in 1789 as secretary of the treasury gave him preeminent influence over the direction of the United States' economy. The controversial fiscal and financial innovations that he introduced became central to the hopes that many federal men—especially in New York—had for realizing the Constitution's economic promise. Hamilton's plans included expanding American manufacturing. Like other New Yorkers motivated by a mixture of patriotic optimism, hopes for profit, and local boosterism, the Crugers embraced and invested in this program despite their former nobodyism and their long history of importing European manufactures. Nicholas Cruger, the elderly ex-speaker John Cruger, and Nicholas's wife, Ann, all subscribed in 1789 to the New York Manufacturing Society (NYMS), a failed early effort to establish mechanized textile manufacturing in the city in the hopes of profits and providing jobs for the urban poor. Nicholas became one of this early joint-stock company's first directors, joining other prominent New Yorkers including his wartime associate Nicholas Low.[62]

Despite the NYMS's failure in 1790, the Crugers joined other New Yorkers and Federalists in supporting Hamilton's even more grandiose plans to create an entire cutting-edge water-powered factory town in Paterson, New Jersey, through another joint-stock company, the Society for the Encouragement of Useful Manufactures (SEUM). There was a strongly nationalist spirit in these projects, which challenged England's dominance in textile manufacturing partly by pirating English technical innovations. Nicholas Cruger was an early investor in the SEUM. Henry Cruger supported it too, meeting in 1790 while still in England with Thomas Marshall, who had worked in the latest English factories. Soon thereafter, Marshall emigrated to New York in violation of protectionist British laws and was appointed manager of the SEUM's planned cotton mill.[63]

The SEUM became a landmark cautionary tale in the history of American capitalism. It floundered due to the project's complexity and the shady dealings of its politically connected director, William Duer, whose mismanagement of company funds and speculation in New York's nascent securities market helped spark the financial panic of 1792.[64] "All sorts and conditions of men and women" were caught up in a mania for investing in stocks and government debt in 1791, and many were ruined when Duer's schemes unraveled, leading to a chain of other failures and a collapse in securities prices.[65] Nicholas and Henry were prominent among Duer's many creditors. Henry told Van Schaack that "the Wound & the Anguish given by Duer is almost incurable, & will long be felt" and that "the subject is too painful for me to dilate upon."[66] Yet, unlike some others wiped out by Duer's fall, the Crugers stayed afloat and managed to preserve their reputations.[67] Neither the NYMS nor the SEUM fulfilled their founders' hopes, but the Crugers' places in these formative episodes in American business history underlined their deepening investment in a shared Federalist vision of securing the republic through economic growth.

In another case of his engagement with fellow Federalists in a novel business, Nicholas Cruger was one of the founders of the joint-stock United Insurance Company in 1796. It aimed to provide merchants with marine insurance policies and investors with profits and the legal protections offered by a corporate structure. Hamilton, after resigning from the Treasury in 1795, reentered private legal practice and served as the company's counsel. When the company received a state corporate charter in 1798, Nicholas Low was its president, while

Nicholas Cruger was a director.[68] In a different undertaking, Henry Cruger was among the original subscribers to the Tontine Coffee House, a landmark in federal New York completed in 1794 by a group of about 150 merchants and other men of business.[69] Intended to benefit subscribers and facilitate business, the Tontine Coffee House became the headquarters for commercial New York: a rendezvous for merchants, insurance brokers, stock jobbers, auctioneers, and many others besides. Not all these novel ventures proved profitable, but enough of them did to make the Crugers among New York's better-known investors in the Federalists' vision for American development.

The Crugers also engaged in formal politics after the Constitution's ratification, running for and serving in local and state government and, especially, acting as local organizers. As with their business activities, a family perspective reveals elements of old and new in the former nobody men's postwar politicking. It built on Cruger traditions of civic engagement and their comfort with the politics of the tavern and the street, but it also reflected the style of the early republic's emerging two-party system. In March 1789, as the new federal government began operating, Nicholas was put forward to represent New York City in the state's annually elected General Assembly.[70] Like Henry in Bristol, Nicholas was touted across his political career as a friend to trade and the working man. Some of this was puffery, but no candidate for office in New York City could win without real popular support. A 1789 piece, for example, claimed "many of the Mechanicks" would support a slate including Cruger.[71] Nicholas was not chosen for the assembly in 1789, but he was voted an inspector of elections, representing the city's Out Ward.[72] Nicholas was again a candidate for the assembly in 1790, when his endorsements included a "meeting of a number of Merchants, at the Coffee-House" and a "meeting of Mechanics, held at Mr. Orson's tavern."[73] Cruger was elected this time, serving from January 1791.[74] On the whole, the type of cross-class and pro-trade urban politics that the Crugers practiced was becoming weaker in New York, partly because the machine-based production that Federalists promoted was very different from the sort of economic growth desired by skilled craftsmen.[75] These developments, however, played out only gradually, and Nicholas benefited from the Crugers' reputations as proponents of New Yorkers' welfare. John Cruger II, known as "the Old Speaker" for his prewar office, spent time in Nicholas's household after the Revolution. By the time of his death at eighty-two in December 1791, when he was eulogized for "the goodness of his character being so universally known," he had witnessed his nephew regain much of the family's old prominence in local affairs.[76] Nicholas, boosted in print by "A Mechanic" as "friendly to arts and manufacture, the sure props of prosperity," was proposed for reelection to the assembly in 1792.[77]

Across the United States, the elections of 1792 were the first "contested on anything resembling a partisan basis."[78] In New York, the governorship was the biggest prize, and the extended Cruger clan supported John Jay against George Clinton. Each candidate's supporters trumpeted his revolutionary credentials, and the election revisited debates over the Constitution. Peter Van Schaack was the first named member of a Kinderhook committee formed to support Jay.[79] Peter summed up his devotion to Jay by lauding him as "a man of first rate character" and a statesman who had completed "a treaty of peace with one of the greatest nations of the world." For Van Schaack, Jay was "a man whom I love, because I know him," and he joined a group of committed organizers working for Jay in 1792.[80] Henry Cruger had resided in America for less than two years, but he signed a pro-Jay public letter in March 1792 and then assured Van Schaack in April that "every Exertion" was being made on Jay's behalf.[81] As he came out for Jay, Henry's name appeared on endorsement lists as a 1792 candidate for state senator.[82]

The results of the 1792 election were mixed for the Crugers and the developing Federalist party. Nicholas lost, outpolled by other Federalist candidates, but Henry was elected a state senator, largely thanks to city voters.[83] Serving in New York's legislature was a future-defining step; Henry was turning his back permanently on English politics and his British subjecthood. Cruger was reportedly elected "without ever having renounced his allegiance to the king," but he definitely did so to take up his seat in November 1792.[84] On the first day of the new legislative session, he took the "oath of abjuration and allegiance as required by a law of this state, and also the oath to support the Constitution of the United States."[85] If this was the moment when Cruger committed once and for all to being an American citizen, then his revolution can be understood to have lasted until 1792.[86]

Family tradition held that Henry was elected despite questions about his eligibility for a New York office.[87] "A Citizen" who wrote a letter that appeared in the press in December 1792, asked, "Can HENRY CRUGER, Esq. be entitled to a seat in the senate of this state?" According to the state constitution, this author claimed, Cruger was required to have been a freeholder, and therefore a citizen, at the time of his election. The letter suggested that a 1789 New York legal case over the amount of interest due on a prewar debt, *Smith v. Ellison*, established a precedent that a New York–born person who had sided with the British after 1776 by going behind British lines was to be considered "a real British subject." On the basis of this precedent, this author argued that because Cruger had "served several years in the British parliament, and as mayor of Bristol, since the declaration of independence," he could not be a citizen unless he had been subsequently naturalized.[88]

The piece raised points that might have forced Cruger to explain himself more fully. In a post-revolutionary period when "volitional allegiance" was the standard through which American governments were sorting out who was and who was not a citizen, the letter's author was pointedly asking—as George Daubeny had done in England a few years earlier—which choice Henry Cruger had made.[89] Yet, in an indication that the crisis of citizenship that the Revolution created was easing, nothing came of these objections to Cruger's election. Neither Henry nor his supporters appear to have responded directly in print; he served in New York's Senate, and the issue was quickly drowned out by other news. Questions about Henry's allegiance, which had followed him since 1775, were fading away.

Following the election of April 1792, New York politics erupted over whether Jay or Clinton had won the governorship. The outcome of their intensely partisan race hinged on the fate of a few hundred ballots. Jay likely received the most votes, but some ballots cast in Otsego County were not handled in full conformity with election regulations, and Clinton's supporters contested them. In June 1792 the state legislature's canvassing committee, a majority of whom were Clinton allies, rejected the disputed ballots and declared Clinton reelected. To Jay's supporters, this was an outrage that invalidated the people's will. They tried—ultimately unsuccessfully—to challenge the canvassing decision and have Jay declared the winner.[90]

Peter and Nicholas were leaders in the Federalists' fight for Jay. Van Schaack thought the "specious casuistry" used to reject the disputed pro-Jay ballots "was only a cover, for a preconcerted design, at all Events, to bring in Clinton." The unpleasant choice, he said, harkening back to wartime dilemmas, was to "sink in passive obedience, or assume a manly resistance," and he wondered what Locke would have made of the situation. Van Schaack and Sedgwick exchanged legal opinions on the case in the hopes of mobilizing precedents on Jay's behalf.[91] Van Schaack and his friends also worked to get pro-Jay items into the press.[92] Peter likely wrote a *Hudson Gazette* piece under the name "An Independent Elector" that blasted pro-Clinton canvassers for showing that "elections are mere puppet shews; by which the *people* are to be juggled out of their liberties."[93] Van Schaack's prominence as a Jay partisan saw him blamed for writing another pseudonymous letter criticizing the canvassers and Clinton himself. An ensuing printed attack characterized Peter and Henry Van Schaack as "two infernal tories who were both within the enemies [*sic*] lines when America was contending for the precious rights which the late revolution has secured to us." The episode illustrated the risks of party politics for former nobodyists like Peter.[94]

Nicholas mobilized street support for Jay. In June 1792, Cruger chaired a pro-Jay New York City committee, and he signed its circular letter urging "fellow citizens" to rally "to preserve our freedom, not only against the attacks of open violence, but against every insidious attempt of artful and unprincipled citizens."[95] Large demonstrations for Jay were organized, and Nicholas, as committee chair, signed an address to him stating that "the Friends of Liberty" regarded Jay as "one of the illustrious defenders of the rights of man" whose cause was "the cause of the People."[96] Populist rhetoric and tactics like this—the language of rights and liberty, committees of correspondence, and street demonstrations—were evocative of the Revolution, but they also had been used by the Crugers and their allies for decades in transatlantic urban politics. In August 1792, as the election controversy continued, Henry Cruger was mooted as a worthy and popular candidate for mayor of New York City, an office that his uncle and grandfather had held but which was appointed by the still Clintonian-controlled legislature.[97] Henry never became mayor, but the Crugers continued to be closely identified with New York City amid the era's intensifying partisanship. Nicholas again became an inspector of elections in September 1792.[98] Ultimately Jay's supporters, calmed by Hamilton and Jay himself, contented themselves with a legislative investigation into the gubernatorial election that changed nothing.[99] Although the Federalists lost this fight, the Crugers were once again fully immersed in their city's politics.

When Nicholas signed a July 1792 letter hailing Jay as a defender of "the rights of man," he echoed common American rhetoric welcoming the early stages of the French Revolution. However, like others, the Crugers grew skeptical of the direction of events in France and alarmed that domestic and international developments might spark Anglo-American war. News of King Louis XVI's execution reached the United States in late March 1793, and soon after the infant French Republic's new ambassador, Edmond Charles Genêt, arrived.[100] France was now at war with Britain and nearly all of Europe, fighting for its revolution's survival. As ambassador, Citizen Genêt worked to undermine British and Spanish imperial power, secure immediate American repayment on French loans, and commission Americans as French privateers. Genêt's mission plunged the United States into controversy, and at stake was not just whether America's foreign policy should favor France or Britain, but whether the nation could maintain real independence rather than become "merely a satellite of a stronger empire."[101] Hamilton's plans for economic development depended on maintaining peace with Britain, and his "commitment to a strict neutrality was absolute, unqualified, and uncompromising."[102] Thomas Jefferson and the Democratic-Republicans were much more sympathetic to France's new government.[103]

Genêt and the radicalized revolution he represented were celebrated in several places upon his arrival in America, and in South Carolina he licensed four ships as French privateers. Hamilton and many Federalists believed that being drawn into Europe's war would be disastrous and that Genêt 's most ardent supporters were "the same men who have been uniformly the enemies and disturbers" of the United States' new federal government.[104] Under Hamilton's influence, and to Jefferson's discomfort, on April 22, Washington issued a neutrality proclamation that outlawed United States citizens "committing, aiding, or abetting hostilities" against any of the belligerent powers. The "sober segments of Republican opinion" also realized there was no real policy alternative to neutrality, and in New York Clinton soon issued a proclamation endorsing the Washington administration's statement.[105]

Following Washington's proclamation, a stymied Genêt threatened to take his appeals directly to the American people. Hamilton, writing as "Pacificus," countered with a series of essays defending the Neutrality Proclamation and the president's authority to direct foreign policy. He also encouraged allies to organize public meetings "everywhere, even in Virginia," to support Washington and strict neutrality.[106] In this charged moment, Nicholas Cruger again emerged as a local organizer. On August 7, newspapers carried an invitation to "the Republican Citizens of New-York, and Friends of the Republic of France" to mark Genêt's impending visit to their city with a public reception, the ringing of church bells, the firing of cannon, and a procession celebrating France's revolution as "the cause of mankind."[107] New York's proponents of neutrality proposed an alternative event. A meeting chaired by Nicholas Cruger invited the public to assemble in front of Trinity Church on the afternoon of Genêt's arrival to express "their approbation of the late Proclamation of the President, and likewise of the conduct of the Governor of this State in respect to the same."[108]

Genêt hoped to win New Yorkers' support for France, but his visit proved a notable success for the cause of maintaining strict neutrality. Perhaps wary of seeming unpatriotic opponents of the president and Clinton, Democratic-Republicans encouraged their supporters to both welcome Genêt and attend the later event.[109] Nicholas Cruger chaired the large afternoon meeting, which adopted resolutions approving Washington's proclamation and pledging support for neutrality. The meeting also resolved, against Genêt and his militant supporters, that it was "repugnant to the laws of the land, and injurious to the best interests of our country" for citizens to participate in privateering against "any nation at peace with these States." Acknowledging Clinton's earlier endorsement of Washington's proclamation, the meeting approved his conduct too, helping make the case that neutrality had bipartisan support.[110] Cruger forwarded the meeting's resolutions to Washington via Hamilton.[111] Federalist Robert Troup told Hamilton that "we have by pursuing a bold & manly line of conduct effected a complete consolidation of parties in favor of the great object of neutrality."[112] Even Jefferson noted in a letter to Madison that "the desire of neutrality" was "universal" as Genêt visited New York.[113]

Those promoting neutrality worked to capitalize on these developments. One widely distributed newspaper report said the New York meeting must have given "the most perfect satisfaction to the friends of order, peace, and national independence."[114] Reports on the meeting also appeared in British newspapers, furthering the cause of preventing Anglo-American war.[115] Washington replied publicly to Cruger, praising the meeting as an example of New Yorkers' "good sense, moderation and patriotic virtue."[116] The cabinet had already decided to ask the French government to replace Genêt, and Jefferson embraced more fully the now clearly popular policy of neutrality.[117] Nicholas Cruger's place within these events is a reminder that opposition to Anglo-American war had a history that stretched back to the 1770s and an appeal beyond the moment's factional politics.

Nicholas continued doing border-crossing business in the hotly contested Caribbean, and his ships became embroiled in disputes with belligerents on both sides. In February 1793 Cruger's schooner *York* was seized when it put in at Port-au-Prince on Saint-Domingue. French customs officials claimed that they believed gunpowder aboard the vessel was intended to be sold to Black revolutionaries. Cruger and Andrew Burke, the vessel's captain and co-owner, denied this, insisting that the *York* had only put in at Saint-Domingue for repairs and provisions and that its cargo was intended for trade in the Spanish Yucatán.

Underlining Cruger's embrace of neutrality, the *York* stopped in Danish, Dutch, Spanish, British, and French Caribbean territory during its final voyage.[118] In 1794, revolutionary French officials detained another vessel of Cruger's, the *Eliza*, for six months in distant Mauritius while it attempted a globe-circling trading voyage.[119] Despite these encounters, trade with France and French territories remained alluring. In 1797 and 1798, for example, Cruger engaged in ventures destined for Bordeaux with Gouverneur and Kemble.[120]

Efforts by the Royal Navy and British privateers to strangle French commerce proved even more dangerous to American shipping. Intensifying British attacks on American ships and crews became an increasingly politicized issue, and, alongside older grievances over the Treaty of Paris, brought the United States and Britain to the brink of war in 1794 despite Washington's Neutrality Proclamation.[121] In February 1794, a British privateer took the ship *Mary*, co-owned by Nicholas, while it was on a typical multi-leg trading voyage out of New York that involved two stops in French Guadeloupe and one in Dutch St. Eustatius before the ship's capture.[122] Nicholas's commercial prominence saw his name used in an anti-British political cartoon from this period that linked George III to the Ottoman sultan Mustafa IV (fig. 20). In the cartoon the two rulers superintend violence against Americans by their surrogates—Pitt, Native Americans, and North African corsairs—while in the foreground plundered goods belonging to American merchants, including Nicholas, are displayed.[123]

France's revolutionary republicanism inspired many Americans, and there was intense anger over Britain's actions at sea, but renewed Anglo-American war in 1794 could have had devastating consequences for the young United States: invasion, occupied or burned cities, perhaps even the loss of independence. Writing as "Pacificus," Hamilton observed that "with the possessions of Great Britain and Spain on both Flanks, the numerous Indian tribes, under the influence and direction of those Powers, along our whole Interior frontier, with a long extended sea coast—with no maritime force of our own, and with the maritime force of all Europe against us, with no fortifications whatever and with a population not exceeding four Millions—it is impossible to imagine a more unequal contest."[124] After much debate, Washington agreed to send an envoy to Britain to press for maritime reparations and attempt to prevent war. On April 15, 1794, he offered John Jay the post.[125] Jay's appointment was protested by critics and, given the public mood, much was made of the fact that his task was securing restitution for American shipping losses.[126] Yet Jay saw his primary mission as preventing war. He wrote his wife, Sarah, that if it pleased "God to make me

Figure 20. Valentine Verax, "The Allied Despots, or the Friendship of Britain for America," c. 1794. Ink and paper. Museum Purchase, acc. no. 1962.0189, Courtesy of Winterthur Museum, Winterthur, DE. In this cartoon, George III and Ottoman sultan Mustafa IV direct subordinates in violence against Americans. Cargoes plundered from American merchants, including a barrel labeled as belonging to Nicholas Cruger, are in the foreground.

instrumental to the continuance of peace and in preventing the Effusion of Blood and other Evils and Miseries incident to War we shall both have Reason to rejoice."[127]

With war and peace in the balance, Nicholas Cruger again became a candidate for the New York General Assembly, an office he had apparently not sought for several years. His reputation as a defender of strict neutrality and a practitioner of freewheeling trade resonated with the moment. A week before Jay's nomination became public, "a large and numerous Meeting of the Cartmen of this city, held at the house of Mrs. Amory" announced support for Cruger, as did a "meeting of the Mechanics." Cruger also appeared on a combined list touted by its supporters as "the Federal Republican Ticket."[128] When a satirical opponent of this slate writing as "Trim" sarcastically urged all the "Tories, Aristocrats, and Moderate men" to turn out, rally "round the Tontine Coffee House," and vote for the Federalists and neutrality in 1794, he knowingly echoed 1775 rhetoric that pro-peace arguments were inherently disloyal.[129]

New York's elections occurred soon after Jay left for his mission in May

1794, and Nicholas, alongside the city's other Federalist candidates, was elected an assemblyman.[130] Concerns over war dominated while Jay negotiated, and Cruger's public profile reached its highest point at a moment when "political discourse exploded in conjunction with innovations in celebration."[131] On July 4, 1794, New Yorkers, like citizens elsewhere, gathered to mark the anniversary of independence with parades and feasts that were widely reported in the press. Members of the city's municipal corporation, the Democratic-Republican Tammany Society, organized artisans, the Sons of the Cincinnati, and other groups all sat down to banquets at which they ate and drank to the nation and their own places in it. "The merchants" held their celebration at the Tontine Coffee House, and, in a testimony to his standing at the moment, Nicholas was placed in the chair. Given his family's profound doubts about independence and his own wartime history, Nicholas chairing a Fourth of July celebration illustrated how a decade of immersion in the city's economic and political life had solidified the Crugers' once precarious place in it. The toasts given at these gatherings expressed New Yorkers' partisan differences through shared political language. Nicholas gave a "volunteer"—a theoretically extemporaneous—toast of his own at the Tontine Coffee House: "Republican Principles: May they resist the arts of pretended friends, and the force of open enemies."[132] In offering this toast at a moment of international crisis, Cruger asserted his party's political views and his own right to participate in the emerging rituals of American nationalism.

While Americans awaited the outcome of Jay's mission, New Yorkers prepared for the state's 1795 gubernatorial election. It was uncertain who would run for either party, as Jay was still in England and Clinton declined nomination.[133] Nicholas Cruger was mooted as a candidate for lieutenant governor on a ticket to be headed by Hamilton.[134] Who floated this ticket is undocumented, but the news was repeated in several other states.[135] These rumors—or perhaps trial balloons—were as close as Nicholas ever got to holding a higher office in state or national government, and it is not even clear that he sought the position. Hamilton, in any case, did not want to be governor, and by March 1795 Nicholas headed a list of names for a committee promoting the candidacy of Jay and his 1792 running mate, Stephen Van Rensselaer, as the men "to secure the peace and advance the honor and prosperity of our Country." Henry Cruger joined this committee too.[136] Jay returned from his diplomatic mission just as the votes were being counted in late May 1795, and he easily defeated the Democratic-Republican nominee, Robert Yates.

The Crugers and their allies, however, had little time for celebrations be-

OBLIVION AND CONCILIATION   261

cause the treaty that Jay negotiated produced impassioned controversy. The treaty reached Philadelphia in March 1795, but only the president and secretary of state knew its contents until Washington formally submitted it to the Senate for its "advice and consent" on June 8. On June 24, 1795, the Senate accepted the treaty—subject to removing one especially controversial article— by a vote of 20–10, exactly reaching the constitutional minimum required for its approval. Angered by the result, one of the opposed senators, the Virginian Stevens Thomson Mason, leaked the treaty to a Philadelphia newspaper editor. The publication of the terms of the Jay Treaty, as it pointedly became known, created a firestorm of anger and protest in print and on the streets, including a campaign to block its ratification by pressuring Washington into not signing it. Critics "charged that the treaty yielded too much to Great Britain and gained far too little for the United States, would harm relations with France, failed to address several substantive issues of controversy, had been negotiated and debated in too much secrecy, and would serve to link the United States closely and subserviently with England."[137] Washington, unswayed, signed the treaty on August 18, 1795, thus making it American law and ending the first round of public controversy over it. The treaty came into effect at the end of February 1796, and then there was a second, intense round of acrimonious public debate as the House of Representatives considered whether to fund the treaty's implementation. The House narrowly voted funding in late April 1796, just under two years after Jay had sailed for London.[138]

The Crugers were not at the forefront of the public fight over the treaty's ratification, but this may have been strategic. Given repeated accusations that the treaty was a tory plot, its backers may not have found it helpful for former nobodyists to speak out. The Crugers and their allies found quieter ways to express their views as the controversy continued. The joint-stock United Insurance Company that Nicholas Cruger helped found in 1796 was dominated by merchants and Federalists.[139] In April 1796, when it seemed that the House of Representatives' Democratic-Republican majority might block funding the treaty, the new United Insurance Company, the New York Insurance Company, and individual underwriters issued a joint resolution stating "that during the present critical and alarming situation of Public Affairs" it would be "inexpedient" for them to "insure American property against Capture or detention by any foreign Power." This resolution was circulated to "the several seaports of the United States." James Madison saw this as a deliberate political maneuver, telling Jefferson that "the Insurance Companies" in Philadelphia and New York had "stopt business, in order to reduce prices & alarm the public" as Congress deliberated. Another anti-treaty correspondent told Madison that "the Treaty or British party are making every exertion to obtain their object; The Cry is war, war, no Insurance to be had, Vessells hauled up, no employment for the people."[140]

Peter Van Schaack also backed the treaty, and his allies kept him abreast of developments.[141] In February 1796 Peter expressed to Henry Cruger how many Federalists felt about the popular furor that surrounded the Jay Treaty. "A systematic opposition to a Government or an Administration, constituted by the People or emanating from them," he wrote, "must be political Heresy, or all the Ideas of Benefit from Union, Concord must be rejected."[142] When the House narrowly approved funding the treaty's implementation, the Federalist congressman John Van Alen described the news to Van Schaack as "an event on which I beg leave to Congratulate you."[143] Renewed war with Britain was narrowly avoided.

The Jay Treaty has often been studied as a point of departure: for American foreign policy, constitutional history, political culture, and issues of sovereignty and citizenship.[144] From the perspective of the Revolution's former nobody men—as an endpoint to their story rather than as a beginning to any number of other histories—there are several striking features about the Jay Treaty. Whatever the merits of its specific terms, the Jay Treaty delivered a period of sustained peace between the young and weak United States and the British Empire, which, unlike in 1775, was already mobilized for war in 1794. In 1775 neither American patriots nor the British government proved willing to make the sorts of genuine, painful, and far-reaching compromises that would have been necessary to preserve peace. In 1794 they did. Ironically, given the charge that the treaty's supporters were "tories," Britain's supporters during the Revolutionary War probably lost the most. Loyalists' hopes for compensation or repossession of American property were simply ignored in the treaty. Likewise, Britain's Native American allies around the Great Lakes were "essentially sold out" by British policymakers in pursuit of "Anglo-American reconciliation."[145] In seeing peace itself as valuable and a good from which many other benefits flowed, Jay shared much with those, like Henry Cruger Jr., who prioritized reconciliation in 1775. Critics at the time and since have wondered whether Jay or another American negotiator could have secured better specific terms, but a focus on the treaty's clauses risks underestimating the overarching value of peace to the fledgling United States.[146]

Jay's treaty prevented war, but at the cost of extraordinarily bitter and personal attacks on those who made and supported it. This too echoed the dynamics of 1775. Henry Jr. and other proponents of peace then were accused of being self-interested, corrupt, devoid of principles, cowardly, and traitorously disloyal by hardliners on both sides; rumors and charges of conspiracy had floated around them. Jay was attacked in strikingly similar ways by critics of the 1794 treaty. Five hundred Philadelphia artisans accompanied a cart containing a representation of Jay carrying a set of scales on which "British gold" outweighed "virtue, liberty, independence."[147] Elsewhere, Jay was hanged in effigy and damned in graffiti. Other treaty supporters also faced vitriolic attacks. Hamilton was asked by one writer whether he aimed at "a re-union with Great Britain; the subversion of the present limited constitution; the establishment of the monarchy; and the eternal annihalism of republicanism, & a republican form of government?"[148] Federalists, more united and better organized than the advocates for peace in 1775 had been, fought back, ridiculing their opponents and defending the treaty through a print campaign that was "massive and widespread."[149] In the end, they managed to convince many Americans that peace and the necessarily painful compromises that secured it were preferable to another Anglo-American war.

Writing from London in 1784, Peter Van Schaack had avowed that "oblivion and conciliation are the great objects of my incessant, most fervent wish."[150] A decade later, the Jay Treaty's prologue claimed that through it the United States and Great Britain aimed to "terminate their differences in such a manner as, without reference to the merits of their respective complaints and pretensions, may be the best calculated to produce mutual satisfaction and good understanding."[151] From former nobodyists' perspectives, the Jay Treaty can be seen as a turn toward the future through a necessary act of forgetting past grievances: a transatlantic form of "oblivion and conciliation." As Eliga Gould has rightly noted, "whatever people at the time said and thought, history has come to regard the Jay Treaty as a decisive moment in consolidating the independence that Congress had unilaterally declared nearly twenty years earlier."[152] In this light, the Crugers' long-standing desire for Anglo-American peace and reconciliation emerges as part of a strain in American life after 1789 that—despite all their doubts about its founding—helped the United States survive.

The Jay Treaty's implementation ended the Crugers' most intense period of political engagement. In April 1796 Henry Cruger informed his fellow Federalists that he declined seeking reelection to the state senate.[153] He never stood for public office again. Nicholas Cruger's organizing work continued. In April 1798, he was the first named member of a New York City committee—Hamilton was named second—formed to support of Jay for governor and a slate of other Federalist candidates.[154] But like his brother, Nicholas never stood again for elected office before his early death in 1800. Peter Van Schaack remained the most politically active member of the family, albeit mostly behind the scenes. In 1800, he wrote in a "desponding style" to Theodore Sedgwick to lament Jefferson's likely election as president.[155] Van Schaack supported Federalist causes and candidates in the Hudson River Valley into the new century.[156]

Britain's wars with revolutionary France gave John Harris Cruger an opportunity to reenter professional life in a small way. His brother-in-law Oliver De Lancey Jr. was appointed the British army's superintendent-general of barracks in 1792 and barrack-master-general in 1794. De Lancey's post enabled him to dispense some patronage, and in 1796 John Harris was named an assistant in Oliver's department.[157] Peter Van Schaack reported to Henry Cruger that he had heard "that our brother the Colonel has lately had a lucky hit, which places him in a State of Independence."[158] De Lancey's tenure ended in controversy in 1804 over discrepancies in his department's accounts, but John Harris kept his place until at least 1806.[159] It was a minor office, but it gave John Harris and Anne a secure income and likely helped them live in London in his final years, where they had a house near Fitzroy Square.[160]

Nicholas Cruger was fifty-six at the time of his death in 1800. An article observed that not only would his family and friends regret his passing, but so too would New York's "tradesmen and men of commercial occupations, who will have great cause to deplore the loss of so universal a merchant."[161] Ironically given his postwar trajectory, Nicholas died in St. Croix, where he went in late 1799 in an apparent final attempt to recover his health. His body was placed in the De Nully family vault at the Peter's Rest plantation in St. Croix.[162] Several of Nicholas's grandchildren were born in St. Croix; in 1808 they were granted the right to purchase land in New York as resident aliens.[163]

It was the Crugers' participation in the intertwined economic and political life of New York in the decade following the Constitution's ratification that made this collective reintegration possible. By linking their family fortunes to the post-revolutionary development of New York City—the center of the Crugers' political engagement across three generations—they contributed to a broader Federalist project that transcended the divides of the war years. When Nicholas Cruger bought shares in the Society for the Encouragement of Useful Manufactures, Peter Van Schaack campaigned on behalf of John Jay, and Henry

Cruger ran for state senate, they demonstrated their appreciation for the willingness of some Americans to put wartime differences behind them and affirmed their loyalty to the United States. The politics of the 1790s were contentious, but to former nobodyists like the Crugers, and to many other people who had doubts about the course of the American Revolution, they were also an opportunity. When the Jay Treaty was secured, the Crugers could celebrate something they had long advocated—Anglo-American peace—alongside other people who now accepted them as fellow citizens.

Conclusion

Henry Cruger Jr.'s longtime commercial partner and political ally, Thomas Mullett, died in 1814. Like Cruger, Mullett resided in Britain and the United States during his life, and he was admired by many on both sides of the Atlantic who shared his commitments to democratizing politics and religious pluralism. Mullett accompanied Cruger on his 1783 visit to the United States, and as the war lurched to a close, Mullett met George Washington. According to one of "the many anecdotes with which Mr. Mullett amused and interested his friends," Washington hosted Mullett at Mount Vernon, where the two had a revealing exchange that crystallizes a feature of nobodyism's place in memories of the Revolution. Washington asked Mullett whether during his extensive travels he had met anyone who might be capable of writing a history of the Revolutionary War. Offering a well-turned compliment, Mullett said he had met only one such person. "Caesar," Mullett reminded the general, "wrote his own Commentaries." Washington, according to the anecdote, bowed to acknowledge the comparison, but then cut to the heart of the matter. "Caesar could write his Commentaries," Washington is said to have replied, "but Sir, *I know* the atrocities committed on both sides have been so great and many, that they cannot be faithfully recorded, and had better be buried in oblivion."[1] What we know about the Revolution, the anecdote insists, has from the start been the subject of much editing, myth-making, and sanitizing.

In the aftermath of what had been a traumatic civil war, it was not just battlefield atrocities that were hard to talk about, and it was not just patriots who thought this way. Loyalists like John Harris Cruger also knew the horrors of the war and understood the value of shaping its history. Because postwar histories were dominated by patriot and loyalist partisans, accounts of those in the middle often went untold, and their perspectives were often ignored. As the Crugers' postwar story illustrates, many nobodyists also had their own powerful reasons to keep silent, or even to hide or obfuscate their wartime choices. After 1783, the nobody men's experiences made uncomfortable histories for the United States, for a refashioned British Empire, and for many of the nobodyists themselves.

Washington's purported call to bury the full history of the Revolutionary War "in oblivion" speaks to the challenges of recovering nobodyist perspectives. This book, in recounting the Crugers' interconnected history, suggests ways of thinking about wider neutralist experiences. The Crugers were strong, even leading, colonial patriots in the political controversies of the 1760s and early 1770s. Fully part of the prewar colonial resistance movement, the Crugers shared—and repeatedly helped to lead—their fellow Americans' opposition to British attempts to more intensively regulate and tax the colonies. The Crugers' parts in events including the disputes over quartering, the Stamp Act crisis, and the assertive 1767 New York merchants' petition showed their readiness to work with many other colonists in pursuit of a common cause. Through their connections to Wilkesite radicalism, the Crugers also contributed to a transatlantic political culture intent on defending English liberty against oligarchic British politicians. Neither aristocratic nor conservative in the circum-Atlantic world they inhabited, the Crugers supported a locally directed vision of trade and liberty within the British Empire that they believed would allow New York City and other maritime communities to flourish. While they sometimes disagreed with other colonists over tactics and priorities in the decade before the Revolution, there was little sign in their prewar political ideology that they would come to break with other Americans.

What changed for the Crugers, and for many other people, is that the constitutional disputes of the previous decade became a shooting war in the spring of 1775. The emergence of militarized violence dramatically transformed the context in which people made decisions. The Crugers, like others, feared war in the aftermath of the Boston Tea Party and worked to prevent it as the political crisis deepened. These efforts, culminating in the New York assembly's 1775 petitions, failed despite the efforts of the family and their allies in America and England. As civil war took hold, the Crugers prioritized containing and ending what they regarded as a mutually disastrous conflict as quickly as possible. The

CONCLUSION

Crugers' history illustrates that for some people who lived through the Revolution, restoring peace was a cause in and of itself: a goal as important as any realistic set of postwar constitutional arrangements. Dedicated to New York and to the prewar political aims of the patriot movement—but largely opposed to participating in civil war—most of the Crugers became nobody men and tried to differentiate themselves from both warring parties.

The Cruger family experienced the war as a period of tragedy and dislocation. The sisters Elizabeth Cruger Van Schaack and Mary Cruger Walton died during it, as did Mary's husband Jacob Walton. The children left behind by these deaths had their lives transformed by the conflict, albeit not in ways that map easily onto wartime politics. Surviving members of the extended Cruger family, like many people from across the political spectrum, endured exile, loss, danger, and fear during the years of fighting. As the experiences of the family's revolutionary generation demonstrate, there were different reasons for being in the middle and varied ways of behaving there. In the face of unwelcome war, some of the family continued to engage in "peace first" politics. Others tried, with mixed results, to keep the conflict at arm's length. Some seem to have regarded the war primarily as an obstacle to be overcome in pursuit of their own self-interests. Unlike their nobodyist Cruger relatives, John Harris Cruger and Anne De Lancey Cruger became committed and militant loyalists in 1776. Their experiences demonstrate the vanishingly thin ideological lines that could separate patriots, loyalists, and nobody men as people made choices from within particular and volatile wartime contexts. Having decided to fight alongside Anne's De Lancey relatives against the rebellion, the couple participated directly in the period's violence. The varied dilemmas that the Crugers confronted and the choices they made as an interdependent family, as people connected to other people, between 1775 and 1783 illustrate the range and complexity of what it meant to be a nobodyist.

For the war's survivors, peace was a blessing and a challenge. Britain's defeat meant permanent exile in England for John Harris Cruger and Anne De Lancey Cruger, their lives forever fenced in by their wartime choices. For the other Crugers, postwar paths led back to New York and they worked to reestablish themselves in a place that they still regarded as the site for their futures. While Nicholas Cruger took over the leadership of the family in New York, Peter Van Schaack relied on the assistance of friends like John Jay to enable his return. Although reelected to Parliament in 1784, Henry Cruger remained tied to New York and emigrated in 1790. Building on their pre-revolutionary expe-

CONCLUSION

riences in politics and commerce, the Crugers joined other like-minded New Yorkers in promoting a Federalist vision of American economic and political development. While challenged by other new citizens of the United States, Federalist politics—including the commitment to preventing renewed conflict with Britain central to the Jay Treaty—provided a means for some people to escape the Revolution's hold.

Nicholas Cruger's death in 1800 marked an endpoint for his family's revolutionary-era history. His business acumen meant that he left a large fortune behind that shaped his children's American futures. All six of Nicholas and his first wife Anna De Nully Cruger's children—three daughters and three sons—had been born on St. Croix in the decade between 1773 and 1782, and by the time of Nicholas's death, they were young adults. Nicholas and his second wife, Ann Markoe Cruger, had three daughters together, the youngest of whom was born less than a year before Nicholas's death.[2] The final settlement of Nicholas's estate was disputed between his adult children on the one hand, and Ann and her second husband, William Rogers, on the other hand, but these complications were settled in the courts in the ensuing years.[3] There was a great deal of money to go around. In 1802, soon after inheriting, Nicholas's eldest son, Bertram Peter Cruger, married Catherine Church. Her English-born father, John Barker Church, had helped provision the Continental Army during the war, returned to England and served in Parliament in the 1790s, and then reemigrated to America. Catherine's mother was a daughter of New York Continental general Philip Schuyler and the sister-in-law to Alexander Hamilton. Another son and a daughter of Nicholas's married their cousins, two of Henry Cruger's children, in 1802.[4]

As the post-revolutionary generation of Crugers melded into New York's elite and memories of the conflict faded, there was little to be gained from preserving the nobody men's stories, which fit poorly with how the republic they inhabited wanted to remember its own origins. Simplifying the past was appealing in England too. John Harris Cruger died in London in 1807, when he was sixty-nine years old. After his death, Anne, "his truly disconsolate widow," had a tablet placed in his memory in St. James Church on London's Hampstead Road. This memorial said nothing about John Harris Cruger's career as a merchant, his role in the pre-revolutionary nonimportation movement, or even his time as a member of New York's Provincial Council. Instead it just stated that "he took up Arms in support of the Rights of this country" and highlighted his military accomplishments including the relief of Augusta, the defense of Ninety Six, and the Battle of Eutaw Springs.[5] It was a glossing of John Harris Cruger and Anne's lives that left out far more than it revealed and conformed to the increasingly regimented stories that Britons and Americans told themselves about the revolutionary past. Anne herself lived until May 1822, when she died in Chelsea at the age of seventy-eight. The *Gentleman's Magazine*, which took note of her death, was even more reductive than the tablet commemorating her husband: she was simply Anne, "relict of Col. Cruger, and dau. of late Brig.-gen De Lancey."[6]

Henry Cruger Jr. kept up a friendship and correspondence with Peter Van Schaack throughout his life. When the two exchanged New Year's wishes in 1812, Henry reflected on what they had experienced, noting that "storms and tempests as well in private as in public life, pains of body and inquietude of mind seem the lot of men. All have a portion. You and I have had a very large share." Given that, Cruger said, "if a retrospect disturbs us, let's confine our thoughts to the present moment and *be happy* if we can."[7] It was a late reminder of how important forgetting was to the lives of postwar nobody men. For them the Revolution remained understandable primarily as a period of rupture and pain rather than national glory. Henry's reputation late in his life was probably brightest in Bristol, where his wartime allegiances were less unsettling and his public persona as a friend of trade and common people endured. According to one account, the supporters of a parliamentary candidate in Bristol in 1812— when Anglo-American conflict again loomed—urged electors to remember "the golden days of honest Harry Cruger," when "Bristol's independent sons broke the fetters of coercion."[8] In 1826, when Henry, then eighty-six, wrote a final preserved letter to Peter Van Schaack, he signed himself "your truly attached, and loving old kinsman." Cruger lived until 1827, some thirty-seven years after returning permanently from England. After he died, he was interred in a Cruger family vault in New York's rebuilt Trinity Church.[9]

Fittingly, much of what remains recoverable about the Crugers' nobody-ism is as much the product of chance and tragedy as planning or pride. In 1797, the oldest surviving child of Elizabeth Cruger and Peter Van Schaack, Henry Cruger Van Schaack, died suddenly at the age of twenty-nine, leaving behind a young family.[10] Peter, who had worried incessantly over his son while exiled and dedicated much attention to him after returning to New York, was deeply affected. In the aftermath of the young man's death, his uncle Henry Cruger Jr., who also was close with him, helped a grieving Peter select a suitable gravestone and epitaph. It was a testimony to family bonds, one that recalled memories of Elizabeth Cruger Van Schaack and the family's wartime sufferings. The letters from this period are among the most emotionally laden of any in the family's surviving correspondence.[11]

When Peter and his second wife had another child in 1802, they named him Henry Cruger Van Schaack after his deceased and still evidently much missed half-brother. It was this second Henry Cruger Van Schaack, born a generation after the Revolution and not related directly to the Cruger family by descent, who worked to preserve, write, and publish family history beginning in the 1840s. His efforts to share these stories, sparked by admiration for his father, Peter, took place as survivors of the Revolution were passing from the scene and when civil war was again emerging as a danger in America. The author Henry Cruger Van Schaack had not experienced the Revolutionary War for himself, but because of his family circumstances, he grew up in its shadow. It was perhaps this peculiar combination of closeness and distance to a story of the nobody men that made him willing to write about their experiences.[12] Few other people in the middle had such dedicated chroniclers.

Peter Van Schaack's world centered on Kinderhook after 1800. According to his son, between 1786 and 1828, when Van Schaack was age eighty-one, he always had one or more aspiring lawyers training under him and instructed nearly one hundred clerks in total. Many of his prominent Federalist friends sent their sons to study under Van Schaack, including Theodore Sedgwick, Rufus King, and others, but he also accepted clerks from more humble backgrounds.[13] He came too to know young Martin Van Buren, also from Kinderhook, who regarded Van Schaack as a learned man, but also a "thorough partisan" whose politics differed greatly from his own.[14] In 1826 Columbia College awarded Van Schaack an honorary doctor of laws. At a meeting of college alumni that year, his old Federalist ally Robert Troup toasted him as "admired for his knowledge of the law, and for his classical attainments, and beloved for the virtues which adorn our nature."[15] In 1829, in a final act of devotion to the recently deceased John Jay, Van Schaack prepared a Latin epitaph for his friend. Van Schaack died in 1832 and was buried in Kinderhook.[16]

With the two hundred and fiftieth anniversary of American independence and the war that brought it, we still have much to learn about the many people who were unwilling to fight for either side. Writing from English exile in 1780, when he was anxious for his distant children's welfare and their future looked grim, Peter Van Schaack reflected on human nature amid the tumults of Revolution and civil war. "The characters of men are mixed;" Van Schaack wrote, "none are perfectly good, and very few totally depraved. Candor, therefore, should lead us to place their good qualities in one scale while the bad are put in the other. Actions *right* and *wrong* in *themselves*, are not always such, as they respect the agent's *motives*."[17] The Crugers' family history—at times ugly, at times inspirational, and at times obscure—reminds us that those who experienced civil war and American independence were people whose own lives and choices were as complex as our own. The nobodyists' stories have a great deal to teach us about the United States' origins, but they have long been hard for the Revolution's children to hear.

Notes

Abbreviations

AHAR	Autographic History of the American Revolution, manuscript compiled by Henry C. Van Schaack, Chicago History Museum, Chicago, Illinois
AH/FO	Alexander Hamilton Papers, Founders Online
AHR	*American Historical Review*
ANB	*American National Biography*, Oxford University Press, Online Edition
AP/FO	Adams Papers, Founders Online
BA	Bristol Archives, Bristol, England
BL	British Library, London, England
CoRI	*Commerce of Rhode Island*, 2 vols. (Boston: Massachusetts Historical Society, 1914–15)
CRNYCC	John Austin Stevens Jr., *Colonial Records of the New York Chamber of Commerce, 1768–1784* (New York: John F. Trow, 1867)
EAS	*Early American Studies*
GBH	Douglas Wright Cruger, *A Genealogical and Biographical History of the Cruger Families in America* (Portland, ME: Published by the author, 1989)
GW/FO	George Washington Papers, Founders Online
HJCAB	"Henry & John Cruger Account Book, 1762–68," New-York Historical Society, New York, New York
HJCLB	"Henry & John Cruger Letter Book, Jun. 1766–Aug. 1767," New-York Historical Society, New York, New York
HoP	*The History of Parliament: The House of Commons 1754–1790*, ed. L. Namier and J. Brooke (1964) Online Edition
HSP	Historical Society of Pennsylvania, Philadelphia, Pennsylvania
HVS	Henry Cruger Van Schaack, *Memoirs of the Life of Henry Van Schaack* [...] (Chicago: A. C. McClurg, 1892)

JAH	*Journal of American History*
JCBL	John Carter Brown Library, Providence, Rhode Island
JER	*Journal of the Early Republic*
JGANY	*Journal of the Votes and Proceedings of the General Assembly of the Colony of New York*, [1691–1775], 3 vols. (1764, 1766, 1820)
JJCU	Papers of John Jay, Columbia University, Digital Collection
JJ/FO	John Jay Papers, Founders Online
LFP	Livingston Family Papers, Gilder Lehrman Institute of American History, "American History, 1493–1945" Database, Adam Matthew
LOC	Library of Congress, Washington, District of Columbia
LP	Liverpool Papers, Add MS 38209, British Library, London, England
NDAR	*Naval Documents of the American Revolution*, 13 vols., Online Edition
NYGBR	*New York Genealogical and Biographical Record*
NYGBS	New York Genealogical and Biographical Society
NYH	*New York History*
NYHS	New-York Historical Society, New York, New York
NYHSQ	*New-York Historical Society Quarterly*
NYPL	New York Public Library, New York, New York
ODNB	*Oxford Dictionary of National Biography*, Oxford University Press, Online Edition
OIEAHC	Omohundro Institute for Early American History and Culture
PFP	Palfrey Family Papers, Houghton Library, Harvard University, Cambridge, Massachusetts
PH	*The Parliamentary History of England from the Earliest Period to the Year 1803* [. . .], 36 vols. (London: T. C. Hansard, 1812–20)
PVS	Henry Cruger Van Schaack, *The Life of Peter Van Schaack, LL. D.* [. . .] (New York: D. Appleton, 1842)
RDAG	*Royal Danish American Gazette*
SLFP	Samuel Ludlow Frey Papers, New York State Library, Albany, New York
TASTD	*Trans-Atlantic Slave Trade Database*, Online Edition
TJ/FO	Thomas Jefferson Papers, Founders Online
UKNA	National Archives (UK), Kew, England
VSFP	Van Schaack Family Papers, Columbia University, New York, New York
WMQ	*William and Mary Quarterly*

Introduction

1. *The Pennsylvania Packet; or, the General Advertiser*, 1 May 1779.

2. Michael A. McDonnell, "The Struggle Within: Colonial Politics on the Eve of Independence," in Edward G. Gray and Jane Kamensky, eds., *The Oxford Handbook of the American Revolution* (New York: Oxford University Press, 2013), 113. Alan Taylor estimated the loyalists as constituting at a maximum about one-fifth of the population, the patriots at about two-fifths, and the "wavering" or neutrals at about two-fifths. See *American Revolutions: A Continental History, 1750–1804* (New York: W. W. Norton, 2016), 212. Robert M. Calhoon assessed that "approximately half the colonists of European ancestry tried to avoid involvement in the struggle." See "Loyalism and Neutrality" in Jack P. Greene and J. R. Pole, eds., *A Companion to the American Revolution* (Malden, MA: Blackwell, 2000), 235. More than forty years ago, John Shy described "a great middle group of Americans" who were "almost certainly a majority of the population" but were "lost from sight in the Revolutionary record or dismissed as 'the timid.'" See *A People Numerous and Armed: Reflections on the Military Struggle for American Independence*, rev. ed. (Ann Arbor: University of Michigan Press, 1990; first edition 1976), 235–36. As Sung Bok Kim put it, "The historical actors of the revolutionary era were not just those who took an active role in directing the wheel of politics and ideology." See "The Limits of Politicization in the American Revolution: The Experience of Westchester County, New York," *JAH* 80, no. 3 (1993): 869.

3. John Adams to Abigail Adams, 23 April 1776, AP/FO.

4. John Adams to Benjamin Rush, 19 March 1812. For other similar assessments of revolutionary-era allegiances by Adams, see John Adams to Benjamin Rush, 31 July 1811; John Adams to Thomas McKean, 26 November 1813. Adams thought a similar rule of thirds applicable to ancient history examples. See John Adams to John Quincy Adams, 5 March 1808. All in AP/FO. He later retroactively applied a similar rule of thirds to American attitudes toward the French Revolution. See Paul H. Smith, "The American Loyalists: Notes on Their Organization and Numerical Strength," *WMQ* 25, no. 2 (1968): 260; John Adams to James Lloyd, 28 January 1815, AP/FO. But Adams was neither precise nor consistent in his estimates during the 1810s, suggesting in another letter to McKean that two-thirds of the American population had "been with us" in the American Revolution. See John Adams to Thomas McKean, 31 November 1813, AP/FO.

5. Michael A. McDonnell, "War Stories: Remembering and Forgetting the American Revolution," in Patrick Spero and Michael Zuckerman, eds., *The American Revolution Reborn* (Philadelphia: University of Pennsylvania Press, 2016), 12.

6. These nobody men's actions could include speech and writing, but I do not consider them limited to that.

7. On the varied factors and forces that went into wartime decision-making, see, for exam-

ple, Taylor, *American Revolutions*, 211–49; Holger Hoock, *Scars of Independence: America's Violent Birth* (New York: Broadway Books, 2017), 29–31; and Maya Jasanoff, *Liberty's Exiles: American Loyalists in the Revolutionary World* (New York: Alfred A. Knopf, 2011), 24. For cogent discussions of the issues focused on New York, see Michael Kammen, "The American Revolution as a *Crise de Conscience:* The Case of New York," in Richard M. Jellison, ed., *Society, Freedom, and Conscience: The American Revolution in Virginia, Massachusetts, and New York* (New York: W. W. Norton, 1976), 125–89; and Daniel J. Hulsebosch, *Constituting Empire: New York and the Transformation of Constitutionalism in the Atlantic World, 1664–1830* (Chapel Hill: University of North Carolina Press, 2005), 156–57. Recent studies of military occupation have been particularly insightful in considering those in the middle. See Aaron Sullivan, *The Disaffected: Britain's Occupation of Philadelphia during the American Revolution* (Philadelphia: University of Pennsylvania Press, 2019); and Donald F. Johnson, *Occupied America: British Military Rule and the Experience of Revolution* (Philadelphia: University of Pennsylvania Press, 2020), especially 6–8, 138–61.

8. On "moderates," see Robert M. Calhoon, *Political Moderation in America's First Two Centuries* (Cambridge: Cambridge University Press, 2009), 6. Calhoon defines moderates as "persons who intentionally undertake civic action, at significant risk or cost, to mediate conflicts, conciliate antagonisms, or find middle ground." This definition certainly applies to several members of the Cruger family, many of whom were politically active, and I use the term to describe some of them, especially before 1775. It does not apply to all of them, however, nor does it apply to other nobodyists who aimed to stay out of or find ways around the Revolution rather than to intervene in order to promote conciliation. It is also important to distinguish, as discussed more below, peacetime political ideology and decision-making from choices made amid violent civil war.

9. For examples of Quaker experiences of neutrality, see Richard Godbeer, *World of Trouble: A Philadelphia Quaker Family's Journey through the American Revolution* (New Haven: Yale University Press, 2019); and Sullivan, *The Disaffected.*

10. Patricia U. Bonomi and Peter R. Eisenstadt, "Church Adherence in the Eighteenth-Century British American Colonies," *WMQ* 39, no. 2 (1982): 272; Alan Taylor, *American Colonies: The Settling of North America* (New York: Penguin, 2001), 443.

11. See, for example, Sullivan, *The Disaffected*, especially 6–9; Michael A. McDonnell, *The Politics of War: Race, Class, and Conflict in Revolutionary Virginia* (Chapel Hill: University of North Carolina Press for the OIEAHC, 2007), 375–81; Judith Van Buskirk, "They Didn't Join the Band: Disaffected Women in Revolutionary Philadelphia," *Pennsylvania History: A Journal of Mid-Atlantic Studies* 62, no. 3 (1995): 306–29; Ronald Hoffman, "The 'Disaffected' in the Revolutionary South," in Alfred F. Young, ed., *The American Revolution: Explorations in the History of American Radicalism* (DeKalb: Northern Illinois University Press, 1976), 273–316. For recent suggestive thoughts on neutrality and the

NOTES TO PAGE 7

"disaffected" in relation to the more established field of loyalist studies, see Kacy Dowd Tillman, *Stripped and Script: Loyalist Women Writers of the American Revolution* (Amherst: University of Massachusetts Press, 2019), 4–11; and Rebecca Brannon, "Introduction," in Rebecca Brannon and Joseph S. Moore, eds., *The Consequences of Loyalism: Essays in Honor of Robert M. Calhoon* (Columbia: University of South Carolina Press, 2019), 2–4.

12. Loyalist historiography is extensive and "lacks a modern synthesis." See Hoock, *Scars of Independence*, 422n6. Estimates of the number of loyalists are provided in Maya Jasanoff, "The Other Side of Revolution: Loyalists in the British Empire," *WMQ* 65, no. 2 (2008): 208; Jasanoff, *Liberty's Exiles*, 351–58; and Smith, "The American Loyalists," 259–77. In addition to Jasanoff, *Liberty's Exiles*, significant overviews include William H. Nelson, *The American Tory* (Oxford: Clarendon Press, 1961); Wallace Brown, *The King's Friends: The Composition and Motives of the American Loyalist Claimants* (Providence, RI: Brown University Press, 1965); Wallace Brown, *The Good Americans: The Loyalists in the American Revolution* (New York: Morrow, 1969); Mary Beth Norton, *The British-Americans: The Loyalist Exiles in England, 1774–1789* (Boston: Little, Brown, 1972); and Robert M. Calhoon, *The Loyalists in Revolutionary America, 1760–1781* (New York: Harcourt Brace Jovanovich, 1973). For a conceptual introduction, see Edward Larkin, "Loyalism," in *Oxford Handbook of the American Revolution*, 291–310.

13. Jasanoff, *Liberty's Exiles*, 8; Christopher F. Minty, "Reexamining Loyalist Identity during the American Revolution," in *Consequences of Loyalism*, 33–47.

14. See, for example, on Black people's experiences, Douglas R. Egerton, *Death or Liberty: African Americans and Revolutionary America* (New York: Oxford University Press, 2009); Cassandra Pybus, *Epic Journeys of Freedom: Runaway Slaves of the American Revolution and Their Global Quest for Liberty* (Boston: Beacon Press, 2006); and Simon Schama, *Rough Crossings: Britain, the Slaves, and the American Revolution* (New York: Ecco, 2006). On Native American peoples' experiences, see, for example, Kathleen DuVal, *Independence Lost: Lives on the Edge of the American Revolution* (New York: Random House, 2015); Alan Taylor, *The Divided Ground: Indians, Settlers, and the Northern Borderland of the American Revolution* (New York: Alfred A. Knopf, 2006); and Colin G. Calloway, *The American Revolution in Indian Country: Crisis and Diversity in Native American Communities* (Cambridge: Cambridge University Press, 1995).

15. Jasanoff, *Liberty's Exiles;* Jerry Bannister and Liam Riordan, eds., *The Loyal Atlantic: Remaking the British Atlantic in the Revolutionary Era* (Toronto: University of Toronto Press, 2012); Jasanoff, "Other Side of Revolution," 205–32.

16. Studies of individuals include S. Scott Rohrer, *The Folly of Revolution: Thomas Bradbury Chandler and the Loyalist Mind in a Democratic Age* (University Park: Pennsylvania State University Press, 2022); John E. Ferling, *The Loyalist Mind: Joseph Galloway and the American Revolution* (University Park: Pennsylvania State University Press, 1977); Carol Berkin,

280 NOTE TO PAGE 7

Jonathan Sewall: Odyssey of an American Loyalist (New York: Columbia University Press, 1974); and Bernard Bailyn, *The Ordeal of Thomas Hutchinson* (Cambridge, MA: Harvard University Press, 1973). New York Loyalists have received particular attention, including from Christopher F. Minty, *Unfriendly to Liberty: Loyalist Networks and the Coming of the American Revolution in New York City* (Ithaca, NY: Cornell University Press, 2023); Ruma Chopra, *Unnatural Rebellion: Loyalists in New York City during the Revolution* (Charlottesville: University of Virginia Press, 2011); Judith L. Van Buskirk, *Generous Enemies: Patriots and Loyalists in Revolutionary New York* (Philadelphia: University of Pennsylvania Press, 2002); Philip Ranlet, *The New York Loyalists* (Knoxville: University of Tennessee Press, 1986); and Robert A. East and Jacob Judd, eds., *The Loyalist Americans: A Focus on Greater New York* (Tarrytown, NY: Sleepy Hollow Restorations, 1975). Other geographically focused studies include Joseph S. Tiedemann, Eugene R. Fingerhut, and Robert W. Venables, eds., *The Other Loyalists: Ordinary People, Royalism, and the Revolution in the Middle Colonies, 1763–1787* (Albany: State University of New York Press, 2009); Jim Piecuch, *Three Peoples, One King: Loyalists, Indians, and Slaves in the Revolutionary South, 1775–1782* (Columbia: University of South Carolina Press, 2008); Robert M. Calhoon, Timothy M. Barnes, and George A. Rawlyk, eds., *Loyalists and Community in North America* (Westport, CT: Greenwood Press, 1994); Anne M. Ousterhout, *A State Divided: Opposition in Pennsylvania to the American Revolution* (Westport, CT: Greenwood Press, 1987); and Robert Stansbury Lambert, *South Carolina Loyalists in the American Revolution* (Columbia: University of South Carolina Press, 1987). Work on the Caribbean has also expanded the geography and actors included in revolutionary history. See especially Andrew Jackson O'Shaughnessy, *An Empire Divided: The American Revolution and the British Caribbean* (Philadelphia: University of Pennsylvania Press, 2000).

17. See, for example, Brad A. Jones, *Resisting Independence: Popular Loyalism in the Revolutionary British Atlantic* (Ithaca, NY: Cornell University Press, 2021); Tillman, *Stripped and Script*; Gregg L. Frazer, *God against the Revolution: The Loyalist Clergy's Case against the American Revolution* (Lawrence: University of Kansas Press, 2018); Allan Blackstock and Frank O'Gorman, eds., *Loyalism and the Formation of the British World, 1775–1914* (Woodbridge, Suffolk: Boydell Press, 2014); Philip Gould, *Writing the Rebellion: Loyalists and the Literature of Politics in British America* (New York: Oxford University Press, 2013); Robert M. Calhoon, Timothy M. Barnes, and Robert Scott Davis, *Tory Insurgents: The Loyalist Perception and Other Essays*, rev. ed. (Columbia: University of South Carolina Press, 2010); Janice Potter, *The Liberty We Seek: Loyalist Ideology in Colonial New York and Massachusetts* (Cambridge, MA: Harvard University Press, 1983); and William Allen Benton, *Whig-Loyalism: An Aspect of Political Ideology in the American Revolutionary Era* (Rutherford, NJ: Fairleigh Dickinson University Press, 1969).

NOTES TO PAGES 7–9

18. Robert M. Calhoon, "The Loyalist Perception," in Calhoon, Barnes, and Davis, *Tory Insurgents*, 3–14.

19. Daniel J. Hulsebosch, "Exile, Choice, and Loyalism: Taking and Restoring Dignity in the American Revolution," *Law & Social Inquiry* 41, no. 4 (2016): 844.

20. Sophie H. Jones, "Steadily Attached to His Majesty? Varieties of Loyalism in Revolutionary New York," *Journal of Early American History* 9, no. 2–3 (2019): 172.

21. Edward Larkin, "What Is a Loyalist?" *Common-Place* 8, no. 1 (2007).

22. Calhoon, *Loyalists in Revolutionary America*, xii. This definition seems even to include the possibility that people who supported the patriot cause but were victimized by patriot authorities might be counted as loyalists.

23. See Brannon, "Introduction," in *Consequences of Loyalism*, 3–4, for a valuable reflection on this issue from within loyalist studies. See also Sullivan, *The Disaffected*, 6–8, 232n6. An evocative recounting of the experiences of people who suffered at the hands of both sides is in Kim, "Limits of Politicization," 868–89.

24. On New York merchant families, see especially Philip L. White, *The Beekmans of New York in Politics and Commerce, 1647–1877* (New York: NYHS, 1956); Philip L. White, ed., *The Beekman Mercantile Papers, 1746–1799*, 3 vols. (New York: NYHS, 1956); and Cynthia A. Kierner, *Traders and Gentlefolk: The Livingstons of New York, 1675–1790* (Ithaca, NY: Cornell University Press, 1992). Valerie H. McKito, *From Loyalists to Loyal Citizens: The De-Peyster Family of New York* (Albany: State University of New York Press, 2015), focuses on the post-revolutionary history of a New York merchant family, especially in Canada. Important studies of merchant families elsewhere in this period include W. T. Baxter, *The House of Hancock: Business in Boston, 1724–1774* (Cambridge, MA: Harvard University Press, 1945); James B. Hedges, *The Browns of Providence Plantations: Colonial Years* (Cambridge, MA: Harvard University Press, 1952); and James B. Hedges, *The Browns of Providence Plantations: The Nineteenth Century* (Providence, RI: Brown University Press, 1968). Also helpful for framing this study have been studies focused on merchant families in the British Empire. See especially Emma Rothschild, *The Inner Life of Empires: An Eighteenth-Century History* (Princeton, NJ: Princeton University Press, 2011); and David Hancock, *Citizens of the World: London Merchants and the Integration of the British Atlantic Community, 1735–1785* (Cambridge: Cambridge University Press, 1995).

25. See, for example, on civil war, Jasanoff, *Liberty's Exiles*, 21–53; T. H. Breen, *American Insurgents, American Patriots: The Revolution of the People* (New York: Hill and Wang, 2010), 42; McDonnell, "War Stories," 9–28. For a recent popular account stressing the conflict as a civil war, see H. W. Brands, *Our First Civil War: Patriots and Loyalists in the American Revolution* (New York: Doubleday, 2021).

26. Shy, *People Numerous and Armed*, 183.

NOTES TO PAGES 9–13

27. For works highlighting the centrality of violence to the Revolution, see, for example, T. Cole Jones, *Captives of Liberty: Prisoners of War and the Politics of Vengeance in the American Revolution* (Philadelphia: University of Pennsylvania Press, 2020); Hoock, *Scars of Independence*; Taylor, *American Revolutions*; McDonnell, "War Stories"; and Wayne E. Lee, *Crowds and Soldiers in Revolutionary North Carolina: The Culture of Violence in Riot and War* (Gainesville: University of Florida Press, 2001).

28. Stathis N. Kalyvas, *The Logic of Violence in Civil War* (Cambridge: Cambridge University Press, 2006), 17.

29. David Armitage, "Every Great Revolution Is a Civil War," in Keith Michael Baker and Dan Edelstein, eds., *Scripting Revolution: A Historical Approach to the Comparative Study of Revolutions* (Stanford: Stanford University Press, 2015), 57–68; Taylor, *American Revolutions*, 212.

30. On neutrals' numbers, see note 2 above.

31. See Kalyvas, *Logic of Violence;* AHR Roundtable, "Ending Civil Wars," *AHR* 120, no. 5 (2015): 1682–1837; and David Armitage, *Civil Wars: A History in Ideas* (New Haven: Yale University Press, 2017), especially 121–47.

32. For these comparisons, see Johnson, *Occupied America*, 7–9.

33. David Underdown, *Somerset in the Civil War and Interregnum* (Newton Abbot: David & Charles, 1973), 117. The work of John Morrill was especially influential in the study of neutralism in England during the civil wars. See, for example, Morrill, *The Revolt of the Provinces: Conservatives and Radicals in the English Civil War, 1630–1650* (London: George Allen & Unwin, 1976).

34. Kalyvas, *Logic of Violence*, 102–4. See also Mark Irving Lichbach, *The Rebel's Dilemma* (Ann Arbor: University of Michigan Press, 1995), 11–19, 350–51.

35. Kalyvas, *Logic of Violence*, 112–13.

36. Kalyvas, *Logic of Violence*, 94, 22.

37. Breen, *American Insurgents*, 13.

38. Kalyvas, *Logic of Violence*, 87–104.

39. Kalyvas, *Logic of Violence*, 94.

40. Stathis N. Kalyvas, "Promises and Pitfalls of an Emerging Research Program: The Microdynamics of Civil War," in Stathis N. Kalyvas, Ian Shapiro, and Tarek Masoud, eds., *Order, Conflict, and Violence* (Cambridge: Cambridge University Press, 2008), 403.

41. Kalyvas, "Promises and Pitfalls," 397–418.

42. Kalyvas, *Logic of Violence*, 44, 365.

43. Kalyvas, *Logic of Violence,* 44–46.

44. This formulation was inspired by Michael J. Braddick and David L. Smith, "Introduction: John Morrill and the Experience of Revolution," in Braddick and Smith, eds., *The*

Experience of Revolution in Stuart Britain and Ireland: Essays for John Morrill (Cambridge: Cambridge University Press, 2011), 9.

45. On these schools and their influence on revolutionary historiography, see Gwenda Morgan, *The Debate on the American Revolution* (Manchester: Manchester University Press, 2007).

46. Patrick Spero, introduction, in *American Revolution Reborn*, 5.

47. DuVal, *Independence Lost*, xxi.

48. In addition to works on merchant families, I have also been encouraged by books that use individual lives as entries into wider revolutionary-era histories, including Jane Kamensky, *A Revolution in Color: The World of John Singleton Copley* (New York: W. W. Norton, 2016); and Alfred F. Young, *The Shoemaker and the Tea Party* (Boston: Beacon Press, 1999).

49. My thinking here has been informed by Mark Peterson, *The City-State of Boston: The Rise and Fall of an Atlantic Power, 1630–1865* (Princeton, NJ: Princeton University Press, 2019), especially 3–10.

1. The Crugers' World

1. Paul R. Huey, "Old Slip and Cruger's Wharf at New York: An Archaeological Perspective of the Colonial American Waterfront," *Historical Archaeology* 18, no. 1 (1984): 15–37.

2. For Cruger genealogies, see Edward F. De Lancey, "Original Family Records: Cruger," *NYGBR* 6 (1875): 74–80, 180–82; and Douglas Wright Cruger, *A Genealogical and Biographical History of the Cruger Families in America* (Portland, ME: Published by the author, [1989]), upon which I have largely relied for genealogical information.

3. DuVal, *Independence Lost*, xxi.

4. Cruger, *GBH*, 1–3. Tileman's burial is recorded on 26 July 1694 in the parish register for St. Dionis Backchurch, London. Accessed through "London, England, Church of England Baptisms, Marriages and Burials, 1538–1812," *Ancestry.com.* See also Henry C. Van Schaack, *Henry Cruger: The Colleague of Edmund Burke in the British Parliament* [. . .] (New York: C. Benjamin Richardson, 1859), 3; De Lancey, "Original Family Records: Cruger," 76.

5. Historical Manuscripts Commission (UK), *The Manuscripts of the House of Lords, 1690–1691* (London: Her Majesty's Stationery Office, 1892), 73.

6. Cruger, *GBH*, 3; William D. Cooper, ed., *Lists of Foreign Protestants, and Aliens, Resident in England 1618–1688* [. . .] (Westminster: Camden Society, 1862), 58; *Calendar of State Papers Colonial, America and West Indies*, vol. 13, *1689–1692*, ed. J. W. Fortescue (London: Her Majesty's Stationery Office, 1901), 612–13. A Valentine Cruger, likely the same person, was married to Mayne Smith in London in 1695. See Parish Register of St. Leonard, Shoreditch, accessed through "London, England, Church of England Baptisms, Marriages

284 NOTES TO PAGE 23

and Burials, 1538–1812," *Ancestry.com*. Valentine Cruger's London-based trading partnership with Francis Terence (Tierens), which ended in bankruptcy, is noted in equity cases recorded in Peter Wilson Coldham, *English Adventurers and Emigrants, 1661–1733* (Baltimore, MD: Genealogical Publishing, 1985), 64, 74. Because of debts owed Dutch correspondents, their partnership is also recorded in Amsterdam City Archives, Notarial Archives, archive number 5075, inventory number 5875, deed number 567949. Accessed through https://archief.amsterdam/indexen/deeds/d0092ad0-e25f-1a7b-e053-b784100aab8a. The parish register recording Tileman's death notes that it occurred in the house of the merchant Francis T[ierens?], likely Valentine's partner. For Valentine's death in 1702, see the parish register for East Bradenham, Norfolk. Accessed through "Norfolk, England, Church of England Baptism, Marriages, and Burials, 1535–1812," *Ancestry.com*.

7. Cruger, *GBH*, 1–3; Joseph F. X. McCarthy, "The Cruger Family in the Eighteenth Century" (PhD diss., Fordham University, 1959), 36.

8. De Lancey, "Original Family Records: Cruger," 74–76; Maud Churchill Nicoll, "The Earliest Cuylers in Holland and America," *NYGBR* 42, no. 4 (1911): 361–66; Thomas Grier Evans, ed., *Records of the Reformed Dutch Church in New Amsterdam and New York: Baptisms from 25 December, 1639, to 27 December, 1730* (New York: NYGBS, 1901), 298, 311, 327, 346, 360, 379, 405, 427; McCarthy, "Cruger Family," 10, 22–24. McCarthy gave particular attention to the family's place in New York politics in earlier periods and to the family's business operations.

9. Cruger, *GBH*, 1–3; Lothrop Withington, "New York Gleanings in England," *NYGBR* 36, no. 1 (1905): 25; William J. Hoffman, "A 'Tumult of the Merchants' of New York in 1698," *NYGBR* 74, no. 3 (1943): 96–100; Thomas J. Archdeacon, *New York City, 1664–1710: Conquest and Change* (Ithaca, NY: Cornell University Press, 1976), 68, 74; Wallace Gandy, ed., *The Association Oath Rolls of the British Plantations* [. . .] (London: Published by the author, 1922), 40–41.

10. Beverly McAnear, "The Place of the Freeman in Old New York," *NYH* 21, no. 4 (1940): 418–30.

11. The genealogical information in this paragraph is based on Cruger, *GBH*, 1–6; Bentley D. Hasell, "Cruger and Hasell: Corrections," *NYGBR* 23 (1892): 147–49; and De Lancey, "Original Family Records: Cruger."

12. See, for example, John Cruger to Philip Livingston, 10 August 1715; John Cruger to Philip Livingston, 22 June 1716; John Cruger to Philip Livingston, 23 June 1716; Marya Cruger to Philip Livingston, November 1716; John Cruger to Philip Livingston, 2 January 1717; Marya Cruger to [Chatrina (Catherine) Livingston], 10 May 1717; "Account of Robert Livingston" [with John Cruger], 14 April 1719; and Henry Cruger to Robert Livingston, 24 May 1724, LFP. On the Cuylers, see Maud Churchill Nicoll, *The Earliest Cuylers in Holland and America* [. . .] (New York: Tobias A. Wright, 1912), especially 12–19.

NOTES TO PAGES 23–26

13. Cathy Matson, *Merchants and Empire: Trading in Colonial New York* (Baltimore, MD: Johns Hopkins University Press, 1998), 373n28.

14. *Minutes of the Common Council of the City of New York, 1675–1776,* 8 vols. (New York: Dodd, Mead, 1905), 2:329, 361, 383.

15. McCarthy, "Cruger Family," 8.

16. Cruger, *GBH*, 5; *Minutes of the Common Council,* 8:42, 50.

17. *New-York Mercury*, 18 August 1755.

18. Julius M. Bloch, ed., *An Account of Her Majesty's Revenue in the Province of New York, 1701–09* (Bridgewood, NJ: Gregg Press, 1966), 24, 56, 68, 81, 120, 125, 139, 163, 174, 230, 269. See also McCarthy, "Cruger Family," 35–38.

19. For example, New York Shipping Returns, CO5/1222, fols. 2, 4, 6, 7, 16, 17, 18, UKNA; Bloch, *Account of Her Majesty's Revenue*, 105, 141, 247, 264, 265, 267, 268, 281, 284, 285.

20. Bloch, *Account of Her Majesty's Revenue*, 96, 107, 115, 127, 143, 167, 232, 239, 250, 271.

21. See "Cornelius Cuyler Letterbooks, 1724–1764," American Antiquarian Society, Worcester, MA. On similar trading by Cruger with another correspondent, see Sally M. Schultz and Joan Hollister, "Jean Cottin, Eighteenth-Century Huguenot Merchant," *NYH* 86, no. 2 (2005): 158–60.

22. McCarthy, "Cruger Family," 36; William I. Roberts III, "Samuel Storke: An Eighteenth-Century London Merchant Trading to the American Colonies," *Business History Review* 39, no. 2 (1965): 148–52.

23. "New York City Assessment Roll, February, 1730," *NYGBR* 95, no. 3 (1964): 168, 172–74.

24. James Grant Wilson, ed., *The Memorial History of the City of New York: From Its First Settlement to the Year 1892*, 4 vols. (New York: New-York History Co., 1892), 2:258.

25. Linda M. Rupert, *Creolization and Contraband: Curaçao in the Early Modern Atlantic* (Athens: University of Georgia Press, 2012), 74–75, 165; Wim Klooster, "Curaçao as a Transit Center to the Spanish Main and the French West Indies," in Gert Oostindie and Jessica V. Roitman, eds., *Dutch Atlantic Connections, 1680–1800: Linking Empires, Bridging Borders* (Leiden: Brill, 2014), 25–51; Wim Klooster, *Illicit Riches: Dutch Trade in the Caribbean, 1648–1795* (Leiden: KITVL Press, 1998), 97–101.

26. Quoted in Wim Klooster and Gert Oostinde, *Realm between Empires: The Second Dutch Atlantic, 1680–1815* (Ithaca, NY: Cornell University Press, 2018), 41.

27. Cruger, *GBH*, 5.

28. New York Shipping Returns, CO5/1227, fol. 12, UKNA.

29. Quoted in Thomas M. Truxes, *The Overseas Trade of British America: A Narrative History* (New Haven: Yale University Press, 2021), 206. See also Virginia D. Harrington, *The New York Merchant on the Eve of the Revolution* (New York, 1935), 192–96.

30. Thomas M. Truxes, *Defying Empire: Trading with the Enemy in Colonial New York* (New Haven: Yale University Press, 2008), 60–61.

286 NOTES TO PAGES 26–27

31. Henry Cruger to Robert Livingston, 21 December 1724, LFP. This may have been the voyage of the sloop *Anne* identified as *TASTD*, Voyage ID# 25367.

32. Cruger, *GBH*, 7.

33. Trevor Burnard and John Garrigus, *The Plantation Machine: Atlantic Capitalism in French Saint-Domingue and British Jamaica* (Philadelphia: University of Pennsylvania Press, 2016), 55–57.

34. "Invoice of Sundry Goods Shipped to Robert Livingston Jr. of New York, 8 June 1732," and "Invoice of Goods Shipped to Robert Livingston Jr. in New York, 28 October 1734," LFP.

35. *Daily Journal* (London), 26 January 1734. See also *Calendar of State Papers Colonial, America and West Indies*, vol. 43, *1737*, ed. K. G. Davies (London: Her Majesty's Stationery Office, 1963), 270–88.

36. Vincent Brown, *The Reaper's Garden: Death and Power in the World of Atlantic Slavery* (Cambridge, MA: Harvard University Press, 2010), 2–5, 10–24.

37. Henry Cruger later became guardian to his first wife's orphaned daughter, also named Hannah. She subsequently married the New Yorker John Van Horn. See Cruger, *GBH*, 7.

38. *Journals of the Assembly of Jamaica*, vol. 3 [1731–1745] (Jamaica: Alexander Aikman, 1747), 415–16, 422–24, 434–36, 439.

39. Cruger, *GBH*, 7.

40. Isaac Samuel Emmanuel, *Precious Stones of the Jews of Curaçao: Curaçaon Jewry, 1656–1957* (New York: Bloch, 1957), 263; *Verzameling stukken bijeengebracht door Cornelis Schryver met betrekking tot de beveiliging van de handel met en scheepvaart op Curaçao en Sint-Maarten* [1739], 16, 25, 34, 37, 118, University of Leiden Digital Collections, https:// digitalcollections.universiteitleiden.nl/view/item/435522/pages; McCarthy, "Cruger Family," 52.

41. Cruger, *GBH*, 11.

42. McCarthy, "Cruger Family," 38.

43. E. B. O'Callaghan, ed., *Calendar of Historical Manuscripts in the Office of Secretary of State, Albany, N.Y.,* part 2 (Albany, NY: Weed, Parsons, 1866), 543.

44. Street names and numbers in lower Manhattan changed repeatedly. For Henry's residence near Hanover Square, likely on Smith Street (later William Street), see, for example, *New-York Evening Post*, 31 March 1746; *New-York Gazette; or, The Weekly Post-Boy*, 13 November 1749. His brother John Cruger also lived on Smith Street. See, for example, *New-York Gazette; or, The Weekly Post-Boy*, 3 January 1757. John Austin Stevens Jr., *Colonial Records of the New York Chamber of Commerce, 1768–1784. With Historical and Biographical Sketches* (New York: John F. Trow, 1867), 129. John Harris Cruger lived at what came to be called no. 8 Hanover Square before the Revolution. See also Van Schaack, *Henry Cruger*, 36, which notes that several generations of Crugers lived at what was called "the

old corner house" at the intersection of "William and Stone Streets, in view of Hanover Square."

45. Cruger, *GBH*, 7–11.

46. On this process, see John M. Murrin, *Rethinking America: From Empire to Republic* (New York: Oxford University Press, 2018); Richard Bushman, *The Refinement of America: Persons, Houses, Cities* (New York: Vintage Books, 1993).

47. De Lancey, "Original Family Records: Cruger," 74; McCarthy, "Cruger Family," 50.

48. McCarthy, "Cruger Family," 50; Cruger, *GBH*, 9–11.

49. On Elizabeth Cruger Van Schaack, see Van Schaack, *PVS*, 104, 479–85.

50. Kathryn C. Buhler and Graham Hood, *American Silver: Garvan and Other Collections in the Yale University Art Gallery*, 2 vols. (New Haven: Yale University Press, 1970), 2:56–57. Other pieces of Cruger silver survive in private and public collections.

51. Henry Cruger Sr. to Thomas Lawrence, New York, 17 October 1753, *Henry Cruger Correspondence 1753*, LOC; "Book of Accounts Belonging to the Academy in Philadelphia," 7 January 1751–26 July 1757, UPA 3, Archives General Collection of the University of Pennsylvania, 1740–1820, University of Pennsylvania, Philadelphia.

52. See accounts referencing John Harris Cruger in HJCAB. John Harris signed a printed July 1761 letter protesting reports that Jamaicans had been keeping up "a constant illegal correspondence" with Hispaniola and requesting more Royal Navy protection. See CO137/61, 49, UKNA. He also signed a 1761 Jamaican letter congratulating George III on his coronation. See CO137/32, 48–49, UKNA.

53. *Collections of the New-York Historical Society for the Year 1885* (New York: NYHS, 1886), 207; *New-York Mercury*, 12 May 1766, 9 June 1766; *New-York Journal; or, The General Advertiser*, 20 November 1766.

54. *The Original Charter of Columbia College* [. . .] (New York: Hall, Clayton, 1854), 8; [Columbia University], *A History of Columbia University, 1754–1904* (New York: Columbia University Press, 1904), 8; McCarthy, "Cruger Family," 70–73.

55. [King's College (New York, NY)], *The matricula or Register of admissions & graduations, & of officers employed in King's College at New-York, 1754–1777,* electronic reproduction (New York: Columbia University Libraries, 2009).

56. McCarthy, "Cruger Family," 81.

57. McCarthy, "Cruger Family," 99–100; Pauline Pruneti Winkel, *Scharloo: A Nineteenth Century Quarter of Willemstad, Curaçao* (Florence: Edizioni Poligrafico Fiorentino, 1990), 204.

58. C. Dallett Hemphill, *Siblings: Brothers and Sisters in American History* (New York: Oxford University Press, 2011), 17–26, 39, 47–63.

59. Nicholas Cruger to Telem[o]n Cruger, 11 July 1772, in Alexander Hamilton Papers: General Correspondence, LOC.

60. Van Schaack, *PVS*, 30–31.

288   NOTES TO PAGES 31–33

61. Laurel Thatcher Ulrich, *Good Wives: Image and Reality in the Lives of Women in Northern New England, 1650–1750* (New York: Vintage Books, 1991), 119.

62. Serena R. Zabin, *Dangerous Economies: Status and Commerce in Imperial New York* (Philadelphia: University of Pennsylvania Press, 2009), 33.

63. Annette Townsend Phillips, *The Walton Family of New York, 1630–1940* (Philadelphia: Historical Publication Society, 1945), 50.

64. On Cruger dealings with Moses Franks, see McCarthy, "Cruger Family," 108, 177–78; *Letter Book of John Watts: Merchant and Councilor of New York, January 1, 1762–December 22, 1765* (New York: NYHS, 1928), 230–31; and entries in HJCAB.

65. Henry C. Van Schaack, "An Old Kinderhook Mansion," *Magazine of American History*, September 1878, 6; Van Schaack, *PVS*, 5; Henry Cruger Jr. to Elizabeth Cruger Van Schaack, 5 January 1767 [1768], SC9829, box 1, folder 29, SLFP.

66. Henry B. Hoff, "Americans Married on Curacao, 1715–1781," *NYGBR* 123, no. 4 (1992): 221. My thanks to Wim Klooster for this reference. Cruger, *GBH*, 18–24.

67. Henry Cruger and Ellin Peach's marriage on November 14, 1765, appears in the records of St. Augustine the Less Parish, Bristol. Her burial on February 6, 1767, is recorded in the register for Christ Church Parish, Bristol. Accessed via "Bristol, England, Church of England Baptisms, Marriages and Burials, 1538–1812," *Ancestry.com*. See also Jeremiah Osborne to Aaron Lopez, 8 February 1767, *CoRI*, 1:180; and Henry Cruger Jr. to Elizabeth Cruger Van Schaack, Bristol, 5 January 1767 [1768], SC9829, box 1, folder 29, SLFP. See also Julie M. Flavell, "Cruger, Henry (1739–1827), merchant and politician," *ODNB*. For mistaken references to Ellin as Hannah, see Cruger, *GBH*, 15–18; Malcolm Lester, "Cruger, Henry, Jr. (1739–1827), merchant, member of Parliament, mayor of Bristol, England, and New York state senator," *ANB*; and John Brooke, "Cruger, Henry (1739–1827), of Bristol," *HoP*. A poem "Verses to the Memory of Mrs. C*****," signed "H." was published immediately under an announcement of Ellin's death in the *New-York Mercury*, 27 April 1767. Seemingly inspired by Ellin's funeral, the poem is full of generic praise for her embodiment of female virtues but provides little insight into who she was as an individual.

68. McCarthy, "Cruger Family," 95. See also Matson, *Merchants and Empire*, 151.

69. For an extended analysis of Cruger trading, see McCarthy, "Cruger Family," 95–134.

70. Truxes, *Defying Empire*, 40–51.

71. Other Dutch correspondents included John Hodshon and John De Neufville. McCarthy, "Cruger Family," 108; Henry & John Cruger to Daniel Crommelin, 14 July 1766, HJCLB; William I. Roberts III, "Ralph Carr: A Newcastle Merchant and the American Colonial Trade," *Business History Review* 42, no. 3 (1968): 273–79.

72. Truxes, *Defying Empire*, 39–44.

73. Klooster, "Curaçao as a Transit Center," 26n6.

NOTES TO PAGES 33–36

74. Ron Chernow, *Alexander Hamilton* (New York: Penguin, 2004), 29.

75. McCarthy, "Cruger Family," 110–12.

76. On the Crugers' logwood and mahogany trading, see HJCAB; McCarthy, "Cruger Family," 54, 106–9; Geoffrey L. Rossano, "Down to the Bay: New York Shippers and the Central American Logwood Trade, 1748–1761," *NYH* 70, no. 3 (1989): 241, 249; and Jennifer L. Anderson, *Mahogany: The Costs of Luxury in Early America* (Cambridge, MA: Harvard University Press, 2012), 129–31.

77. McCarthy, "Cruger Family," 109–12.

78. Cathy D. Matson, "Fair Trade, Free Trade: Economic Ideas and Opportunities in Eighteenth-Century New York City Commerce" (PhD diss., Columbia University, 1985), 145, 159.

79. "Petition and Memorial of the Merchants of New York Trading to the Bay of Honduras," CO137/67, 63–64, UKNA.

80. On Madeira trading, see John Harris Cruger to William Palfrey, 12 July 1774, PFP. On the whaling venture, see, among others, Henry Cruger to William Palfrey, 5 August 1773, PFP.

81. New York Shipping Returns, CO5/1228, fols. 2–32, UKNA.

82. McCarthy, "Cruger Family," 90.

83. See various letters in HJCLB.

84. James G. Lydon, "New York and the Slave Trade, 1700 to 1774," *WMQ* 35, no. 2 (1978): 390.

85. *TASTD*, Voyage ID nos. 24543 and 37068; New York Shipping Returns, CO5/1228, fol. 54, UKNA; *New-York Mercury*, 10 August 1761, 27 June 1763.

86. *TASTD*, Voyage ID nos. 17708, 17737, 17422, 17460; *New-York Gazette; or, The Weekly Post-Boy*, 9 July 1770.

87. Erik Gobel, *The Danish Slave Trade and Its Abolition* (Leiden: Brill, 2016), 31.

88. *RDAG*, 23 January 1771.

89. James Thomas Flexner, *The Young Hamilton: A Biography* (Boston: Little, Brown, 1979), 39; Broadus Mitchell, *Alexander Hamilton: Youth to Maturity, 1755–1788* (New York: Macmillan, 1957), 23.

90. *Intra-American Slave Trade Database*, Voyage ID nos. 107157, 107606, 107646, 107841, 107843, 107910, 107949. See also Henry and John Cruger to Daniel Hewlett, New York, 18 June 1766, in HJCLB.

91. Nicholas Cruger to Messrs. Walton and Cruger, 5 June 1772, in Alexander Hamilton Papers: General Correspondence, LOC. See also Kortright & Cruger to Henry Cruger Jr., 6 June [1772?], in Alexander Hamilton Papers: General Correspondence, LOC.

92. [Daniel Horsmanden], *A journal of the proceedings in the detection of the conspiracy formed by some white people, in conjunction with Negro and other slaves, for burning the city of New-York* [. . .] (New York: James Parker, 1744), 89, 92, 99, 104, 109, 114, 116, 124; appendix:

"A List of Negroes Committed on Account of the Conspiracy"; appendix: "Negroes Indicted Who Were Not to Be Found."

93. Edward B. Callaghan, *Lists of Inhabitants of Colonial New York Excerpted from the Documentary History of the State of New-York*, indexed by Rosanne Conway (Baltimore, MD: Genealogical Publishing, 2007), 209.

94. Will of Henry Cruger Sr., proved 2 March 1780, Prob 11/1062, UKNA.

95. Jack P. Greene, *Settler Jamaica in the 1750s: A Social Portrait* (Charlottesville: University of Virginia Press, 2016), 257–58.

96. "St. Andrew, Quantity of Land Cultivated [. . .] 1753," CO137/28, 173, UKNA. See also David B. Ryden, "'One of the Fertilest Pleasentest Spotts': An Analysis of the Slave Economy in Jamaica's St. Andrew Parish, 1753," *Slavery and Abolition* 21, no. 1 (April 2000): 32–55.

97. Details of Henry Cruger's Jamaica property from "Legacies of British Slave-ownership Database," University College London, https://www.ucl.ac.uk/lbs/person/view/2146655317.

98. Will of Henry Cruger Sr., proved 2 March 1780, Prob 11/1062, UKNA. See also entry for John Harris Cruger, "Legacies of British Slave-ownership Database," https://www.ucl .ac.uk/lbs/person/view/2146658685.

99. McCarthy, "Cruger Family," 100, 113, 228–29, 255; *RDAG*, 15 May 1773, 1 July 1775, 14 February 1776.

100. Telemon Cruger's involvement with Anna Mariana's manumission is recorded in "Curaçao: Free from slavery (manumissions) 1722–1863," access number 1.05.12.01, inventory number 203, fol. 66, National Archives, The Hague. Accessed via https://www.nationaa larchief.nl/onderzoeken/zoekhulpen/curacao-vrij-van-slavernij-manumissies-1722-1863. Telemon's involvement in other manumissions is also recorded in this dataset. My thanks to Wim Klooster for suggesting these records.

101. McCarthy, "Cruger Family," 127–28; Harrington, *New York Merchant*, 132, 153.

102. I. N. Phelps Stokes, *The Iconography of Manhattan Island, 1498–1909*, 6 vols. (New York: Robert H. Dodd, 1915–28), 4:561. Cruger's partners were Henry Cuyler, Joseph Scott, and Gerardus Duycking.

103. Huey, "Old Slip and Cruger's Wharf," 15. See, for example, Henry Cruger's advertisement for a house for rent in *New-York Gazette; or, The Weekly Post-Boy*, 9 March 1752.

104. James Sullivan et al., eds., *The Papers of Sir William Johnson*, 13 vols. (Albany: University of the State of New York, 1921–1962), 3:654–56, 7:1143, 8:157–58, 12:221–22, 12:896. On Cruger land acquisitions, see McCarthy, "Cruger Family," 17–19, 55, 158–60, 172–74.

105. On merchants and politics, see Arthur Meier Schlesinger, *The Colonial Merchants and the American Revolution, 1763–1776* (New York: Columbia University, 1918), 29; Edward Countryman, *A People in Revolution: The American Revolution and Political Society in New York, 1760–1790* (Baltimore, MD: Johns Hopkins University Press, 1981), 113; Thomas M.

NOTES TO PAGES 39–41

Doerflinger, "Philadelphia Merchants and the Logic of Moderation, 1760–1775," *WMQ* 40, no. 2 (1983): 210; and Gordon S. Wood, *The Radicalism of the American Revolution* (New York: Vintage, 1993), 120.

106. *Minutes of the Common Council*, 3:15, 4:42; Wilson, *Memorial History*, 2:190–94, 243, 258; McCarthy, "Cruger Family," 12, 41–42; John Franklin Jameson, "Origin and Development of the Municipal Government of New York City, Part Second—The English and American Period," *Magazine of American History* 8, no. 9 (1882): 607–11; Richard B. Morris, ed., *Select Cases of the Mayor's Court of New York City, 1674–1784* (Washington, DC: American Historical Association, 1935), 1–62.

107. McCarthy, "Cruger Family," 55–70.

108. *New-York Gazette; or, The Weekly Post-Boy,* 27 January 1752.

109. Wilson, *Memorial History*, 4:522; McCarthy, "Cruger Family," 73–82.

110. Benjamin Franklin to William Parsons, 28 June 1756, Franklin Papers, Founders Online.

111. Harrington, *New York Merchant*, 295; McCarthy, "Cruger Family," 77–81.

112. McCarthy, "Cruger Family," 90–92; *Letter Book of John Watts*, 88–93, 229–31.

113. François Weil, *A History of New York*, trans. Jody Gladding (New York: Columbia University Press, 2004), 21.

114. McCarthy, "Cruger Family," 43, 53–54, 91; "Petition of John Cruger and Company to James De Lancey," 28 June 1757, NYPL Digital Collections; Stuyvesant Fish, *The New York Privateers, 1756–1763* [...] (New York: George Grady Press, 1945), 92; Entry for 14 February 1763, HJCAB.

115. On quartering controversies, including John Cruger's role, see John Gilbert McCurdy, *Quarters: The Accommodation of the British Army and the Coming of the American Revolution* (Ithaca, NY: Cornell University Press, 2019), 89–126; Truxes, *Defying Empire*, 30–32; J. Alan Rogers, *Empire and Liberty: American Resistance to British Authority 1755–1763* (Berkeley: University of California Press, 1974), 75–89; J. Alan Rogers, "Colonial Opposition to the Quartering of Troops during the French and Indian War," *Military Affairs* 34, no. 1 (1970): 7–9; Shy, *Toward Lexington*, 166; Lawrence Henry Gipson, *The British Empire before the American Revolution*, 14 vols. (New York: Alfred A. Knopf, 1965–69), 11:39–41.

116. Quotations in paragraph from William Smith, *The History of the late Province of New-York* [...], 2 vols. (New York: NYHS, 1830), 2:292–94.

117. Truxes, *Defying Empire*, 43–48.

118. Truxes, *Defying Empire*, 194; Thomas M. Truxes, "Transnational Trade in the Wartime North Atlantic: The Voyage of the Snow *Recovery*," *Business History Review* 79, no. 4 (2005): 756.

119. Truxes, *Defying Empire*, 7, 13, 62–64, 101.

292   NOTES TO PAGES 41–44

120. Truxes, *Defying Empire*, 195.

121. New York Shipping Returns, CO5/1228, fol. 70, UKNA; Truxes, *Defying Empire*, 44, 62–63, 83, 127, 156–71.

122. Carl L. Becker, *The History of Political Parties in the Province of New York, 1760–1776* (Madison: University of Wisconsin Press, 1909), 8–14, 22.

123. Hemphill, *Siblings*, 16–26.

124. Van Schaack, *PVS*, 204.

2. Stamps and People

1. Because the events of the 1770s have loomed so large in interpretations of 1765, scholarship treating the Stamp Act crisis has been shaped primarily by major trends in the interpretation of the Revolution and its causes. Edmund S. Morgan and Helen M. Morgan, *The Stamp Act Crisis: Prologue to Revolution* (Chapel Hill: University of North Carolina Press for the OIEAHC, 1995) remains the most comprehensive account. Originally published in 1953, it supported wider neo-Whig interpretations of the revolutionary era. A subsequent influential work in this tradition, which connected the Stamp Act crisis to other events to provide an account of the Revolution's origins, is Pauline Maier, *From Resistance to Revolution: Colonial Radicals and the Development of American Opposition to Britain, 1765–1776* (New York: Knopf, 1972). Many scholars have emphasized the role of colonial port cities in the crisis. In answer to the Morgans' work and the wider neo-Whig interpretation of the Revolution, social, labor, and left historians published scholarship from the 1960s emphasizing the autonomy and power of common people and the urban crowd in the events of 1765. Important works in this direction include Jesse Lemisch, *Jack Tar vs. John Bull: The Role of New York's Seamen in Precipitating the Revolution* (New York: Garland, 1997), based on a 1962 PhD dissertation and notable for its focus on New York rather on the more typical Boston; Gary B. Nash, *The Urban Crucible: Social Change, Political Consciousness, and the Origins of the American Revolution* (Cambridge, MA: Harvard University Press, 1979); and Alfred F. Young, *Liberty Tree: Ordinary People and the American Revolution* (New York: New York University Press, 2006). For all their differences, these accounts shared a fundamental tendency to interpret the Stamp Act crisis as part of forward-looking national stories of the United States. The fullest account of the controversy within the framework of British political history is P. D. G. Thomas, *British Politics and the Stamp Act Crisis: The First Phase of the American Revolution, 1763–1767* (Oxford: Oxford University Press, 1975). Joseph Tiedemann, *Reluctant Revolutionaries: New York City and the Road to Independence, 1763–1776* (Ithaca, NY: Cornell University Press, 1997) provides an account of 1765 within the context of New York history. A recent edited volume has offered valuable fresh interpretations. Zachary

NOTES TO PAGES 45–50

McLeod Hutchins, ed., *Community without Consent: New Perspectives on the Stamp Act* (Hanover, NH: Dartmouth College Press, 2016).

2. Quoted in Robert J. Christen, *King Sears: Politician and Patriot in a Decade of Revolution* (New York: Arno Press, 1982), 44.

3. C. A. Weslager, *The Stamp Act Congress, with an Exact Copy of the Complete Journal* (Newark: University of Delaware Press, 1976), 24.

4. Morgan and Morgan, *Stamp Act*, 37–38.

5. *JGANY*, 2:749–50.

6. Weslager, *Stamp Act Congress*, 80–81. On John Cruger's part in corresponding with New York's London agent, see, for example, *JGANY*, 2:746, 750, 753.

7. *JGANY*, 2:754.

8. The Assembly's petitions can be found in *JGANY*, 2:769–79.

9. *JGANY*, 2:776–77.

10. Thomas, *British Politics and the Stamp Act Crisis*, 88.

11. Morgan and Morgan, *Stamp Act*, 26–27; Weslager, *Stamp Act Congress*, 34, 50.

12. Jack P. Greene and Richard Jellison, "The Currency Act of 1764 in Imperial-Colonial Relations, 1764–1776," *WMQ* 18, no. 4 (1961): 485–91. See also Joseph Albert Ernst, "The Currency Act Repeal Movement: A Study of Imperial Politics and Revolutionary Crisis, 1764–1767," *WMQ* 25, no. 2 (1968): 177–211.

13. *New-York Mercury*, 3 December 1764; *New York Gazette*, 10 December 1764, 17 December 1764.

14. Morgan and Morgan, *Stamp Act*, 54–72; Weslager, *Stamp Act Congress*, 34.

15. Morgan and Morgan, *Stamp Act*, 108.

16. Weslager, *Stamp Act Congress*, 80–81, 187–89.

17. Lewis Cruger, ed., *Journal of the First Congress of the American Colonies in Opposition to the Tyrannical Acts of the British Parliament Held at New-York, October 7, 1765* (New York: E. Winchester, 1845), iii–vi. Lewis Cruger (1803–1879) was born in South Carolina, where his father owned a plantation, and graduated from Columbia College in 1823. After publishing on the Stamp Act Congress, he produced several works sympathetic to Southern secessionism and became the Confederacy's comptroller of the treasury in 1861. See Cruger, *GBH*, 46–48, 79–80. On the various, sometimes differing, early printings of the Stamp Act Congress's journal, see Weslager, *Stamp Act Congress*, 170–73.

18. Weslager, *Stamp Act Congress*, 59.

19. Weslager, *Stamp Act Congress*, 124.

20. For the influence of nationalist paradigms on interpretations of the Stamp Act crisis, see Zachary McLeod Hutchins, "Introduction: The Stamp Act, from Beginning to End," in Hutchins, *Community without Consent*, xiii.

294   NOTES TO PAGES 50–54

21. On John Cruger as supposed drafter of the Declaration of Rights, see Cruger, ed., *Journal of the First Congress*, iv. This claim was echoed in, for example, Benson John Lossing, *History of New York City* [. . .], 2 vols. (New York: Perine Engraving and Publishing, 1884), 1:208; and Wilson, *Memorial History*, 2:356.

22. Weslager, *Stamp Act Congress*, 139–40. On Dickinson as its author, see, for example, Elaine K. Ginsberg. "Dickinson, John (1732–1808), statesman and political pamphleteer," *ANB*.

23. Weslager, *Stamp Act Congress*, 81.

24. On the power of Boston's people during the early phase of the Stamp Act crisis, see, for example, Nash, *Urban Crucible*, 292–311; and Young, *Liberty Tree*, 325–44. On the historiography of "popular" versus "elite" agency in these events, see J. Patrick Mullins, "The Sermon That Didn't Start the Revolution: Jonathan Mayhew's Role in the Boston Stamp Act Riots," in Hutchins, *Community without Consent*, 28–29.

25. Henry B. Dawson, *The Sons of Liberty in New York* ([New York]: Published by the author, 1859), 72.

26. F. L. Engelman, "Cadwallader Colden and the Stamp Act Riots," *WMQ* 10, no. 4 (1953): 560–78, 568 (quotation).

27. On the importance of a "vertically aligned mercantile interest" encompassing poorer working people and better-off merchants to events in Boston in the Stamp Act crisis, see Mullins, "The Sermon That Didn't Start the Revolution," 29. For an earlier account stressing the role of common sailors in the New York Stamp Act crisis but framing it primarily as a class story of "Left vs. Right," see Lemisch, *Jack Tar vs. John Bull*, 73–104. On sailors and maritime culture in the Stamp Act Crisis and the coming of the Revolution, see also Paul A. Gilje, *Liberty on the Waterfront: American Maritime Culture in the Age of Revolutions* (Philadelphia: University of Pennsylvania Press, 2004).

28. Gilje, *Liberty on the Waterfront*, 101; Denver Brunsman, *The Evil Necessity: British Naval Impressment in the Eighteenth-Century Atlantic World* (Charlottesville: University of Virginia Press, 2013), 54–55, 179.

29. Christen, *King Sears*, 15–17. On Sears's career, see also Pauline Maeir, *The Old Revolutionaries: Political Lives in the Age of Samuel Adams* (New York: Vintage Books, 1982), 51–100.

30. Weslager, *Stamp Act Congress*, 148–57, 200–218.

31. Dawson, *Sons of Liberty*, 79–84; Engelman, "Cadwallader Colden," 568–69.

32. *New-York Mercury*, 7 November 1765.

33. Dawson, *Sons of Liberty*, 88.

34. On performative protest, see Molly Perry, "Buried Liberties and Hanging Effigies: Imperial Persuasion, Intimidation, and Performance during the Stamp Act Crisis," in Hutchins, *Community without Consent*, 36–66.

NOTES TO PAGES 54–62

35. On the complementary nature of street protests and colonists soliciting "assistance from power brokers in England," see Perry, "Buried Liberties," 36–37.

36. Dawson, *Sons of Liberty*, 83.

37. Dawson, *Sons of Liberty*, 84; Engelman, "Cadwallader Colden," 568–70.

38. Dawson, *Sons of Liberty*, 89–99; Engelman, "Cadwallader Colden," 571–73.

39. Neil R. Stout, "Captain Kennedy and the Stamp Act," *NYH* 45, no. 1 (1964): 48–49; Engelman, "Cadwallader Colden," 573–75.

40. Dawson, *Sons of Liberty*, 99.

41. Engelman, "Cadwallader Colden," 573–77; Dawson, *Sons of Liberty*, 99–104.

42. Dawson, *Sons of Liberty*, 101.

43. *The Letters and Papers of Cadwallader Colden*, 9 vols. (New York: NYHS, 1918–37), 7:64–71.

44. Tiedemann, *Reluctant Revolutionaries*, 27.

45. Dawson, *Sons of Liberty*, 104.

46. Morgan and Morgan, *Stamp Act*, 187–88.

47. Dawson, *Sons of Liberty*, 94.

48. Engelman, "Cadwallader Colden," 569, 573–76.

49. Quoted in Morgan and Morgan, *Stamp Act*, 192.

50. Robert R. Livingston to Robert Monckton, 8 November 1765, *Collections of the Massachusetts Historical Society*, 4th ser., vol. 10 (Boston: Massachusetts Historical Society, 1871), 561.

51. Stout, "Captain Kennedy," 48–49.

52. Dawson, *Sons of Liberty*, 104. McCarthy argued that some evidence strongly suggested that John Cruger had "leadership of the major faction involved in the Stamp Act riots." See McCarthy, "Cruger Family," 147–49.

53. Wilson, *Memorial History*, 2:366.

54. *Letters and Papers of Cadwallader Colden*, 7:93.

55. *JGANY*, 2:783.

56. For the public meeting, see *New-York Gazette*, 2 December 1765, and for the critical account of it, see *New-York Mercury*, 2 December 1765. On Sears's role in this meeting, see Christen, *King Sears*, 52–55.

57. Morgan and Morgan, *Stamp Act*, 168–73.

58. Morgan and Morgan, *Stamp Act*, 277.

59. Morgan and Morgan, *Stamp Act*, 279–87.

60. Christen, *King Sears*, 70–73.

61. Morgan and Morgan, *Stamp Act*, 287.

62. Henry Cruger Jr. to Aaron Lopez, 4 September 1765, *CoRI*, 1:119.

296 NOTES TO PAGES 63–68

63. Quoted in L. Stuart Sutherland, "Edmund Burke and the First Rockingham Ministry," *English Historical Review* 47, no. 185 (1932): 64.

64. On the British context for repeal, see Morgan and Morgan, *Stamp Act*, 279–92; and Thomas, *British Politics and the Stamp Act Crisis*, 181–84 on Rockinghamite policy, and 185–252 on the process of repeal. The *Virginia Gazette* reported two petitions came from Bristol and that Cruger was involved with the second, which seems to have been more forceful. See *Virginia Gazette*, 28 March 1766; and Walter E. Minchinton, "The Political Activities of Bristol Merchants with Respect to the Southern Colonies before the Revolution," *Virginia Magazine of History and Biography* 79, no. 2 (1971): 180–81.

65. Henry Cruger Jr. to Aaron Lopez, 1 March 1766, *CoRI*, 1:146.

66. Henry Cruger Jr. to Henry Cruger Sr., 14 February 1766, *CoRI*, 1:139–43; Michael G. Kammen, *A Rope of Sand: The Colonial Agents, British Politics, and the American Revolution* (Ithaca, NY: Cornell University Press, 1968), 92.

67. Morgan and Morgan, *Stamp Act*, 293.

68. "Letter from the Committee of Merchants in London, trading to North-America, directed to John Cruger, Esq; and the Rest of the Merchants in New-York," 28 February 1766. Published as a supplement to the *New-York Mercury*, 21 April 1766.

69. Compare the London merchants' letter with the analysis of repeal in Morgan and Morgan, *Stamp Act*, 271–92.

70. Henry Cruger Jr. to Aaron Lopez, 1 March 1766, *CoRI*, 1:145.

71. *Newport Mercury*, 30 June–7 July 1766.

72. "Annual Report," *NYHSQ* 58, no. 5 (1974): 25–26.

73. Young, *Liberty Tree*, 351.

74. *Pennsylvania Gazette*, 3 July 1766; see also Joan Coutu, *Persuasion and Propaganda: Monuments and the Eighteenth-Century British Empire* (Montreal: McGill–Queen's University Press, 2006), 195–234.

75. Alexander James Wall, *The Equestrian Statue of George III and the Pedestrian Statue of William Pitt Erected in the City of New York, 1770* (New York: NYHS, 1920), 38–57.

3. Transatlantic Patriots

1. Scholarship on the Townshend Acts crisis is vast. Many accounts have stressed the central role of merchants and markets in the period's politics and treated events in New York. Important works for this study include the progressive interpretations of Becker, *Political Parties*, and Schlesinger, *Colonial Merchants*, both of which stress economic roots of the American Revolution and consider New York politics in depth. Meier, *Resistance to Revolution* offers a classic "neo-Whig" overview of the period, emphasizing the perspective of militant patriots. Peter D. G. Thomas, *The Townshend Duties Crisis: The Second Phase of the American Revolution, 1767–1773* (Oxford: Clarendon Press, 1987) analyzes British

NOTES TO PAGES 69–71

politics. Leopold S. Launitz-Schürer Jr., *Loyal Whigs and Revolutionaries: The Making of the Revolution in New York, 1765–1776* (New York: New York University Press, 1980); Tiedemann, *Reluctant Revolutionaries*; and Minty, *Unfriendly to Liberty* focus on New York. Benjamin Carp, *Rebels Rising: Cities and the American Revolution* (New York: Oxford University Press, 2007), situates New York within a wider urban-oriented history. T. H. Breen, *The Marketplace of Revolution: How Consumer Politics Shaped the American Revolution* (New York: Oxford University Press, 2004), places the period at the center of a wider and influential interpretation arguing for the centrality of the politics of consumption to the coming of the Revolution. Patrick Griffin, *The Townshend Moment: The Making of Empire and Revolution in the Eighteenth Century* (New Haven: Yale University Press, 2017), connects events in North America, Britain, and Ireland.

2. McCurdy, *Quarters*, 89–126; Peter D. G. Thomas, "The Stamp Act Crisis and Its Repercussions, Including the Quartering Act Controversy," in Jack P. Greene and J. R. Pole, eds., *A Companion to the American Revolution* (Malden, MA: Blackwell, 2000), 132–33.

3. Thomas, "Stamp Act Crisis," 132; Thomas, *British Politics and the Stamp Act Crisis*, 101–8, 293–94; Nicholas Varga, "The New York Restraining Act: Its Passage and Some Effects, 1766–1768," *NYH* 37, no. 3 (1956): 237–38.

4. Christen, *King Sears*, 96–98.

5. Thomas, "Stamp Act Crisis," 132.

6. Wilson, *Memorial History*, 2:384.

7. Varga, "New York Restraining Act," 239; Thomas, *British Politics and the Stamp Act Crisis*, 220–21, 257–58, 300–303. On the Crugers' support for the petition, see Henry & John Cruger to Moses Franks, 22 December 1766, same to Daniel Crommelin, 23 December 1766, and same to Moses Franks, 22 April 1767, HJCLB.

8. On the Free Port Act, see Adrian J. Pearce, *British Trade with Spanish America, 1763–1808* (Liverpool: Liverpool University Press, 2014), 42–51; and Thomas, *British Politics and the Stamp Act Crisis*, 253–75. Bristol merchants campaigned around the Free Port Act, and Henry Cruger Jr. was in London when it was considered. See Jeremiah Osborne to Aaron Lopez, 29 April 1766; Henry Cruger to Aaron Lopez, 9 April 1766; Henry Cruger to Aaron Lopez, 20 May 1766, all in *CoRI*, 1:151–60. See also Henry & John Cruger to Moses Franks, 14 July 1766, HJCLB.

9. Christen, *King Sears*, 102–3.

10. For the petition, see *A Collection of Interesting, Authentic Papers, Relative to the dispute between Great Britain and America* [. . .] (London: John Almon, 1777), 163–67.

11. Lawrence Henry Gipson, *The Coming of the Revolution* (New York: Harper & Row, 1954), 133.

12. William Stanhope Taylor and John Henry Pringle, eds., *Correspondence of William Pitt, Earl of Chatham*, 4 vols. (London: John Murray, 1839), 3:188–94. On the petition's trans-

298   NOTES TO PAGES 71–74

atlantic dynamics, see Christen, *King Sears*, 82–96; Varga, "New York Restraining Act," 239–43; and Thomas, *British Politics and the Stamp Act Crisis*, 300–309.

13. Varga, "New York Restraining Act," 240–42.

14. Thomas, *Townshend Duties*, 8.

15. Robert J. Chaffin, "The Townshend Act Crisis, 1767–1770," in Greene and Pole, *Companion to the American Revolution*, 138.

16. Thomas, *British Politics and the Stamp Act Crisis*, 337–63; Thomas, *Townshend Duties*, 18–35; Jonathan Eacott, *Selling Empire: India in the Making of Britain and America, 1600–1830* (Chapel Hill: University of North Carolina Press for the OIEAHC, 2016), 189–91.

17. Chaffin, "Townshend Act Crisis," 138–39.

18. E. B. O'Callaghan, ed., *Journal of the Legislative Council of the Colony of New-York. Began the 8th Day of December 1743; and Ended the 3d of April 1775*, 2 parts (Albany, NY: Weed, Parsons, 1861), 2:1622.

19. McCarthy, "Cruger Family," 160–61; Henry Moore to the Earl of Dartmouth, 21 December 1765, CO5/1072, part 1, 19–20, UKNA.

20. Useful articles on these elections include Roger Champagne, "Family Politics versus Constitutional Principles: The New York Assembly Elections of 1768 and 1769," *WMQ* 20, no. 1 (1963): 57–79; Lawrence H. Leder, "The New York Elections of 1769: An Assault on Privilege," *Mississippi Valley Historical Review* 49, no. 4 (1963): 675–82; Bernard Friedman, "The New York Assembly Elections of 1768 and 1769: The Disruption of Family Politics," *NYH* 46, no. 1 (1965): 3–24; Patricia Bonomi, "Political Patterns in Colonial New York City: The General Assembly Election of 1768," *Political Science Quarterly* 81, no. 3 (1966): 432–47; James S. Olson, "The New York Assembly, the Politics of Religion, and the Origins of the American Revolution, 1768–1771," *Historical Magazine of the Protestant Episcopal Church* 43, no. 1 (1974): 21–28; Luke J. Feder, "'No Lawyer in the Assembly!' Character Politics and the Elections of 1768 in New York City," *NYH* 95, no. 2 (2014): 154–71; Christopher F. Minty, "Republicanism and the Public Good: A Re-examination of the DeLanceys, c. 1768–1769," *NYH* 97, no. 1 (2016): 55–81; and Christopher F. Minty, "Loyalism and the Liberty Boys: Popular Politics and Allegiance in British New York," *NYH* 101, no. 1 (2020): 68–69, 77. The De Lancey faction's politics between these elections and 1777 receive extended treatment in Minty, *Unfriendly to Liberty*.

21. Christen, *King Sears*, 122–23.

22. Christen, *King Sears*, 118–20.

23. Champagne, "Family Politics," 68.

24. *New York Journal*, 17 December 1767.

25. Stevens, *CRNYCC*, 3–8, 42, 100. On the chamber's founding and De Lanceyite politics, see Minty, "Republicanism," 66–68, and Minty, *Unfriendly to Liberty*, 96–102.

NOTES TO PAGES 74–79

26. Stevens, *CRNYCC*, 3, 99.

27. For nonimportation as background to the chamber's founding, see Wilson, *Memorial History*, 4:516; Schlesinger, *Colonial Merchants*, 116.

28. Becker, *Political Parties*, 58n28.

29. Christen, *King Sears*, 144–45, 158n3; McCarthy, "Cruger Family," 170.

30. Schlesinger, *Colonial Merchants*, 114–31, 156.

31. On the meaning of "free trade," see Matson, *Merchants and Empire*, 6–10.

32. Stevens, *CRNYCC*, 14, 15, 17, 21–23, 32–34.

33. On the chamber and arbitration, see Eben Moglen, "Commercial Arbitration in the Eighteenth Century: Searching for the Transformation of American Law," *Yale Law Journal* 93, no. 1 (1983): 140–44; Stevens, *CRNYCC*, 47.

34. Truxes, *Defying Empire*, 190–192; Hulsebosch, *Constituting Empire*, 118–20; Gregory Afinogenov, "Lawyers and Politics in Eighteenth-Century New York," *NYH* 89, no. 2 (2008): 160–62; Jack P. Greene, *The Constitutional Origins of the American Revolution* (Cambridge: Cambridge University Press, 2011), 134–39.

35. Tiedemann, *Reluctant Revolutionaries*, 121–22.

36. Thomas, *Townshend Duties*, 81–85.

37. Christen, *King Sears*, 125–29; Launitz-Schürer, *Loyal Whigs*, 58–61.

38. Christen, *King Sears*, 124–25.

39. *JGANY*, 3:70–71; Christen, *King Sears*, 131–33; Launitz-Schürer, *Loyal Whigs*, 63.

40. Historians have given varying interpretations of these developments. See Champagne, "Family Politics," 68–69; Friedman, "The New York Assembly Elections," 14; Tiedemann, *Reluctant Revolutionaries*, 129–31; Minty, *Unfriendly to Liberty*, 39–42.

41. Friedman, "New York Assembly Elections," 14, 22n37.

42. Christen, *King Sears*, 142–43n41; Thomas, *Townshend Duties*, 127.

43. Tiedemann, *Reluctant Revolutionaries*, 132.

44. Launitz-Schürer, *Loyal Whigs*, 66–68; Christen, *King Sears*, 136–38; quotation in Champagne, "Family Politics," 60.

45. Minty, *Unfriendly to Liberty*, 57.

46. Becker, *Political Parties*, 75n106.

47. Compare members of the Committee of Inspection in Becker, *Political Parties*, 75n106, with chamber members in Stevens, *CRNYCC*, 300–304. A sixteenth member of the Committee of Inspection, Joseph Bull, joined the chamber in June 1769.

48. For Cooley's own account, see *Scots Magazine*, 1 September 1769, 477–79. See also Schlesinger, *Colonial Merchants*, 189n1. Because of evidence documenting John Harris Cruger's role in nonimportation, I have identified him rather than his uncle John as the member of the family likely most directly involved in the Cooley affair. For the letter attacking Cooley, see *New-York Chronicle*, 20 July 1769; also printed as a broadside, *New-*

NOTES TO PAGES 79–83

York, July 20th, Advertisement of greater importance to the public [. . .] (New York, 1769), https://www.loc.gov/item/rbpe.10302400/. For reports on Cooley's treatment, see *New-York Gazette and the Weekly Mercury*, 24 July 1769; *New-York Gazette; or, The Weekly Post-Boy*, 24 July 1769; *New-York Journal; or, The General Advertiser*, 27 July 1769. Unlike Cooley's own account, none of the New York newspaper reports name John Harris Cruger or any other committee members. Cruger's name did appear, however, when Cooley's letter was republished in the *Massachusetts Gazette: and the Boston Weekly News-Letter*, 23 November 1769. See also Tiedemann, *Reluctant Revolutionaries*, 156; Jones, *Resisting Independence*, 90–92; Schlesinger, *Colonial Merchants*, 188–89; and Breen, *Marketplace of Revolution*, 257–67.

49. Breen, *Marketplace of Revolution*, 254–67. In November 1769, John Harris Cruger, Jacob Walton, Isaac Sears, and others formed a "Private Association" to protect their "common Rights." See Minty, *Unfriendly to Liberty*, 78.

50. Schlesinger, *Colonial Merchant*, 190.

51. Quoted in Breen, *Marketplace of Revolution*, 255.

52. Tiedemann, *Reluctant Revolutionaries*, 136–40; Christen, *King Sears*, 161–64.

53. Christen, *King Sears*, 163–64.

54. Tiedemann, *Reluctant Revolutionaries*, 139–43; Minty, *Unfriendly to Liberty*, 65–79.

55. Christen, *King Sears*, 161–67; Launitz-Schürer, *Loyal Whigs*, 79–83; Tiedemann, *Reluctant Revolutionaries*, 139–45; Thomas *Townshend Duties*, 200–201.

56. Edward Countryman, "McDougall, Alexander (1732–1786), revolutionary leader and banker," *ANB;* Roger J. Champagne, *Alexander McDougall and the American Revolution* (Schenectady, NY: Union College Press, 1975), 5–10.

57. [Alexander McDougall], "To the betrayed inhabitants of the city and colony of New-York" ([New York: James Parker, 1769]); Champagne, *Alexander McDougall*, 16–23; Launitz-Schürer, *Loyal Whigs*, 83–87; Tiedemann, *Reluctant Revolutionaries*, 143–45.

58. Christen, *King Sears*, 167. On the De Lancey faction's dealings with McDougall and his supporters, with an emphasis on their ideological differences, see Minty, *Unfriendly to Liberty*, 79–95, 107–32.

59. On soldier/civilian tensions, see Lemisch, *Jack Tar*, 121–42.

60. Christen, *King Sears*, 181–90; Tiedemann, *Reluctant Revolutionaries*, 147–49.

61. *New-York Journal; or, The General Advertiser*, 12 April 1770; Christen, *King Sears*, 192–96.

62. Thomas, *Townshend Duties*, 161–79.

63. Schlesinger, *Colonial Merchants*, 215–16; Christen, *King Sears*, 211–14; Launitz-Schürer, *Loyal Whigs*, 87–88; Tiedemann, *Reluctant Revolutionaries*, 161–62.

64. On this point, see Christen, *King Sears*, 214–16, 239n27.

65. Schlesinger, *Colonial Merchants*, 221–22; Christen, *King Sears*, 214–17; Launitz-Schürer, *Loyal Whigs*, 88; Tiedemann, *Reluctant Revolutionaries*, 161–62.

NOTES TO PAGES 83–86   301

66. The names of John, Henry, and John Harris Cruger appeared in a list of those supporting resuming imports in *New-York Gazette; or, The Weekly Post-Boy*, 23 July 1770. The list further marked "persons who were very assiduous in bringing about the late resolution to import." None of the Crugers were so marked. However, all three Crugers were listed in a hostile letter published in Boston naming over one hundred New Yorkers working to end total nonimportation. See *Boston Gazette, and Country Journal*, 23 July 1770.

67. Schlesinger, *Colonial Merchants*, 222–23; Christen, *King Sears*, 217–22; Launitz-Schürer, *Loyal Whigs*, 88–89; Tiedemann, *Reluctant Revolutionaries*, 162–63; Minty, *Unfriendly to Liberty*, 121–30.

68. Henry Cruger Sr. to Peter Van Schaack, 18 June 1770, American Revolutionary War Manuscripts, Boston Public Library. On the *Ellin*, see *New-York Journal; or, The General Advertiser*, 31 May 1770, 7 June 1770, 14 June 1770, 22 November 1770, 13 June 1771.

69. Schlesinger, *Colonial Merchants*, 223–27; Christen, *King Sears*, 222–28; Tiedemann, *Reluctant Revolutionaries*, 164–65.

70. Breen, *Marketplace of Revolution*, 238–39.

71. Michael D. Hattem, "'As Serves Our Interest Best': Political Economy and the Logic of Popular Resistance in New York City, 1765–1776," *NYH* 98, no. 1 (2017): 42.

72. Hattem, "As Serves Our Interest Best," 68.

73. Tiedemann, *Reluctant Revolutionaries*, 165.

74. Greene and Jellison, "Currency Act of 1764," 513; Schlesinger, *Colonial Merchants*, 223–24; Christen, *King Sears*, 227; Henry Cruger Sr. to Peter Van Schaack, 18 June 1770, American Revolutionary War Manuscripts, Boston Public Library.

75. Christen, *King Sears*, 224.

76. Schlesinger, *Colonial Merchants*, 225–27; Christen, *King Sears*, 226–27; Tiedemann, *Reluctant Revolutionaries*, 164–65.

77. Leopold S. Launitz-Schürer Jr., "Whig-Loyalists: The De Lanceys of New York," *NYHSQ* 56, no. 3 (1972): 192.

78. Hattem, "As Serves Our Interest Best," 68. For a more skeptical assessment of the democratic credentials of those for importing, see Breen, *Marketplace of Revolution*, 276–79.

79. Christen, *King Sears*, 231–37; Schlesinger, *Colonial Merchants*, 227–36.

80. On the De Lancey faction's role in developing popular politics and political associationism, especially in this period, see Minty, *Unfriendly to Liberty*, 6, 115–39.

81. Benjamin Carp, "Did Dutch Smugglers Provoke the Boston Tea Party?" *Early American Studies* 10, no. 2 (2012): 346.

82. Eacott, *Selling Empire*, 194.

83. Schlesinger, *Colonial Merchants*, 251.

84. Schlesinger, *Colonial Merchants*, 244–50; Carp, "Dutch Smugglers," 335–59.

85. Schlesinger, *Colonial Merchants*, 247.

NOTES TO PAGES 86–89

86. McCarthy, "Cruger Family," 129; Nicholas Cruger to Messrs. Walton & Cruger, 5 June 1772, in Alexander Hamilton Papers: General Correspondence, LOC.

87. *New-York Gazette and the Weekly Mercury*, 5 October 1772.

88. George William Edwards, *New York as an Eighteenth Century Municipality, 1731–1776* (New York: Columbia University Press, 1917), 192–95.

89. John Latimer, *The History of the Society of Merchant Venturers of Bristol, with Some Account of the Anterior Merchants' Guilds* (Bristol: J. W. Arrowsmith, 1903); and W. E. Minchinton, *Politics and the Port of Bristol in the Eighteenth Century: The Petitions of the Society of Merchant Venturers, 1698–1803* (Bristol: Bristol Record Society, 1963).

90. Henry Cruger Jr. to Elizabeth Van Schaack, 5 January 1767 [1768], Box 1, Folder 29, SLFP.

91. Latimer, *Merchant Venturers*, 330.

92. For an overview of Wilkes's career, see Peter D. G. Thomas, "Wilkes, John (1725–1797), politician," *ODNB*. On Wilkes and America, see Arthur H. Cash, *John Wilkes: The Scandalous Father of Civil Liberty* (New Haven: Yale University Press, 2006), 230–35.

93. *New-York Gazette and the Weekly Mercury*, 26 March 1770.

94. *London Chronicle*, 11–14 March 1769.

95. Steve Poole and Nicholas Rogers, *Bristol from Below: Law, Authority and Protest in a Georgian City* (Woodbridge: Boydell Press, 2017), 99; P. T. Underdown, "Henry Cruger and Edmund Burke: Colleagues and Rivals at the Bristol Election of 1774," *WMQ* 15, no. 1 (1958): 15–16.

96. For the petition, see *Independent Chronicle,* 5–8 January 1770. For Cruger's speech, see *Gazetteer and New Daily Advertiser*, 25 July 1769. This speech was reprinted in *New-York Gazette and the Weekly Mercury*, 18 September 1769.

97. *General Evening Post*, 4–6 January 1770; *Independent Chronicle*, 5–8 January 1770; *New-York Journal; or, The General Advertiser*, 15 March 1770; and *Newport Mercury*, 19 March 1770.

98. John Gorham Palfrey, "Life of William Palfrey, Paymaster-General in the Army of the Revolution," in Jared Sparks, ed., *The Library of American Biography*, 2nd ser., vol. 7 (Boston: Charles C. Little and James Brown, 1852), 337–75; Robin Eagles, ed., *The Diaries of John Wilkes, 1770–1797* (London: Boydell Press, 2014), 17, 18.

99. See Henry Cruger Jr. to William Palfrey, 14 March 1772; Henry Cruger Jr. to William Palfrey, 14 October 1772; Henry Cruger Jr. to William Palfrey, 28 March 1774, PFP.

100. Henry Cruger Jr. to Horatio Gates, 6 July 1770, Horatio Gates Papers, NYHS.

101. John Latimer, *The Annals of Bristol in the Eighteenth Century* ([London?]: Printed for the author, 1893), 397. See also *The London Magazine, or Gentleman's Monthly Intelligencer*, January 1772, 38–40.

102. Supplement to *Massachusetts Spy*, 3 April 1772.

NOTES TO PAGES 89–94 303

103. *Middlesex Journal or Chronicle of Liberty*, 22–25 February 1772; *Public Advertiser*, 25 February 1772.

4. The Center Fails

1. Thomas, *Townshend Duties*, 214–25.

2. *Massachusetts Gazette and Boston Weekly News-Letter*, 17 December 1772; Alan C. Aimone and Eric I. Manders, "A Note on New York City's Independent Companies, 1775–1776," *NYH* 63, no. 1 (1982): 60; and Solomon Henner, "The Career of William Tryon as Governor of the Province of New York, 1771–1780" (PhD diss., New York University, 1968), 70–76.

3. William H. W. Sabine, ed., *Historical Memoirs from 16 March 1763 to 9 July 1776 of William Smith* (New York: Colburn and Tegg, 1956), 140; McCarthy, "Cruger Family," 176.

4. McCarthy, "Cruger Family," 177–78; Ross J. S. Hoffman, *Edmund Burke, New York Agent with His Letters to the New York Assembly and Intimate Correspondence with Charles O'Hara, 1761–1776* (Philadelphia: American Philosophical Society, 1956), 121–22.

5. On these maneuverings, see William Tryon to (Earl of Hillsborough), 5 March 1771, CO5/1075, 197–98, UKNA; William Tryon to Earl of Hillsborough, 5 March 1772, CO5/1075, 247–48, UKNA; *Journal of the Legislative Council of the Colony of New-York* [1743–1775] (Albany, NY: Weed, Parsons, 1861), 1887, 1897; *New-York Gazette and the Weekly Mercury*, 2 August 1773.

6. *Rivington's New-York Gazetteer*, 12 August, 1773.

7. *New-York Gazette and the Weekly Mercury*, 5 April 1773, 12 April 1773, 26 April 1773; *Rivington's New-York Gazetteer*, 1 July 1773.

8. McCarthy, "Cruger Family," 158–60, 173–74. Henry Cruger Sr. was also involved in Vermont land dealings in this period. See Nathaniel Chipman, *Reports and Dissertations in Two Parts* [. . .] (Rutland, VT: Anthony Haswell, 1793), 99–110.

9. Van Schaack, *PVS*, 15. The resulting publication was [Peter Van Schaack, ed.], *Laws of New-York from the Year 1691, to 1773 inclusive* [. . .], 2 vols. (New York: Hugh Gaine, 1774).

10. Chernow, *Alexander Hamilton*, 37–39; Mitchell, *Alexander Hamilton: Youth to Maturity*, 34–35.

11. Eacott, *Selling Empire*, 205–6; Thomas, *Townshend Duties*, 246–57.

12. Benjamin W. Labaree, *The Boston Tea Party* (New York: Oxford University Press, 1964), 77, 87–103.

13. Tiedemann, *Reluctant Revolutionaries*, 176.

14. Tiedemann, *Reluctant Revolutionaries*, 179–80; Christen, *King Sears*, 284–94.

15. Labaree, *Boston Tea Party*, 97–103.

16. Carp, "Dutch Smugglers," 355.

304   NOTES TO PAGES 94–96

17. Labaree, *Boston Tea Party*, 138–45.

18. Peter D. G. Thomas, *Tea Party to Independence: The Third Phase of the American Revolution, 1773–1776* (Oxford: Oxford University Press, 1991), 22–23; Labaree, *Boston Tea Party*, 154–60; Tiedemann, *Reluctant Revolutionaries*, 182.

19. Thomas, *Tea Party*, 30.

20. Thomas, *Tea Party*, 48–61; Labaree, *Boston Tea Party*, 170–93; Boston Port Act, 31 March 1774, at *The Avalon Project: Documents in Law, History, and Diplomacy*, Yale Law School, https://avalon.law.yale.edu/18th_century/boston_port_act.asp.

21. Thomas, *Tea Party*, 62–87; Labaree, *Boston Tea Party*, 194–203.

22. Thomas, *Tea Party*, 88–117.

23. Tiedemann, *Reluctant Revolutionaries*, 183.

24. Tiedemann, *Reluctant Revolutionaries*, 186.

25. Sabine, *Historical Memoirs of William Smith*, 186.

26. Launitz-Schürer, "Whig-Loyalists," 194.

27. Van Schaack, *PVS*, 28.

28. For an account of this period emphasizing a growing ideological divide between De Lanceyites and McDougallites, see Minty, *Unfriendly to Liberty*, 153–66.

29. Champagne, *Alexander McDougall*, 55.

30. Tiedemann, *Reluctant Revolutionaries*, 187–91; Becker, *Political Parties*, 112–17; Champagne, *Alexander McDougall*, 56.

31. On Low's career, see Robert Ernst, "Isaac Low and the American Revolution," *NYH* 74, no. 2 (1993): 133–57.

32. Robert G. Parkinson, *The Common Cause: Creating Race and Nation in the American Revolution* (Chapel Hill: University of North Carolina Press for the OIEAHC, 2016), 6.

33. Becker, *Political Parties*, 114.

34. "Resolution of the New York Committee of Safety Adopted May 1774," AHAR, fol. 97; Van Schaack, *PVS*, 16–17; Peter Force, ed., *The American Archives*, 4th ser., 6 vols. (Washington, DC: M. St. Clair Clarke and Peter Force, 1837–1846), 1:293–301.

35. Launitz-Schürer, *Loyal Whigs*, 113–15; Becker, *Political Parties*, 118–20.

36. John Jay to John Vardill, 23 May 1774, JJ/FO.

37. Launitz-Schürer, *Loyal Whigs*, 113–19. See also Minty, *Unfriendly to Liberty*, 153–66.

38. Thomas Jones, *History of New York during the Revolutionary War* [. . .], ed. Edward Floyd De Lancey, 2 vols. (New York: NYHS, 1879), 1:34.

39. Diary of John Adams, 23 August 1774, AP/FO; John Jay to Peter Van Schaack, 2 October 1774; and Peter Van Schaack to John Jay, 12 October 1774, fols. 111–13, AHAR. See also James Duane to Peter Van Schaack, 2 September 1774, fol. 137, AHAR; Van Schaack, *PVS*, 21–22.

40. Jones, *Resisting Independence*, 113.

NOTES TO PAGES 97–99

41. "Journal of the Continental Congress—The Articles of Association, October 20, 1774," at *The Avalon Project: Documents in Law, History, and Diplomacy,* Yale Law School, https://avalon.law.yale.edu/18th_century/contcong_10-20-74.asp.

42. Jones, *History of New York,* 1:34.

43. *Supplement to the Massachusetts-Gazette (Massachusetts Gazette: and the Boston Weekly News-Letter,* 15 September 1774; Labaree, *Boston Tea Party,* 252; Thomas, *Tea Party,* 158–59.

44. Paul H. Smith et al., eds., *Letters of Delegates to Congress, 1774–1789,* 25 vols. (Washington, DC: Library of Congress, 1976–2000), 1:110, 113–15.

45. Julian P. Boyd, *Anglo-American Union: Joseph Galloway's Plans to Preserve the British Empire, 1774–1778* (Philadelphia: University of Pennsylvania Press, 1941), 37–38; Chopra, *Unnatural Rebellion,* 31–32.

46. On the congress's procedural handling of Galloway's plan, see Smith et al., *Letters of Delegates,* 1:113–19; Boyd, *Anglo-American Union,* 38. Galloway subsequently viewed himself as the victim of a conspiracy within the congress to unfairly squash his plan.

47. Van Schaack, *PVS,* 47.

48. On the Committee of Sixty's formation, see Launitz-Schürer, *Loyal Whigs,* 121–23, 127n41; *New-York Journal; or, The General Advertiser,* 24 November 1774. For an alternative interpretation to mine, see Becker, *Political Parties,* 163–69.

49. McCarthy, "Cruger Family," 188–89. According to letters he sent to William Palfrey, Henry Cruger Jr. was in America by June 1773 and remained there until at least April 10, 1774. Cruger planned to sail for England on May 1. News of the Boston Port Act arrived in New York on May 11. See Henry Cruger to William Palfrey, 21 June 1773, 7 March 1774, 28 March 1774, 10 April 1774, PFP.

50. On 1774's election, see John Brooke, "Introductory Survey," in *HoP;* Peter D. G. Thomas, *Lord North* (New York: St. Martin's Press, 1976), 80–81.

51. Lewis Namier and John Brooke, eds., *History of Parliament. The House of Commons, 1754–1790,* 3 vols. (New York: Oxford University Press, 1964), 1:284.

52. Henry Cruger to William Palfrey, 7 March 1774, PFP.

53. John Gorham Palfrey, "Life of William Palfrey, Paymaster-General in the Army of the Revolution," in *The Library of American Biography,* edited by Jared Sparks, Second Series, vol. 7 (Boston: Little & Brown, 1845), 368–88. See also William Palfrey to Henry Cruger, 18 May 1774, PFP.

54. *Public Advertiser,* 4 October 1774.

55. On this election, see Poole and Rogers, *Bristol from Below,* 252–58; P. T. Underdown, "Henry Cruger and Edmund Burke," 14–34.

56. John Brooke, "Nugent, Robert (1709–88), of Gosfield, Essex," *HoP.*

57. Henry Cruger to Peter Van Schaack, 4 November 1774, fol. 119, AHAR.

306 NOTES TO PAGES 100–103

58. G. E. Weare, *Edmund Burke's Connection with Bristol from 1774 till 1780* [. . .] (Bristol: William Bennett, 1894), 81; Namier and Brooke, *History of Parliament*, 1:286.

59. Namier and Brooke, *History of Parliament*, 1:286–87; Edmund Burke to the Duke of Portland, 3 September 1780, in Thomas W. Copeland et al., eds., *The Correspondence of Edmund Burke*, 10 vols. (Chicago: University of Chicago Press, 1958–1978), 4:274.

60. Weare, *Burke's Connection*, 79.

61. Weare, *Burke's Connection*, 89. On the influence of Burke's formulation, see Gordon S. Wood, *Representation in the American Revolution* (Charlottesville: University Press of Virginia, 1969), 4.

62. McCarthy, "Cruger Family," 176.

63. Hoffman, *Edmund Burke*, 139–40.

64. Van Schaack, *Henry Cruger*, 19–20. On Burke as New York's agent, see Jack M. Sosin, *Agents and Merchants: British Colonial Policy and the Origins of the American Revolution, 1763–1775* (Lincoln: University of Nebraska Press, 1965), 222–23.

65. Julie M. Flavell, "Americans of Patriot Sympathies in London and the Colonial Strategy for Opposition, 1774–1775" (PhD diss., University College London, 1988), 12.

66. Van Schaack, *PVS*, 30. See also Van Schaack, *Henry Cruger*, 13–15.

67. Van Schaack, *PVS*, 31.

68. Van Schaack, *PVS*, 31.

69. On Quincy, see Richard D. Brown, "Quincy, Josiah Jr. (1744–1775), lawyer and political leader," *ANB;* George H. Nash III, "From Radicalism to Revolution: The Political Career of Josiah Quincy Jr.," *Proceedings of the American Antiquarian Society* 79, no. 2 (1969): 253–90; Julie M. Flavell, "American Patriots in London and the Quest for Talks, 1774–1775," *Journal of Imperial and Commonwealth History* 20, no. 3 (1992): 335–69; and Daniel R. Coquillette and Neil Longley York, eds., *Portrait of a Patriot: The Major Political and Legal Papers of Josiah Quincy Junior*, 6 vols. (Boston: Colonial Society of Massachusetts, 2005–14). For Cruger's meeting with Quincy, see Coquillette and York, *Portrait of a Patriot*, 1:250.

70. Novanglus [John Adams], "III. To the Inhabitants of the Colony of Massachusetts-Bay, 6 February 1775," AP/FO.

71. Van Schaack, *Henry Cruger*, 55.

72. *The Speeches in the Last Session of the Present Parliament, delivered by several of the principal advocates in the House of Commons, in favour of the rights of America* [. . .] (New York: James Rivington, 1775).

73. Van Schaack, *Henry Cruger*, 52–55.

74. Van Schaack, *Henry Cruger*, 22.

75. *Pennsylvania Ledger*, 11 February 1775.

76. Becker, *Political Parties*, 168; Launitz-Schürer, *Loyal Whigs*, 145–46.

NOTES TO PAGES 104–109

77. Launitz-Schürer, *Loyal Whigs*, 130.

78. On these maneuverings, see Launitz-Schürer, *Loyal Whigs*, 130–34; Becker, *Political Parties*, 174–78; Minty, *Unfriendly to Liberty*, 181–85.

79. Henry Van Schaack to Peter Van Schaack, 16 January 1775 (cataloged as 16 July 1775), in "Henry Van Schaack Papers, 1734–1896," box 2, Edward E. Ayer Manuscript Collection, Newberry Library, Chicago. Available in Edward E. Ayer Digital Collection, https://collections.carli.illinois.edu/digital/collection/nby_eeayer/id/32803/rec/1; Van Schaack, *HVS*, 33–35, 37–44.

80. Van Schaack, *HVS*, 36–37.

81. *PH* 18:149–60; quotation: 18:154.

82. Van Schaack, *Henry Cruger*, 25–26; Flavell, "Americans of Patriot Sympathies," 199.

83. *PH* 18:168–98, Bristol Petition at 18:180–81. See also Thomas, *Tea Party*, 181–89.

84. Julie M. Flavell, "Lord North's Conciliatory Proposal and the Patriots in London," *English Historical Review* 107, no. 423 (1992): 315.

85. Flavell, "Conciliatory Proposal," 307.

86. Thomas, *Tea Party*, 199–201.

87. Flavell, "Conciliatory Proposal," 302.

88. Thomas, *Tea Party*, 195–212.

89. Flavell, "Conciliatory Proposal," 311–16.

90. Thomas, *Tea Party*, 177.

91. Thomas, *Tea Party*, 208–9, 215.

92. *The Plot discovered, Communicated by Letter from a worthy American Patriot in London, to his Friends in this Country, dated March 15, 1775.* ([New York?], [1775?]).

93. William Lee to Josiah Quincy, London, 3 April 1775, in Coquillette and York, *Portrait of a Patriot*, 6:387–88; Launitz-Schürer, *Loyal Whigs*, 137–42; Flavell, "Americans of Patriot Sympathies," 79n54, 184–86.

94. On the debated issue of ministerial bribery in New York, see Launitz-Schürer, *Loyal Whigs*, 137–45; and Bernard Mason, *The Road to Independence: The Revolutionary Movement in New York, 1773–1777* (Lexington: University of Kentucky Press, 1966), 50–54.

95. For another claim that De Lanceyites including the Crugers were offered baronetcies for supporting North's proposals, see *Morning Chronicle, and London Advertiser*, 27 June 1775.

96. Henry Cruger to Ralph Izard, 21 March 1775, in Anne Izard Deas, ed., *Correspondence of Mr. Ralph Izard* [. . .] (New York: Charles S. Francis, 1844), 57–60; see also Flavell, "Americans of Patriot Sympathies," 33.

97. Van Schaack, *Henry Cruger*, 18–21.

98. Deas, *Ralph Izard*, 57–60.

99. Deas, *Ralph Izard*, 57–60.

308 NOTES TO PAGES 110–120

100. Jones, *History of New York*, 1:37–39; Launitz-Schürer, *Loyal Whigs*, 146–55.

101. Flavell, "Americans of Patriot Sympathies," 221–22.

102. Launitz-Schürer, *Loyal Whigs*, 148–55; *PH* 18:643; Thomas, *Tea Party*, 228; Troy Bickham, *Making Headlines: The American Revolution as Seen through the British Press* (DeKalb: Northern Illinois University Press, 2009), 71.

103. Thomas, *Tea Party*, 230–31.

104. *JGANY*, 3:109–17; *PH* 18:650–55.

105. *PH* 18:644.

106. *PH* 18:647.

107. *PH* 18:644–46.

108. Thomas, *Tea Party*, 230–31.

109. Force, *American Archives*, 4th ser., 2:513.

110. Becker, *Political Parties*, 233–43.

5. Whigs Killing for the King

1. Jones, *History of New York*, 1:39–41; Christen, *King Sears*, 379–93.

2. See family information provided by Edward Floyd De Lancey as editor of Jones, *History of New York*, 1:649–63.

3. Launitz-Schürer, "Whig-Loyalists," 179–98. On the wider phenomenon, see Benton, *Whig-Loyalism*.

4. See, for example, John Adams to Joseph Warren, 21 June 1775; John Adams to Joseph Palmer, 5 July 1775, AP/FO. Four Pennsylvania Delegates in Congress to the Philadelphia Committee of Inspection and Observation, 3[–5?] July 1775, Franklin Papers, Founders Online. Doris Begor Morton, *Philip Skene of Skenesborough* (Granville, NY: Grastorf Press, 1959); and Philip Ranlet, "Skene, Philip (1725–1810), British officer and loyalist," *ANB*.

5. John Harris Cruger to [James Duane?], 13 July 1775, Duane Family Papers, ser. 1, box 3, NYHS. Accessed via New York Heritage Digital Collections, https://nyheritage.content dm.oclc.org/digital/collection/p16124coll1/id/35835/rec/30. The recipient of this letter from Cruger was presumably James Duane because of its inclusion in his papers, where it is among other letters to and from him. The recipient is not named on the letter itself, however. Moreover, although Cruger makes clear that he is responding to a June letter sent by his correspondent containing the accusations against his family, that letter is apparently not preserved in Duane's papers. I have therefore reconstructed the accusations made against the Crugers from John Harris Cruger's detailed refutation of them.

6. Abstract of Letter from Henry Cruger Jr. to Henry Cruger, 3 May 1775, in *The Manuscripts of the Earl of Dartmouth*, vol. 2, *American Papers* (London: Her Majesty's Stationery Office, 1895), 296.

NOTES TO PAGES 120–123

7. Van Schaack, *PVS*, 44–45.

8. Useful accounts among the many on New York's revolution include Joshua Canale, "'When a State Abounds in Rascals': New York's Revolutionary Era Committees for Public Safety, 1775–1783," *JER* 39, no. 2 (2019): 203–38; Chopra, *Unnatural Rebellion*; Edward Countryman, *A People in Revolution: The American Revolution and Political Society in New York, 1760–1790* (Baltimore, MD: Johns Hopkins University Press, 1981); Matthew P. Dziennik, "New York's Refugees and Political Authority in Revolutionary America," *WMQ* 77, no. 1 (2020): 65–96; Richard M. Ketchum, *Divided Loyalties: How the American Revolution Came to New York* (New York: Henry Holt, 2002); Jones, "Steadily Attached to His Majesty?," 163–98; Kammen, "American Revolution as a *Crise de Conscience*," 125–89; Kim, "Limits of Politicization," 868–89; Minty, *Unfriendly to Liberty*, 191–224; Christopher F. Minty, "Of One Hart and One Mind: Local Institutions and Allegiance during the American Revolution," *EAS* 15, no. 1 (2017): 99–132; Ranlet, *New York Loyalists*; Barnet Schecter, *The Battle for New York: The City at the Heart of the American Revolution* (New York: Walker, 2002); Tiedemann, *Reluctant Revolutionaries*; and Van Buskirk, *Generous Enemies*.

9. "The Memorial of Lt. Col. J. H. Cruger," 9 February 1784, AO12/20, fols. 143–46, UKNA. Hereafter "Memorial of J. H. Cruger." Further supporting evidence and related documents at AO12/20, fols, 146–50; AO12/89, fols. 122–27; AO12/90, fol. 109; AO12/109, 107; AO13/54, fols. 204–30; AO13/64, fols. 158–67; AO13/83, 95–96.

10. On the danger of reading too much into loyalists' retrospective claims, see also Calhoon, "The Loyalist Perception," in Calhoon, Barnes, and Davis, *Tory Insurgents*, 3.

11. John Harris Cruger to Peter Van Schaack, 27 June 1775, AHAR, fol. 145. See also Van Schaack, *PVS*, 52.

12. Julie M. Flavell, "Government Interception of Letters from America and the Quest for Colonial Opinion in 1775," *WMQ* 58, no. 2 (2001): 403–30; and Richard A. Roberts, ed., *Calendar of Home Office Papers of the Reign of George III, 1773–1775* (London: Her Majesty's Stationery Office, 1899), xxiv–xxvi.

13. Copy of intercepted letter of (John) Harris Cruger to Henry Cruger Jr., 3 November 1775, CO5/134, fols. 41–43.

14. Hoock, *Scars of Independence*, 38–39; Christen, *King Sears*, 410; Jones, *Resisting Independence*, 148–49.

15. John Richard Alden, *General Charles Lee: Traitor or Patriot?* (Baton Rouge: Louisiana State University Press, 1951), 97.

16. Alden, *Charles Lee*, 88–103; Dominick Mazzagetti, *Charles Lee: Self before Country* (New Brunswick, NJ: Rutgers University Press, 2013), 104–12; Philip Papas, *Renegade Revolutionary: The Life of General Charles Lee* (New York: New York University Press, 2014), 130–41.

17. Chopra, *Unnatural Rebellion*, 45–46.

310   NOTES TO PAGES 123–130

18. Van Schaack, *HVS*, 54–55.

19. Van Schaack, *HVS*, 54–55.

20. Papas, *Renegade Revolutionary*, 143–44.

21. *The Lee Papers*, vol. 1, *1754–1776* (New York: NYHS, 1872), 345–47.

22. Alden, *Charles Lee*, 100–101.

23. On these developments, see, for example, Van Buskirk, *Generous Enemies*, 2–16; Calhoon, *Loyalists in Revolutionary America*, 370–73.

24. Force, *American Archives*, 4th ser., 6:1363–71.

25. Jones, *History of New York*, 1:101–3.

26. "Memorial of J. H. Cruger."

27. "Memorial of J. H. Cruger."

28. Jones, *History of New York*, 1:108–9.

29. Chopra, *Unnatural Rebellion*, 51.

30. *New-York Gazette and the Weekly Mercury*, 4 November 1776; *New York City during the American Revolution: Being a collection [. . .] from the manuscripts in the possession of the Mercantile Library Association [. . .]* ([New York]: Published by the author, 1861), 117–37. See also Chopra, *Unnatural Rebellion*, 65–66.

31. "Petition of 547 Loyalist from New York City, November 28, 1776," NYHS Digital Collections; R. W. G. Vail, "The Loyalist Declaration of Dependence of November 28, 1776," *NYHSQ* 31, no. 2 (1947): 68–71.

32. De Lancey, "Original Family Records: Cruger," 77.

33. Jones, *History of New York*, 1:264–67.

34. A searing account is Kim, "Limits of Politicization," 868–89.

35. "Memorial of J. H. Cruger."

36. Jones, *History of New York*, 1:185–87. According to an even more graphic report, two unnamed infants died in the house. See *New-York Gazette and the Weekly Mercury*, 1 December 1777.

37. Jones, *History of New York*, 1:187.

38. Cruger, *GBH*, 7–11.

39. See Benjamin L. Carp, "The Night the Yankees Burned Broadway: The New York City Fire of 1776," *Early American Studies* 4, no. 2 (2006): 471–511.

40. For a list of sufferers, see *Pennsylvania Evening Post*, 26 August 1778.

41. G. D. Scull, ed., *The Montresor Journals* (New York: NYHS, 1881), 8, 126, 508.

42. *Royal Gazette*, 8 August 1778. See also *Royal Gazette*, 5 August 1778, 12 August 1778.

43. "Memorial of Henry Cruger, Esq," 22 January 1789 and 12 July 1789, AO13/95, fols. 22–25, UKNA. Hereafter "Memorial of Henry Cruger." Newspaper accounts reported that six houses, owned by John and Henry Cruger, were destroyed.

44. W. O. Raymond, "A Brave Soldier of the Revolution," *Acadiensis* 2, no. 4 (1902): 238–44;

NOTES TO PAGES 132–135

Benson J. Lossing, *The Pictorial Field-book of the Revolution* [. . .], 2 vols. (New York: Harper & Bros., 1860), 2:528; McCarthy, "Cruger Family," 237–38; Major Archibald McArthur to Major Thomas Pinckney, 8 July 1779, Thomas Addis Emmet Collection, doc. no. 7659, NYPL; *Gazetteer and New Daily Advertiser* (London), 25 September 1779.

45. John Harris Cruger to Henry Cruger, 8 November 1779, VSFP; Alexander A. Lawrence, *Storm over Savannah: The Story of Count d'Estaing and the Siege of the Town in 1779* (Athens: University of Georgia Press, 1951).

46. "Memorial of J. H. Cruger."

47. Catherine S. Crary, ed., *The Price of Loyalty: Tory Writings from the Revolutionary Era* (New York: McGraw-Hill, 1973), 274–75.

48. John Harris Cruger to Henry Cruger, 8 November 1779, with "Memorandum" on siege of Savannah, VSFP.

49. Crary, *Price of Loyalty*, 275.

50. Jones, *History of New York*, 2:383–86.

51. Richard C. Cole, "The Siege of Savannah and the British Press, 1779–1780," *Georgia Historical Quarterly* 65, no. 3 (1981): 189–202.

52. On the Franco-American alliance as consolidating loyalism, see Jones, *Resisting Independence*, 166–75.

53. For the act, see *Laws of the Legislature of the State of New York, In Force Against the Loyalists* [. . .] (London: H. Reynell, 1786), 9–27. On seizures of loyalist property, see Howard Pashman, "The People's Property Law: A Step toward Building a New Legal Order in Revolutionary New York," *Law and History Review* 31, no. 3 (August 2013): 587–626; Brett Palfreyman, "The Loyalists and the Federal Constitution: The Origins of the Bill of Attainder Clause," *JER* 35, no. 3 (2015): 451–73; and Chopra, *Unnatural Rebellion*, 160.

54. Chopra, *Unnatural Rebellion*, 161.

55. John Jay to George Clinton, 6 May 1780, JJCU; Jones, *History of New York*, 2:538.

56. For an overview of the military history, see John S. Pancake, *This Destructive War: The British Campaign in the Carolinas, 1780–1782* (University: University of Alabama Press, 1985). On regional revolutionary violence, see Lee, *Crowds and Soldiers*, 164–211.

57. George Smith McCowen Jr., *The British Occupation of Charleston, 1780–82* (Columbia: University of South Carolina Press, 1972), 52–56.

58. Marvin L. Cann, "War in the Backcountry: The Siege of Ninety Six, May 22 – June 19, 1781," *South Carolina Historical Magazine* 72, no. 1 (1971): 2.

59. "Memorial of J. H. Cruger."

60. Jasanoff, *Liberties Exiles*, 21–23, 45; and Edward J. Cashin, *The King's Ranger: Thomas Brown and the American Revolution on the Southern Frontier* (New York: Fordham University Press, 1999).

312 NOTES TO PAGES 135–140

61. Heard Robertson, "The Second British Occupation of Augusta, 1780–81," *Georgia Historical Quarterly* 58, no. 4 (1974): 434.

62. Leslie Hall, *Land & Allegiance in Revolutionary Georgia* (Athens: University of Georgia Press, 2001), 106.

63. Piecuch, *Three Peoples, One King*, 203; Hall, *Land & Allegiance*, 104–5; Cashin, *King's Ranger*, 107–14.

64. Robertson, "Second British Occupation," 434.

65. Cashin, *King's Ranger*, 114–21.

66. Cornwallis to John Harris Cruger, 18 August 1780, CO5/101, fol. 210–11, UKNA.

67. *Whitehall Evening Post*, 27–30 January 1781.

68. See, for example, *The Freeman's Journal; or, The North-American Intelligencer*, 27 June 1781. On atrocities and propaganda, see Holger Hoock, "Mangled Bodies: Atrocity in the American Revolutionary War," *Past and Present* 230 (2016): 123–59; Lee, *Crowds and Soldiers*, 194–99.

69. On the Ceded Lands, see Hall, *Land & Allegiance*, 11–15.

70. Robertson, "Second British Occupation," 434–36.

71. Robert Middlekauff, *The Glorious Cause: The American Revolution, 1763–1789* (New York: Oxford University Press, 1982), 461–62.

72. Jones, *History of New York*, 2:385.

73. Joseph Johnson, *Traditions and Reminisces Chiefly of the American Revolution in the South* [. . .] (Charleston, SC: Walker and James, 1851), 471; Jerome A. Greene, *Historic Resource Study and Historic Structure Report, Ninety Six: A Historical Narrative* (Denver: Denver Service Center, US Dept of the Interior, 1978), 123; Jones, *History of New York*, 2:385; John Buchanan, *The Road to Charleston: Nathaniel Greene and the American Revolution* (Charlottesville: University of Virginia Press, 2019), 106.

74. On the siege's military history, see Greene, *Ninety Six*, 123–72.

75. "Memorial of J. H. Cruger."

76. Jones, *History of New York*, 2:385.

77. For statements by Cornwallis and Carleton, see AO12/20, fol, 150, AO13/54, fols. 216–17, UKNA.

78. Robert M. Dunkerly and Irene B. Boland, *Eutaw Springs: The Final Battle of the American Revolution's Southern Campaign* (Columbia: University of South Carolina Press, 2017), 112–13.

79. Chopra, *Unnatural Rebellion*, 197.

80. *New-York Gazette and the Weekly Mercury*, 20 August 1781. On Polly's illness, Nicholas Cruger to Peter Van Schaack, 17 August 1780, VSFP.

81. Loyalist claim on behalf of the children of Jacob and Mary Walton, 24 March 1784, AO12/24, fols. 144–45, UKNA.

NOTES TO PAGES 140–143

82. McCowen, *British Occupation*, 19.

83. *The Pennsylvania Packet; or, The General Advertiser*, 17 August 1782.

84. *Royal Gazette*, 14 August 1782.

85. Chopra, *Unnatural Rebellion*, 209.

86. John Harris Cruger to Peter Van Schaack, 9 April 1783, VSFP.

87. *Royal Gazette*, 4 June 1783.

88. John Harris Cruger Statement before the Loyalist Claims Commission, 3 June 1785, AO12/20, fol. 147, UKNA; and Ward Chipman to Edward Winslow, New York, 25 June 1783, in W. O. Raymond, ed., *Winslow Papers, A.D. 1776–1826* (St. John, N.B.: Sun Printing, 1901), 91–93; *Morning Herald and Daily Advertiser*, 30 July 1783.

6. The Price of Neutrality

1. Van Schaack's career is summarized in Ronald W. Howard, "Van Schaack, Peter (1747–1832), lawyer," *ANB*, and treated at length in William A. Benton, "Peter Van Schaack: The Conscience of a Loyalist," in East and Judd, *Loyalist Americans*, 44–55; Paul M. Hamlin, "Peter Van Schaack," *Columbia University Quarterly* 24 (1932): 66–105; Maxwell H. Bloomfield, *American Lawyers in a Changing Society* (Cambridge, MA: Harvard University Press, 1976), 1–31; and in a full-length biography by his admiring son: Henry C. Van Schaack, *The Life of Peter Van Schaack, LL.D* [...] (New York: D. Appleton, 1842). This last reprints entirely many of Peter's letters and other writings, the originals of which I have also consulted in the Van Schaack Family Papers at Columbia University. To ease readers' access and simplify references, I have cited this published work rather than the manuscript collection when possible.

2. The *Oxford English Dictionary* dates the first use of "conscientious objection" to 1790, describing an English religious Dissenter's unwillingness to hold a local government office. The *OED*'s first reference for "conscientious objector" dates to 1825 and a similar context. Its first reference for the concept in relation to refusing military service dates to 1863 and the United States Civil War.

3. The key work in this regard is Benton, *Whig-Loyalism*. Classing Van Schaack as a loyalist stretches back to Lorenzo Sabine, *Biographical Sketches of Loyalists of the American Revolution with An Historical Essay*, 2 vols. (Boston: Little, Brown, 1864), 2:379–81. Such categorizations have continued in modern work. See, for example, Calhoon, *Loyalists in Revolutionary America*, 186–87; Chopra, *Unnatural Rebellion*, 48–49, 58. One of the most insightful assessments of Van Schaack's experiences, which emphasizes his neutrality, is Kammen, "American Revolution as a *Crise de Conscience*," 167–73, 182–87.

4. Van Schaack, *PVS*, 302.

5. Force, *American* Archives, 4th ser., 2:471; Becker, *Political Parties*, 196; Launitz-Schürer, *Loyal Whigs*, 159; Jones, *History of New York*, 1:505–6.

NOTES TO PAGES 143–150

6. Chopra, *Unnatural Rebellion*, 36–37; Jones, *History of New York,* 1:41–42.

7. Van Schaack, *PVS*, 38.

8. "Letter from John Cruger and Jacob Walton [. . .]," 3 May 1775, in Force, *American Archives*, 4th ser., 2:479–80.

9. Minty, *Unfriendly to Liberty*, 191.

10. Van Schaack, *HVS*, 44–45; Hamlin, "Peter Van Schaack," 77.

11. Van Schaack, *PVS*, 51. The Van Schaacks returned to the city briefly after their sons' deaths but then moved to Kinderhook more permanently. See Peter Van Schaack to Henry Cruger Sr., 6 September 1775, VSFP.

12. Van Schaack, *PVS*, 52–53.

13. Peter Van Schaack to Henry Cruger Sr., 6 September 1775, VSFP.

14. Elizabeth Van Schaack to Henry Cruger Sr., 7 September 1775, VSFP.

15. Van Schaack, *PVS*, 48–51.

16. Elizabeth A. Fenn, *Pox Americana: The Great Smallpox Epidemic of 1775–82* (New York: Hill and Wang, 2001), 3.

17. Jeannie F. J. Robison and Henrietta C. Bartlett, eds., *Genealogical Records: Manuscript Records of Births, Deaths, and Marriages, Taken from Family Bibles, 1581–1917* (New York: Colonial Dames of the State of New York, 1917), 258–60.

18. Van Schaack, *PVS*, 15.

19. Van Schaack, *PVS*, 58.

20. Van Schaack, *PVS*, 195.

21. For Van Schaack as "extraordinarily legalistic," see Chopra, *Unnatural Rebellion*, 48. On how Van Schaack's personality may have shaped his revolution, see also Carl Becker, "John Jay and Peter Van Schaack," *Quarterly Journal of the New York State Historical Association* 1, no. 1 (1919): 1–12.

22. Van Schaack, *PVS*, 9.

23. See his observations on the Banishing Act in Van Schaack, *PVS*, 112.

24. On the centrality of oaths to many neutrals' difficulties, see Kammen, "American Revolution as a *Crise de Conscience*," 155–84.

25. Hamlin, "Peter Van Schaack," 77.

26. For these January 1776 reflections, from which the quotations in this and the preceding paragraphs are taken, see Van Schaack, *PVS*, 54–58.

27. Bernard Bailyn, *The Ideological Origins of the American Revolution*, enlarged ed. (Cambridge, MA: Harvard University Press, 1992), 94, 95.

28. In this respect, it is significant that Bailyn used excerpts from Van Schaack's "tormented meditations," as an example of how "thoughtful and informed people" responded to anti-ministerial rhetoric. See Bailyn, *Ideological Origins*, 149–50.

29. For the quotations in the preceding paragraphs, see Van Schaack, *PVS*, 54–58.

NOTES TO PAGES 150–159

30. For violence as a defining feature of the Revolution, see Hoock, *Scars of Independence*, especially 11–20.

31. Van Schaack, *PVS*, 304.

32. Van Schaack, *PVS*, 59; *Journals of the Provincial Congress, Provincial Convention, Committee of Safety and Council of Safety of the State of New-York: 1775–1776–1777*, vol. 1 (Albany, NY: Thurlow Weed, 1842), 389.

33. Van Schaack, *PVS*, 58–60.

34. Van Schaack, *HVS*, especially 24–64.

35. Van Schaack, *HVS*, 57–61.

36. *Journals of the Provincial Congress* [. . .], 699.

37. Quotations from Kalyvas, *Logic of Violence*, 176–80.

38. Van Schaack, *PVS*, 70.

39. Van Schaack, *PVS*, 70–77.

40. Van Schaack, *PVS*, 71–76.

41. Van Schaack, *PVS*, 78.

42. Hamlin, "Peter Van Schaack," 79–80; Van Schaack, *PVS*, 85–86.

43. Van Schaack, *PVS*, 86–91.

44. Van Schaack, *HVS*, 74–75; Nicoll, *Earliest Cuylers*, 26.

45. Van Schaack, *HVS*, 74.

46. John Burgoyne to the Commissioners for American Sufferers, 7 January 1783, AO13/67, fols. 415–16, UKNA; Van Schaack, "Old Kinderhook Mansion," 523–25.

47. On the increased persecution of loyalists after Saratoga, see Jasanoff, *Liberty's Exiles*, 40–41.

48. Van Schaack, *PVS*, 60, 95.

49. Van Schaack, *PVS*, 104.

50. John McNamara Hayes to Peter Van Schaack, 13 April 1778, VSFP.

51. Van Schaack, *PVS*, 479–85; "Minutes of Peter Van Schaack relating to the death of his wife," box 1, folder 1, SLFP.

52. Hamlin, "Peter Van Schaack," 83; *New-York Gazette and the Weekly Mercury*, 25 May 1778.

53. Van Schaack mentioned this court martial to John Jay but said little about it. Van Schaack, *PVS*, 124. See also Hamlin, "Peter Van Schaack," 84n2.

54. Van Schaack, *PVS*, 109–10.

55. Van Schaack, *PVS*, 110–13.

56. Van Schaack, *PVS*, 110.

57. Van Schaack, *PVS*, 118–19.

58. Van Schaack, *PVS*, 122–24.

59. Van Schaack, *PVS*, 120.

60. Van Schaack, *PVS*, 132–34.

61. Van Schaack, *PVS*, 134–59; quotations at 158, 139.

62. Van Schaack, *PVS*, 265–66.

63. Peter Van Schaack to Henry Cruger Sr., 4 February 1779, VSFP.

64. Van Schaack, *PVS*, 195.

65. Van Schaack, *PVS*, 165.

66. For Van Schaack's initial 1779 petition, see AO13/67, fol. 404. Hereafter "Petition of Peter Van Schaack." Ensuing documents at AO13/67, fols. 402–3, 405–18; AO12/20, fols. 135–37; AO12/109, fol. 298; AO12/101, 202–203; AO12/103, fol. 73, UKNA.

67. "Petition of Peter Van Schaack."

68. "Petition of Peter Van Schaack."

69. For more on the Carlisle Commission, see chapter 7 below.

70. Peter Van Schaack to Henry Cruger Sr., 31 July 1779, box 1, folder 31, item no. 270, SLFP.

71. Peter Van Schaack to William Eden, 9 September 1779, AO13/67, fols. 405–6, UKNA.

72. "Petition of Peter Van Schaack"; George Johnstone to Germain, 2 February 1781, AO13/67, fols. 407–8, UKNA.

73. AO13/67, fol. 409; AO12/103, fol. 73, UKNA.

74. AO12/101, 202, UKNA. The delay in Van Schaack's claim is noted in AO12/103, fol. 73, UKNA. On Henry Cruger Sr.'s legacies, see Van Schaack, *PVS*, 305.

75. Jasanoff, *Liberty's Exiles*, 119–20.

76. Peter Van Schaack to John Wilmot and Daniel Parker Coke, 16 January 1783, AO13/67, fols. 417–18, UKNA.

77. AO13/67, fols. 411–16, UKNA.

78. William Tryon to "To All Whom It May Concern," 27 November 1782, AO13/67, fol. 411, UKNA.

79. AO12/103, fol. 73, UKNA.

80. Jasanoff, *Liberty's Exiles*, 120.

81. Van Schaack, *PVS*, 259–60.

82. Van Schaack, *PVS*, 260–63.

83. Van Schaack, *PVS*, 349–51.

84. Van Schaack, *PVS*, 318.

85. Van Schaack, *PVS*, 338.

86. Van Schaack, *PVS*, 301–3.

87. Van Schaack, *PVS*, 308.

88. Van Schaack, *PVS*, 324.

7. The Search for Peace

1. Van Schaack, *PVS*, 43–44.

2. *Dunlap's Pennsylvania Packet; or, The General Advertiser*, 28 August 1775.

NOTES TO PAGES 167–172

3. Van Schaack, *Henry Cruger*, 6; *Royal Gazette* (New York), 14 June 1780.

4. Van Schaack, *PVS*, 43–44.

5. "Interviews with Edmund Burke and Lord North in 1775," AHAR, fols. 196–97. Also published in Henry Van Schaack, "Diary and Memoranda of Henry Cruger: Conversations with Edmund Burke and Lord North, 1775," in *Magazine of American History* [. . .] 7 (1881): 358–63. For the August 23 proclamation, see "By the King, A Proclamation, For suppressing Rebellion and Sedition" (London: Charles Eyre and William Strahan, 1775).

6. For rumors on who might be sent, see Ralph Izard to "A Friend in Bath," 27 October 1775, in Deas, *Correspondence of Mr. Ralph Izard*, 135. See also Ira D. Gruber, *The Howe Brothers and the American Revolution* (Chapel Hill: University of North Carolina Press for the OIEAHC, 1974), 32–34.

7. Flavell, "Cruger, Henry (1739–1827)." For quotations, "Interviews with Edmund Burke and Lord North in 1775," AHAR, fols. 196–97. See also Flavell, "Conciliatory Proposal," 302–22.

8. *The Statutes at Large From the Thirteenth Year of the Reign of King George the Third* [. . .], vol. 12 (London: Charles Eyre and William Strahan, 1776), 432–41. For a more sympathetic reading of North and the Prohibitory Act, see Thomas, *Tea Party*, 297–98.

9. The Crugers long held that the seizure of the *George* by the HMS *Argo* was unjust, partly because it occurred before the Prohibitory Act was supposed to be in effect. Henry Cruger Jr. pursued an ultimately unsuccessful British appeal all the way to the Privy Council regarding the incident. See *Cruger v. Garnier*, STC_1777_02, in Sharon Hamby O'Connor, Mary Sarah Bilder, and Charles Donahue, eds., *Appeals to the Privy Council from the American Colonies: An Annotated Digital Catalogue*, part 2 (Ames Foundation, 2020), https://amesfoundation.law.harvard.edu/ColonialAppeals/.

10. Copy of a letter from Peter S. Curtenius to Messrs. Cruger & Mallard, 27 March 1776, CO5/40, Part 2, fols. 235–36, UKNA.

11. John Adams to Horatio Gates, 23 March 1776, AP/FO.

12. *PH* 18:1143–45.

13. *PH* 18:1148–54.

14. "Postcript" to *Dunlap's Pennsylvania Packet; or, The General Advertiser*, 6 May 1776. This item seems to have first appeared in the London press. See *General Evening Post* (London), 20–22 February 1776; and *Middlesex Journal and Evening Advertiser*, 20–22 February 1776. On reprinted newspaper stories and the mobilization of American opinion in 1775, see Parkinson, *Common Cause*, 15.

15. "Postscript" to *Dunlap's Pennsylvania Packet; or, The General Advertiser*, 6 May 1776. The editorial remarks labeling Cruger a traitor also appeared, for example, in *New-York Journal; or, The General Advertiser*, 9 May 1776; *Newport Mercury*, 20 May 1776; and *Freeman's*

318 NOTES TO PAGES 172–174

Journal; or, New-Hampshire Gazette, 25 May 1776. The editorial remarks were not included, for example, in *Pennsylvania Evening Post*, 7 May 1776; *Pennsylvania Ledger*, 11 May 1776; *New-York Gazette and the Weekly Mercury*, 13 May 1776; and *Maryland Gazette*, 16 May 1776. The editorial remarks also do not appear in what seems to be the original London newspaper item on which these colonial reprintings were based. See *General Evening Post* (London), 20–22 February 1776.

16. *Pennsylvania Evening Post*, 7 May 1776. See also a related critique of Cruger's supposed inconstancy in *The Remembrancer; or, Impartial Repository of Public Events*, part 2, *For the Year 1776* (London: J. Almon, 1776), 224–27.

17. Pauline Maier, *American Scripture: Making the Declaration of Independence* (New York: Vintage Books, 1998), 38.

18. Gruber, *Howe Brothers*, 63–88.

19. Brooke, "Cruger, Henry."

20. W. E. Minchinton, ed., *The Trade of Bristol in the Eighteenth Century* (Bristol: Bristol Record Society, 1957), x–xi; Poole and Rogers, *Bristol from Below*, 241–42.

21. More than two hundred Bristol ships operated as privateers during the war. Poole and Rogers, *Bristol from Below*, 242, 246; Walter Minchinton, *The Port of Bristol in the Eighteenth Century* (Bristol: Bristol Branch of the Historical Association, 1962), 5.

22. Peter Marshall, *Bristol and the War of American Independence* (Bristol: Bristol Branch of the Historical Association, 1977), 5.

23. Marshall, *Bristol and the War*, 5.

24. Based on a review of the surviving but very incomplete "Bristol Presentments" recording the port's imports and exports. The cargo for New York traveled aboard the *Swift*, under John Clark, which left Bristol on 21 February 1778. See database "Bristol Shipping Records: Imports and Exports, 1770–1917," *British Online Archives*. See also *NDAR*, 12:351.

25. *New-Jersey Gazette*, 2 September 1778. For advertisements by Perry, see *New-York Gazette and the Weekly Mercury*, 29 December 1777, 9 March 1778, 29 June 1778, 27 July 1778.

26. On the *Love and Unity*, see *New-Jersey Gazette*, 26 August 1778, 2 September 1778, 23 September 1778, 30 September 1778, 10 March 1779.

27. *New-Jersey Gazette*, 2 September 1778.

28. *New-Jersey Gazette*, 2 September 1778.

29. On Mallard's bankruptcy, see *Correspondence of Edmund Burke*, 4:268–69n2.

30. John Brooke, "Jenkinson, Charles (1729–1808), of Addiscombe, Surr.," *HoP;* Lewis B. Namier, *Personalities and Powers* (London: H. Hamilton, 1955), 21; Ben Gilding and Richard Connors, "'Chatham's Ghost' and the Enduring Spectre of Lord Bute's Secret Influence: A Political Negotiation of 1778," *Parliamentary History* 38, part 2 (2019): 175–202; and John Brewer, "Party and the Double Cabinet: Two Facets of Burke's *Thoughts*," *Historical Journal* 14, no. 3 (1971): 479–501.

NOTES TO PAGES 175–179

31. John Cannon, "Robinson, John (1727–1802), politician," *ODNB.*

32. Brooke, "Jenkinson, Charles"; John Cannon, "Jenkinson, Charles, first Earl of Liverpool (1729–1808), politician," *ODNB.*

33. Henry Cruger to [Charles Jenkinson], 11 May 1777, vol. 20, fol. 120, LP.

34. "Extract of a Letter rec'd from Mr. Cruger," [undated], vol. 20, fol. 178, LP. A reference to Burgoyne's capture indicates that this letter was written after October 17, 1777.

35. Brooke, "Cruger, Henry"; Henry Cruger to Charles Jenkinson, 31 October 1781, vol. 28, fol. 108, LP; Charles Jenkinson to Henry Cruger, 4 November 1781, vol. 119, fol. 195, LP.

36. *PH* 19:563–84, quotations at 566, 565.

37. *Public Advertiser*, 13 December 1777; *PH* 19:584–89.

38. *PH* 19:588–89.

39. Thomas, *Lord North*, 108–9; I. R. Christie, "Eden, William (1744–1814), of Beckenham, Kent," *HoP.*

40. Anthony Gregory, "'Formed for Empire': The Continental Congress Responds to the Carlisle Peace Commission," *JER* 38, no. 4 (2018): 643–72. See also Reginald E. Rabb, "The Role of William Eden in the British Peace Commission of 1778," *The Historian* 20, no. 2 (1958): 153–78.

41. On these maneuverings, see Weldon A. Brown, *Empire or Independence: A Study in the Failure of Reconciliation, 1774–1783* (Port Washington, NY: Kennikat Press, 1966), 211–27.

42. There are no extant division lists for these bills, but in 1780 Cruger claimed he had been "much blamed for voting for Lord North's conciliatory bill." See *General Evening Post*, 4–6 May 1780.

43. Van Schaack, *Henry Cruger*, 25–26.

44. On these developments, see Richard W. Van Alstyne, *Empire and Independence: The International History of the American Revolution* (New York: John Wiley & Sons, 1965), 149; Brown, *Empire or Independence*, 226.

45. H. M. Scott, *British Foreign Policy in the Age of the American Revolution* (Oxford: Clarendon Press, 1990), 259–64.

46. "Memorial of Henry Cruger."

47. Gregory, "Formed for Empire," 652.

48. *Journals of the Continental Congress, 1774–1789*, 34 vols. (Washington DC: Government Printing Office, 1904–37), 22 April 1778, 10:374–80.

49. Henry Cruger to Charles Jenkinson, 8 June 1778, and the accompanying extract, vol. 21, fol. 59–61, LP.

50. Gregory, "Formed for Empire," 659–64.

51. See "Manifesto and Proclamation of the Carlisle Commissioners," 3 October 1778, in *Remembrancer; or, Impartial Repository of Public Events for the Year 1779* (London: J. Almon, 1779), 66–70.

320 NOTES TO PAGES 180–181

52. On these debates over Irish trade, see Padhraig Higgins, *A Nation of Politicians: Gender, Patriotism, and Political Culture in Late Eighteenth-Century Ireland* (Madison: University of Wisconsin Press, 2010); Daniel I. O'Neill, *Edmund Burke and the Conservative Logic of Empire* (Berkeley: University of California Press, 2016); and Minchinton, *Politics and the Port of Bristol*, xxxii–xxxiii. For speeches by Cruger on Irish trade, see *Public Advertiser*, 9 May 1778, 13 March 1779; *General Evening Post*, 20 March 1779. For Burke's views, see Edmund Burke, *Two Letters from Mr. Burke to Gentlemen in the City of Bristol, on the Bills Depending in Parliament Relative to the Trade of Ireland* (London: J. Dodsley, 1778).

53. Given the limited nature of parliamentary reporting, Cruger's voting record is somewhat uncertain in this period. Having voted for Fox's opposition motion regarding the "old corps" in February 1778—a clear vote against the ministry's failing American war effort— Cruger's name is not among the minority of members of Parliament who in December 1778 voted to censure the Carlisle Commission for its late belligerent proclamation. Surviving records make it impossible to tell whether he voted with the majority or was absent. Cruger, along with Burke, Fox, and others, was listed as absent when a "call of the House" was made to enforce members' attendance on February 11, 1779. See *Journals of the House of Commons*, vol. 37, [1778–80], 135, 178. In 1780, Burke noted bitterly that Cruger had secured the support of Bristol's lower-class voters "by a diligent attendance on *them*, and a total Neglect of attendance in Parliament." See Brooke, "Cruger, Henry."

54. Edmund Burke to the Duke of Portland, 3 September 1780, *Correspondence of Edmund Burke*, 4:268.

55. William Thomas Laprade, ed., *Parliamentary Papers of John Robinson, 1774–1784* (London: Royal Historical Society, 1922), 49–50; Brooke, "Cruger, Henry." See also F. P. Lock, *Edmund Burke*, vol. 1, *1730–1784* (Oxford: Oxford University Press, 2008), 413, 442n46.

56. On this pension, see Poole and Rogers, *Bristol from Below*, 267, which argues that "Cruger was not a government spy or patriotic turncoat."

57. On money spent against Cruger in the 1780 and 1781 elections, see Laprade, *John Robinson*, 37, 57, 58; and "Minutes about Bristol Expenses," 20 April 1782, RA GEO/MAIN/4650, *Georgian Papers Online*.

58. On Crown spending and its influence in Parliament, see E. A. Reitan, "The Civil List in Eighteenth-Century British Politics: Parliamentary Supremacy versus the Independence of the Crown," *Historical Journal* 9, no. 3 (1966): 318–37; E. A. Reitan, "Edmund Burke and Economical Reform, 1779–83," *Studies in Eighteenth-Century Culture* 14 (1985): 129–58; and Warwick Funnell, "The 'Proper Trust of Liberty': Economical Reform, the English Constitution and the Protections of Accounting during the American War of Independence," *Accounting History* 13, no. 1 (2008): 7–32. On Cruger's vote for reform, see *The London Courant and Westminster Chronicle*, 13 March 1780.

59. "Memorial of Henry Cruger."

NOTES TO PAGES 181–184

60. "Memorial of Henry Cruger"; Kalyvas, *Logic of Violence*, 44–46.

61. "Memorial of Henry Cruger."

62. "Memorial of Henry Cruger."

63. On Eden's role in intelligence, see Samuel Flagg Bemis, "British Secret Service and the French-American Alliance," *AHR* 29, no. 3 (1924): 474–95.

64. *The General Evening Post*, 4–6 May 1780. See also *PH* 21:570–91.

65. *The General Evening Post*, 4–6 May 1780.

66. *The General Evening Post*, 4–6 May 1780. For other coverage of the debate on Conway's bill, see *Public Advertiser*, 6 May 1780; *Gazetteer and New Daily Advertiser*, 16 May 1780. An extensive report on Cruger's speech appeared in *Remembrancer; or, Impartial Repository of Public Events for the Year 1781*, part 1 (London: J. Almon, 1780 [*sic*]), 233–39. It is not entirely clear whether Cruger was referencing voting for North's conciliatory proposals of 1775 or 1778.

67. *London Evening-Post*, 23–25 May 1780. See also *PH* 21:627.

68. For this election, see John Brooke, "Bristol" (1754–1790), *HoP*. See also Poole and Rogers, *Bristol from Below*, 268–72.

69. On these developments, see P. D. G. Thomas, "Brickdale, Matthew (1735–1831), of Clifton, Glos. and Taunton, Som."; I. R. Christie, "Lippincott, Sir Henry, 1st Bt. (1737–80), of Littleton-upon-Severn, Glos."; Brooke, "Cruger, Henry"; Brooke, "Burke, Edmund (1729–97), of Beaconsfield, Bucks."; Mary M. Drummond, "Combe, Richard (?1728–80), of Earnshill, nr. Langport, Som."; and Brooke, "Bristol," all in *HoP*.

70. Van Schaack, *Henry Cruger*, 27.

71. For the original letter, see *Dunlap's Pennsylvania Packet; or, The General Advertiser*, 3 October 1774. It was separately reprinted as a broadside. See "From the *Pennsylvania Packet, Philadelphia, October 3*," American Antiquarian Society, Worcester, MA. For an assessment of the election, noting this letter's impact, see *St. James's Chronicle; or, British Evening-Post*, 19–21 October 1780.

72. John Brooke, "Introductory Survey," in Lewis Namier and John Brooke, *History of Parliament*, 1:85; "Minutes about Bristol Expenses," 20 April 1782, RA GEO/MAIN/4650, *Georgian Papers Online*.

73. *The Bristol Contest; Containing a Particular Account of the Proceedings of Both Parties* [. . .] *in 1781* (Bristol: W. Pine, [1781]), 7.

74. Brooke, "Bristol," *HoP*; "Minutes about Bristol Expenses," 20 April 1782, RA GEO/MAIN/4650, *Georgian Papers Online*; Latimer, *Annals of Bristol*, 447; Poole and Rogers, *Bristol from Below*, 269–72.

75. Latimer, *Annals of Bristol*, 447. See also *The Bristol Poll-Book, Being a List of Persons Who Voted at the Election of a Member to Serve in Parliament* [. . .] ([Bristol?], [1781?]).

76. Poole and Rogers note that while some poorer Bristolians supported Daubeny, Cruger's

322   NOTES TO PAGES 185-194

core backers were "small masters and journeymen who would not be browbeaten into voting as their masters dictated." See Poole and Rogers, *Bristol from Below*, 271–72.

77. *Bristol Contest*, 9–12, 37.

78. *Bristol Contest*, 31, 26–27, 44.

79. References to the 1774 letter in the *Pennsylvania Packet* recurred in the 1781 election. See, for example, *Bristol Contest*, 42–46.

80. Members of the Corporation voted 22–7 for Cruger over Daubeny in 1781. See *Bristol Poll-Book*, iii–iv.

81. *Felix Farley's Bristol Journal*, 26 January 1782; Poole and Rogers, *Bristol from Below*, 272–73.

82. Carrie Rebora Barratt and Ellen G. Miles, *Gilbert Stuart* (New York: Metropolitan Museum of Art, 2004), 113–14.

83. Shelburne invited Cruger in September 1782 to submit proposals for supplying military provisions. Norman Baker, *Government and Contractors: The British Treasury and War Supplies, 1775–1783* (London: Athlone Press, 1971), 136.

84. David Hancock, "Oswald, Richard (1705?–1784), merchant and diplomat," *ODNB*.

85. *Felix Farley's Bristol Journal*, 7 June 1783; *English Chronicle; or, Universal Evening-Post*, 18–21 October 1783.

8. Friend of Washington?

1. Van Schaack, *Henry Cruger*, 6.

2. Margherita Arlina Hamm, *Famous Families of New York* [. . .], 2 vols. (New York: G. P. Putnam's Sons, 1902), 1:71–72. For a more cautious early assertion that Nicholas "leaned to the American side" during the Revolution, see De Lancey, "Original Family Records, Cruger," 78.

3. Account entry for 14 June 1765, HJCAB.

4. Michael E. Newton, *Discovering Hamilton: New Discoveries in the Lives of Alexander Hamilton, His Family, Friends, and Colleagues from Various Archives around the World* (Phoenix, AZ: Eleftheria, 2019), 172–73; Chernow, *Alexander Hamilton*, 31; Jean Louise Willis, "The Trade between North America and the Danish West Indies, 1756–1807, with Special Reference to St. Croix" (PhD diss., Columbia University, 1963), 41–45.

5. For the development of St. Croix, see Neville A. T. Hall, *Slave Society in the Danish West Indies: St. Thomas, St. John, and St. Croix*, ed. B. W. Higman (Baltimore, MD: Johns Hopkins University Press, 1992), 2–17; Willis, "Trade between North America and the Danish West Indies," 1–23; Waldemar Westergaard, *The Danish West Indies under Company Rule (1671–1754)* [. . .] (New York: Macmillan, 1917); and Florence Lewisohn, *St. Croix under Seven Flags* (Hollywood, FL: Dukane Press, 1970).

6. William Cissel, "Alexander Hamilton: The West Indian 'Founding Father,'" Christiansted

NOTES TO PAGES 195–199

National Historic Site, National Park Service, US Department of the Interior (July 2004), 14.

7. Willis, "Trade between North America and the Danish West Indies," 3, 41–49, 63. See also Truxes, *Defying Empire*, 61–62.

8. Hall, *Slave Society*, 11.

9. On these dynamics, see Jeppe Mulich, "Microregionalism and Intercolonial Relations: the Case of the Danish West Indies, 1730–1830," *Journal of Global History* 8 (2013): 73.

10. Hall, *Slave Society*, 5, 11–19; Willis, "Trade between North America and the Danish West Indies," 73–82.

11. Hall, *Slave Society*, 11–17.

12. Hall, *Slave Society*, 15–16.

13. Hall, *Slave Society*, 17.

14. Truxes, *Defying Empire*, 61–62.

15. Henry & John Cruger and G. W. Beekman to [David] Beekman and [Nicholas] Cruger, 2 August 1766; and Henry & John Cruger and G. W. Beekman to Messrs. [Telemon] Cruger and [Isaac] Gouverneur, 2 August 1766, HJCLB.

16. Hamilton's work for Nicholas Cruger is documented multiple letters from 1771 and 1772 in AH/FO. See also, among many works on Hamilton, Chernow, *Alexander Hamilton*, 23–38.

17. Quotation from Chernow, *Alexander Hamilton*, 29.

18. *RDAG*, 30 October 1773.

19. *RDAG*, 4 December 1773.

20. *RDAG*, 30 October 1773, 4 December 1773,

21. *RDAG*, 5 January 1774, 26 February 1774.

22. Willis, "Trade between North America and the Danish West Indies," 95.

23. Quotation in Alexander Hamilton to Tileman (Telemon) Cruger, 1 February 177[2], AH/FO. Other letters on the *Thunderbolt*'s travels include Alexander Hamilton to Nicholas Cruger, 12 November 1771; Alexander Hamilton to Tileman Cruger, 16 November 1771; Alexander Hamilton to Nicholas Cruger, 27 November 1771; Alexander Hamilton to [Jacob] Walton and [John Harris] Cruger, 27 November 1771, AH/FO.

24. Alexander Hamilton to Tileman Cruger, 16 November 1771, AH/FO.

25. Lewisohn, *St. Croix*, 90–91, 149; Westergaard, *Danish West Indies*, 226.

26. On de Nully's death, see *RDAG*, 30 September 1772.

27. Willis, "Trade between North America and the Danish West Indies," 95n3.

28. *Dunlap's Pennsylvania Packet; or, The General Advertiser*, 2 January 1775.

29. *RDAG*, 19 April 1775. See also *RDAG*, 24 May 1775.

30. Michael Jarvis, *In the Eye of All Trade: Bermuda, Bermudians, and the Maritime Atlantic World, 1680–1783* (Chapel Hill: University of North Carolina Press for the OIEAHC, 2012), 403.

324 NOTES TO PAGES 199–202

31. This Danish salute of the American flag is said to have preceded the better-known one at Dutch St. Eustatius, which happened in November 1776. See J. Franklin Jameson, "St. Eustatius in the American Revolution," *American Historical Review* 8, no. 4 (July 1903): 691.

32. Willis, "Trade between North America and the Danish West Indies," 100, 113–14.

33. Willis, "Trade between North America and the Danish West Indies," 81–82.

34. Willis, "Trade between North America and the Danish West Indies," 126.

35. Willis, "Trade between North America and the Danish West Indies," 131.

36. Samuel Flagg Bemis, *The Diplomacy of the American Revolution* (Bloomington: Indiana University Press, 1957), 149–63; Willis, "Trade between North America and the Danish West Indies," 107–11.

37. Victor Enthoven, "'That Abominable Nest of Pirates': St. Eustatius and the North Americans, 1680–1780," *EAS* 10, no. 2 (2012): 241–42; Jameson, "St. Eustatius," 696–708; Andrew Jackson O'Shaughnessy, *An Empire Divided: The American Revolution and the British Caribbean* (Philadelphia: University of Pennsylvania Press, 2000), 214–32.

38. Nicholas Cruger to Tench Coxe, 13 April 1781, Coxe Family Papers, Box 10, Folder 11, HSP.

39. Willis, "Trade between North America and the Danish West Indies," 139–43.

40. *RDAG*, 8 July 1775, 10 July 1776, 17 August 1776.

41. On Cruger's relationship with Willcocks and Low, see Nicholas Cruger to John Willcocks, 16 December 1778, Nicholas Low Papers, 1728–1893, NYHS; and Nicholas Low and John Willcocks to Nicholas Cruger, Philadelphia, 18 June 1779, Nicholas Low Papers, LOC. On the Willcocks and Low partnership, see Thomas Doerflinger, *A Vigorous Spirit of Enterprise: Merchants and Economic Development in Revolutionary Philadelphia* (Chapel Hill: University of North Carolina Press, 2012), 289–90.

42. For Willcocks's investments in privateering, see entries in Donald Grady Shomette, *Privateers of the Revolution: War on the New Jersey Coast, 1775–1783* (Atglen, PA: Schiffer, 2016), Appendix A, 325–61.

43. Jacob E. Cooke, *Tench Coxe and the Early Republic* (Chapel Hill: University of North Carolina Press, 1978), 16–61; on his trade with Nicholas Cruger, 45–47. On Coxe's war and his destruction of records, see also Johnson, *Occupied America*, 116, 158–69.

44. Nicholas Cruger to John Willcocks, 16 December 1778, Nicholas Low Papers, 1728–1893, NYHS.

45. For the deposition, see CO318/5, fols. 113–14, UKNA.

46. Nicholas Cruger to Peter Van Schaack, 17 August 1780, VSFP.

47. Customs Journal of Arrival & Clearances of Vessels, Christiansted, St. Croix, V.I., January–July 1779, entry no. 280, T39, Microfilm, Roll 9, United States National Archives, College Park, MD.

48. On prewar salt trading, see McCarthy, "Cruger Family," 122. A mariner told a patriot court

NOTES TO PAGES 203–205

that he had been master of a vessel owned by "Nathaniel Cruger" that was captured by the Royal Navy while on a salt trading voyage between St. Croix and Edenton, North Carolina, in December 1777. This owner was almost certainly Nicholas Cruger. Walter L. Clark, *The State Records of North Carolina* [...], vol. 13, *1778–79* (Winston, NC: I. & J. C. Stewart, 1896), 95–96, 454.

49. Jarvis, *Eye of All Trade*, 397.

50. Michael S. Adelberg, "'Long in the Hand and Altogether Fruitless': The Pennsylvania Salt Works and Salt-Making on the New Jersey Shore during the American Revolution," *Pennsylvania History: A Journal of Mid-Atlantic Studies* 80, no. 2 (2013): 215–42; Larry G. Bowman, "The Scarcity of Salt in Virginia during the American Revolution," *Virginia Magazine of History and Biography* 77, no. 4 (1969): 464–72; and R. L. Hilldrup, "The Salt Supply of North Carolina during the American Revolution," *North Carolina Historical Review* 22, no. 4 (1945): 393–417.

51. Jarvis, *Eye of All Trade*, 188–99, 397–403.

52. Willis, "Trade between North America and the Danish West Indies," 135.

53. Thomas Shirley to George Germain, 30 August 1781, CO152/61, 127–28, UKNA.

54. Thomas Shirley to Peter Parker, 30 August 1781, CO152/61, 129–30, UKNA.

55. Jarvis, *Eye of All Trade*, 400.

56. James Fenimore Cooper, *The Spy: A Tale of the Neutral Ground* (1821).

57. Anne Bezanson et al., *Prices and Inflation during the American Revolution, Pennsylvania, 1770–1790* (Philadelphia: University of Pennsylvania Press, 1951), 158.

58. Adelberg, "'Long in the Hand,'" 217.

59. Jarvis, *Eye of All Trade*, 399.

60. Bezanson, *Prices and Inflation*, 142–58. Bezanson noted that despite various records, "regrettably, no continuous series of prices of salt can be made for the war years." See Bezanson, *Prices and Inflation*, 157–58.

61. Bezanson, *Prices and Inflation*, 148.

62. Bezanson, *Prices and Inflation*, 148–51.

63. Bezanson, *Prices and Inflation*, 151–53.

64. Bezanson, *Prices and Inflation*, 154.

65. Nicholas Cruger to John Willcocks, 16 December 1778, Nicholas Low Papers, 1728–1893, NYHS. These shifts in instructions coincide with a period when Philadelphia's salt prices cooled somewhat. See Bezanson, *Prices and Inflation*, 148–50. The salt that Nicholas shipped via Thomas Guion in late 1778 was sold in New London, Connecticut. See Guion's advertisement in the *Connecticut Gazette*, 1 January 1779.

66. In August 1780, Nicholas told Peter Van Schaack that he had "a fine cold winter indeed" in New York that had "thank God perfectly reestablished my health." Nicholas Cruger to Peter Van Schaack, 17 August 1780, VSFP.

NOTES TO PAGES 205–213

67. The crucial account can be found in *New-York Packet and the American Advertiser*, 19 January 1784. For the circumstances surrounding this publication, see chapter 9 below.

68. Jacob Walton to Peter Van Schaack, 29 August 1780, VSFP; HCA/32/262/1, UKNA.

69. Willis, "Trade between North America and the Danish West Indies," 133–34.

70. *The Pennsylvania Packet; or, The General Advertiser*, 8 February 1780.

71. Nicholas Cruger to George Washington, 18 April 1780, GW/FO.

72. George Washington to Nicholas Cruger, 22 April 1780, [Washington's reply in notes to Nicholas Cruger to George Washington, 18 April 1780], GW/FO.

73. Another of Washington's aides, Tench Tilghman, wrote a letter of introduction on Nicholas's behalf to patriot financier Robert Morris in February 1780. I have been unable to locate this letter, but for reference to it, see *American Book-Prices Current* (New York: Robert H. Dodd, 1917), 1063.

74. *Royal Gazette*, 31 May 1780. See also *New-York Gazette and the Weekly Mercury*, 5 June 1780. British vice-admiralty court records relating to the *Active*'s capture accord with the story relating to Nicholas Cruger but make no mention of him. See HCA/32/261/4, UKNA.

75. *New York Packet and the American Advertiser*, 19 January 1784.

76. Nicholas Cruger to Peter Van Schaack, 17 August 1780, VSFP.

77. Nicholas Cruger to Peter Van Schaack, 17 August 1780, VSFP.

78. Will of Henry Cruger, Prob 11/1062, UKNA. Henry Cruger Sr.'s death date has been given as February 5, 1780. See Cruger, *GBH*, 7. His death was reported in London's *The General Evening Post*, 10–12 February 1780. From February 14, 1780, the *New-York Gazette and the Weekly Mercury* contained advertisements for the sale of houses in New York that were "part of the estate" of "the Hon. Henry Cruger, Esq." He was in ill health, and evidently efforts to sell his New York property began prior to his death. See also Nicholas Cruger to Peter Van Schaack, 17 August 1780, VSFP.

79. Nicholas Cruger to Peter Van Schaack, 17 August 1780, VSFP.

80. De Lancey, "Original Family Records, Cruger," 78. No further information about the circumstances or the vessels involved is recorded in accounts that I have found.

81. McCarthy, "Cruger Family," 113.

82. Cissel, "Alexander Hamilton," 7.

83. Nicholas Cruger to Peter Van Schaack, 17 August 1780, VSFP.

84. For the *Harmony*'s history, see Louis Frank Middlebrook, *History of Maritime Connecticut during the American Revolution, 1775–1783*, 2 vols. (Salem, MA: The Essex Institute, 1925), 2:119–20.

85. "Cruger vs. the Captor of the Brig *Cumberland*," *Revolutionary War Prize Cases: Records of the Court of Appeals in Cases of Capture, 1776–1787*, Microfilm, M162, reel 13, case no. 109, United States National Archives. Hereafter "Cruger vs. the Captor."

NOTES TO PAGES 213–223

86. Thomas Hayes to Peter Van Schaack, 13 April 1782, VSFP.

87. *Connecticut Journal*, 10 October 1782; "Cruger vs. the Captor."

88. "Cruger vs. the Captor"; *Connecticut Journal*, 22 May 1783.

89. Willis, "Trade between North America and the Danish West Indies," 147.

90. McCarthy, "Cruger Family," 254.

9. Subjects and Citizens

1. Van Schaack, *HVS*, 105.

2. Jasanoff, "Other Side of Revolution," 208.

3. John Harris Cruger to Edward Winslow, London, 28 March 1784, in W. O. Raymond, ed., *Winslow Papers, A.D. 1776–1826* (St. John, N.B.: Sun Printing, 1901), 173–74.

4. Jasanoff, *Liberty's Exiles*, 114–15.

5. A. P. Baggs et al., "Beverley, 1700–1835: Social Life and Conditions," in *A History of the County of York East Riding*, vol. 6, *The Borough and Liberties of Beverley*, ed. K. J. Allison (London: Victoria County History, 1989), 131–35. *British History Online,* https://www.british-history.ac.uk/vch/yorks/east/vol6.

6. Van Schaack, *PVS*, 297, 367.

7. Eugene R. Fingerhut, "De Lancey, Oliver (1718–1785), colonial politician and Loyalist," *ANB;* H. M. Stephens, rev. by Troy of Bickham, "Lancey, Oliver De (c. 1749–1822), army officer and politician in America," *ODNB;* Brian Murphy, "De Lancey, Oliver (c.1749–1822), of Effingham Hill, Surr.," *HoP;* S. G. P. Ward, "Lancey, Sir William Howe De Lancey (c. 1778–1815), army officer," *ODNB;* and H. M. Stephens, rev. by James Lunt, "Lancey, Oliver De (1803–1837), army officer," *ODNB.*

8. Chopra, *Unnatural Rebellion*, 267n111; John Harris Cruger to Edward Winslow, New York, 18 April 1783, *Winslow Papers*, 80–81.

9. *Winslow Papers*, 136–38.

10. Jasanoff, "Other Side of Revolution," 216.

11. Fingerhut, "De Lancey, Oliver," *ANB.*

12. "Memorial of J. H. Cruger."

13. "The Paris Peace Treaty of September 30, 1783," at *The Avalon Project: Documents in Law, History, and Diplomacy*, Yale Law School, https://avalon.law.yale.edu/18th_century/paris.asp; John Harris Cruger to the Loyalist Claims Commission, 2 November 1788, AO13/64, fols. 164–65, UKNA.

14. See submissions at AO12/20, fols. 147–50, UKNA.

15. The "houses and lots, late the property of John Harris Cruger" on the north side of Little Queen Street, were advertised for sale in the *New-York Journal and State Gazette*, 22 April 1784.

NOTES TO PAGES 223–225

16. New York State Commissioners of Forfeiture, *Sales of Forfeited Lands in City & County of New York, 1784–1787*, vol. 2, 9, NYHS.

17. Hans-Jürgen Grabbe, "European Immigration to the United States in the Early National Period, 1783–1820," *Proceedings of the American Philosophical Society* 133, no. 2 (1989): 194, 198 (quotation).

18. Robert Ernst, "A Tory-Eye View of the Evacuation of New York," *NYH* 64, no. 4 (1983): 382.

19. Jasanoff, *Liberty's Exiles*, 92.

20. Thomas Jones claimed that at least two thousand "rebels" came into New York between the announcement of the provisional peace terms and the completion of the British withdrawal in November 1783 and that they "were taking care of their property, and receiving back their houses." See Jones, *History of New York*, 2:260.

21. See Nicholas Cruger to Tench Coxe, 2 September 1783, Coxe Family Papers, col. 2049, box 16, folder 7, HSP; *Connecticut Courant and Weekly Intelligencer*, 9 September 1783.

22. This claim appears most often in accounts by Cruger descendants. See Van Schaack, *Henry Cruger*, 7; De Lancey, "Original Family Records: Cruger," 78. See also Hamm, *Famous Families of New York*, 1:72. This claim has also sometimes arisen in relation to Nicholas's connection to Hamilton. Mitchell, for example, wrote that Cruger was "chairman of the committee of New Yorkers that escorted Washington in his triumphant entry into the city in 1783." See Mitchell, *Alexander Hamilton: Youth to Maturity*, 24. However, I have found no documentation for this. A newspaper account naming people to have leading roles in welcoming Washington and Governor Clinton into the city does not mention Cruger, nor was he a signer of addresses from "the Citizens of New York, who have returned from Exile" presented to Washington and Clinton. See *Rivington's New-York Gazette, and Universal Advertiser*, 22 November 1783, 29 November 1783.

23. *New-Jersey Gazette*, 20 January 1784.

24. Draft of Letter from Robert Livingston to John Jay, 25 January 1784, in Richard B. Morris, ed. *John Jay, The Winning of the Peace: Unpublished Papers 1780–1784*, 2 vols. (New York: Harper and Row, 1980), 1:678–81.

25. *New York Packet and the American Advertiser*, 19 January 1784.

26. *New York Packet and the American Advertiser*, 19 January 1784.

27. Carol Sue Humphrey, "Rivington, James (1724–1802), journalist and newspaper publisher," *ANB;* Catherine Snell Crary, "The Tory and the Spy: The Double Life of James Rivington," *WMQ* 16, no. 1 (1959): 61–72; and Todd Andrlik, "James Rivington: King's Printer and Patriot Spy?" *Journal of the American Revolution*, March 2014, https://allthings liberty.com/2014/03/james-rivington-kings-printer-patriot-spy/.

28. *Massachusetts Gazette*, 16 December 1783, quoted in Andrlik, "James Rivington."

29. *New-York Packet and the American Advertiser*, 19 January 1784; *Independent Gazette; or the*

NOTES TO PAGES 226–230

New-York Journal Revived, 22 January 1784; *Independent Journal; or, The General Advertiser*, 24 January 1784.

30. For the circulation of accounts of Cruger's attack on Rivington, see, for example, *Independent Ledger*, 26 January 1784; *Continental Journal and Weekly Advertiser*, 29 January 1784; *South-Carolina Gazette and General Advertiser*, 14 February 1784.

31. Cruger, *GBH*, 21.

32. On privateering and federal law, see Deirdre Mask and Paul MacMahon, "The Revolutionary War Prize Cases and the Origins of Diversity Jurisdiction," *Buffalo Law Review* 63, no. 3 (2015): 477–547.

33. "Cruger vs. the Captor."

34. *New-York Packet*, 12 December 1785.

35. Worthington Chauncey Ford, ed., *Some Social Notes Addressed to Samuel Blachley Webb, 1776–1791* (Boston: University Press, 1911), 122, 127; Wilson, *Memorial History*, 3:87–101.

36. Cruger, *GBH*, 22–23.

37. "Cruger vs. the Captor."

38. Van Schaack, *PVS*, 287, 329.

39. Van Schaack, *PVS*, 231.

40. Van Schaack, *PVS*, 231.

41. Van Schaack, *PVS*, 372–73.

42. Van Schaack, *PVS*, 335.

43. Van Schaack, *PVS*, 310.

44. Van Schaack, *PVS*, 329.

45. Van Schaack, *PVS*, 312.

46. Van Schaack, *PVS*, 373.

47. *Boston Evening–Post: and the General Advertiser*, 31 May 1783.

48. Van Schaack, *PVS*, 339.

49. For a compendium of anti-loyalist measures, including those passed after the war's end, see *Laws of the Legislature of the State of New York, In Force Against the Loyalists* [. . .].

50. Quoted in Jared Sparks, *The Life of Gouverneur Morris: with selections from his correspondence and miscellaneous papers* [. . .], 3 vols. (Boston: Gray & Bowen, 1832), 1:269; on Morris and Van Schaack's friendship, see William Howard Adams, *Gouverneur Morris: An Independent Life* (New Haven: Yale University Press, 2003), 23, 32, 57, 70.

51. [Alexander Hamilton], "A Letter from Phocion to the Considerate Citizens of New York, [1–27 January 1784]"; and [Alexander Hamilton], "Second Letter from Phocion, [April 1784]," AH/FO.

52. Van Schaack, *HVS*, 105; Henry Cruger to Peter Van Schaack, 6 February 1784, VSFP.

53. Henry Cruger to Peter Van Schaack, 6 February 1784, VSFP.

330   NOTES TO PAGES 231–235

54. *Laws of the Legislature of the State of New York in Force Against the Loyalists* [. . .], 111–16. See also Oscar Zeichner, "The Loyalist Problem in New York after the Revolution," *NYH* 21, no. 3 (1940): 284–302.

55. Van Schaack, *HVS*, 98–121.

56. Henry Cruger to Peter Van Schaack, 6 February 1784, VSFP.

57. Van Schaack, *PVS*, 376–78.

58. Van Schaack, *PVS*, 378–79.

59. *Laws of the Legislature of the State of New York in Force Against the Loyalists* [. . .], 117–20; Van Schaack, *PVS*, 379–82.

60. AO12/20, fol. 135–37; AO12/101, fol. 203; AO12/103, fol. 73, UKNA.

61. Van Schaack, *PVS*, 389–90.

62. Van Schaack, *PVS*, 389.

63. Van Schaack, *PVS*, 401–3.

64. Hamlin, "Peter Van Schaack," 96.

65. Van Schaack, *PVS*, 406; Hamlin, "Peter Van Schaack," 101.

66. See, for example, *Newport Mercury*, 16 August 1783; *Connecticut Journal*, 20 August 1783.

67. Thomas Blount to [John Gray Blount], 23 September 1783, in Alice Barnwell Keith, *The John Gray Blount Papers*, vol. 1, *1764–1789* (Raleigh, NC: State Department of Archives and History, 1952), 110.

68. Van Schaack, *HVS*, 105.

69. *Lowndes's London Directory for the Year 1784* [. . .] (London: T. & W. Lowndes, 1784), 41.

70. On Mullett's career, see Timothy D. Whelan, ed., *Baptist Autographs in the John Rylands University Library of Manchester, 1741–1845* (Macon, GA: Mercer University Press, 2009), 423–26; John Wilkes to John Hancock, 15 May 1783, in *Proceedings of the Massachusetts Historical Society, 1864–1865* (Boston: Massachusetts Historical Society, 1866), 459–60.

71. For a summary of the postwar economic situation, see Cathy Matson, "The Revolution, the Constitution, and the New Nation," in Stanley L. Engerman and Robert E. Gallman, eds., *The Cambridge Economic History of the United States*, vol. 1, *The Colonial Era* (Cambridge: Cambridge University Press, 1996), 372–82.

72. Henry Cruger to John Hancock, 5 March 1783, in *New England Historical and Genealogical Register* 28 (1874): 51–52.

73. Cruger, Lediard and Mullett, "Sir Uniting in Sentiment [. . .]," Philadelphia, 1 September 1783; "Goods Exported from Bristol, by Henry Cruger, and Comp." ([Philadelphia]: E. Oswald and D. Humphreys, [1783?]); and Henry Cruger to Messrs. Brown & Benson, New York, 15 December 1783; all in Nicholas Brown Papers, JCBL. The "Sir Uniting in Sentiment [. . .]" printed circular was also sent, for example, to Philadelphia merchants Reed

NOTES TO PAGES 236–240

and Forde. See Reed and Forde Papers, collection 541, box 2, folder 2, HSP. My thanks to Kim Gruenwald to pointing me to the Reed and Forde Papers for Cruger material.

74. Van Schaack, *HVS*, 133.

75. Henry Cruger & Co. to Messrs. Reed & Forde, Bristol, 31 July 1784, Reed and Forde Papers, collection 541, box 2, folder 3, HSP.

76. *London Gazette*, 30 September–4 October 1788.

77. *Independent Journal; or, The General Advertiser*, 27 April 1785; *Maryland Journal and Baltimore Advertiser*, 27 May 1785; *Independent Gazetteer; or, The Chronicle of Freedom*, 11 June 1785. See also 1785 letters in Reed and Forde Papers, collection 541, box 2, folder 4, HSP.

78. Henry Cruger to Peter Van Schaack, 7 October 1785, VSFP.

79. Kenneth Morgan, *Bristol and the Atlantic Trade in the Eighteenth Century* (Cambridge: Cambridge University Press, 1993), 113. On Henry's extended difficulties collecting from one American firm, see Arthur P. Whitaker, "Reed and Forde: Merchant Adventurers of Philadelphia: Their Trade with Spanish New Orleans," *Pennsylvania Magazine of History and Biography* 61, no. 3 (1937): 237–62.

80. See, for example, *Felix Farley's Bristol Journal*, 3 April 1784.

81. Van Schaack, *Henry Cruger*, 31–32. On this election, see Poole and Rogers, *Bristol from Below*, 274–76.

82. *Felix Farley's Bristol Journal*, 12 June 1784.

83. See letters in *Felix Farley's Bristol Journal*, 10 April 1784, 17 April 1784, and 24 April 1784.

84. *Gazetteer and New Daily Advertiser*, 12 May 1780; *Felix Farley's Bristol Journal*, 11 October 1783. See also *General Evening Post*, 11 October 1783.

85. Van Schaack, *PVS*, 327.

86. *Felix Farley's Bristol Journal*, 24 April 1784 and 1 May 1784.

87. M[annaseh] Dawes, *Observations on the Mode of Electing Representatives in Parliament for the City of Bristol* [. . .] (Bristol: J. Lloyd, 1784), 36–37.

88. Dawes, *Observations*, 36–38.

89. 16 March 1786, *Journals of the House of Commons* (London, 1803), vol. 41, 325.

90. For example, *Northampton Mercury*, 18 March 1786; *Maryland Journal and Baltimore Advertiser*, 23 May 1786.

91. 24 March 1786, *Journals of the House of Commons*, vol. 41, 439.

92. *Loudon's New-York Packet*, 8 June 1786.

93. *PH* 25:283–84.

94. On Cruger and the Corn Law, see for example Henry Cruger Jr. to Jeremiah Osborne, 28 April 1789, SMV/7/2/1/15, BA.

332 NOTES TO PAGES 240-245

95. John Frederick Bryant, *Verses by John Frederick Bryant* (London: Printed for the author, 1787), 32.

96. McCarthy, "Cruger Family," 258.

10. Oblivion and Conciliation

1. Henry Cruger to Peter Van Schaack, 19 September 1788, Henry Cruger (1739–1827) Papers, 1745–1803, NYHS.

2. Stanley Elkins and Eric McKittrick, *The Age of Federalism* (New York: Oxford University Press, 1993), 4.

3. Henry Cruger to Peter Van Schaack, 7 October 1785, VSFP.

4. Van Schaack, *PVS*, 327.

5. Van Schaack, *PVS*, 325.

6. Van Schaack, *PVS*, 429–30.

7. *Daily Advertiser*, 16 February 1788.

8. Van Schaack, *PVS*, 426–28.

9. Hamlin, "Peter Van Schaack," 94; Van Schaack, *PVS*, 441.

10. Van Schaack, *PVS*, 425–26; *New-York Journal*, 5 June 1788.

11. Van Schaack, *PVS*, 429.

12. David Waldstreicher, *In the Midst of Perpetual Fetes: The Making of American Nationalism, 1776–1820* (Chapel Hill: University of North Carolina Press for OIEAHC, 1997), 86–107; Simon P. Newman, *Parades and the Politics of the Street: Festive Culture in the Early American Republic* (Philadelphia: University of Pennsylvania Press, 1997), 40–43; Lawrence A. Peskin, "From Protection to Encouragement: Manufacturing and Mercantilism in New York City's Public Sphere, 1783–1795," *JER* 18, no. 4 (1998): 589–615; and Paul A. Gilje, "The Common People and the Constitution: Popular Culture in New York City in the Late Eighteenth Century," in Paul A. Gilje and William Pencak, eds., *New York in the Age of the Constitution, 1775–1800* (Rutherford, NJ: Fairleigh Dickinson University Press, 1992), 48–73.

13. Whitfield J. Bell Jr., "The Federal Processions of 1788," *NYHSQ* 46, no. 1 (1962): 29–39; and Sarah H. J. Simpson, "The Federal Procession in the City of New York," *NYHSQ* 9, no. 2 (1925): 39–57.

14. *Independent Journal; or, The General Advertiser*, 2 August 1788.

15. *A Correct List of those Members Who Voted with the Right Hon. William Pitt, on Monday, the 18th Day of April, 1785, for a Parliamentary Reform* (London: John Stockdale, 1785), 4.

16. James Livesey, "Free Trade and Empire in the Anglo-Irish Commercial Propositions of 1785," *Journal of British Studies* 52, no. 1 (2013): 119; Brooke, "Cruger, Henry."

17. Brooke, "Cruger, Henry." See, for example, 20 February 1786, *Parliamentary Register* [. . .],

NOTES TO PAGES 246–248

vol. 19 (London: J. Debrett, 1787), 46; 3 March 1786, *Journals of the House of Commons*, vol. 41, 281–82. On Cruger and the Shop Tax, see *General Advertiser*, 16 February 1786; and *Felix Farley's Bristol Journal*, 4 April 1789.

18. *State Gazette of South-Carolina*, 17 May 1787; *Daily Advertiser*, 23 January 1788

19. "Henry Cruger & Company Account Book, 1784–1793," MssCol NYGB 18210, vol. 1, NYPL.

20. Henry Cruger to Peter Van Schaack, 14 July 1787, VSFP.

21. *London Gazette*, 30 September–4 October 1788.

22. *Bath Chronicle*, 21 August 1788.

23. Capel Lofft, *An History of the Corporation and Test Acts* [. . .] ([Bury St Edmunds]: J. Rackham, 1790), 38. See also G. M. Ditchfield, "The Parliamentary Struggle over the Repeal of the Test and Corporation Actions, 1787–1790," *English Historical Review* 89, no. 352 (1974): 551–77.

24. P. J. Marshall, *Edmund Burke and the British Empire in the West Indies: Wealth, Power, and Slavery* (Oxford: Oxford University Press, 2019), 98.

25. Henry Cruger to Jeremiah Osborne, 28 April 1789, SMV/7/2/1/15, BA.

26. *The Parliamentary Register; of History of the Proceedings and Debates of the House of Commons* [. . .], vol. 26 (London: J. Debrett, 1789), 130–54.

27. *Gazetteer and New Daily Advertiser*, 13 May 1789.

28. Henry Cruger to Jeremiah Osborne, 18 May 1789, SMV/7/2/1/15, BA.

29. *Felix Farley's Bristol Journal*, 30 May 1789.

30. *Parliamentary Register* [. . .], vol. 26, 198–99. See also *Morning Star*, 22 May 1789; *Felix Farley's Bristol Journal*, 30 May 1789; Latimer, *Annals of Bristol*, 477.

31. *Parliamentary Register* [. . .], vol. 26, 200–202.

32. Henry Cruger to Peter Van Schaack, 14 July 1787, VSFP.

33. Brooke, "Cruger, Henry."

34. Minchinton, *Trade of Bristol*, 49.

35. *London Gazette*, 6–10 May 1788.

36. *London Chronicle*, 23–26 August 1788. In some sources her name is given as Clarissa.

37. Cruger, *GBH*, 18.

38. *Daily Advertiser*, 4 June 1790; *Gazetteer and New Daily Advertiser*, 13 March 1790; Brooke, "Cruger, Henry."

39. *Public Advertiser*, 22 April 1790; *Daily Advertiser*, 4 June 1790; Minchinton, *Trade of Bristol*, 57; Van Schaack, *Henry Cruger*, 36.

40. Van Schaack, *Henry Cruger*, 40.

41. See Henry Cruger to Reed and Forde, 26 September 1790, Reed and Forde Papers, collection 541, box 3, folder 2, HSP.

42. See, for example, *New-York Daily Gazette*, 26 March 1792, 21 February 1793.

334 NOTES TO PAGES 248–250

43. *New York Price Current*, 13 December 1800.

44. *Daily Advertiser*, 26 May 1788, 2 January 1795, 13 May 1797.

45. "Inventory of the Estate Real & Personal of the late Nicholas Cruger, Esq. taken at New York the 11th March 1800," Nicholas Cruger Estate Papers, 1800–1821, LOC.

46. Dael A. Norwood, *Trading Freedom: How Trade with China Defined Early America* (Chicago: University of Chicago Press, 2021), 15–23.

47. "Cargo of the Ship Jenny of New York [. . .]," India Office Records, H/MISC/337, BL.

48. Lynch & Stoughton Journal, 1783–1788, 277, 296–97, 313, BV Lynch & Stoughton, NYHS.

49. *New-York Packet*, 29 February 1788.

50. John Temple to Francis Osborne [Marquess of Carmarthen], 3 April 1788; Extract of a Letter from Phineas Bond to Francis Osborne, 5 May 1788; "Cargo of the Ship Jenny of New York [. . .]," India Office Records, H/MISC/337, BL.

51. *Journals of the Continental Congress*, 11 February 1788, 34:34–35.

52. Lynch and Stoughton to Isaac Gouverneur, 3 July 1794, Lynch & Stoughton Letterbook, 1791–1794, BV Lynch & Stoughton, NYHS; Nicholas Cruger to Ebenezer Stevens, 18 December 1792, NYHS Digital Collections.

53. Gouverneur and Kemble to Nicholas Cruger, 9 March 1795, BV Gouverneur & Kemble Letterbook, NYHS; *Daily Advertiser*, 13 May 1797.

54. *Daily Advertiser*, 3 June 1793.

55. *Daily Advertiser*, 24 September 1792, 1 July 1793, 30 July 1793, 17 August 1793; *Commercial Advertiser*, 14 April 1798.

56. Gouverneur and Kemble to Joseph Gouverneur and Peter Cruger, 20 January 1795, BV Gouverneur & Kemble Letterbook, NYHS; Lisa Sturm-Lind, *Actors of Globalization: New York Merchants in Global Trade, 1784–1812* (Leiden: Brill, 2018), 70–74; Diary of John Adams, 27 July 1796, AP/FO.

57. Norwood, *Trading Freedom*, 16.

58. Robert E. Wright, *Origins of Commercial Banking in America, 1750–1800* (Lanham, MD: Rowman & Littlefield, 2001), 77–95.

59. Wright, *Origins of Commercial Banking*, 92–95, 108n156.

60. Wright, *Origins of Commercial Banking*, 83. On the politics of the bank, see also Alfred F. Young, *The Democratic Republicans of New York: The Origins, 1763–1797* (Chapel Hill: University of North Carolina Press for the Institute of Early American History and Culture, 1967), 211–14.

61. "Inventory of the Estate Real & Personal of the Late Nicholas Cruger [. . .]," Nicholas Cruger Estate Papers, LOC. Cruger is not in two early lists of bank shareholders from 1784/5 and 1791. See Robert A. East, *Business Enterprise in the American Revolutionary*

NOTES TO PAGES 251–253

Era (New York: Columbia University Press, 1938), 327–29; and Henry Williams Domett, *A History of the Bank of New York, 1784–1884* (New York: G.B. Putnam, 1884), 132–35.

62. *Daily Advertiser*, 17 March 1789, 21 March 1789, 28 March 1789, 30 March 1789; Joseph S. Davis, *Essays in the Earlier History of American Corporations*, 2 vols. (Cambridge, MA: Harvard University Press, 1917), 2:275; Peskin, "From Protection to Encouragement," 589–615.

63. Thomas Marshall to Alexander Hamilton, 19 July 1791, AH/FO; Davis, *Earlier History*, 1:400–401.

64. On the SEUM and Duer, see Davis, *Earlier History*, 1:111–345; and Cathy Matson, "Public Vices, Private Benefit: William Duer and His Circle, 1776–1792," in William Pencak and Conrad Edick Wright, eds., *New York and the Rise of American Capitalism: Economic Development and the Social and Political History of an American State, 1780–1870* (New York: NYHS, 1989), 72–123.

65. Davis, *Earlier History*, 1:286.

66. Henry Cruger to Peter Van Schaack, 20 April 1792, Small Manuscripts Collection, Chicago History Museum, Chicago, IL.

67. Davis, *Earlier History*, 1:296.

68. *American Minerva: An Evening Advertiser*, 17 March 1796; Julius Goebel Jr., ed., *The Law Practice of Alexander Hamilton: Documents and Commentary*, 5 vols. (New York: Columbia University Press, 1964–81), 2:404–6; *Laws of the State of New-York. Passed at the Twenty-First Session of the Legislature* [. . .] (Albany, NY: Loring Andrews, 1798), 339.

69. *The Constitution and Nominations of the Subscribers to the Tontine Coffee-House* (New York, 1796), 32.

70. *New-York Daily Gazette*, 30 March 1789, 4 April 1789.

71. *New-York Daily Gazette*, 8 April 1789.

72. *New-York Daily Gazette*, 9 April 1789; *Journal of the Assembly of the State of New-York* [. . .], *1789* (New York: Samuel and John Loudon, 1789).

73. *Daily Advertiser*, 19 April 1790, 20 April 1790. See also *New-York Daily Gazette*, 20 April 1790; *Daily Advertiser*, 26 April 1790, 27 April 1790.

74. *Daily Advertiser*, 26 May 1790; *Journal of the Assembly of the State of New-York, Fourteenth Session* (New York: Francis Childs and John Swaine, 1791).

75. On mechanics' support for the Constitution, see Young, *Democratic Republicans*, 100–102; and Sean Wilentz, *Chants Democratic: New York City and the Rise of the American Working Class, 1788–1850* (Oxford: Oxford University Press, 2004), 67–68.

76. Cruger, *GBH*, 11; *Daily Advertiser*, 21 December 1791.

77. *The Weekly Museum*, 7 April 1792.

78. Elkins and McKittrick, *Age of Federalism*, 288.

NOTES TO PAGES 253–255

79. *Albany Gazette*, 16 April 1792. See also Young, *Democratic Republicans*, 284–86.

80. Van Schaack, *PVS*, 437–39; Robert Troup to John Jay, 6 May 1792, JJ/FO; Egbert Benson to Peter Van Schaack, 14 March 1792, VSFP; Young, *Democratic Republicans*, 284–86.

81. Supplement to *New-York Journal, & Patriotic Register*, 24 March 1792; Henry Cruger to Peter Van Schaack, 20 April 1792, Small Manuscripts Collection, Chicago History Museum, Chicago, IL.

82. For endorsements of Henry and sometimes Nicholas in 1792, see *Diary; or, Loudon's Register*, 7 April 1792; *New-York Journal, & Patriotic Register*, 7 April 1792; *Daily Advertiser*, 25 April 1792.

83. New York Assembly, New York County Election Results, 1792; and New York State Senate, Southern District Election Results, 1792, in *A New Nation Votes: American Election Returns, 1787–1825*, https://elections.lib.tufts.edu/.

84. Lester, "Cruger, Henry Jr."

85. *Journal of the Senate of the State of New-York. Sixteenth Session* (New York: Francis Childs and John Swaine, [1793]), [3].

86. Cruger apparently retained at least a token political connection to Bristol, never resigning from the city's Common Council and therefore formally remaining a member until his death. See Latimer, *Annals of Bristol*, 489.

87. Van Schaack, *Henry Cruger*, 38–40.

88. *New-York Journal, & Patriotic Register*, 22 December 1792.

89. On volitional allegiance, see James H. Kettner, *The Development of American Citizenship, 1608–1870* (Chapel Hill: University of North Carolina Press, 1978), 213–47.

90. "The Disputed Election of 1792: Editorial Note," JJ/FO; Alan Taylor, *William Cooper's Town: Power and Persuasion on the Frontier of the Early American Republic* (New York: Alfred A. Knopf, 1995), 167–98; and Edward B. Foley, "The Founders' *Bush v. Gore*: The 1792 Election Dispute and Its Continuing Relevance," *Indiana Law Review* 44, no. 1 (2010): 23–84.

91. Peter Van Schaack to Theodore Sedgwick, 19 June 1792, 25 June 1792, 31 August 1792, JJCU.

92. See, for example, Barent Gardenier to Henry Van Schaack, 24 September 1792, VSFP.

93. *Hudson Gazette*, 19 July 1792. A manuscript version is in Van Schaack's papers. See "An Independent Elector" [1792] in VSFP. See also Henry Van Schaack to Peter Van Schaack, 1 September 1792, VSFP.

94. *Daily Advertiser*, 1 August 1792, and, for a defense of Van Schaack, *Hudson Gazette*, 16 August 1792.

95. *Daily Advertiser*, 30 June 1792. On Nicholas Cruger organizing for Jay, see *Daily Advertiser*, 10 July 1792, 14 July 1792, 24 July 1792, 26 July 1792.

96. *Daily Advertiser*, 14 July 1792.

NOTES TO PAGES 255–258

97. *Daily Advertiser*, 23 August 1792.

98. *Daily Advertiser*, 12 September 1792.

99. Van Schaack chaired a Kinderhook committee that petitioned for an investigation of the canvassers. See Philip Schuyler to Alexander Hamilton, 28 November 1792, AH/FO.

100. Elkins and McKittrick, *Age of Federalism*, 310–11.

101. Carol Berkin, *A Sovereign People: The Crises of the 1790s and the Birth of American Nationalism* (New York: Basic Books, 2017), 82–83.

102. Elkins and McKittrick, *Age of Federalism*, 360.

103. Matthew Schoenbachler, "Republicanism in the Age of Democratic Revolution: The Democratic-Republican Societies of the 1790s," *JER* 18, no. 2 (1998): 237–61; Elkins and McKittrick, *Age of Federalism*, 342, 363.

104. Elkins and McKittrick, *Age of Federalism*, 360. See also Douglas Bradburn, *The Citizenship Revolution: Politics and the Creation of the American Union, 1774–1804* (Charlottesville: University of Virginia Press, 2009), 107–23.

105. Young, *Democratic Republicans*, 351.

106. Elkins and McKittrick, *Age of Federalism*, 362.

107. *New-York Daily Gazette*, 7 August 1793; Young, *Democratic Republicans*, 355–57.

108. *New-York Daily Gazette*, 7 August 1793.

109. Young, *Democratic Republicans*, 355–57; *Daily Advertiser*, 8 August 1793.

110. *Daily Advertiser*, 9 August 1793.

111. "Address from the Citizens of New York City," 8 August 1793; and Alexander Hamilton to George Washington, 9 August 1793, GW/FO.

112. Robert Troup to Alexander Hamilton, 8 August 1793, AH/FO.

113. Thomas Jefferson to James Madison, 11 August 1793, TJ/FO.

114. *Daily Advertiser*, 9 August 1793. For reprinting examples, *Federal Gazette and Philadelphia Daily Advertiser*, 10 August 1793; *Columbian Centinel*, 14 August 1793; *Oracle of the Day*, 17 August 1793. See also *Gazette of the United States*, 14 August 1793.

115. *General Evening Post*, 26–28 September 1793; *Evening Mail*, 27–30 September 1793.

116. *Diary; or, Loudon's Register*, 14 August 1793. Hamilton likely drafted Washington's reply. See George Washington to Alexander Hamilton, 10 August 1793, GW/FO. For a reply from Clinton, see *Diary; or, Loudon's Register*, 17 August 1793.

117. Elkins and McKittrick, *Age of Federalism*, 362–65. Nicholas Cruger and others accused the Jeffersonian publisher Thomas Greenleaf of libeling Washington as the Genêt affair concluded. See Greenleaf's *New-York Journal, & Patriotic Register*, 7 December 1793; and *American Minerva*, 10 December 1793, 13 December 1793.

118. *Diary; or, Loudon's Register*, 21 August 1793; "Memorial from Nicholas Cruger and Others, 26 June 1793," John Nixon to Thomas Jefferson, 29 May 1793, and Thomas Jefferson to Edmond Charles Genêt, 12 July 1793, TJ/FO; "Cruger v. Ward, Ward and Ward,"

338 NOTES TO PAGES 258–259

Legal File, 1708–1804, Alexander Hamilton Papers, LOC. For subsequent efforts to collect damages from France for the *York*, see Walter Lowrie and Matthew St. Clair Clarke, eds., *American State Papers. Documents, Legislative and Executive, of the Congress of the United States* [. . .], vol. 1 (Washington, DC: Gales and Seaton, 1832), 678, 756–57. One 1794 report included Cruger's *York* in a list of American vessels taken by British, rather than French, cruisers. See *Philadelphia Gazette and Universal Daily Advertiser*, 1 September 1794. This seems a mistake.

119. *Baltimore Daily Intelligencer*, 12 March 1794; *Diary; or Evening Register*, 24 March 1794. On the *Eliza*'s voyage, see Amasa Delano, *A Narrative of Voyages and Travels, in the Northern and Southern Hemispheres* [. . .] (Boston: E. G. House, 1817), 196–207.

120. Sturm-Lind, *Actors of Globalization*, 82–83; *Abstract of Cases Transmitted to the Secretary of the Treasury, Pursuant to the Sixth Section of the Act* [. . .] ([Philadelphia, 1800]).

121. Elkins and McKittrick, *Age of Federalism*, 375–96.

122. This case was subsequently appealed in London by the American agent Samuel Bayard. See "Before the Most Noble and Right Honorable the Lords Commissioners of Appeals in Prize Causes. Brigantine Mary, James Codwise, Master [. . .] Appellant's Case" (1798); "Before the Most Noble and Right Honorable the Lords Commissioners of Appeals in Prize Causes. Brigantine Mary, James Codwise, Master [. . .] Respondent's Case"; "Before the Most Noble and Right Honorable the Lords Commissioners of Appeals in Prize Causes. Brigantine Mary, James Codwise, Master [. . .], Appendix: Preparatory Examinations," all in database The Making of the Modern Law: Trials, 1600–1926 (Gale).

123. On this cartoon, see Matthew Rainbow Hale, "'Many Who Wandered in Darkness': The Contest over American National Identity, 1795–1798," *EAS* 1, no. 1 (2003): 134–36; Jasper M. Trautsch, "'Mr. Madison's War' or the Dynamic of Early American Nationalism?" *EAS* 10, no. 3 (2012): 638–40.

124. "Pacificus No. III," [6 July 1793], AH/FO; Jerald A. Combs, *The Jay Treaty: Political Battleground of the Founding Fathers* (Berkeley: University of California Press, 1970), 108.

125. Elkins and McKittrick, *Age of Federalism*, 388–95; Samuel Flagg Bemis, *Jay's Treaty: A Study in Commerce and Diplomacy* (New York: Macmillan, 1923), 184–99.

126. See, for example, *General Advertiser*, 19 April 1794, 28 April 1794; *Gazette of the United States*, 24 April 1794.

127. John Jay to Sarah Livingston Jay, 15 April 1794, JJ/FO.

128. *New-York Daily Gazette*, 11 April 1794; *Daily Advertiser*, 12 April 1794; *Diary; or, Evening Register*, 12 April 1794, 15 April 1794. On cartmen's politics, see Graham Russell Hodges, *New York City Cartmen, 1667–1850* (New York: New York University Press, 2012), 81–92.

129. For Trim's letter and a response, see *Diary; or, Evening Register*, 17 April 1794, 18 April 1794.

NOTES TO PAGES 260–262

130. "The Jay Treaty: Appointment and Instructions: Editorial Note," JJ/FO; New York Assembly, New York County Election Results, 1794, *New Nation Votes*.

131. Waldstreicher, *Midst of Perpetual Fetes*, 129–30.

132. *Diary; or, Evening Register*, 5 July 1794; *Daily Advertiser*, 5 July 1794. These reports also appeared in many other newspapers. See also Newman, *Parades and the Politics of the Street*, 92–99.

133. Young, *Democratic Republicans*, 429–35.

134. Ezekiel Gilbert to Peter Van Schaack, 16 December 1794, VSFP; *Daily Advertiser*, 28 January 1795.

135. See, for example, *Philadelphia Gazette and Universal Daily Advertiser*, 29 January 1795; *Federal Intelligencer and Baltimore Daily Gazette*, 3 February 1795; *Norwich Packet*, 5 February 1795; *Columbian Centinel*, 7 February 1795.

136. *American Minerva, and the New-York (Evening) Advertiser*, 5 March 1795. See also the printed "To the Electors of the State of New-York," (1795) containing this list, JJCU. Nicholas Cruger politicked to reassure the public that Jay would be back in time to serve as governor if elected. *American Minerva, and the New-York (Evening) Advertiser*, 22 April 1795, 27 April 1795. John Jay to Nicholas Cruger, 11 September 1794, JJCU, documents their friendly relationship.

137. Todd Estes, *The Jay Treaty Debate, Public Opinion, and the Evolution of Early American Political Culture* (Amherst: University of Massachusetts Press, 2006), 3.

138. Amanda C. Demmer, "Trick or Constitutional Treaty? The Jay Treaty and the Quarrel over the Diplomatic Separation of Powers," *JER* 35 (2015): 579–95; Elkins and McKittrick, *Age of Federalism*, 417–32.

139. See the list of founders in *American Minerva: An Evening Advertiser*, 17 March 1796.

140. *Gazette of the United States*, 20 April 1796; Combs, *Jay Treaty*, 178–80; James Madison to Thomas Jefferson, 23 April 1796, and John Langdon to James Madison, 28 April 1796, Papers of James Madison, Founders Online.

141. Theodore Sedgwick to Peter Van Schaack, 14 January 1795 and 3 August 1795; Ezekiel Gilbert to Peter Van Schaack, 16 April 1796, VSFP.

142. Peter Van Schaack to Henry Cruger, 29 February 1796, VSFP.

143. John Evert Van Alen to Peter Van Schaack, 2 May 1796, VSFP.

144. See, among many other works, Estes, *Jay Treaty Debate;* Demmer, "Trick or Constitutional Treaty"; Lawrence B. A. Hatter, *Citizens of Convenience: The Imperial Origins of American Nationhood on the U.S.-Canadian Border* (Charlottesville: University of Virginia Press, 2017).

145. Jasanoff, *Liberty's Exiles*, 320.

146. Eliga H. Gould, *Among the Powers of the Earth: The American Revolution and the Making of a New World Empire* (Cambridge, MA: Harvard University Press, 2012), 136–38. See

340   NOTES TO PAGES 263–270

also Elkins and McKittrick, *Age of Federalism*, 410–14; Combs, *Jay Treaty*, 150–58; Bemis, *Jay's Treaty*, 252–71.

147. Waldstreicher, *Perpetual Fetes*, 138–39.

148. Estes, *Jay Treaty Debate*, 104–17, 121 (quotation).

149. Estes, *Jay Treaty Debate*, 125.

150. Van Schaack, *PVS*, 372–73.

151. Bemis, *Jay's Treaty*, 321.

152. Gould, *Among the Powers*, 138.

153. *Daily Advertiser*, 11 April 1796.

154. *Greenleaf's New York Journal and Patriotic Register*, 21 April 1798.

155. Theodore Sedgwick to Peter Van Schaack, 30 March 1800, VSFP.

156. See, for example, *Hudson Gazette*, 16 April 1799; *Albany Centinel*, 14 April 1801; *The Bee* (Hudson, NY), 21 April 1807.

157. *Morning Post and Fashionable World*, 10 February 1796; *Oracle, and Public Advertiser*, 11 February 1796; *Oracle, and the Daily Advertiser*, 4 September 1799.

158. Peter Van Schaack to Henry Cruger, 29 February 1796, VSFP.

159. Stephens and Bickham, "Lancey, Oliver De (c. 1749–1822)"; [House of Commons], *The Second Report of the Commissioners of Military Enquiry. Appointed by Act of 45 George III. cap. 47* [. . .] (London, 1806), 119.

160. "Fitzroy Street," in *Survey of London*, vol. 21, *The Parish of St Pancras*, part 3: *Tottenham Court Road and Neighbourhood*, ed. J. R. Howard Roberts and Walter H. Godfrey (London: London County Council, 1949), 44–46. *British History Online*, https://www.british-history.ac.uk/survey-london/vol21/pt3.

161. *Daily Advertiser*, 26 April 1800.

162. Cruger, *GBH*, 21. See also *New-York Gazette and General Advertiser*, 26 April 1800.

163. Cruger, *GBH*, 41.

Conclusion

1. John Evans, "Memoirs of Mr. Thomas Mullett," *The Gentleman's Magazine: And Historical Chronicle. From January to June, 1815,* vol. 85, part 1 (London: Nichols, Son, and Bentley, 1815), 83–85.

2. Cruger, *GBH*, 21–24.

3. Will and Codicil of Nicholas Cruger, 1791 and 1800, Folder AC 120, J0038–82, New York State Archives, Albany, New York. See also Prob 11/1419, 75–77, UKNA. Nicholas Cruger Estate Papers, 1800–1821, LOC; "Rogers and Rogers v. Cruger et al," Legal File, 1708–1804, Alexander Hamilton Papers, LOC; William Johnson, *Reports of Cases Argued and Determined in the Supreme Court of Judicature and in the Court for the Trial of*

NOTES TO PAGES 270–273

Impeachments and the Correction of Errors in the State of New-York, vol. 7 (New York: Isaac Riley, 1811), 557–635.

4. Cruger, *GBH*, 28–45. On Church's career, see David R. Fisher, "Church, John Barker (1748–1818), of Down Place, Berks.," *HoP.*

5. For the contents of this memorial to John Harris Cruger, see "St. James Church, Hampstead Road," in *Survey of London*, vol. 21, *The Parish of St Pancras*, part 3: *Tottenham Court Road and Neighbourhood*, ed. J. R. Howard Roberts and Walter H. Godfrey (London: London County Council, 1949), 123–36. *British History Online*, https://www.british-history.ac.uk/survey-london/vol21/pt3. This church was demolished in 1964.

6. *The Gentleman's Magazine: And Historical Chronicle. From January to June, 1822*, vol. 92, part 1 (London: John Nichols and Son, 1822), 572.

7. Van Schaack, *Henry Cruger*, 42–43.

8. "Henry Cruger," in Evert A. Duyckinck and George L. Duyckinck, *Cyclopaedia of American Literature* [. . .], 2 vols. (New York: Charles Scribner, 1866), 1:223; Van Schaack, *Henry Cruger*, 41.

9. Van Schaack, *Henry Cruger*, 47–48.

10. Cruger, *GBH*, 25; Van Schaack, *PVS*, 447.

11. Peter Van Schaack to Henry Cruger, 5 February 1797; Peter Van Schaack to Henry Cruger, 9 September 1797, VSFP.

12. On Henry Cruger Van Schaack's biography, see George Van Santvoord, "Henry Cruger Van Schaack," *Dictionary of American Biography*, 22 vols. (New York: Charles Scribner's Sons, 1928–58), 19:213.

13. Van Schaack, *Peter Van Schaack*, 443–46.

14. Martin Van Buren, *The Autobiography of Martin Van Buren*, ed. John C. Fitzpatrick (Washington, DC: Government Printing Office, 1920), 19–20.

15. Hamlin, "Peter Van Schaack," 98–99.

16. Van Schaack, *PVS*, 460–61.

17. Van Schaack, *PVS*, 249.

Acknowledgments

Nobody Men stresses the interconnectedness of people as they move through their times. Such ties have been central to the history of this book and its author too. I researched and wrote *Nobody Men* while working at Temple University and am grateful for the institutional and personal support I have received there. Two valuable sabbaticals aided me at different stages and a fellowship from the Center for the Humanities at Temple offered both focused time and a stimulating interdisciplinary forum for sharing work. A LAURA grant from Temple's College of Liberal Arts enabled me to work with Maureen Iplenski as a research assistant, and I appreciate her work in newspaper research that contributed to chapters 9 and 10. My thanks to current and former colleagues in the History Department, especially my encouraging writing-group friends Peter Lavelle, Harvey Neptune, and Eileen Ryan. Jess Roney, besides being part of this circle, has been consistently generous as a reader, a sounding board, a colleague, and a friend.

Many other scholars read, listened, provided critiques, and helped me to develop my ideas. Thank you to organizers and participants in the following: the Temple Early Atlantic Seminar; the Early American Republic Seminar at the City University of New York; the Washington Area Early American History Seminar and the Washington Library at Mount Vernon; the Consortium on the Revolutionary Era; the Annual Meeting of the Omohundro Institute for Early American History and Culture; the Annual Meeting of the Organization of American Historians; the "On Edge: New Frontiers in Atlantic History" Conference held at the University of Southampton; the Georgetown University Early Modern Global History Seminar; the "Zones and Lines, Water and Land: New Conversations on Borders" Conference at the University of Cardiff; the New York University Atlantic World Workshop; the Annual Meeting of the North American Conference on British Studies; the Delaware Valley British Studies Seminar; and the Triangle Early American History Seminar, the Triangle Global British

344 ACKNOWLEDGMENTS

History Seminar, and the National Humanities Center. A Visiting Fellowship at Clare Hall and the opportunity to be a Visiting Scholar in the Faculty of History at the University of Cambridge helped me complete the book.

Many other people offered intellectual aid and moral support. The good people of Hobbs in Swarthmore gave me coffee and community as I wrote. Stephen Hague first mentioned the career of Henry Cruger to me when I expressed a still-new interest in people in the middle during the Revolution. My friend Philip Stern arranged for an early forum to help me articulate some ideas, was a comrade on research forays in the United Kingdom, and has been a source of much appreciated encouragement. Kate Carté swapped drafts with me and offered insightful critiques of two chapters. Rebecca Goetz's friendship and positivity have been uplifting. My thanks to Charles Wilson for his keen listening and his kind counsel. Jennifer Garfall shared her expert design advice and assistance. Rebecca Lloyd aided me in obtaining access to sources through Temple's library. Wim Klooster and Kim Gruenwald generously pointed me to useful archival materials. David Armitage provided sage mentorship on how to frame and propose the book. Insightful anonymous readers offered learned and appreciated advice. Thank you to Bill Nelson for his work on the maps and to Adina Popescu and her colleagues at Yale University Press.

Family is a major theme in this book. Writing and researching it have repeatedly brought home to me how fortunate I am in my own kin. My warm thanks to Donald and Nancy Fowler for their abiding support and good humor. Siiri Fowler has been there time and again, and I thank her for such unflagging generosity. My siblings and their families have been boosters, respites, and inspirations. Thanks to Sofia, Mark, Fiona, and young Mark Sakson; to Maura, Siddharth, Rohan, Kian, and Lekha Velamoor; to Evan Glasson and Chase Currier; and to Brendan Glasson and Sabrina Ramos. My mother, Mary Sue Mulligan, and stepfather, Bill Eccleston, have offered counsel and provided much care for our family as I have worked on this project. My love and thanks go to them.

Hilary Glasson and Ned Glasson have lived with this, their father's book, from the start. Standing alongside them as they grow into themselves has helped me to reflect on the interconnected lives of the people of the past in different and, I hope, deeper ways. I am grateful for that and proud of them. I thank Hilary for her perceptive thoughtfulness, consistent backing, and witty intelligence. I thank Ned for sharing both his knowledgeable, energizing enthusiasm for history and his sense of fun. Lucy Glasson has provided many years of steadfast support and encouragement as I have worked on this project and we have raised our family. Without Lucy this book would not exist: her intellect, compassion, and labor are inscribed on every page. My thanks are not enough, Lucy, but I give them with all my heart. This book is for Lucy, Hilary, and Ned, with love, gratitude, and hope.

Index

Page references followed by an f indicate a figure.

Abrahamson, Pieter Heyliger, 207

Adams, Abigail, 3

Adams, John, 3, 5, 96, 102, 123, 170, 277n4

Administration of Justice Act (1774), 94

Albany County Committee of Safety, 151–52

Albany County's Committee to Detect Conspiracies, 152–53

Alsop, John, 96

American Crisis (Paine), 152

American immigration, 223

American Mutiny Act (1765). *See* Quartering Act

American Revolution: attitudinal or behavioral support, 11; cessation of hostilities, 224; as civil war, 9; decision-making in, 2–3, 12–13, 15, 193, 268; histories of, 5–14, 267–68; ideological origins of, 149; violence and, 2, 9–11, 69, 91, 105, 110, 118, 125

American Revolutionary battles: Boston siege, 119, 122, 143; Bunker Hill, 119; Cornwallis in Virginia, 138, 140; Eutaw Springs, South Carolina, 139–40; Kings Mountain, 137; Lexington and Concord, 101, 109–11, 117, 144, 152; Long Island, 126; Ninety Six, South Carolina, 135–39; Saratoga battles, 127, 155; Savannah battle and siege, 129–30, 132, 133f, 134; Yorktown, Cornwallis defeat, 138, 140, 191

Armitage, David, 9

Asia trade, 249–50

Bailyn, Bernard, 149, 314n28

Bancker, Christopher, 246

Bank of New York, 250

Barry & Cruger (firm), 27

Battle of Golden Hill (New York City), 81

Bayard, Samuel, 338n122

Bayard, William, 49

Becker, Carl, 41–42

Beekman, David, 193, 196

Beekman family, 52, 95

Benson, Egbert, 228

Bernard, Francis, 77

Blount, Thomas, 234

Boston Massacre, 81

Boston Port Act (1774), 94–95, 98, 305n49

Boston Tea Party, 91, 94, 98, 268

Bramin (pseudonym), 1, 7

Breen, Timothy, 11

Brickdale, Matthew, 99, 184–85

Bristol: election propaganda, 186f–89f; Independent Society, 87; parliamentary elections, 98–100, 180, 184–85, 236–40; politics, 86–90, 106, 173, 177, 190; trade, 169, 173, 180

British Army: evacuation of New York, 234; John Harris Cruger joining, 126–27; military supply contracts, 40; New York and, 80–81, 126–27, 155–56; offensive actions, 127; Oliver De Lancey joining, 126–27; quartering and billeting, 40, 46, 69, 71, 77, 79–81, 94

British Empire: constitutional crisis of, 42, 45, 50, 69, 91; France and, 183–84, 255, 264; mercantilism of, 37, 41, 68, 76; North American colonies and, 8, 44, 93; "patriots" and, 5; restrictions on postwar trade, 234–35

Brown, Nicholas, 235
Brown, Thomas, 135–36
Bryant, John Frederick, 240
Bull, Frederick, 89
Burgoyne, John, 155–58, 161, 163, 175
Burke, Andrew, 257
Burke, Edmund: Henry Cruger Jr. relations with, 100–101, 175–76; Henry Cruger Sr. meeting, 167; Irish reform supporter, 180; Jenkinson's influence at court, 174; New York Assembly agent, 92, 101, 110, 167; New York petitions (1775), 110–11; "Olive Branch Petition" and, 167; Parliamentary elections, 99–101, 184; Parliamentary role, 106; Rockinghamites and, 175, 178, 191; on the slave trade, 247
Burns' Coffee House, 54, 58

Calhoon, Robert M., 8, 277n2, 278n8, 281n22
Campbell, John (Earl of Loudon). *See* Loudon, Earl of
Caribbean islands, 2, 7, 21, 26, 33–36, 192–96, 199–201, 203, 257
Carleton, Guy, 140, 222
Carlisle, Lord, 161, 178–79
Carlisle Peace Commission, 161, 164, 177–79, 320n53
Chatham, Lord, 70–72, 106, 177–78. *See also* Pitt, William
Church, Catherine, 270
Church, John Barker, 270
Church of England, 6, 29, 96, 246
civil war: American Revolution as, 9–12, 14–15, 112–13, 117, 127, 129, 267–69; denunciation in, 152; microdynamics of, 11–12, 118, 137, 141, 152, 173; neutrals in, 10; retroactive explanations for participation, 12, 120, 181; in Southern backcountry, 129, 135–37; Van Schaack on, 105, 142, 148–50, 154, 163; violence central to, 11
Clarke, Elijah, 135–37
Clinton, George, 157–59, 231–32, 253–57, 260, 328n22
Clinton, Henry, 129, 134, 155
Coercive (Intolerable) Acts (1774), 91, 94–95, 98–99, 105–6
Coke, Daniel Parker, 162–63
Colden, Alexander, 59, 84

Colden, Cadwallader, 41, 46, 49, 51, 53, 55–59, 79–80, 108
Collins, Isaac, 174
Commissioners for Detecting and Defeating Conspiracies, 158
Committee of Fifty-One, 95–98
Committee of Sixty, 98, 109–10
Common Council (New York), 56–57, 87, 96
"Common Sense" (Paine), 123–24
conscientious objector, 142, 313n2
Conway, Henry, 183
Cooley, Simeon, 78–79, 299n48
Cooper, James Fenimore, 204
Corn Laws, 240
Cornwallis, Charles, 134–38, 140, 191, 222
Court of Appeals in Cases of Capture, 226–27
Coxe, Tench, 201–2
Crommelin, Daniel, 33
Cruger, Anna de Nully, 32, 198, 205, 207, 226, 270
Cruger, Anna (John and Marya's daughter), 24
Cruger, Anne De Lancey: in Beverly, England postwar, 219–21, 223; death in England, 270–71; death of, 271; De Lancey family and, 32, 118, 124, 126–27, 134, 219–21, 269; to England postwar, 141; family house attacked, 127–28; in London postwar, 264; loss of New York property, 222; marriage to John Harris Cruger, 3, 32; in Ninety Six, South Carolina, 137–39; prisoner of French, 132–33; to Savannah, 132; in South Carolina backcountry, 137; wartime travel, 131f
Cruger, Ann Markoe, 32, 226–27, 270
Cruger, Bertram Peter, 270
Cruger, Caroline Smith, 32
Cruger, Dorothea Kier, 32
Cruger, Elizabeth Blair, 32, 248
Cruger, Elizabeth Harris, 2, 27, 29, 30f, 129
Cruger, Ellin Peach, 32, 247, 288n67
Cruger, Hannah (Sloughter) Montgomery, 27
Cruger, Henrietta Crisson, 32
Cruger, Henry, Jr.: in Bristol, England, 31, 33, 35, 173–74, 180, 240; Bristol Common Council member, 87, 336n86; Bristol Independent Society, 87; Bristol mayor, 190–91; Bristol's Society of Merchant Venturers, 86–87; British troops provisioning

INDEX

conspiracy, 120; Charles Jenkinson and, 174–75, 179–80, 182; Chatham and, 106, 177–78; citizenship question, 237–40, 253, 336n86; Crown pension, 175, 180–81; Declaration of Independence and, 173; Edmond Burke and, 106, 175, 184, 247; emigration to New York, 242, 245, 247, 269; English radicalism of, 89; family of, 27, 247–48; Irish trade and, 180; Jay Treaty and, 263; John Hancock and, 34, 89, 235; John Jay and, 253; King's College education, 30–31; Loyalist Claims Commission petition, 181–82, 247; marriages of, 32, 247, 288n67; military conflict likely, 109; to New York in 1783, 224, 234; New York oath of allegiance, 253; on New York petitions (1775), 111–12, 181–82; New York state senator, 253, 263; in Parliament, 102–3, 239, 245; in Parliament and Conway proposal, 183; in Parliament and Wilkes, 176; Parliamentary elections, 98–100, 180, 184–85, 187, 188f, 191, 237, 248, 321n76; in Parliament postwar, 240, 245–46; in Parliament voting record, 320n53; Philip Skene and, 119; political career of, 42; portrait of, 88f, 104f, 190f; postwar adjustments, 219; postwar financial situation, 236, 248; postwar life of, 271; postwar trade partnerships, 234–36; Prohibitory Act and, 169–72; as pro-peace, 2, 103, 106, 166, 173, 176–77, 180–83, 235, 263; *Royal Danish American Gazette* and, 199; seizure of the *George*, 317n9; SEUM investment and failure, 251; slave trade and, 35, 246–47; Stamp Act and, 62–65; Tontine Coffee House, 252; trade and finances of, 33–34, 169–70, 173–74, 181, 191, 234–36, 245–48; travel to America, 93, 98, 220f, 234, 240; West India interest and, 246; William Pitt the younger and, 237

Cruger, Henry, Sr.: Cruger's Wharf and, 21, 37; in England, 144, 167–68; family of, 2, 27; French wartime commerce and, 41; General Assembly member, 39; health issues, 167; Jamaica and, 26–27; King's College governor, 30; land purchases in New York and Vermont, 37; Loyalist Claims Commission and, 181; nonimportation and, 84–85;

privateer investments, 40; Provincial Council member, 73, 78, 92; slave trade and ownership, 26, 36; Stamp Act and, 60; trade of, 32–37; underwriting maritime insurance, 37; will and property distribution, 210–11, 326n78

Cruger, John Harris: Bay of Honduras petition and, 34; in Beverly, England postwar, 220, 223; British lieutenant colonel, 126; British patronage, 264; in Charleston, South Carolina, 140–41; conspiracy theory refutation, 119; death in London, 270–71; De Lancey family and, 31–32, 118, 126–27, 220–21, 264; Eutaw Springs, South Carolina, 139–40; exile in England, 141, 219–20; extralegal "Committee of Inspection," 78; Forfeiture Act and, 134, 223; French wartime commerce and, 41; Governor's Guard lieutenant colonel, 92; horrors of war, 267–68; house raid by patriots, 127–29; inheritance of Jamaica property, 36; in Jamaica, 29, 35, 286n4; land purchases in New York and Vermont, 37; as loyalist, 118, 125–27, 133–34, 139, 141, 170, 220, 269; loyalist army officer, 3, 127; Loyalist Claims Commission and, 221–23; loyalist diaspora postwar, 220; marriage of, 31, 132; moderate patriot, 121–23; New York Chamber of Commerce and, 74, 76; New York City chamberlain, 86, 222; New York City freeman, 29; in Ninety Six, South Carolina, 137–39, 175; nonimportation and, 78–79; "Olive Branch Petition" and, 121–22; Parliamentary election and, 237; Philadelphia Academy education, 29; Philip Skene and, 119; Provincial Congress named loyalist, 124, 126; Provincial Council member, 92, 108, 118, 121; in Savannah, 129–30, 131f, 132; seizure of property, 223, 327n15; slave trade and, 36; Stamp Act and, 82; treatment of patriots in Ninety Six, 135–36; Vermont landholdings, 92; violence and, 117–18, 125–26, 129, 134–37, 141

Cruger, John I: background of, 2; birthplace and origin of, 22–23; career of, 23–24; death of, 27; Dutch Curaçao and, 24–26; marriage of, 23; Philip Livingston, cosyn, 23; political offices of, 23, 39; portrait of,

350   INDEX

Cruger, John I (*continued*)
25f; *Prophet Daniel* (ship) and, 23; slave
trade and, 27; trade of, 23–26
Cruger, John II: bachelorhood, 27, 49; British
military supply contracts, 40–41, 119;
Committee of Correspondence member, 46;
family of, 24, 27–28, 49; General Assembly
(New York) Speaker, 2, 29, 78–81, 92, 105,
112; at Kinderhook, 144, 151; King's College governor, 30; land purchases in New
York and Vermont, 37; named as disaffected,
151; New York Chamber of Commerce and,
74–76; New York City freeman, 27; New
York City mayor, 45, 55, 69, 76; New York
petition on trade (1766), 69–73; "the Old
Speaker," 252; political offices and politics
of, 39, 49–50, 80; portrait of, 47f; quartering and, 40, 56, 71; Sons of Liberty and,
51; Stamp Act and, 54–58, 82; Stamp Act
Congress and, 45, 49–55
Cruger, Lediard, and Mullett (firm), 236, 246
Cruger, Lewis, 49–50, 293n17
Cruger, Maria, 24
Cruger, Marya Cuyler, 23–24, 26
Cruger, Nicholas: *Adriane* seized by British,
207–8; Asia trade, 249–50; British prisoner,
207–10, 212; British wartime trade, 212–13;
on the *Bumper* to Jamaica, 193; Citizen
Genêt and, 256–57; *Cumberland* privateer
capture, 213–14, 226–27; Danish citizenship, 202, 211, 226–27, 249; death in St.
Croix, 264, 270; "Dutch" tea, 86; family of,
27–28, 32, 198, 226, 270; Federalist party
and, 259; "federal man," 243; French vessel
seizures, 257–58; General Assembly (New
York) candidate, 252, 259–60; Hamilton
and, 3, 192, 196–97; health issues, 197,
207, 264, 325n66; Henry Sr. executor, 211;
John Jay and, 255; July 4th celebration, 260;
marriages of, 32; *Mary* privateer capture,
258, 338n122; *Nancy* privateer capture,
202; Neutrality Proclamation and, 255–61;
New York City freeman, 29; to New York
postwar, 212, 223–24; New York ratification
convention and, 244–45; New York real
estate and, 227, 249; North American wartime trade, 201–3; partnerships, 193–94;
political beliefs unknown, 214–15; postwar

Caribbean trade, 257; postwar in New York,
225–27; postwar trading and business,
248–52, 257–58, 264, 270; public office
and, 264; questionable loyalties, 193; and
Rivington, 210–11, 224–26; Rose Hill, 227;
salt trade, 203–5, 325n48; SEUM investment and failure, 251; slave trade and,
35–36, 197, 212; St. Croix merchant, 31,
33, 36, 192–98, 212–14, 226, 248–49;
Thunderbolt cargo and travel, 197–98;
United Insurance Company, 251–52, 261;
wartime travel to British North America,
205, 206f, 207–10; Washington and, 193,
208–9, 224, 257, 328n22
Cruger, Rachel, 24
Cruger, Samuel Peach. *See* Peach, Samuel
Cruger, Telemon: in Curaçao, 31, 33, 36, 196,
211; family of, 27; King's College education,
31; marriages of, 32; and *Thunderbolt*,
197–98
Cruger, Tileman (d. 1694), 22, 283n4
Cruger, Tileman (d. 1730), 24, 26
Cruger, Valentine, 22, 283n6
Cruger and Mallard (firm), 174, 234
Cruger family: anglicization of, 28–29; Anglo-
American movement, 89–90; antidemocratic aristocracy label, 42; collective history of, 16; commercial interests of, 9, 21;
commercial networks of, 26; commercial
success of, 68–69; dock workers and, 52;
Dutch Curaçao and, 26, 29; family tree, 2,
4f; Federalist party and, 242, 270; interdependence and trade by, 22, 32–34, 37,
39, 43; Jay Treaty, 261; kin-keeping, 31;
letters reviewed by British government,
121; motivation of, 9; neutralist experience,
268–69; neutralist stories of, 15; New York
City development and, 15–16; patriot leadership and, 97; politics of, 15, 22, 39–43,
68–69, 90, 243, 252, 268; postwar commitment to United States, 242; postwar New
York and, 269; Prohibitory Act and trade,
169; Provincial Congress named loyalists,
125; rebuilding after war, 17; reintegration
into New York, 264–65; residences and
trading, 28f; slave traders and owners, 16,
23, 29, 35–36; Sons of Liberty and, 52;
Stamp Act and, 63–67; wartime decision-

INDEX   351

making, 2–3, 15, 37, 69; wartime nobodyists, 6, 91–92
Cruger's Wharf, 21, 37, 38f, 92, 129, 130f, 181
Cruger women: archive and, 16, 32; marriage
market and, 29, 31–32; material refinement
and, 29, 30f
Curaçao: John Cruger II in, 27; neutral port
in, 41; Telemon Cruger in, 31–33, 36,
196–97, 211; trading center, 24–26, 34–35,
214, 249
Currency Act (1764), 48, 79–80, 84
Curtenius, Peter, 169
Cuyler family, 23–24, 37, 40, 156

Danish West India and Guinea Company, 194
Dartmouth, Lord, 92, 101, 107
Daubeny, George, 184, 187, 237–40, 254
Dawes, Mannaseh, 238–39
Deane, Silas, 176
DeBrosses, Elias, 179
Declaration of Independence: British actions
in response, 126; British pro-Americans and,
174; Cruger's speech in Parliament and, 176;
moderation and reconciliation eliminated,
172; no referenda on, 10; overall nature of
the conflict, 6; Prohibitory Act and, 172–73;
Second Continental Congress and, 3; Van
Schaack response to, 152
Declaratory Act (1766), 63–64, 66, 101, 111,
176
De Lancey, Charlotte, 127–28, 221
De Lancey, James, 40, 62, 73, 78, 144
De Lancey, John, 82, 98
De Lancey, Oliver: to Beverly, England postwar, 220; Boston Port Act and, 94; British
army officer, 126–27; British government
compensation, 221; British troops pro-
visioning and, 40; Crugers and, 32; death
of, 220; and De Lancey's brigade, 127;
Forfeiture Act and, 134; house raid by
patriots, 127–29, 310n36; loyalist stance,
126–27; Provincial Council member, 92;
Stamp Act and, 82
De Lancey, Oliver, Jr., 220, 264
De Lancey, Phila Franks, 32, 127–28, 220–21
De Lancey, Stephen, 126
De Lancey family: British military officers,
118, 221; Cruger marriage links, 31–32; in

England postwar, 220; loyalist stance of,
118
De Lanceyites: General Assembly (New York)
election, 73, 78, 80; politics of, 103; reconciliation possibility, 112; Second Continental Congress and, 110; Sons of Liberty and,
77, 81, 87; Stamp Act repeal celebrations,
82; tea sales stance, 93
De Lancey's Brigade, 127, 129, 132, 134–35,
137, 141, 221
de Nully, Bertram Pieter, 198
Deshon, John, 213
d'Estaing, Charles Henri, comte, 132–33
Dickinson, John, 50, 73
disaffected as term, 1, 6–7, 125–26, 151–52.
See also nobodyists and nobodyism
Duane, James, 95–97, 119–20, 143, 308n5
Duer, William, 251
Duke, Henry, 136
Durant, Cornelius, 203
Dutch Reformed Church, 6, 23–24, 29–30,
198
"Dutch" tea, 86
Dutch trade, 33, 41
Dutch West India Company, 24–25
DuVal, Kathleen, 13

East India Company, 72, 93, 249
Eden, William, 161–62, 176, 178–80, 182
Evacuation Day (1783), 224, 328n22

Federalist party: Cruger support for, 242–43,
252–61, 264, 270; European war and
neutrality, 256–57, 259; Hamilton and
economic growth, 250–52, 270; Jay Treaty
and, 263; New York Governor election fight,
253–55; United Insurance Company in-
fluence, 261–62
First Continental Congress, 96–98, 104–5,
110, 168
Floyd, Elizabeth, 128
Forfeiture Act (1779), 134, 223
Forsey v. Cunningham (1764), 76
Fox, Charles, 170–72, 176, 191, 237, 320n53
Franco-American alliance, 177–79
Franklin, Benjamin, 29, 40, 63, 176
Franklin, William, 97
Franks, Moses, 32

352   INDEX

Free Port Act (1766), 70, 297n8
French Revolution, 10, 242, 255–56, 258
Friends (Quakers), 6, 126, 148
Friends of Liberty and Trade, 82, 84–85, 87

Gage, Thomas, 56–58, 79, 106, 112, 117
Galloway, Joseph, 97–98, 305n46
Gansevoort, Hester Cuyler, 156
Gansevoort, Leonard, 156, 158
Gates, Horatio, 89, 137, 170, 227
General Assembly (New York): billeting law,
    69, 71; bills of credit, 79–80, 84; Committee
    of Correspondence of, 46, 49; elections in,
    73–74, 78; fear of violence and war, 105–6;
    First Continental Congress and, 103–7;
    Moore and disputes, 77; paper money and,
    79; party politics and, 77; petitions (1775),
    105, 110–12, 268; Stamp Act petitions, 59;
    Sugar Act petitions, 46–47
Genêt, Edmond Charles, 255–57, 337n117
Gentleman's Magazine, 271
George III (king), 66, 87, 94, 122, 167, 172,
    224, 258, 259f
Germain, George, 155, 162
Gipson, Lawrence Henry, 70
Gould, Eliga, 263
Gouverneur, Nicholas, 24
Gouverneur, Sarah Cruger, 24
Gouverneur and Kemble (firm), 249, 258
Grant, Alexander, 213
Greene, Nathanael, 137–40
Greenleaf, Thomas, 337n117
Greg and Cunningham (firm), 41
Grenville, George, 45, 47–48, 59, 61–62, 64
Guion, Thomas, 202, 325n65

Haldane, Henry, 135
Hamilton, Alexander: Bank of New York and,
    250; Cruger employment in St. Croix, 3, 93;
    Cruger family and, 243; economic develop-
    ment and, 256; family of, 270; Jay Treaty
    and, 263; John Jay and, 230, 255, 264; New
    York politics and, 260; Nicholas Cruger and,
    3, 43, 192–93, 196–98, 208; peace with
    Britain, 256; pseudonym "Pacificus," 258;
    pseudonym "Phocion," 230; secretary of the
    treasury, 250–51; SEUM, 251; Washington
    and, 208, 257

Hancock, John, 34, 43, 75, 89, 234–35
Hansler, Hans, 23
Harris, Nicholas and Saye, 27
Hattem, Michael, 84
Hayes, Thomas, 213
Henry & John Cruger (firm), 26, 32–35, 49,
    119, 169, 196
Henry Cruger and Company, 234, 246
Heyliger, Catherine, 198
Hillsborough, Lord, 77–78
Hoare, Henry, 160
Hopkins, Thomas, 213
Howe, Richard, 127, 172
Howe, William, 126–27, 155, 172
Hudson Gazette, 254
Hudson's Bay Company, 22
Hunter, John, 160
Hutchinson, Thomas, 86

Inglis, Charles, 96
interdependence: in colonial America, 13, 15,
    22; Crugers and, 32, 118, 156, 196, 219,
    237, 243
Irish trade, 180, 245
Izard, Ralph, 109

Jamaica: Cruger family and, 21, 24, 26–27,
    34–36, 174, 193; Cruger property and
    slaves, 36; free port in, 70; Henry Moore
    and, 59; inheritance of Jamaica property,
    211, 223; John Harris Cruger and, 35, 211,
    233; New York commerce, 26
James, Thomas, 55
Jauncey, James, 74
Jay, John: ambassador to Spain, 134; American
    shipping losses, 258; attacked for Jay Treaty,
    263; Commissioners for Detecting and De-
    feating Conspiracies, 158–59; Committee
    of Fifty-One and, 95–96; Cruger family and,
    43; Cruger support for, 243; Cruger support
    for governor, 253; former loyalists and, 230;
    New York governor candidate, 254, 260,
    339n136; Nicholas Cruger and, 227; Second
    Continental Congress, 146; Van Schaack
    and, 143, 153, 156–57, 164, 228–29,
    231–32, 255
Jay, Sarah, 227, 258
Jay Treaty, 261–63, 265, 270

INDEX

Jefferson, Thomas, 256–57, 261, 264
Jenkinson, Charles, 111, 174–76, 179–80, 182
Johnstone, George, 161–62, 178–79
Jones, Thomas, 96–97, 110, 125–26, 128, 137–38, 143, 328n20

Kelly, William, 69–70
Kennedy, Archibald, 55, 58, 61
Kinderhook. *See* Van Schaack, Peter
King's College (New York), 30–31, 146, 196
Knox, Hugh, 196
Kortright, Cornelius, 194
Kortright, Lawrence, 74
Kortright and Cruger (firm), 35

League of Armed Neutrality, 200
Lediard, Thomas, 234
Lee, Arthur and William, 108
Lee, Charles, 121–24, 139
Lee, Henry, 139
Leisler's Rebellion, 22
Letters from a Farmer in Pennsylvania (Dickinson), 73
Liberty Boys, 51, 60, 69, 96, 98, 110, 143. *See also* Sons of Liberty
liberty pole, 66, 69, 78–79, 81
Lincoln, Benjamin, 132
Lippincott, Henry, 184–85
Lispenard, Leonard, 49
Livingston, Philip, 49, 53, 74, 78, 96
Livingston, Robert, Jr., 27
Livingston, Robert R. (d. 1775), 45, 49, 53, 56
Livingston, Robert R. (d. 1813), 225
Livingston faction, 60, 62, 73–74, 77–78, 80–82, 92–93, 95, 98
Livingston family, 23, 26, 32, 121
Locke, John, 143, 148, 163, 215
Lopez, Aaron, 65
Loudon, Earl of, 40, 56
Louis XVI (king of France), 255
Low, Isaac, Committee of Fifty-One chairman, 95–96
Low, Nicholas, 201, 251
Loyalist Claims Commission, 120, 181, 221–23, 232, 247
Loyalist Declaration of Dependence (1776), 127
loyalists and loyalism: anti-loyalist laws, 230–31; in backcountry South, 135,

137–38; colonial population of, 4–5, 277n2; definition of, 5, 7–8, 281n22; emigration postwar, 220, 223–24; histories of, 7–8; peace treaty and defeat of, 141; recovery of property postwar, 229–30; in the United States, 11; Whigs and, 118
Lynch, Dominick, 249

Madison, James, 261
Mallard, John, 174, 234
Markoe family, 32, 226
Marshall, Thomas, 251
Marston, Nathaniel, 27
Marston, Thomas, 27
Mason, Stevens Thomson, 261
Massachusetts Government Act (1774), 94
Matthews, David, 129
McDonnell, Michael, 5
McDougall, Alexander, 80–82, 84–85, 93, 95–96, 98, 105, 250
McEvers, James, 51–52
McFarlane, David, 213–14
Meredith, William, 65, 168
Mesnard, Thomas, 209
Montresor, John, 129
Moore, Henry, 55–56, 59–60, 70, 73, 77, 79
Morgan, Edmund S. and Helen M., 292n1
Morrice, John, 213
Morrill, John, 282n33
Morris, Gouverneur, 228, 230
Morris, Richard, 232
Mullett, Thomas, 234–36, 246, 267

Naturalization Act (1790), 236
Navigation Acts (Britain), 33, 41, 45
neutralist studies, 16
Neutrality Proclamation (1793), 256–58
neutrals and neutralism. *See* nobodyists and nobodyism
New England Trade and Fishery Bill (1775), 107
New-Jersey Gazette, 174
New York Chamber of Commerce, 74–76, 78, 95, 179, 240
New York citizenship law postwar, 231–32
New York City: British and Dutch in, 23; fires in, 129; wartime control of, 118, 122–23, 125–26, 174, 224–25

New York Committee of Inspection, 78, 83–85, 299n47
New York Committee of Safety, 152
New York Convention, 153–54
New York governor elections, 253–55, 260
New York Manufacturing Society (NYMS), 250–51
New York Restraining Act (1767), 71–74, 77
New York's Committee of Public Safety, 123
New York slave conspiracy (1741), 36
nobodyists and nobodyism: conscientious objector stance, 142; Crugers as representative of, 16; definition of, 5–6, 277n6, 278n8; diverse actions of, 14; loyalists and, 7–8; motivation of, 13–15; motives and bribes questioned, 108–9; numbers of, 1, 10, 277n2; peace seeking, 166–67; perspective on Revolutionary War, 268; "The Plot Discovered" broadside, 118; study of, 14; warring parties and, 7
nonexportation, 97
nonimportation: Boston merchants and, 75, 84, 95; Boston Port Act and, 75, 95–96; British exporters and, 62–63; Committee of Fifty-One and, 96–97; Continental Association, 97–98, 103, 105–7; effective action and support, 79, 82; ending of, 86; enforcement of, 79; extralegal "Committee of Inspection," 78, 83–85; John Harris Cruger and, 270, 299n48; New York Chamber of Commerce and, 74; New York disputes and, 87; New York merchants and, 60, 83–85, 301n66; Philadelphia merchants and, 75, 85; Rhode Island and, 83; Stamp Act and, 54–55, 60, 62–63; Townshend Acts and, 73, 78
North, Lord and North's government: Bristol elections and, 184; Burgoyne's surrender and, 175; challenges in Parliament, 170–71; Coercive (Intolerable)Acts (1774) and, 98–99; Committee of Oblivion, 106; conciliatory measures, 109, 111, 177–78, 182–83; Continental Congresses and, 102; Henry Cruger Jr. and information, 180, 182; Henry Cruger Jr. criticism of, 102, 109, 112, 171–72, 183, 190; Henry Cruger Sr. meeting with, 168; New York petitions (1775) and, 111–12; "Olive Branch Petition" and, 167;

Prohibitory Act and, 168–69; resignation, 191; Restraining Acts (1775), 107–9; Townshend Acts and, 82; waging a pointless lost war, 163
The North Briton (Wilkes), 87
"Novanglus" (John Adams), 102
Nugent, Robert, 99

oaths and oath taking: Charles Lee and, 124, 192; civil war and, 11; Henry Cruger Jr. and, 237–40, 253; John Harris Cruger and, 134–37; Peter Van Schaack and, 146, 151, 153–54, 158–59, 233; Van Schaack family and, 231
"Olive Branch Petition," 121–22, 167–69
Oswald, Richard, 191

Paine, Thomas, 123–24, 152
Palfrey, William, 89, 98–99
patriots, definition of, 5
Pattison, James, 208
Peach, Clara Partridge, 248, 333n36
Peach, Samuel, 32, 35, 87, 89, 99, 184, 187, 236, 247
Peach, Samuel Peach (grandson), 247–48
Pennsylvania Packet, 171–72, 184, 187
Perry, John, 174
Pitt, William, 45, 61, 66, 70. *See also* Chatham, Lord
Pitt, William, the younger, 237, 245–47
"Plan of Union" (Galloway), 97–98
Pownall, Thomas, 183
privateers and privateering, 40, 172–74, 201–2, 213, 256–58
Prohibitory Act (1775), 168–70, 172, 199, 201, 317n9
Provincial Congress (New York), 124–26, 151–52
Provincial Council (New York): Boston Port Act and, 94; Committee of Sixty and, 110; conspiracy theory and, 108; Henry Sr. and, 73, 78; John Harris Cruger and, 92, 118, 121, 134, 270; Oliver De Lancey and, 92; Stamp Act and, 53, 55–58; tea issue and, 93; Valentine Cruger and, 22

Quartering Act (1765), 69, 77, 94
quartering and billeting, 40, 46, 69, 71, 79–81

INDEX

355

Quebec Act (1774), 94, 111
Quincy, Josiah, 102

ratification and ratification conventions, 244–45, 249
Rawdon, Lord, 138–39
reconciliationists, 6, 102, 122, 124, 144, 161, 168–69, 172, 178–79, 181, 231
Restraining Acts (1775), 107–9, 111, 168
Riedelle, John, 34
Rivington, James, 122, 157, 210–11, 224–26
Robinson, Beverly, 40
Robinson, John, 174
Rockingham and Rockinghamites, 61–64, 71, 100–101, 175–78, 184, 191
Rogers, William, 270
Royal Danish American Gazette, 195, 199

salt trade, 202–5, 325n65
Schuyler, Philip, 105, 121, 270
Scott, John Morin, 78, 82
Seabury, Samuel, 96
Sears, Isaac: anti-British activist, 52; Boston Port Act and, 95; chamber of commerce member, 73; Committee of Fifty-One, 96; Committee of Inspection, 78; Committee of Sixty member, 98; Lee's Connecticut militia and, 123; Liberty Boys and, 69; nonimportation and, 79, 83–85; patriot oaths and, 124; quartering issue and, 80–81; Rivington's press raid, 122; Sons of Liberty and, 73, 77; Stamp Act and, 60, 62, 82; support for Massachusetts, 77; Tea Act and, 93; Townshend Acts protest, 80; transatlantic trade petition, 70
Second Continental Congress, 110, 119, 121–22, 146, 167–69
Sedgley, Samuel, 65
Sedgwick, Theodore, 158, 228, 231, 235, 243, 254, 264, 272
Seven Years' War: Cruger business during, 34–35, 39–41; dangers and opportunities of, 39; Denmark's neutrality, 194, 196; East India Company and Asian territories, 72; New York Chamber of Commerce after, 74; privateers and, 52; Stamp Act after, 44–45, 51; trade with French during, 41
Shays's Rebellion (1786/87), 235–36

Shelburne, Lord and his government, 162, 164, 178, 191, 322n83
Shirley, Thomas, 203
Shy, John, 9, 277n2
Silvester, Peter, 160
Skene, Philip, 118–20
slavery and slave trade: Crugers and, 23, 26, 29, 35–36, 135, 196; Curaçao and, 25–26; enslaved people owned by Crugers, 36; Henry Cruger Jr. and, 246–47; St. Croix and, 194–97
Sluyter, John Jacob, 246
Smith, William, 92
Smith v. Ellison, 254
Society for the Encouragement of Useful Manufactures (SEUM), 251
Society for the Promotion of Arts, Agriculture, and Oeconomy, 48
Society of Merchant Venturers (Bristol), 63, 86–87
Sons of Liberty: Committee of Fifty-One endorsement, 96; De Lanceyites and, 77; General Assembly electioneering, 73; Josiah Quincy and, 102; Lexington and Concord reaction, 117; liberty pole and, 81; merchant leaders and, 54; nonimportation and, 83; quartering issue and, 80; "real" Sons of Liberty, 82; Sears and, 52; Second Continental Congress and, 110; Stamp Act and, 62; Stamp Act and Kennedy, 58; street protesters, 51; support for Massachusetts, 77; Wilkesites and, 89. *See also* Liberty Boys
Soumaine, Simeon, 29, 30f
The Spy (Cooper), 204
Stamp Act (1765): celebrations of repeal, 65–66, 69, 81–82; Committee of Merchants in London letter, 64–65; Declaratory Act (1766), 63–64, 66; Henry Cruger Jr. and, 63–65; John Cruger and, 54–59, 64–65; legacies of resistance to, 66–67, 70–71, 73, 79, 93, 105–06; Moore and, 59; nonimportation and, 54–55, 62; opposition and resistance, 2, 8, 47–49, 51, 54–55, 57–59; political theater and, 54, 60, 65; repeal of, 59–68
Stamp Act Congress: circular letter, 48–49; colonial resistance coordinated, 57; Declaration of Rights, 50, 52–53; delegates to, 49;

356 INDEX

Stamp Act Congress (*continued*)
John Cruger at, 54; John Cruger participation, 44–45, 49, 54; John Harris Cruger and, 66; Lewis Cruger and, 293n17; New York delegation, 59; New York meeting, 50; petitions of, 52–54, 59
St. Croix, 194–96, 198–200, 214, 226, 248, 264, 324n31
St. Eustatius, 198, 200–201, 203–4, 209, 226, 258, 324n31
Stoughton, Thomas, 249
Stuart, Gilbert, 190
Suffolk Resolves (Massachusetts), 97
Sugar Act (1764), 45–47
Sung Bok Kim, 277n2

Taylor, Alan, 9, 277n2
Tea Act (1773), 84, 93, 98–99, 177, 181–82
Test and Corporation Acts (1789), 246
Tilghman, Tench, 326n73
Tontine Coffee House, 252, 259–60
Townshend, Charles, 69, 71–72
Townshend Acts: Bristol trade and, 87, 89; description, 72; nonimportation and, 73, 75, 77–79, 82–86; repeal of, 82, 92; tax on tea retained, 82–83
Treat, Malachi, 223
Treaty of Amity, Commerce, and Navigation. *See* Jay Treaty
Treaty of Paris (1783), 164, 191, 219, 222–24, 229–30, 235–37, 240, 258
Trecothick, Barlow, 63–64
Troup, Robert, 257, 272
Tryon, William, 92, 120–21, 163

Underdown, David, 10
United Insurance Company, 251, 261

Van Alen, John, 262
Van Buren, Martin, 272
Van Horn, Hannah, 286n37
Van Schaack, Cornelius, 31, 144–45
Van Schaack, David, 144, 151–53, 156, 231
Van Schaack, Elizabeth Cruger (Bess), 2, 27, 29, 32, 142, 144–45, 157, 269
Van Schaack, Henry (brother to Peter), 105, 151–52, 163–64, 231, 235–36

Van Schaack, Henry Cruger "Harry," 160, 192, 228, 232–33, 271–72
Van Schaack, Henry Cruger (second son), 272
Van Schaack, Peter: "Association" of, 143–44; Banishment Act (New York), 158–59; banishments of, 2, 153–54, 158–59; Boston Port Act and, 94; British financial aid petition, 161–63; citizen of the United States, 164–65; Committee of Fifty-One, 95; Committee of safety, correspondence, and protection, 151–52; Committee of Sixty, 98, 110; Cruger family and, 32, 159–60; death of, 272; death of Harry, 272; Declaration of Independence viewpoint, 152; in England postwar, 227–28; English exile during the revolution, 159–61; "federal man," 243; health problems of, 145, 158–60; Henry Sr. executor, 211; to his son Harry, 42, 145–46; Jay Treaty and, 262–63; John Adams and, 96; John Jay and, 243, 253–55, 337n99; at Kinderhook, 124, 144–46, 151–52, 154, 157, 233, 272; loyalism and, 142–43, 163–64; marriages of, 29, 32, 243, 272; memos to himself on the war, 147–50, 154; New York Bar and, 233; New York Convention and, 153–54; nobodyism and character of, 142, 145–48, 150, 152–53, 156–57, 159; oaths and, 146, 153; peace treaty and defeat of, 141; portrait of, 147f; postwar law clerks, 272; postwar loyalty to New York State, 233; postwar New Yorker resentment, 244; Provincial Congress label, 151; return to New York postwar, 3, 229–33; Stamp Act and, 82; statute law compilation, 92–93, 146; violence and the Revolution, 150–51; visit to Beverly postwar, 220; Whig-Loyalism and, 142–43
Van Swieten, Ouziel, 23

Waddell, William, 222
Walton, Henry, 160, 227–29
Walton, Jacob: British troops and, 123; Committee of Inspection, 85; Committee of Sixty member, 98; death of, 269; French wartime commerce, 41; General Assembly (New York), 73, 78; Henry Sr. executor, 211;

INDEX 357

loyalist stance, 127; marriage of, 31; New York Chamber of Commerce, 74; in New York post war, 140; Nicholas Cruger's capture, 207–8; Provincial Congress named loyalist, 126; slave trade and, 36; Stamp Act and, 82; St. Croix smuggling, 86
Walton, Mary Cruger, 2, 27, 31, 140, 269
Walton, Polly, 140
Walton, William, 74–75, 92, 98
Walton family, 31, 33, 62
War of 1812, 8
War of Austrian Succession, 40
Washington, George: army in Pennsylvania, 152; British in New York and, 124; Continental General through New York, 121; Genêt affair and, 337n117; history of the Revolutionary War, 267–68; Jay Treaty and, 260–61; and John Hancock, 237; Lee urges New York's destruction, 122–23; Neutrality Proclamation, 256–58; Nicholas Cruger

and, 193, 208–11, 213, 227; Rivington and, 225; victorious army in New York, 224
Watts, John, 34, 40, 73, 94, 108, 227
Watts family, 40, 108, 227, 245
Webb, Samuel B., 227
Wenzel, Michael de, 160
West, Benjamin, 160
West India interest, 246
Whig-Loyalists, 118, 142
Wilberforce, William, 246–47
Wilkes, John, and Wilkesites, 81, 87, 89, 102, 166, 176, 179, 245, 268
Willcocks, John, 201–2, 205
Wilmot, John, 162–63
Wilton, Joseph, 66
Worcester Resolves (1783), 230–31
Wright, James, 130, 137

Yates, Robert, 260